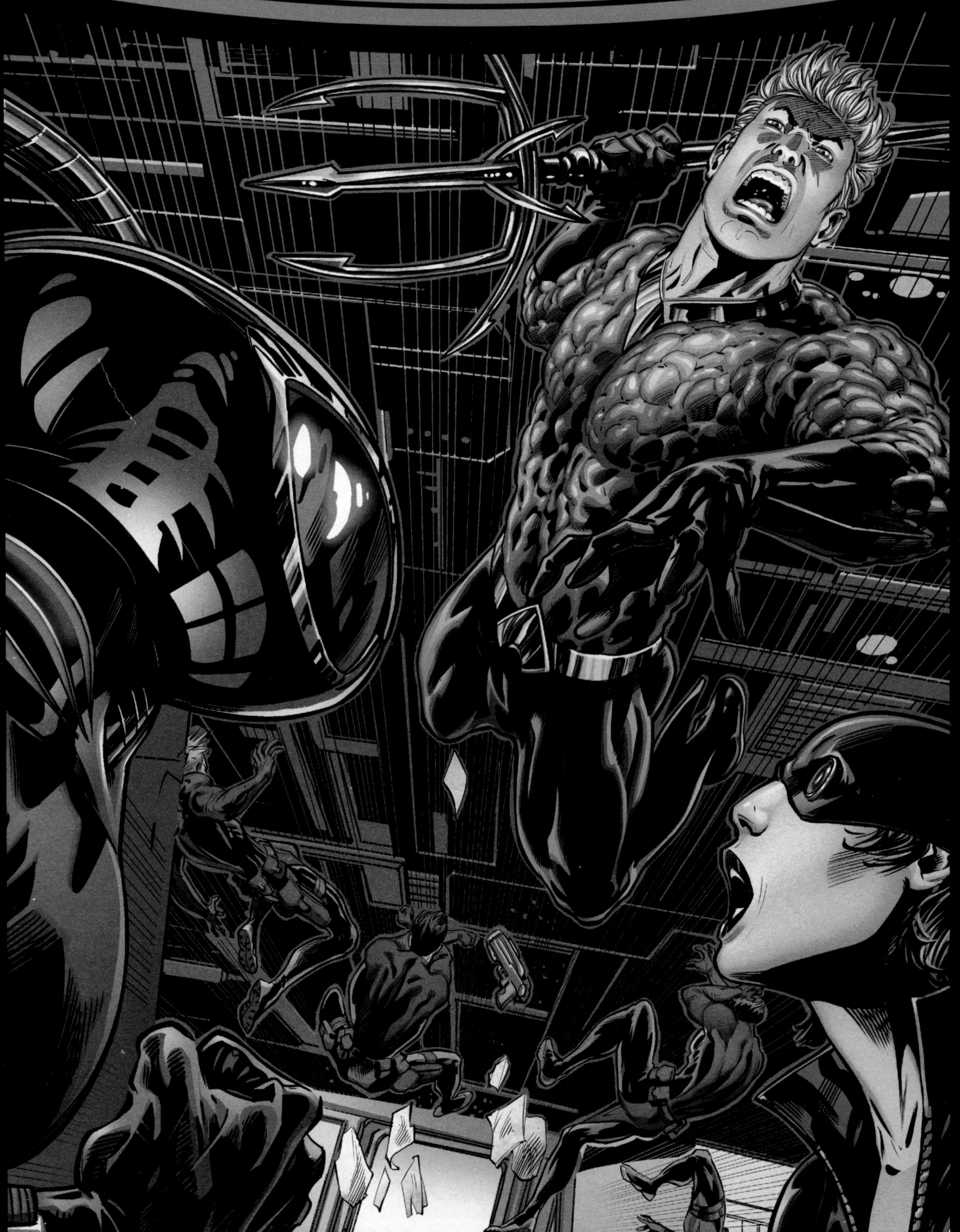

AQUAMAN

VOL. 2 BLACK MANTA RISING

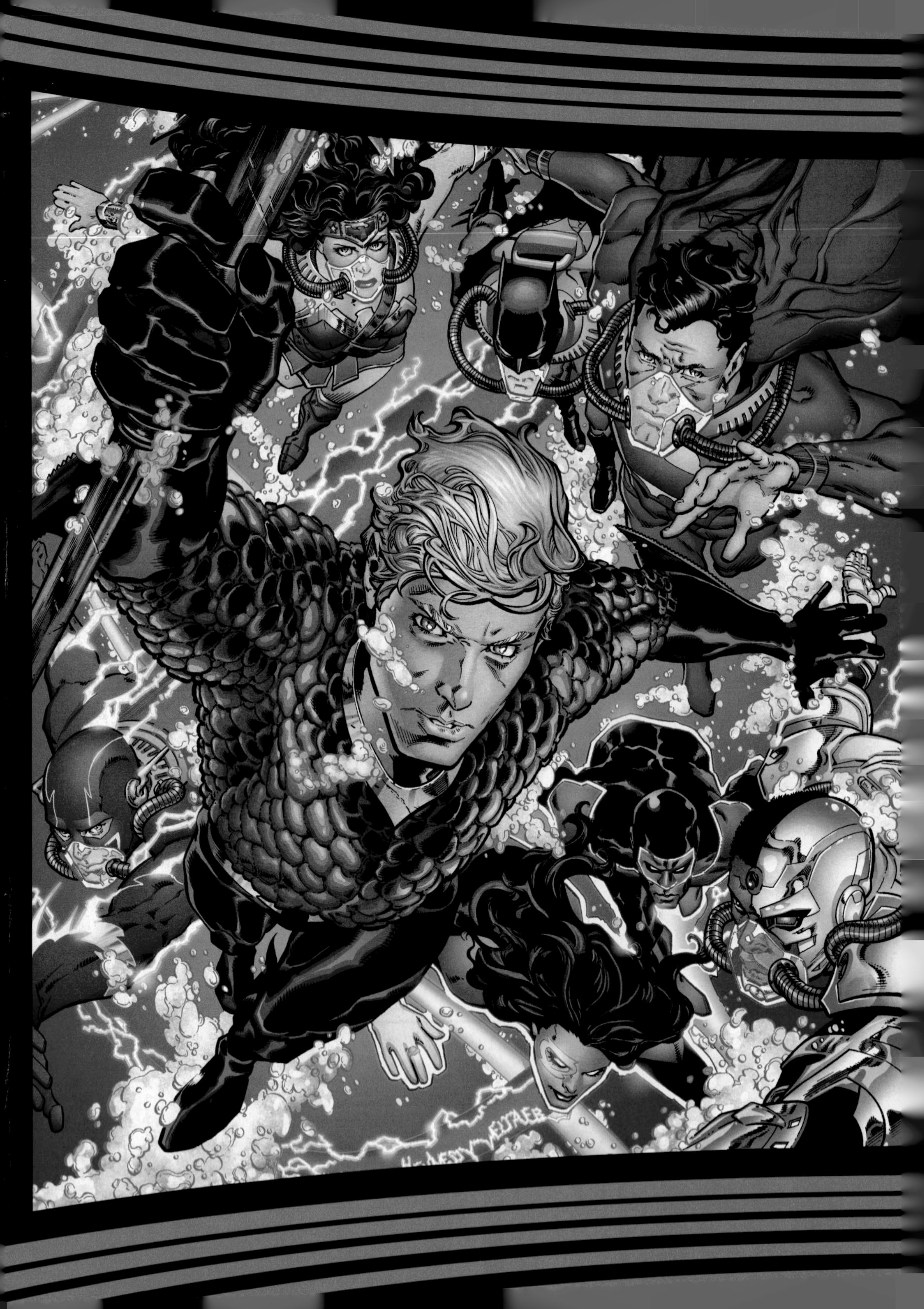

BRIAN CUNNINGHAM Editor - Original Series ◦ **AMEDEO TURTURRO DIEGO LOPEZ** Assistant Editors - Original Series
JEB WOODARD Group Editor - Collected Editions ◦ **LIZ ERICKSON** Editor - Collected Edition
STEVE COOK Design Director - Books

BOB HARRAS Senior VP - Editor-in-Chief, DC Comics

DIANE NELSON President ◦ **DAN DiDIO** Publisher ◦ **JIM LEE** Publisher ◦ **GEOFF JOHNS** President & Chief Creative Officer
AMIT DESAI Executive VP - Business & Marketing Strategy, Direct to Consumer & Global Franchise Management ◦ **SAM ADES** Senior VP - Direct to Consumer
BOBBIE CHASE VP - Talent Development ◦ **MARK CHIARELLO** Senior VP - Art, Design & Collected Editions
JOHN CUNNINGHAM Senior VP - Sales & Trade Marketing ◦ **ANNE DePIES** Senior VP - Business Strategy, Finance & Administration
DON FALLETTI VP - Manufacturing Operations ◦ **LAWRENCE GANEM** VP - Editorial Administration & Talent Relations
ALISON GILL Senior VP - Manufacturing & Operations ◦ **HANK KANALZ** Senior VP - Editorial Strategy & Administration
JAY KOGAN VP - Legal Affairs ◦ **THOMAS LOFTUS** VP - Business Affairs
JACK MAHAN VP - Business Affairs ◦ **NICK J. NAPOLITANO** VP - Manufacturing Administration
EDDIE SCANNELL VP - Consumer Marketing ◦ **COURTNEY SIMMONS** Senior VP - Publicity & Communications
JIM (SKI) SOKOLOWSKI VP - Comic Book Specialty Sales & Trade Marketing ◦ **NANCY SPEARS** VP - Mass, Book, Digital Sales & Trade Marketing

AQUAMAN VOL. 2: BLACK MANTA RISING

DC Comics, 2900 West Alameda Ave., Burbank, CA 91505
Printed by LSC Communications, Salem, VA, USA. 3/10/17. First Printing.
ISBN: 978-1-4012-7227-2

Library of Congress Cataloging-in-Publication Data is Available.

AQUAMAN
VOL. 2 BLACK MANTA RISING

DAN ABNETT
writer

SCOT EATON * **BRAD WALKER**
PHILIPPE BRIONES
pencillers

WAYNE FAUCHER * **ANDREW HENNESSY**
DANIEL HENRIQUES * **PHILIPPE BRIONES**
inkers

GABE ELTAEB
colorist

PAT BROSSEAU
letterer

BRAD WALKER, ANDREW HENNESSY
& GABE ELTAEB
collection cover artists

AQUAMAN created by **PAUL NORRIS**

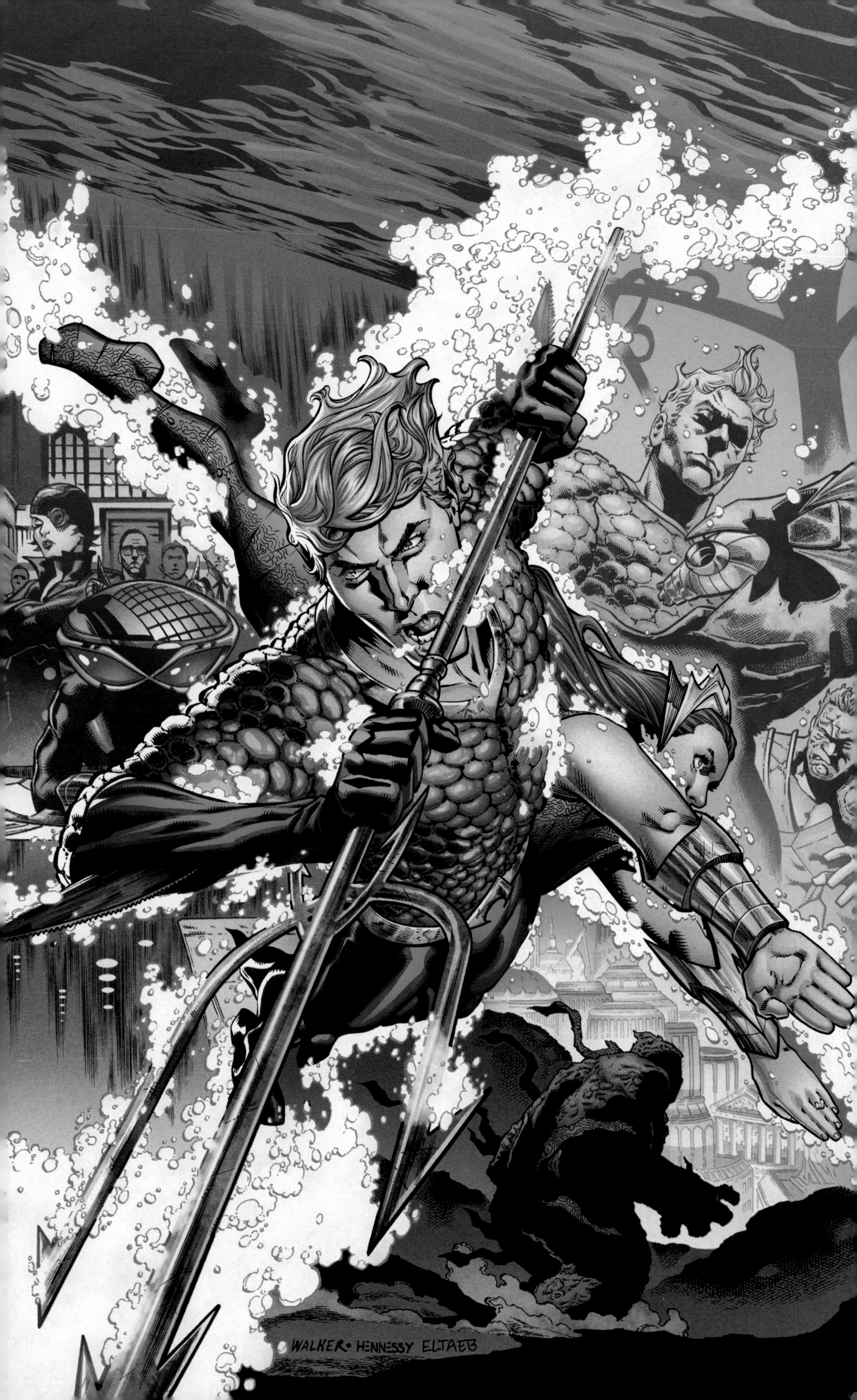
WALKER• HENNESSY ELTAEB

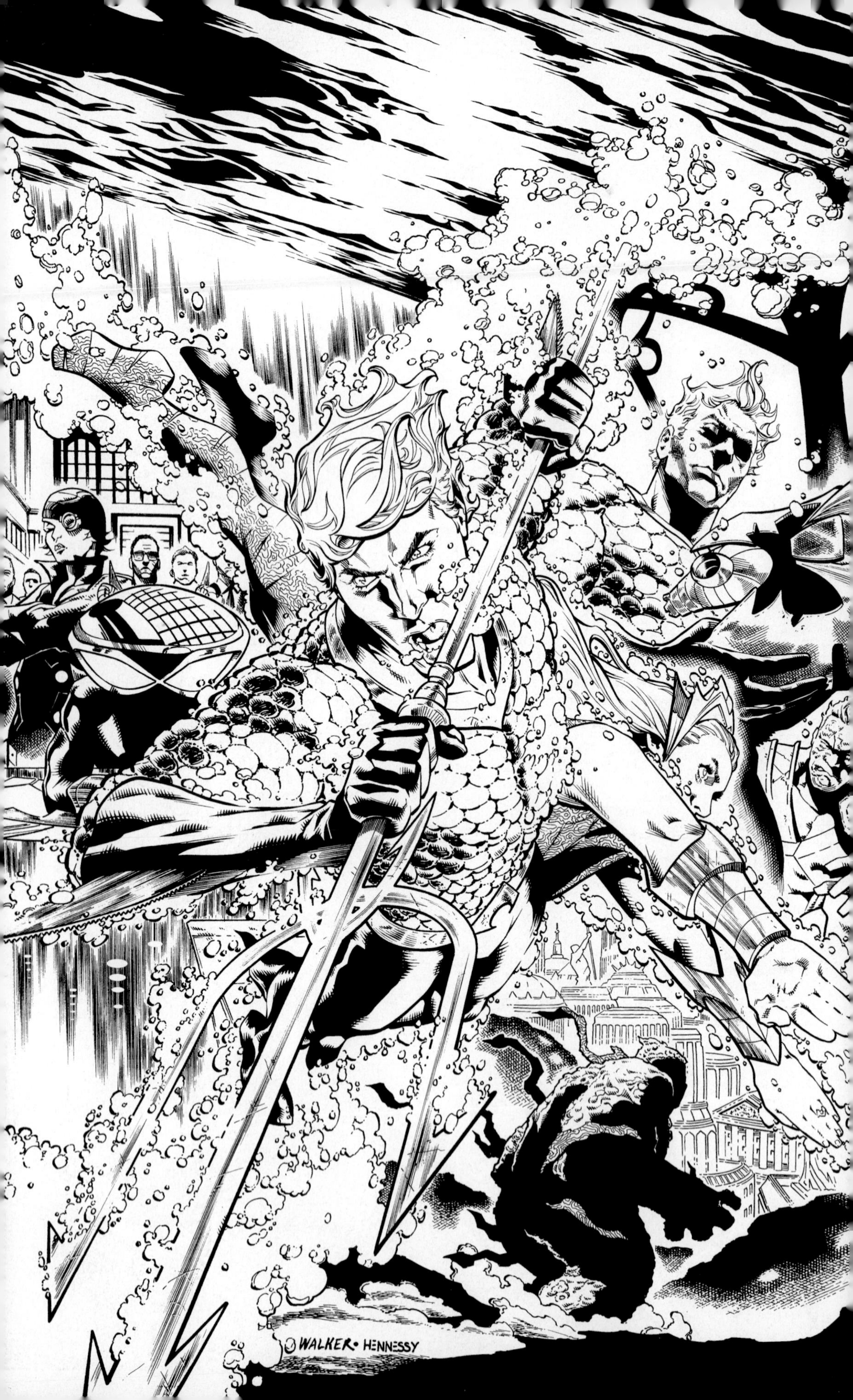
WALKER• HENNESSY

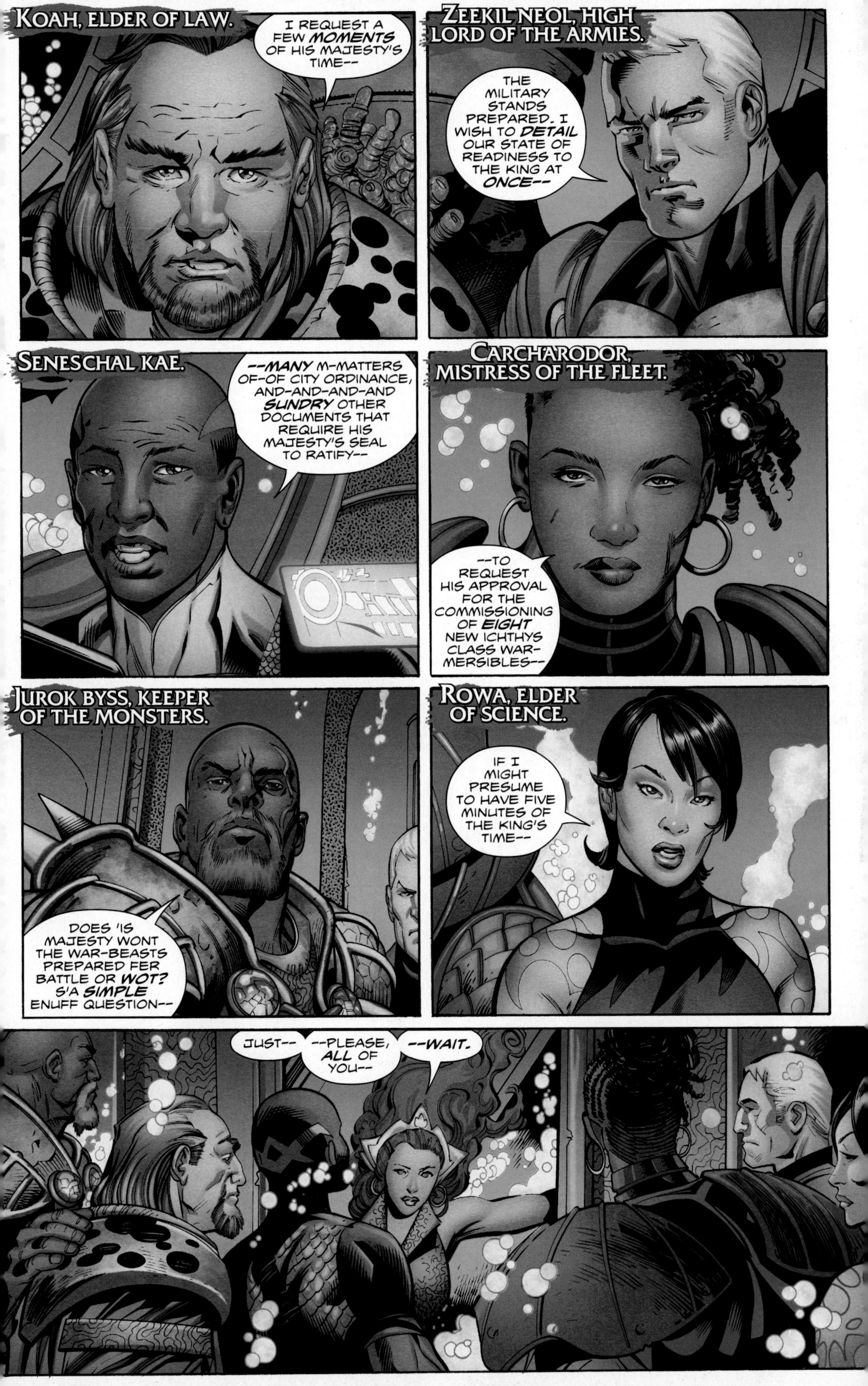
KOAH, ELDER OF LAW.
I REQUEST A FEW MOMENTS OF HIS MAJESTY'S TIME--
ZEEKIL NEOL, HIGH LORD OF THE ARMIES.
THE MILITARY STANDS PREPARED. I WISH TO DETAIL OUR STATE OF READINESS TO THE KING AT ONCE--
SENESCHAL KAE.
--MANY M-MATTERS OF--OF CITY ORDINANCE, AND--AND--AND--AND SUNDRY OTHER DOCUMENTS THAT REQUIRE HIS MAJESTY'S SEAL TO RATIFY--
CARCHARODOR, MISTRESS OF THE FLEET.
--TO REQUEST HIS APPROVAL FOR THE COMMISSIONING OF EIGHT NEW ICHTHYS CLASS WAR-MERSIBLES--
JUROK BYSS, KEEPER OF THE MONSTERS.
DOES 'IS MAJESTY WONT THE WAR-BEASTS PREPARED FER BATTLE OR WOT? S'A SIMPLE ENUFF QUESTION--
ROWA, ELDER OF SCIENCE.
IF I MIGHT PRESUME TO HAVE FIVE MINUTES OF THE KING'S TIME--
JUST--
--PLEASE, ALL OF YOU--
--WAIT.

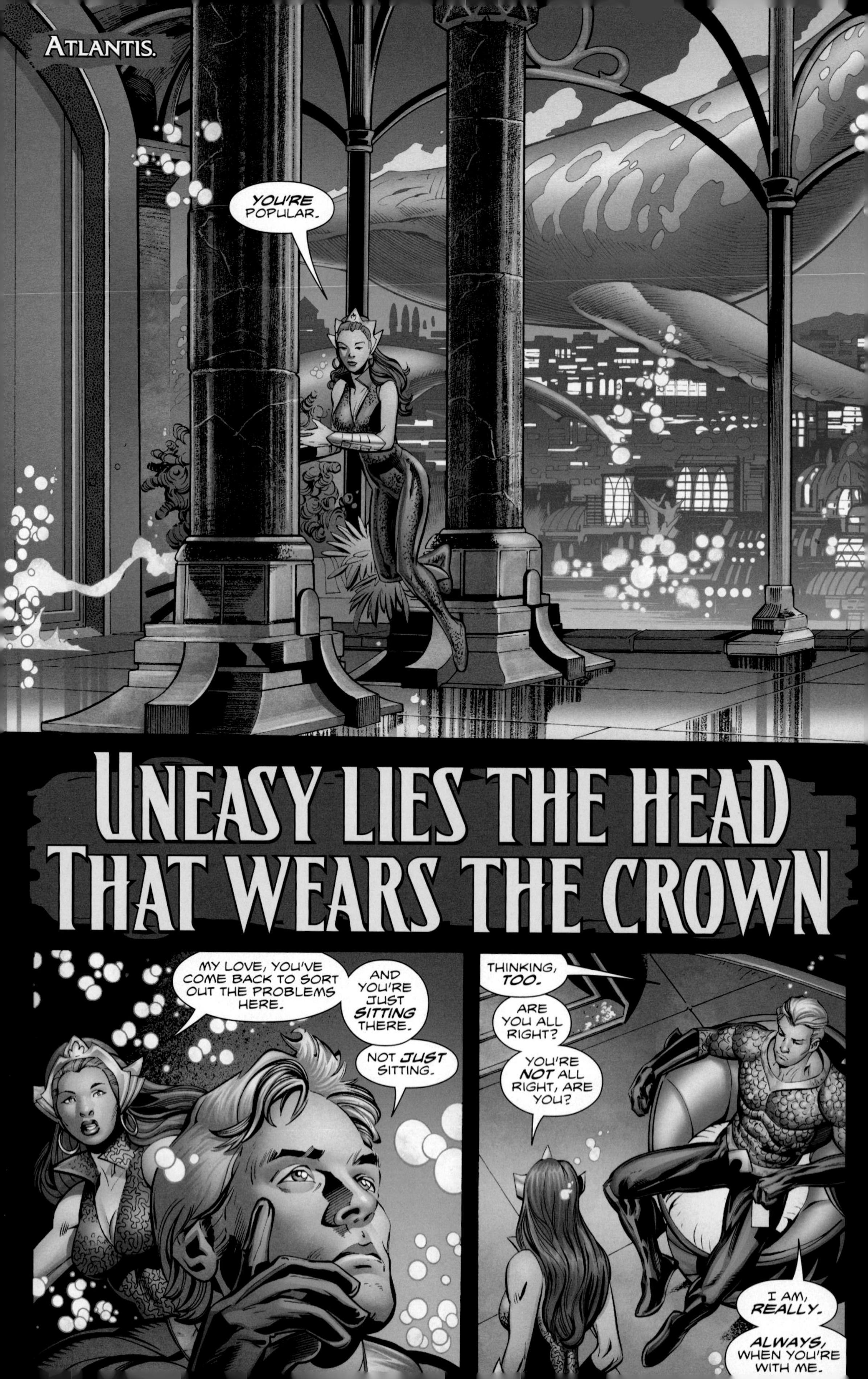
ATLANTIS.
YOU'RE POPULAR.
UNEASY LIES THE HEAD THAT WEARS THE CROWN
MY LOVE, YOU'VE COME BACK TO SORT OUT THE PROBLEMS HERE.
AND YOU'RE JUST SITTING THERE.
NOT JUST SITTING.
THINKING, TOO.
ARE YOU ALL RIGHT?
YOU'RE NOT ALL RIGHT, ARE YOU?
I AM, REALLY.
ALWAYS, WHEN YOU'RE WITH ME.

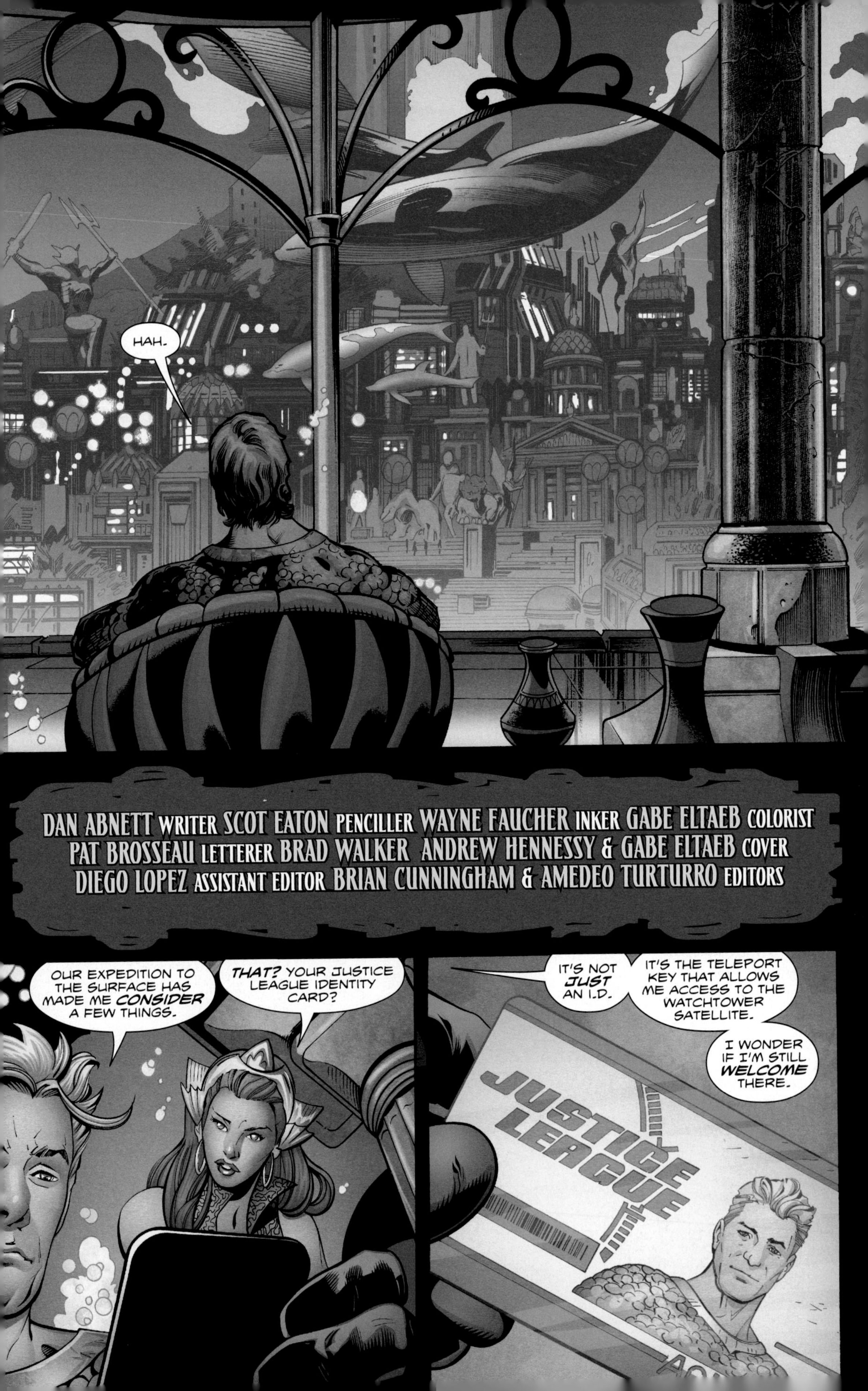
HAH.
DAN ABNETT WRITER SCOT EATON PENCILLER WAYNE FAUCHER INKER GABE ELTAEB COLORIST
PAT BROSSEAU LETTERER BRAD WALKER ANDREW HENNESSY & GABE ELTAEB COVER
DIEGO LOPEZ ASSISTANT EDITOR BRIAN CUNNINGHAM & AMEDEO TURTURRO EDITORS
OUR EXPEDITION TO THE SURFACE HAS MADE ME CONSIDER A FEW THINGS.
THAT? YOUR JUSTICE LEAGUE IDENTITY CARD?
IT'S NOT JUST AN I.D.
IT'S THE TELEPORT KEY THAT ALLOWS ME ACCESS TO THE WATCHTOWER SATELLITE.
I WONDER IF I'M STILL WELCOME THERE.
JUSTICE LEAGUE

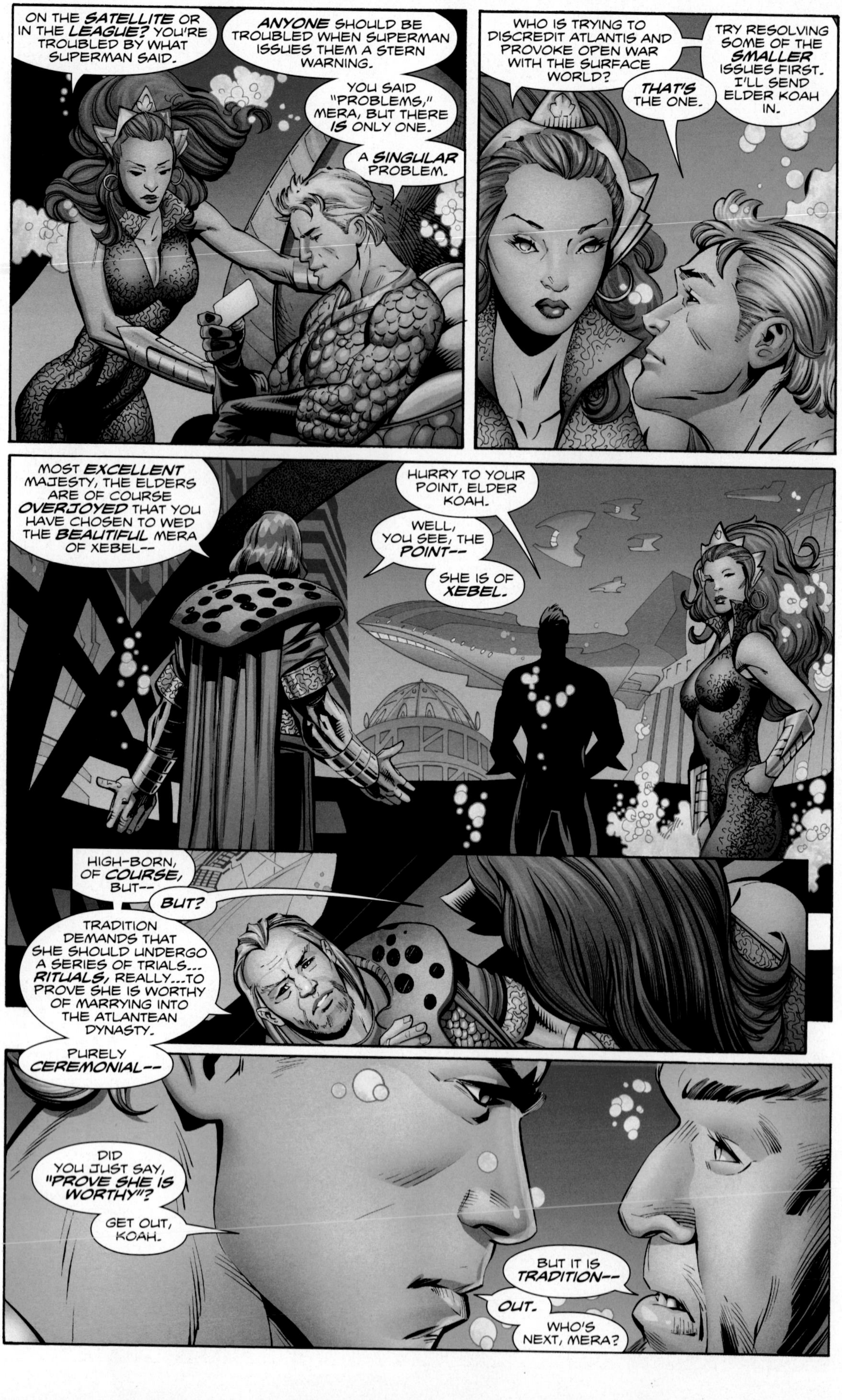

ON THE SATELLITE OR IN THE LEAGUE? YOU'RE TROUBLED BY WHAT SUPERMAN SAID.
ANYONE SHOULD BE TROUBLED WHEN SUPERMAN ISSUES THEM A STERN WARNING.
YOU SAID "PROBLEMS," MERA, BUT THERE IS ONLY ONE.
A SINGULAR PROBLEM.
WHO IS TRYING TO DISCREDIT ATLANTIS AND PROVOKE OPEN WAR WITH THE SURFACE WORLD?
THAT'S THE ONE.
TRY RESOLVING SOME OF THE SMALLER ISSUES FIRST. I'LL SEND ELDER KOAH IN.
MOST EXCELLENT MAJESTY, THE ELDERS ARE OF COURSE OVERJOYED THAT YOU HAVE CHOSEN TO WED THE BEAUTIFUL MERA OF XEBEL--
HURRY TO YOUR POINT, ELDER KOAH.
WELL, YOU SEE, THE POINT--
SHE IS OF XEBEL.
HIGH-BORN, OF COURSE, BUT--
BUT?
TRADITION DEMANDS THAT SHE SHOULD UNDERGO A SERIES OF TRIALS... RITUALS, REALLY...TO PROVE SHE IS WORTHY OF MARRYING INTO THE ATLANTEAN DYNASTY.
PURELY CEREMONIAL--
DID YOU JUST SAY, "PROVE SHE IS WORTHY"?
GET OUT, KOAH.
BUT IT IS TRADITION--
OUT.
WHO'S NEXT, MERA?

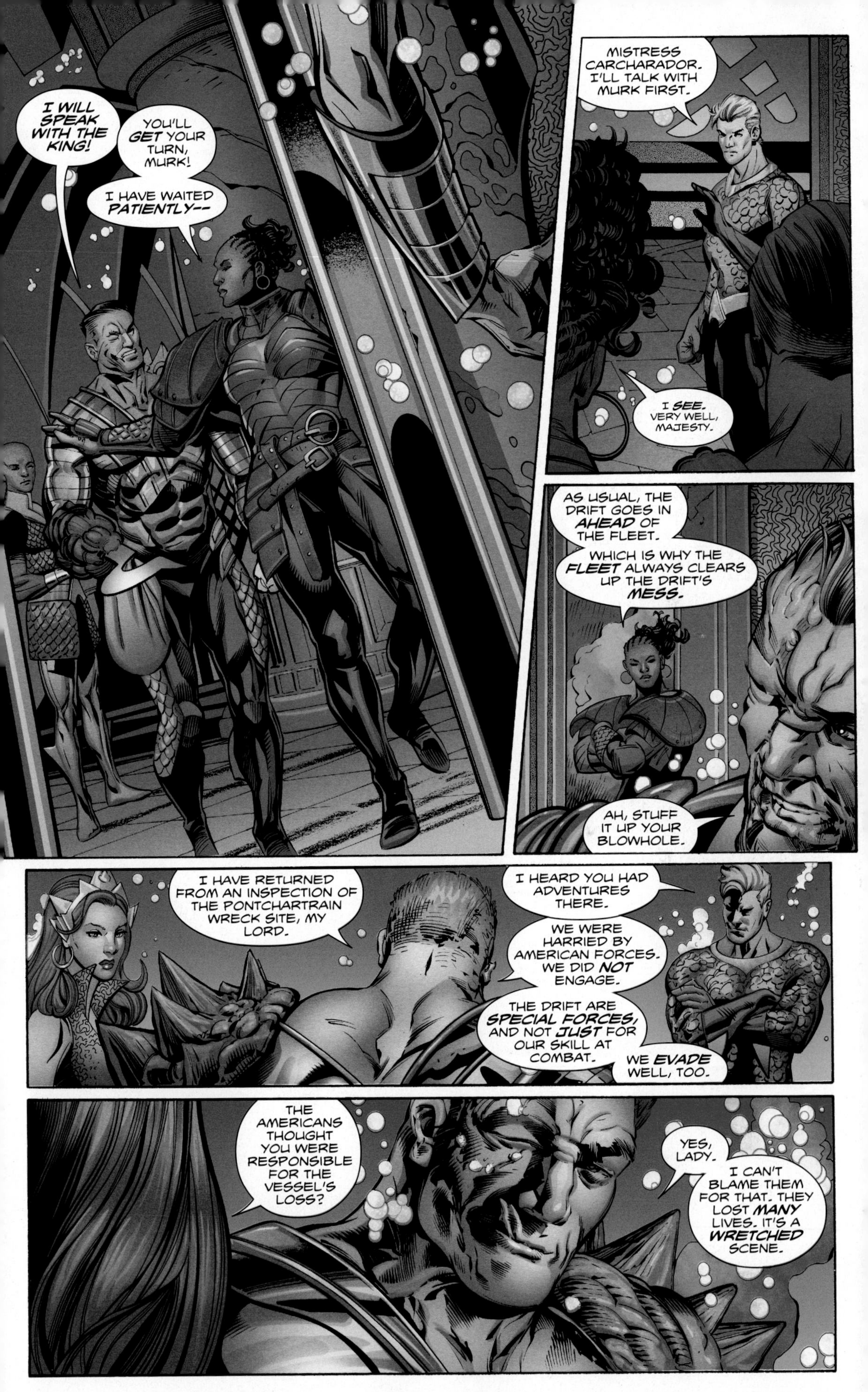
I WILL SPEAK WITH THE KING!
YOU'LL GET YOUR TURN, MURK!
I HAVE WAITED PATIENTLY--
MISTRESS CARCHARADOR. I'LL TALK WITH MURK FIRST.
I SEE. VERY WELL, MAJESTY.
AS USUAL, THE DRIFT GOES IN AHEAD OF THE FLEET.
WHICH IS WHY THE FLEET ALWAYS CLEARS UP THE DRIFT'S MESS.
AH, STUFF IT UP YOUR BLOWHOLE.
I HAVE RETURNED FROM AN INSPECTION OF THE PONTCHARTRAIN WRECK SITE, MY LORD.
I HEARD YOU HAD ADVENTURES THERE.
WE WERE HARRIED BY AMERICAN FORCES. WE DID NOT ENGAGE.
THE DRIFT ARE SPECIAL FORCES, AND NOT JUST FOR OUR SKILL AT COMBAT.
WE EVADE WELL, TOO.
THE AMERICANS THOUGHT YOU WERE RESPONSIBLE FOR THE VESSEL'S LOSS?
YES, LADY.
I CAN'T BLAME THEM FOR THAT. THEY LOST MANY LIVES. IT'S A WRETCHED SCENE.

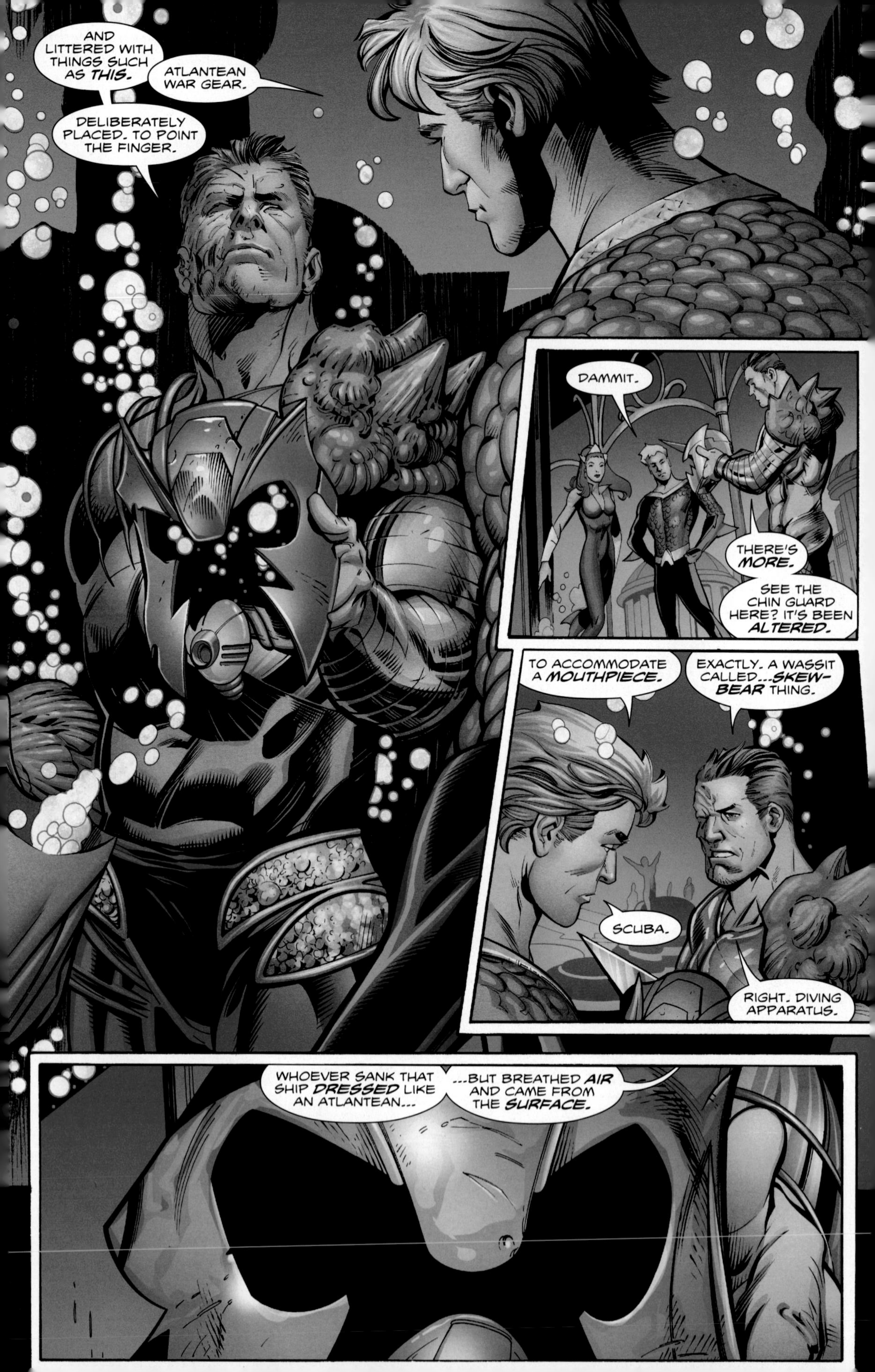
AND LITTERED WITH THINGS SUCH AS THIS.
ATLANTEAN WAR GEAR.
DELIBERATELY PLACED. TO POINT THE FINGER.
DAMMIT.
THERE'S MORE.
SEE THE CHIN GUARD HERE? IT'S BEEN ALTERED.
TO ACCOMMODATE A MOUTHPIECE.
EXACTLY. A WASSIT CALLED...SKEW-BEAR THING.
SCUBA.
RIGHT. DIVING APPARATUS.
WHOEVER SANK THAT SHIP DRESSED LIKE AN ATLANTEAN...
...BUT BREATHED AIR AND CAME FROM THE SURFACE.

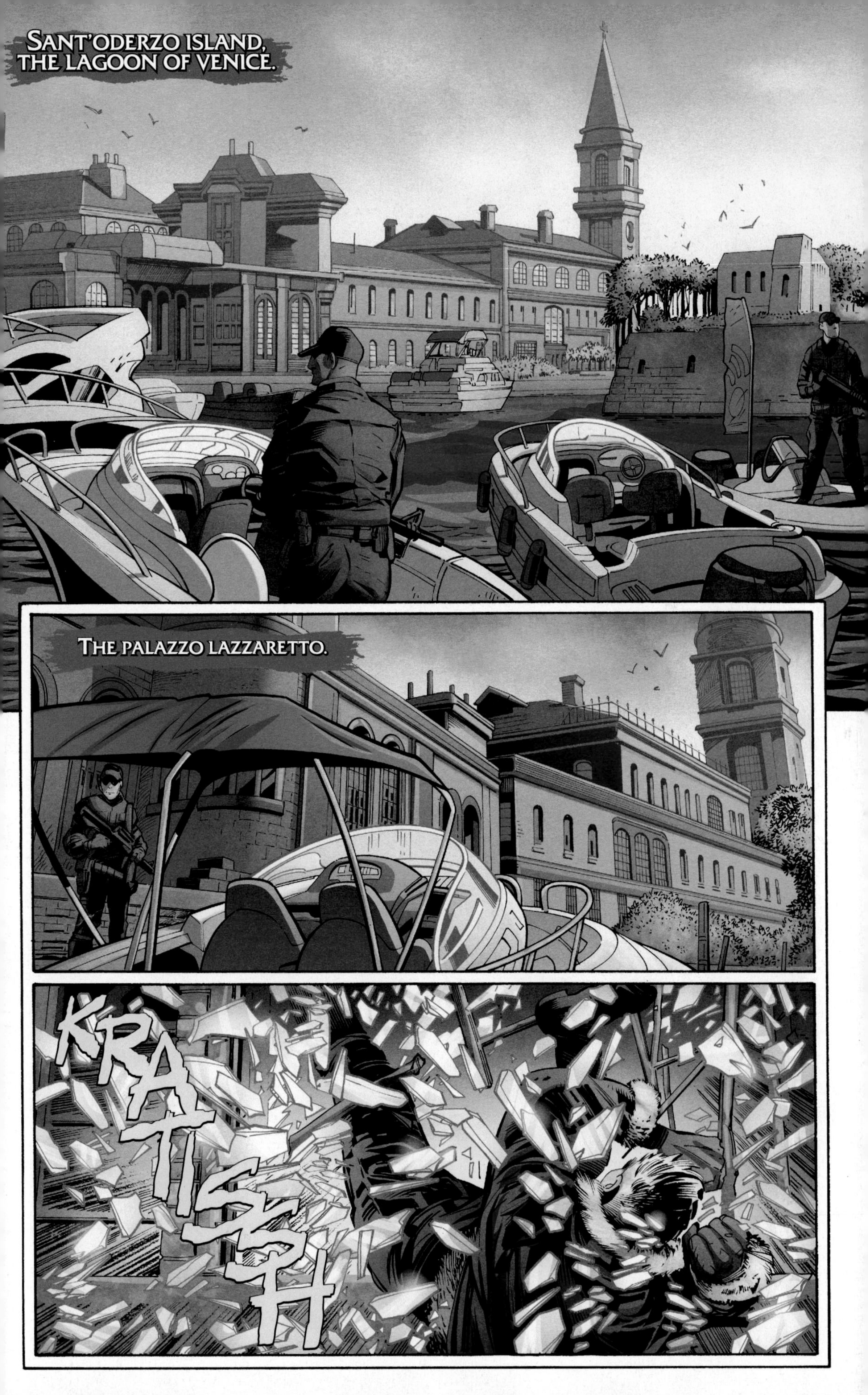
SANT'ODERZO ISLAND, THE LAGOON OF VENICE.
THE PALAZZO LAZZARETTO.
KRATTISSH

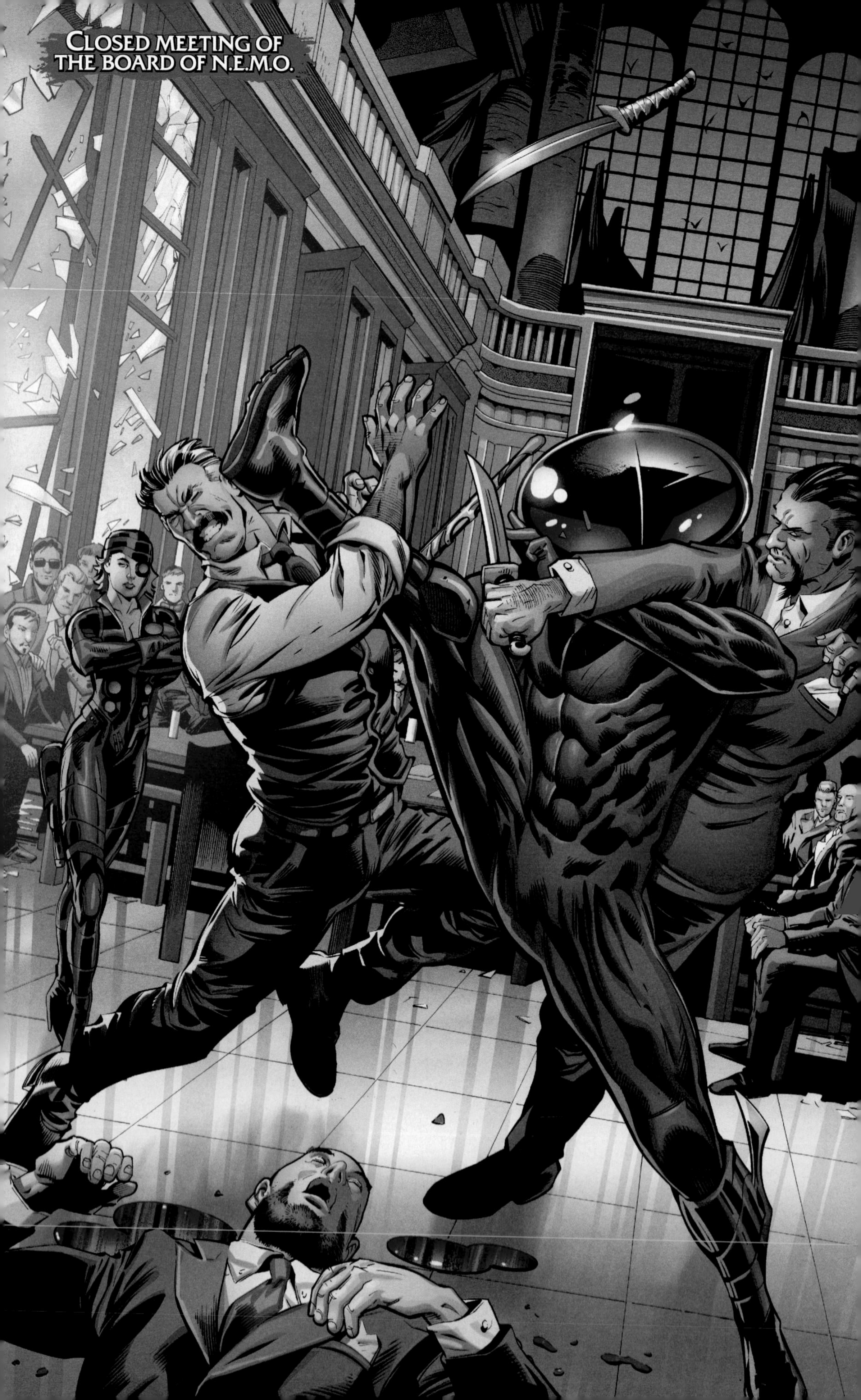
CLOSED MEETING OF
THE BOARD OF N.E.M.O.

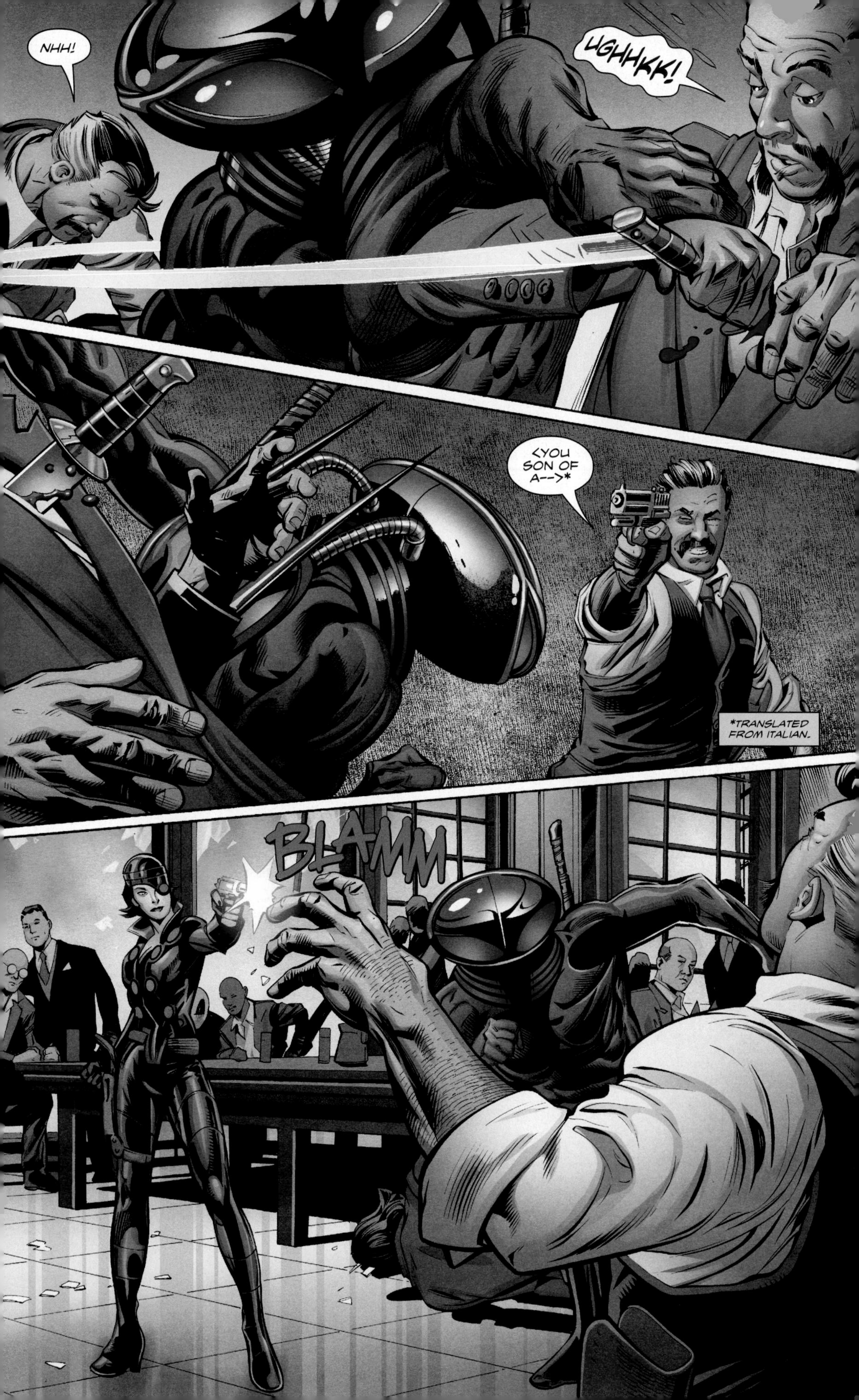
NHH!
UGHHKK!
<YOU SON OF A-->*
*TRANSLATED FROM ITALIAN.
BLAMM

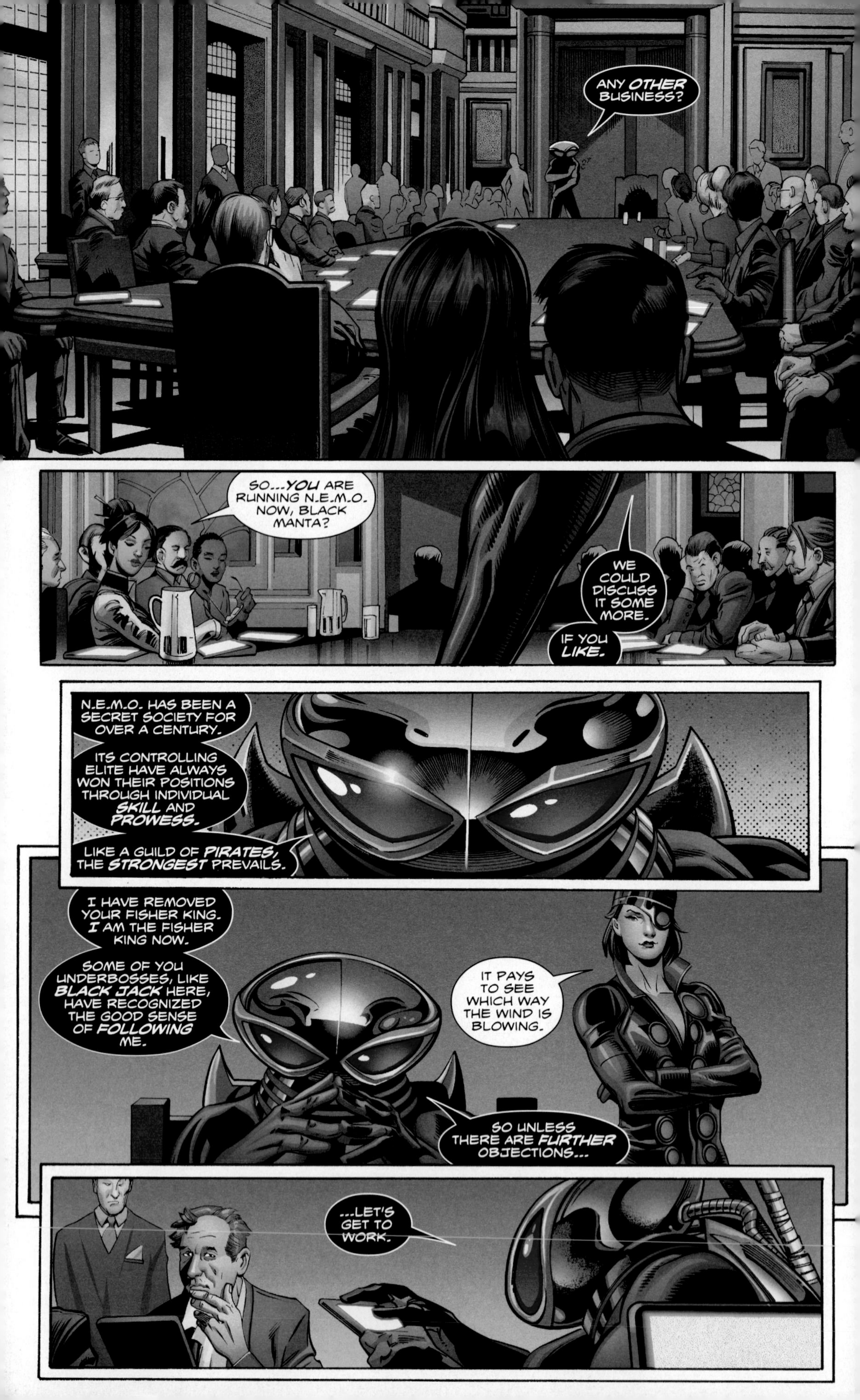

ANY OTHER BUSINESS?
SO...YOU ARE RUNNING N.E.M.O. NOW, BLACK MANTA?
WE COULD DISCUSS IT SOME MORE.
IF YOU LIKE.
N.E.M.O. HAS BEEN A SECRET SOCIETY FOR OVER A CENTURY.
ITS CONTROLLING ELITE HAVE ALWAYS WON THEIR POSITIONS THROUGH INDIVIDUAL SKILL AND PROWESS.
LIKE A GUILD OF PIRATES, THE STRONGEST PREVAILS.
I HAVE REMOVED YOUR FISHER KING. I AM THE FISHER KING NOW.
SOME OF YOU UNDERBOSSES, LIKE BLACK JACK HERE, HAVE RECOGNIZED THE GOOD SENSE OF FOLLOWING ME.
IT PAYS TO SEE WHICH WAY THE WIND IS BLOWING.
SO UNLESS THERE ARE FURTHER OBJECTIONS...
...LET'S GET TO WORK.

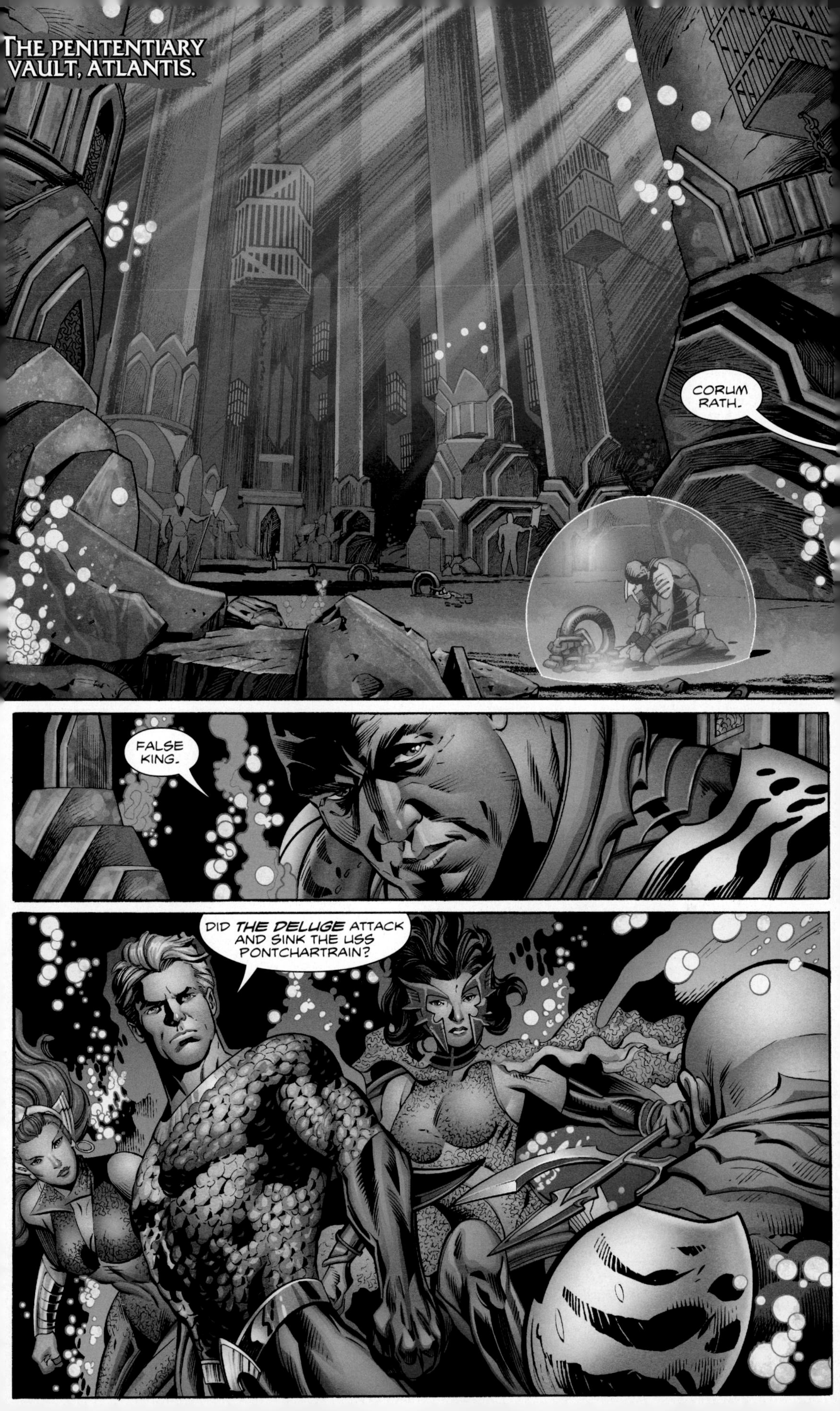
THE PENITENTIARY VAULT, ATLANTIS.
CORUM RATH.
FALSE KING.
DID THE DELUGE ATTACK AND SINK THE USS PONTCHARTRAIN?

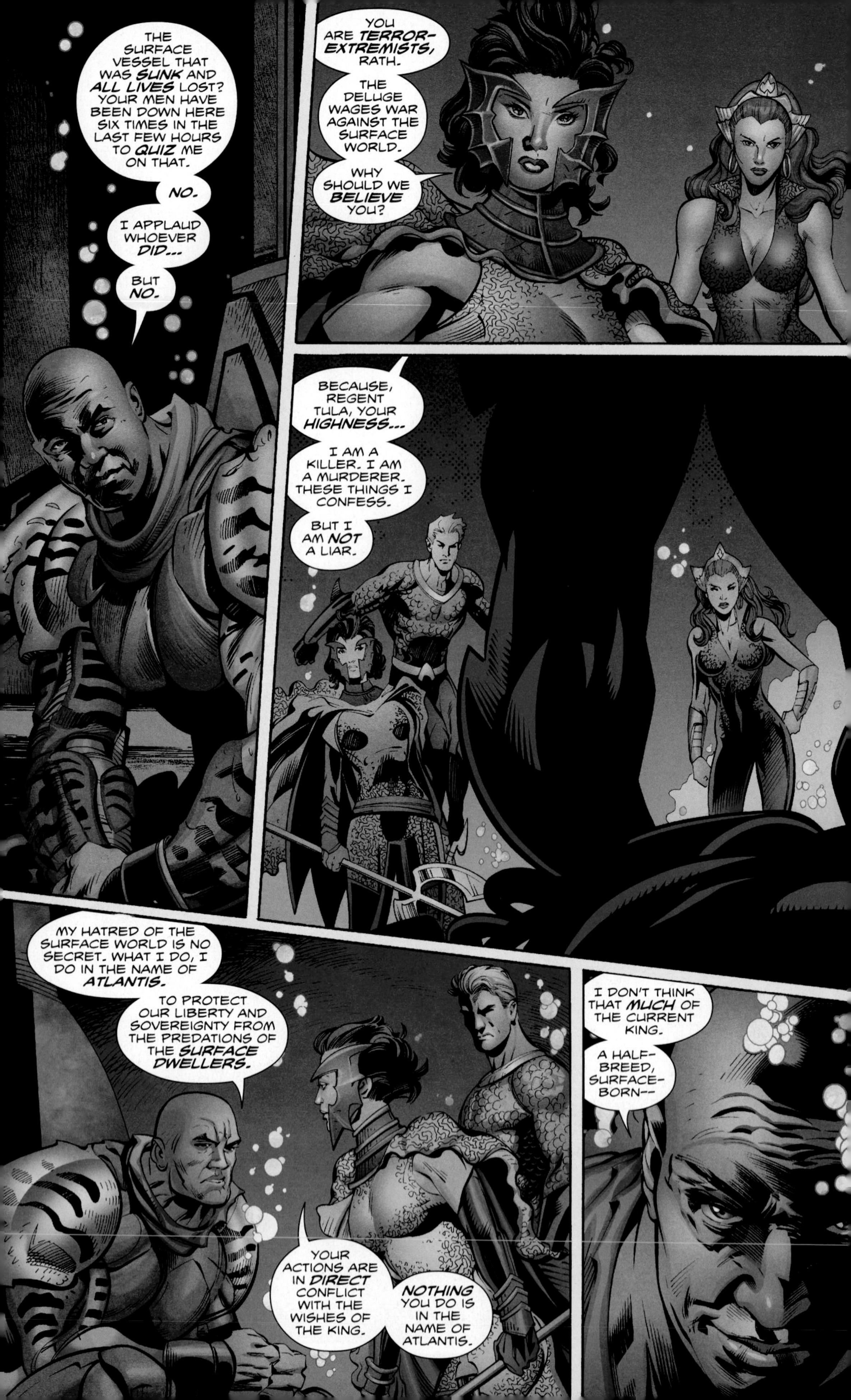
THE SURFACE VESSEL THAT WAS SUNK AND ALL LIVES LOST? YOUR MEN HAVE BEEN DOWN HERE SIX TIMES IN THE LAST FEW HOURS TO QUIZ ME ON THAT.
NO.
I APPLAUD WHOEVER DID...
BUT NO.
YOU ARE TERROR-EXTREMISTS, RATH.
THE DELUGE WAGES WAR AGAINST THE SURFACE WORLD.
WHY SHOULD WE BELIEVE YOU?
BECAUSE, REGENT TULA, YOUR HIGHNESS...
I AM A KILLER. I AM A MURDERER. THESE THINGS I CONFESS.
BUT I AM NOT A LIAR.
MY HATRED OF THE SURFACE WORLD IS NO SECRET. WHAT I DO, I DO IN THE NAME OF ATLANTIS.
TO PROTECT OUR LIBERTY AND SOVEREIGNTY FROM THE PREDATIONS OF THE SURFACE DWELLERS.
YOUR ACTIONS ARE IN DIRECT CONFLICT WITH THE WISHES OF THE KING.
NOTHING YOU DO IS IN THE NAME OF ATLANTIS.
I DON'T THINK THAT MUCH OF THE CURRENT KING.
A HALF-BREED, SURFACE-BORN--

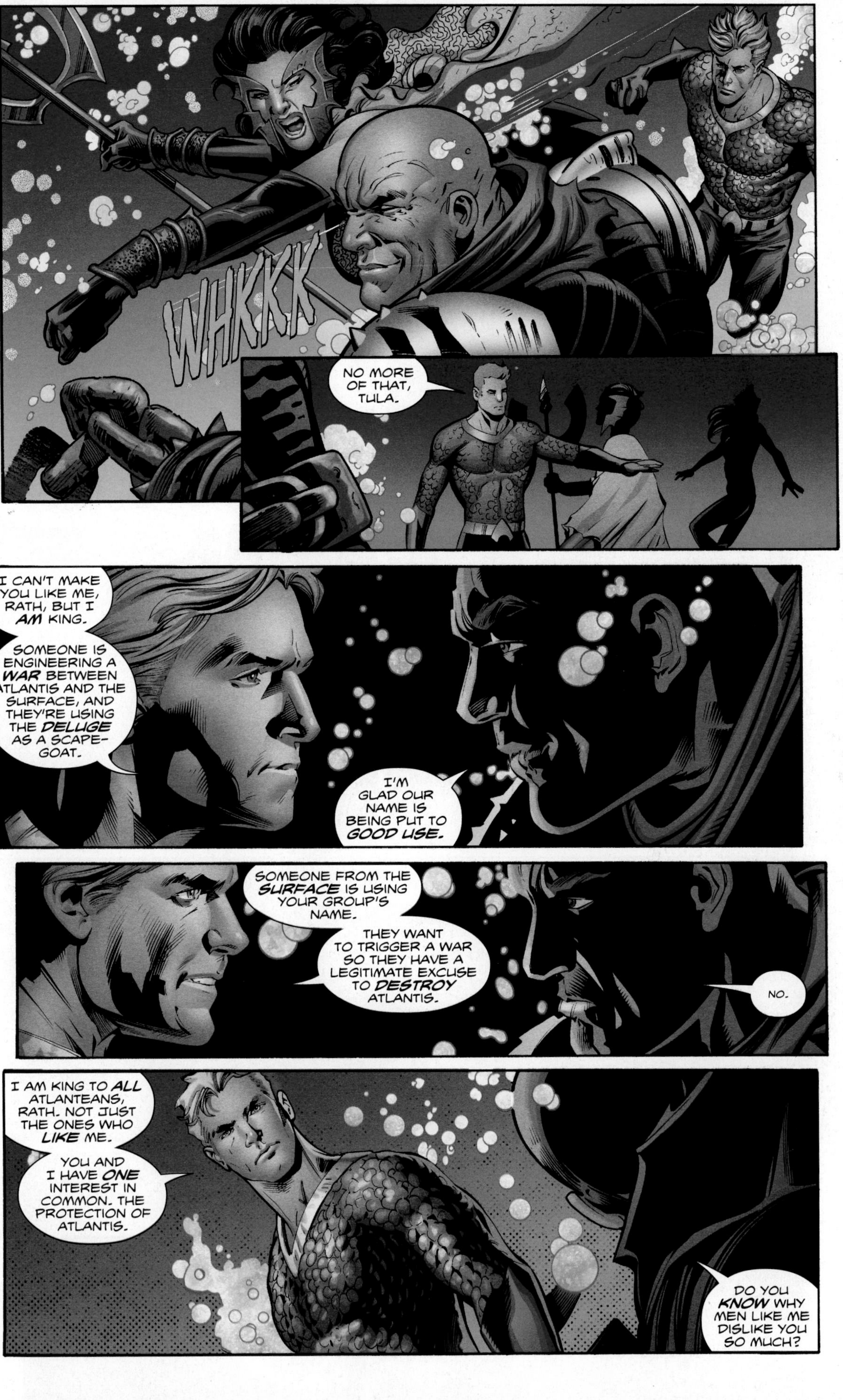
WHKKK
NO MORE OF THAT, TULA.
I CAN'T MAKE YOU LIKE ME, RATH, BUT I AM KING.
SOMEONE IS ENGINEERING A WAR BETWEEN ATLANTIS AND THE SURFACE, AND THEY'RE USING THE DELUGE AS A SCAPE-GOAT.
I'M GLAD OUR NAME IS BEING PUT TO GOOD USE.
SOMEONE FROM THE SURFACE IS USING YOUR GROUP'S NAME.
THEY WANT TO TRIGGER A WAR SO THEY HAVE A LEGITIMATE EXCUSE TO DESTROY ATLANTIS.
NO.
I AM KING TO ALL ATLANTEANS, RATH. NOT JUST THE ONES WHO LIKE ME.
YOU AND I HAVE ONE INTEREST IN COMMON. THE PROTECTION OF ATLANTIS.
DO YOU KNOW WHY MEN LIKE ME DISLIKE YOU SO MUCH?

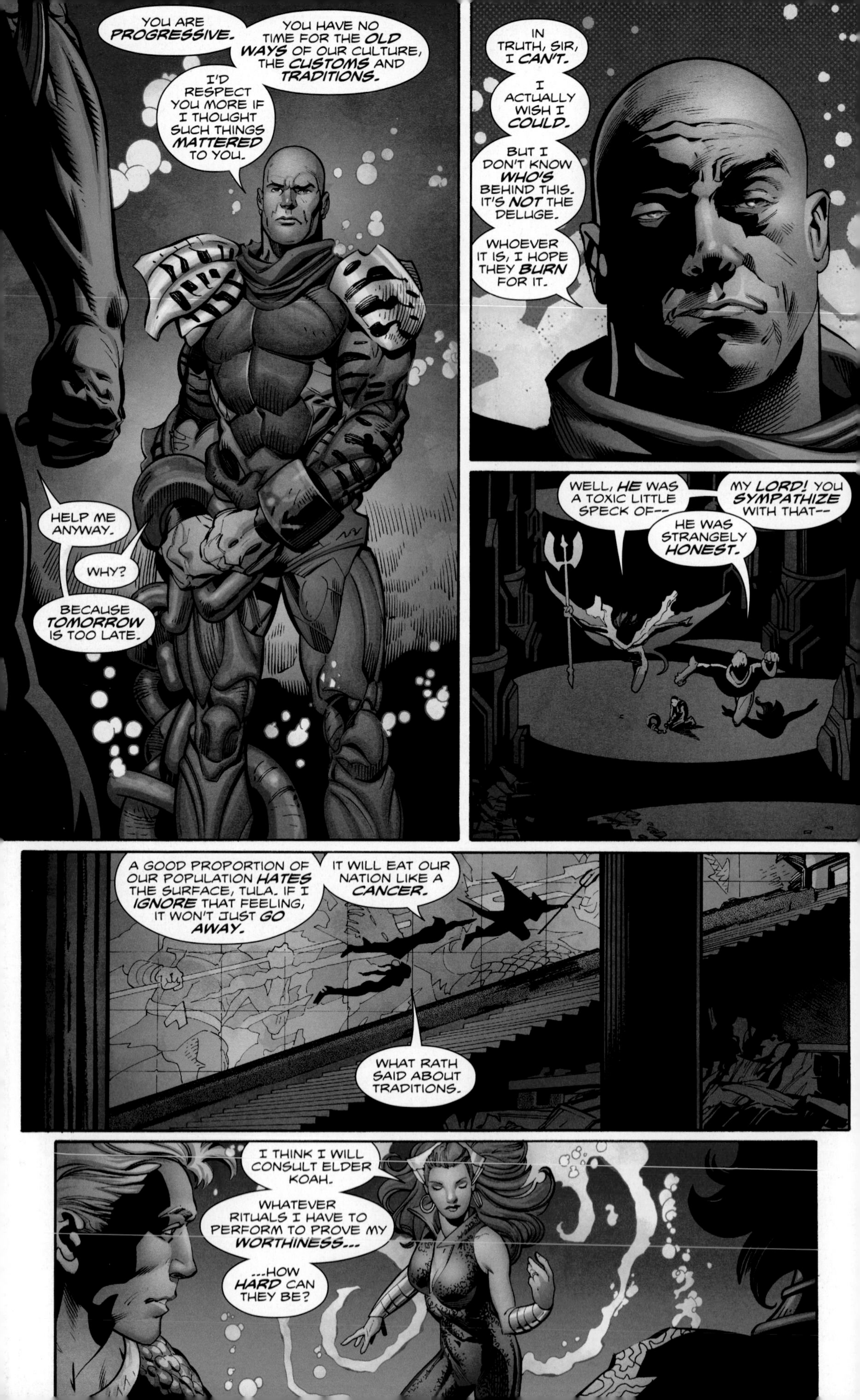
YOU ARE PROGRESSIVE.
YOU HAVE NO TIME FOR THE OLD WAYS OF OUR CULTURE, THE CUSTOMS AND TRADITIONS.
I'D RESPECT YOU MORE IF I THOUGHT SUCH THINGS MATTERED TO YOU.
HELP ME ANYWAY.
WHY?
BECAUSE TOMORROW IS TOO LATE.
IN TRUTH, SIR, I CAN'T.
I ACTUALLY WISH I COULD.
BUT I DON'T KNOW WHO'S BEHIND THIS. IT'S NOT THE DELUGE.
WHOEVER IT IS, I HOPE THEY BURN FOR IT.
WELL, HE WAS A TOXIC LITTLE SPECK OF--
MY LORD! YOU SYMPATHIZE WITH THAT--
HE WAS STRANGELY HONEST.
A GOOD PROPORTION OF OUR POPULATION HATES THE SURFACE, TULA. IF I IGNORE THAT FEELING, IT WON'T JUST GO AWAY.
IT WILL EAT OUR NATION LIKE A CANCER.
WHAT RATH SAID ABOUT TRADITIONS.
I THINK I WILL CONSULT ELDER KOAH.
WHATEVER RITUALS I HAVE TO PERFORM TO PROVE MY WORTHINESS...
...HOW HARD CAN THEY BE?

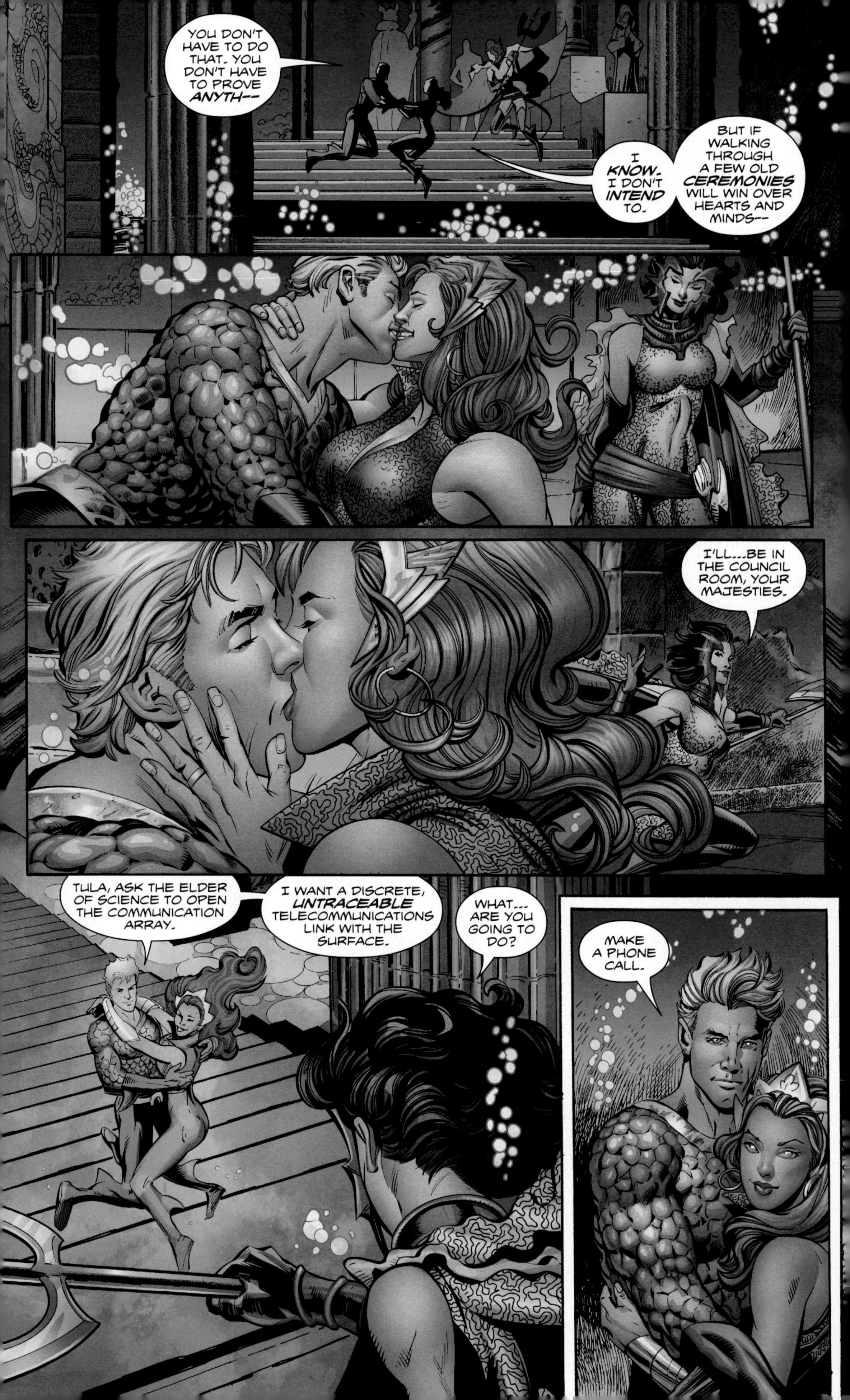
YOU DON'T HAVE TO DO THAT. YOU DON'T HAVE TO PROVE ANYTH--
I KNOW. I DON'T INTEND TO.
BUT IF WALKING THROUGH A FEW OLD CEREMONIES WILL WIN OVER HEARTS AND MINDS--
I'LL...BE IN THE COUNCIL ROOM, YOUR MAJESTIES.
TULA, ASK THE ELDER OF SCIENCE TO OPEN THE COMMUNICATION ARRAY.
I WANT A DISCRETE, UNTRACEABLE TELECOMMUNICATIONS LINK WITH THE SURFACE.
WHAT... ARE YOU GOING TO DO?
MAKE A PHONE CALL.

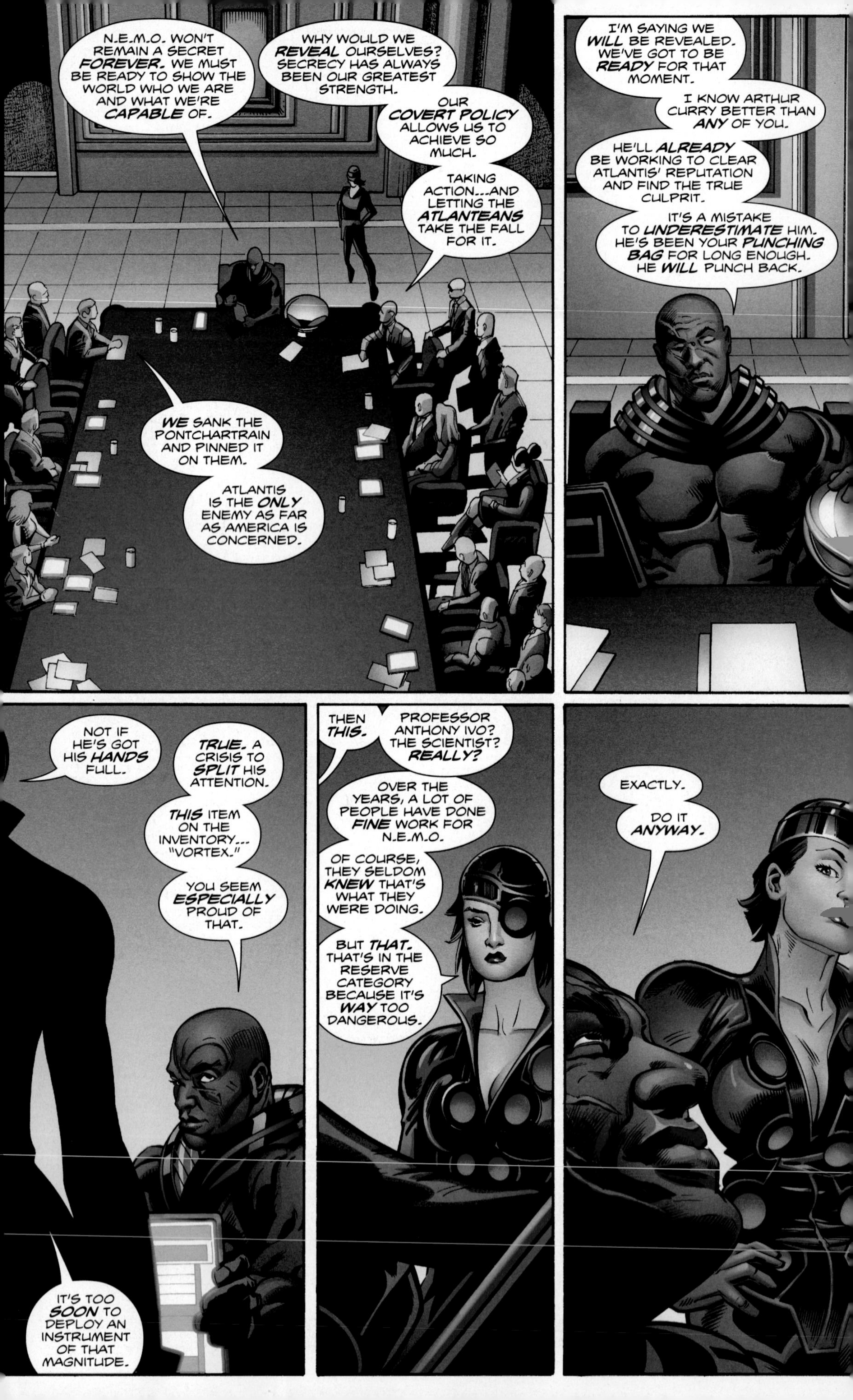
N.E.M.O. WON'T REMAIN A SECRET FOREVER. WE MUST BE READY TO SHOW THE WORLD WHO WE ARE AND WHAT WE'RE CAPABLE OF.
WHY WOULD WE REVEAL OURSELVES? SECRECY HAS ALWAYS BEEN OUR GREATEST STRENGTH.
OUR COVERT POLICY ALLOWS US TO ACHIEVE SO MUCH.
TAKING ACTION...AND LETTING THE ATLANTEANS TAKE THE FALL FOR IT.
WE SANK THE PONTCHARTRAIN AND PINNED IT ON THEM.
ATLANTIS IS THE ONLY ENEMY AS FAR AS AMERICA IS CONCERNED.
I'M SAYING WE WILL BE REVEALED. WE'VE GOT TO BE READY FOR THAT MOMENT.
I KNOW ARTHUR CURRY BETTER THAN ANY OF YOU.
HE'LL ALREADY BE WORKING TO CLEAR ATLANTIS' REPUTATION AND FIND THE TRUE CULPRIT.
IT'S A MISTAKE TO UNDERESTIMATE HIM. HE'S BEEN YOUR PUNCHING BAG FOR LONG ENOUGH. HE WILL PUNCH BACK.
NOT IF HE'S GOT HIS HANDS FULL.
TRUE. A CRISIS TO SPLIT HIS ATTENTION.
THIS ITEM ON THE INVENTORY... "VORTEX."
YOU SEEM ESPECIALLY PROUD OF THAT.
IT'S TOO SOON TO DEPLOY AN INSTRUMENT OF THAT MAGNITUDE.
THEN THIS.
PROFESSOR ANTHONY IVO? THE SCIENTIST? REALLY?
OVER THE YEARS, A LOT OF PEOPLE HAVE DONE FINE WORK FOR N.E.M.O.
OF COURSE, THEY SELDOM KNEW THAT'S WHAT THEY WERE DOING.
BUT THAT. THAT'S IN THE RESERVE CATEGORY BECAUSE IT'S WAY TOO DANGEROUS.
EXACTLY.
DO IT ANYWAY.

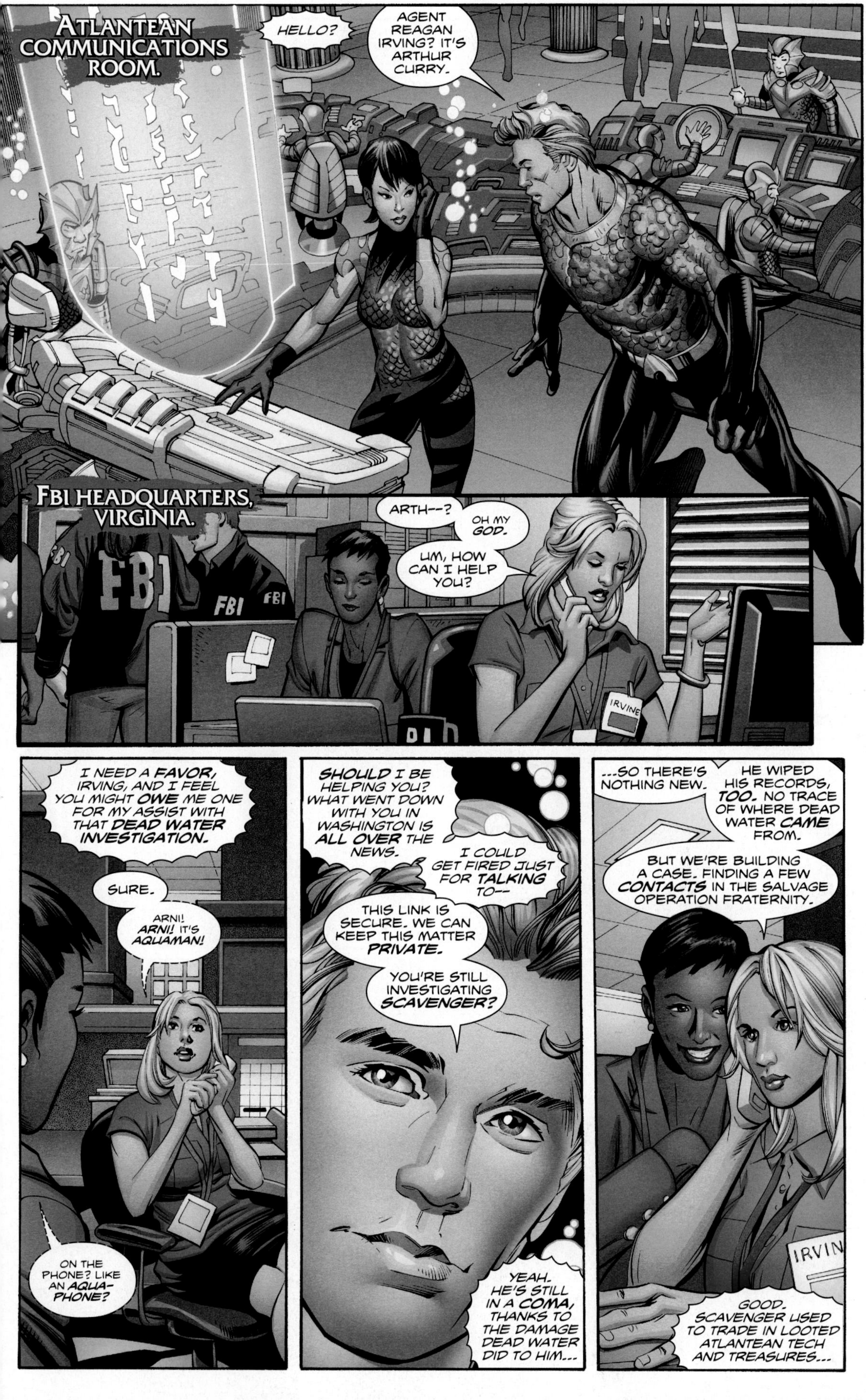
ATLANTEAN COMMUNICATIONS ROOM.
HELLO?
AGENT REAGAN IRVING? IT'S ARTHUR CURRY.
FBI HEADQUARTERS, VIRGINIA.
ARTH--?
OH MY GOD.
UM, HOW CAN I HELP YOU?
IRVINE
I NEED A FAVOR, IRVING, AND I FEEL YOU MIGHT OWE ME ONE FOR MY ASSIST WITH THAT DEAD WATER INVESTIGATION.
SURE.
ARNI! ARNI! IT'S AQUAMAN!
ON THE PHONE? LIKE AN AQUA-PHONE?
SHOULD I BE HELPING YOU? WHAT WENT DOWN WITH YOU IN WASHINGTON IS ALL OVER THE NEWS.
I COULD GET FIRED JUST FOR TALKING TO--
THIS LINK IS SECURE. WE CAN KEEP THIS MATTER PRIVATE.
YOU'RE STILL INVESTIGATING SCAVENGER?
YEAH. HE'S STILL IN A COMA, THANKS TO THE DAMAGE DEAD WATER DID TO HIM...
...SO THERE'S NOTHING NEW.
HE WIPED HIS RECORDS, TOO. NO TRACE OF WHERE DEAD WATER CAME FROM.
BUT WE'RE BUILDING A CASE. FINDING A FEW CONTACTS IN THE SALVAGE OPERATION FRATERNITY.
IRVIN
GOOD. SCAVENGER USED TO TRADE IN LOOTED ATLANTEAN TECH AND TREASURES...

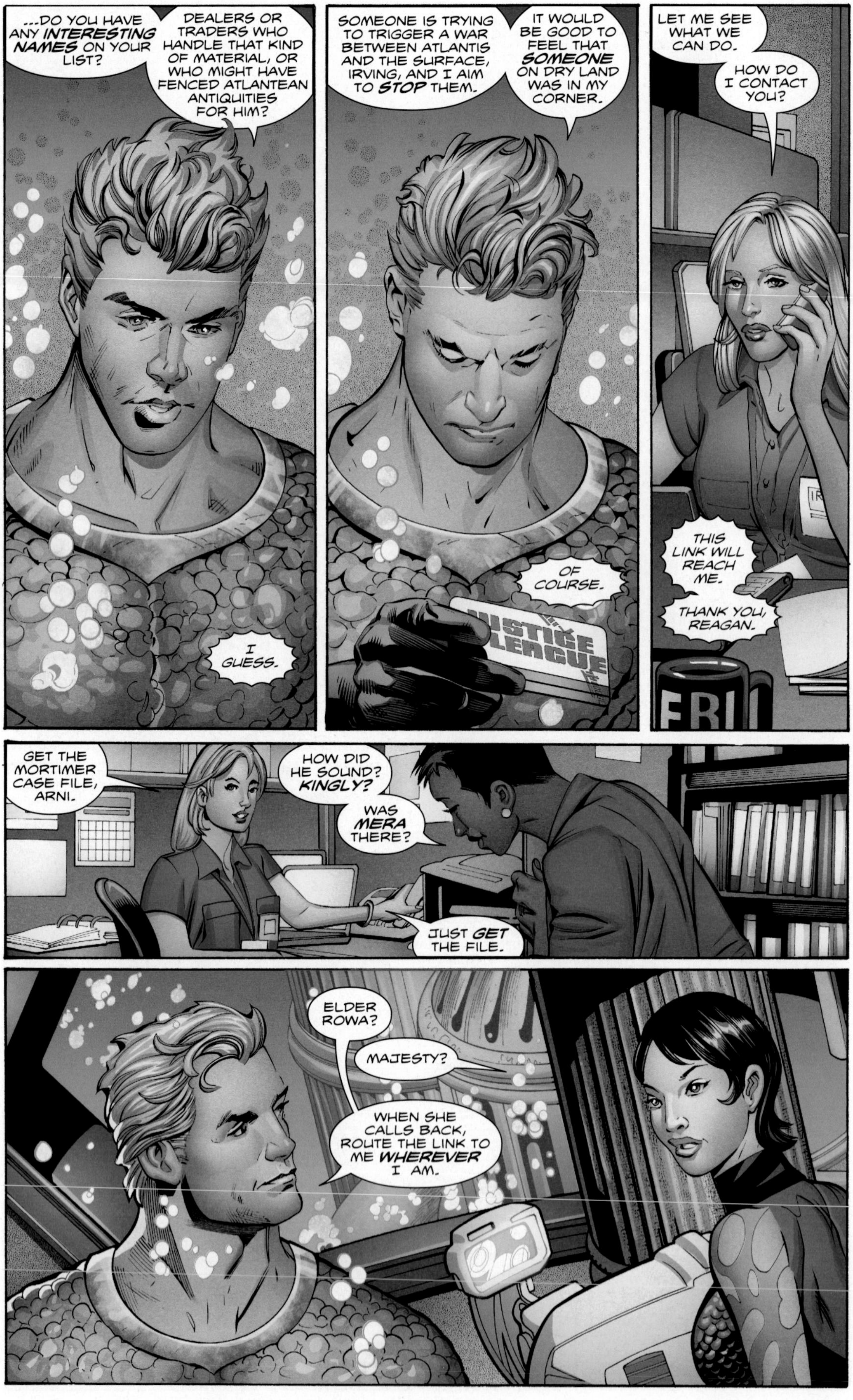
...DO YOU HAVE ANY INTERESTING NAMES ON YOUR LIST?
DEALERS OR TRADERS WHO HANDLE THAT KIND OF MATERIAL, OR WHO MIGHT HAVE FENCED ATLANTEAN ANTIQUITIES FOR HIM?
I GUESS.
SOMEONE IS TRYING TO TRIGGER A WAR BETWEEN ATLANTIS AND THE SURFACE, IRVING, AND I AIM TO STOP THEM.
IT WOULD BE GOOD TO FEEL THAT SOMEONE ON DRY LAND WAS IN MY CORNER.
OF COURSE.
JUSTICE LEAGUE
LET ME SEE WHAT WE CAN DO.
HOW DO I CONTACT YOU?
THIS LINK WILL REACH ME.
THANK YOU, REAGAN.
FBI
GET THE MORTIMER CASE FILE, ARNI.
HOW DID HE SOUND? KINGLY?
WAS MERA THERE?
JUST GET THE FILE.
ELDER ROWA?
MAJESTY?
WHEN SHE CALLS BACK, ROUTE THE LINK TO ME WHEREVER I AM.

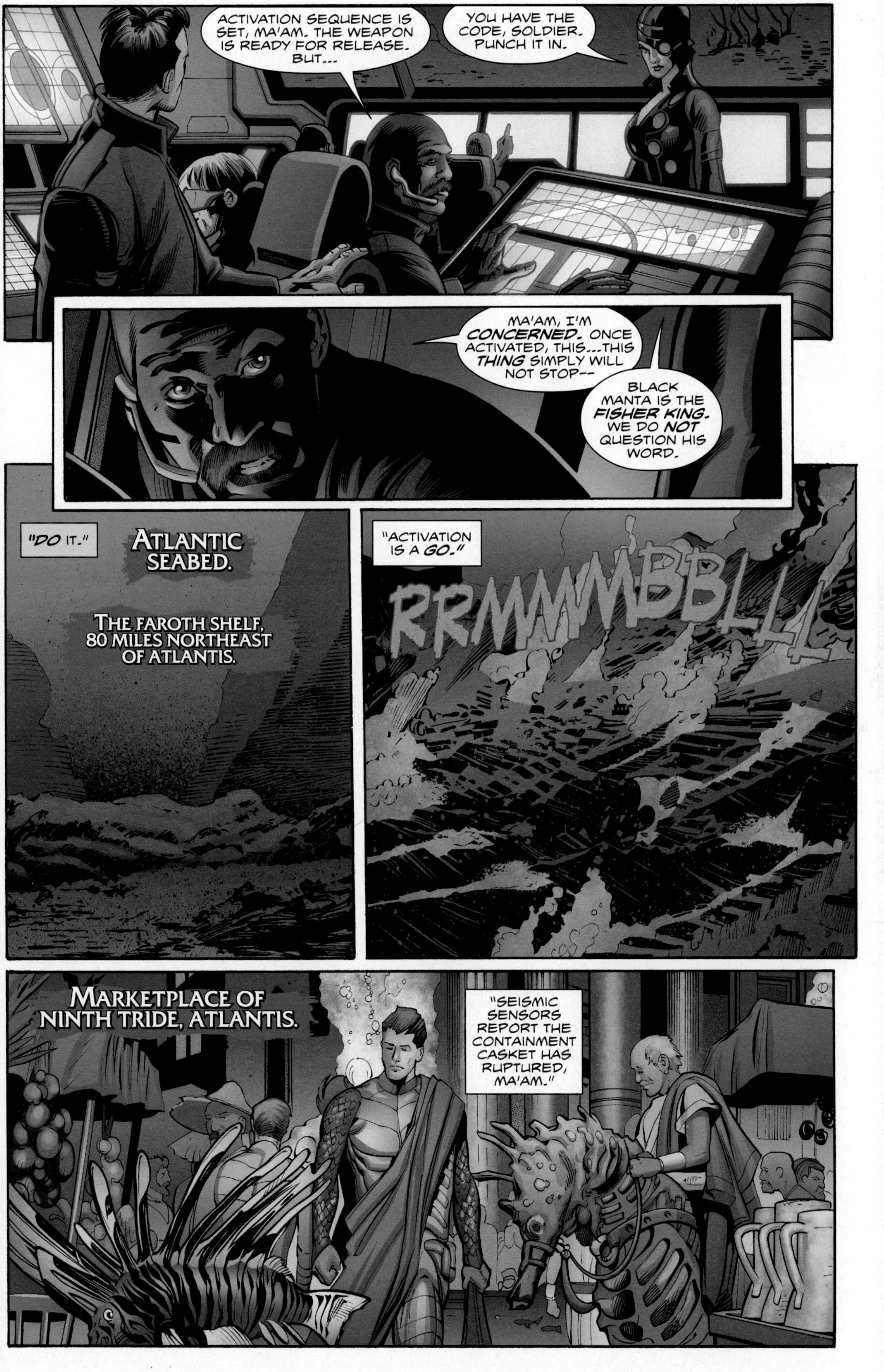
ACTIVATION SEQUENCE IS SET, MA'AM. THE WEAPON IS READY FOR RELEASE. BUT...
YOU HAVE THE CODE, SOLDIER. PUNCH IT IN.
MA'AM, I'M CONCERNED. ONCE ACTIVATED, THIS...THIS THING SIMPLY WILL NOT STOP--
BLACK MANTA IS THE FISHER KING. WE DO NOT QUESTION HIS WORD.
"DO IT."
ATLANTIC SEABED.
THE FAROTH SHELF, 80 MILES NORTHEAST OF ATLANTIS.
"ACTIVATION IS A GO."
RRMMMMBBLLL
MARKETPLACE OF NINTH TRIDE, ATLANTIS.
"SEISMIC SENSORS REPORT THE CONTAINMENT CASKET HAS RUPTURED, MA'AM."

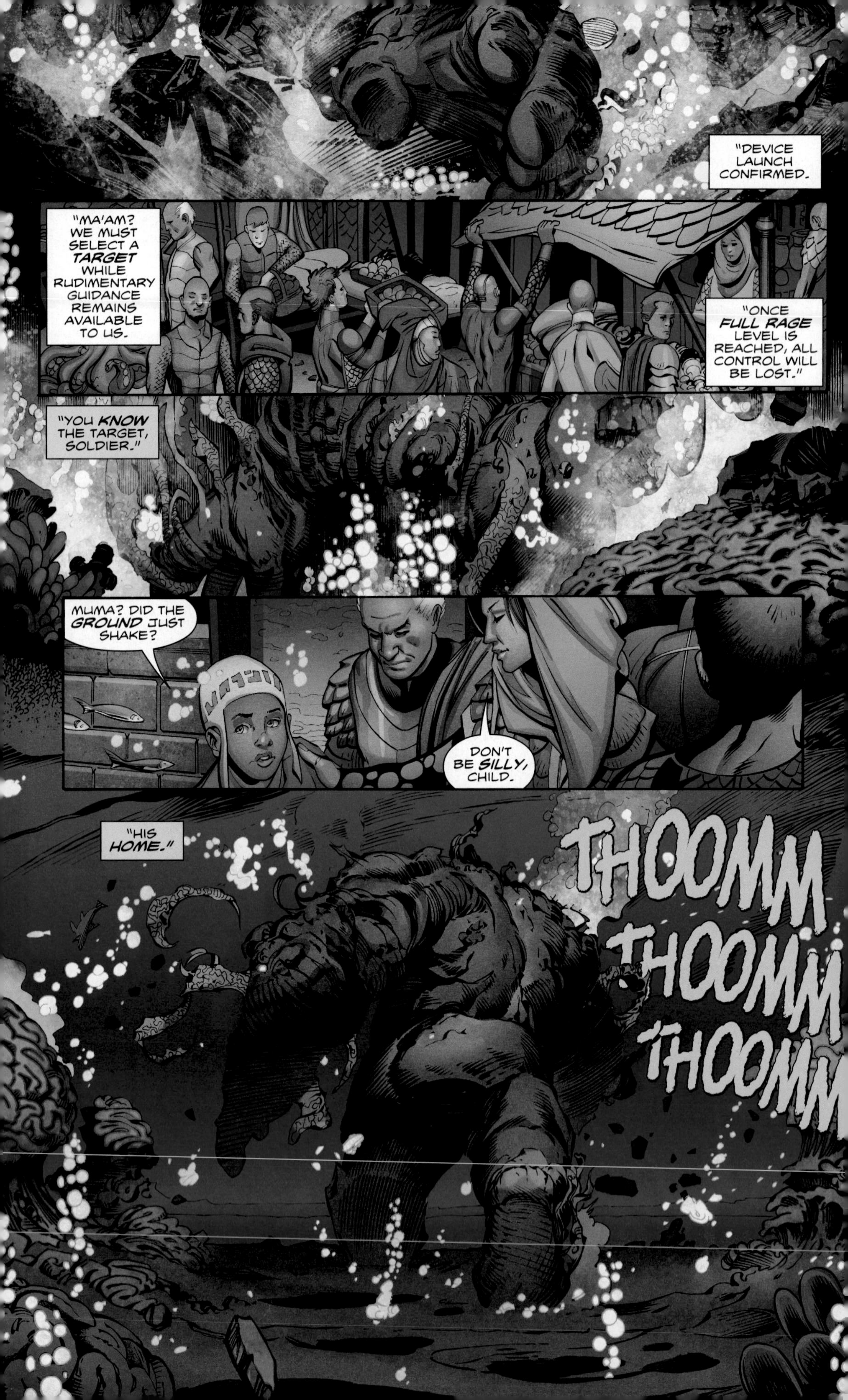
"DEVICE LAUNCH CONFIRMED.
"MA'AM? WE MUST SELECT A TARGET WHILE RUDIMENTARY GUIDANCE REMAINS AVAILABLE TO US.
"ONCE FULL RAGE LEVEL IS REACHED, ALL CONTROL WILL BE LOST."
"YOU KNOW THE TARGET, SOLDIER."
MUMA? DID THE GROUND JUST SHAKE?
DON'T BE SILLY, CHILD.
"HIS HOME."
THOOMM
THOOMM
THOOMM

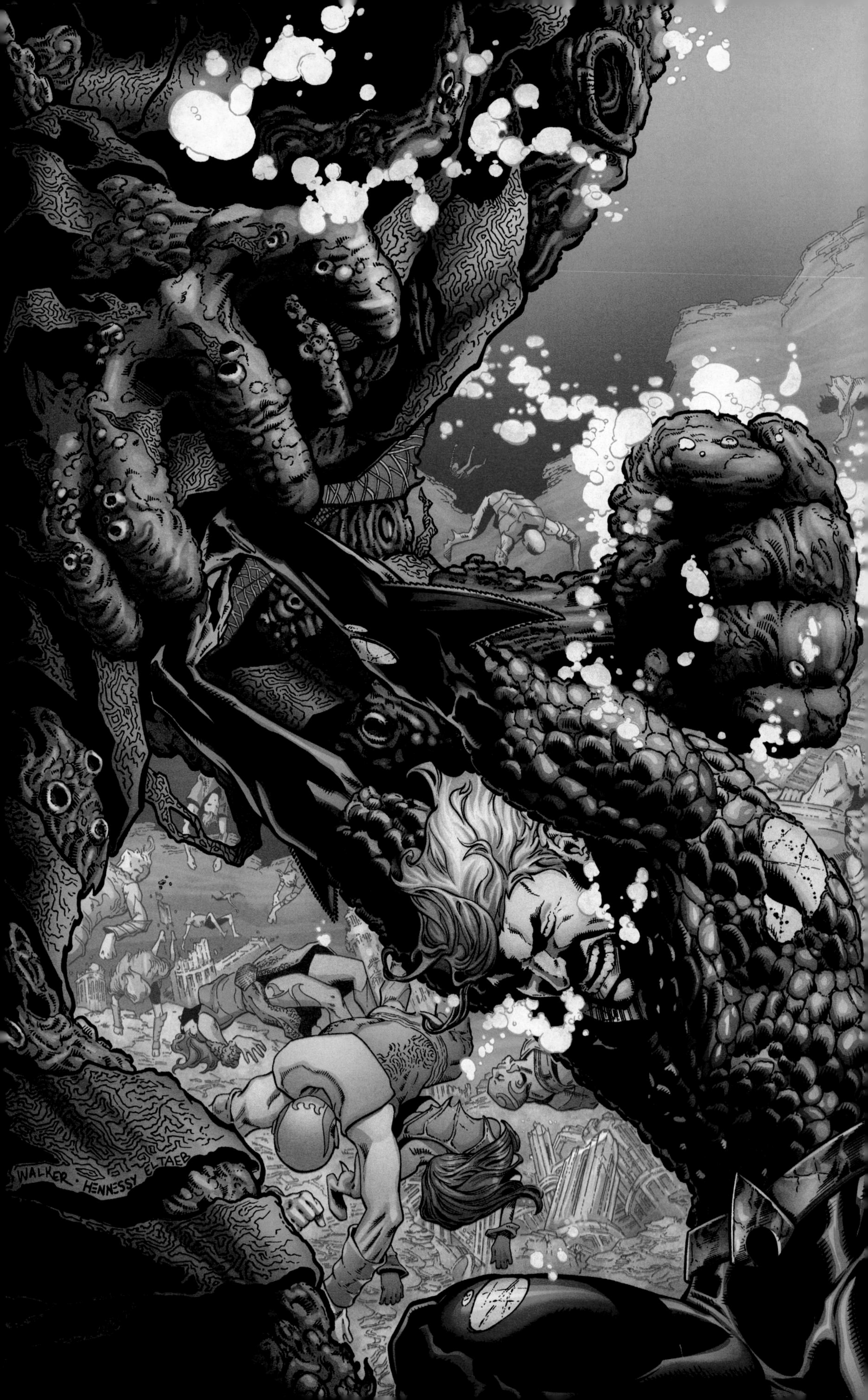
WALKER HENNESSY & TAEB

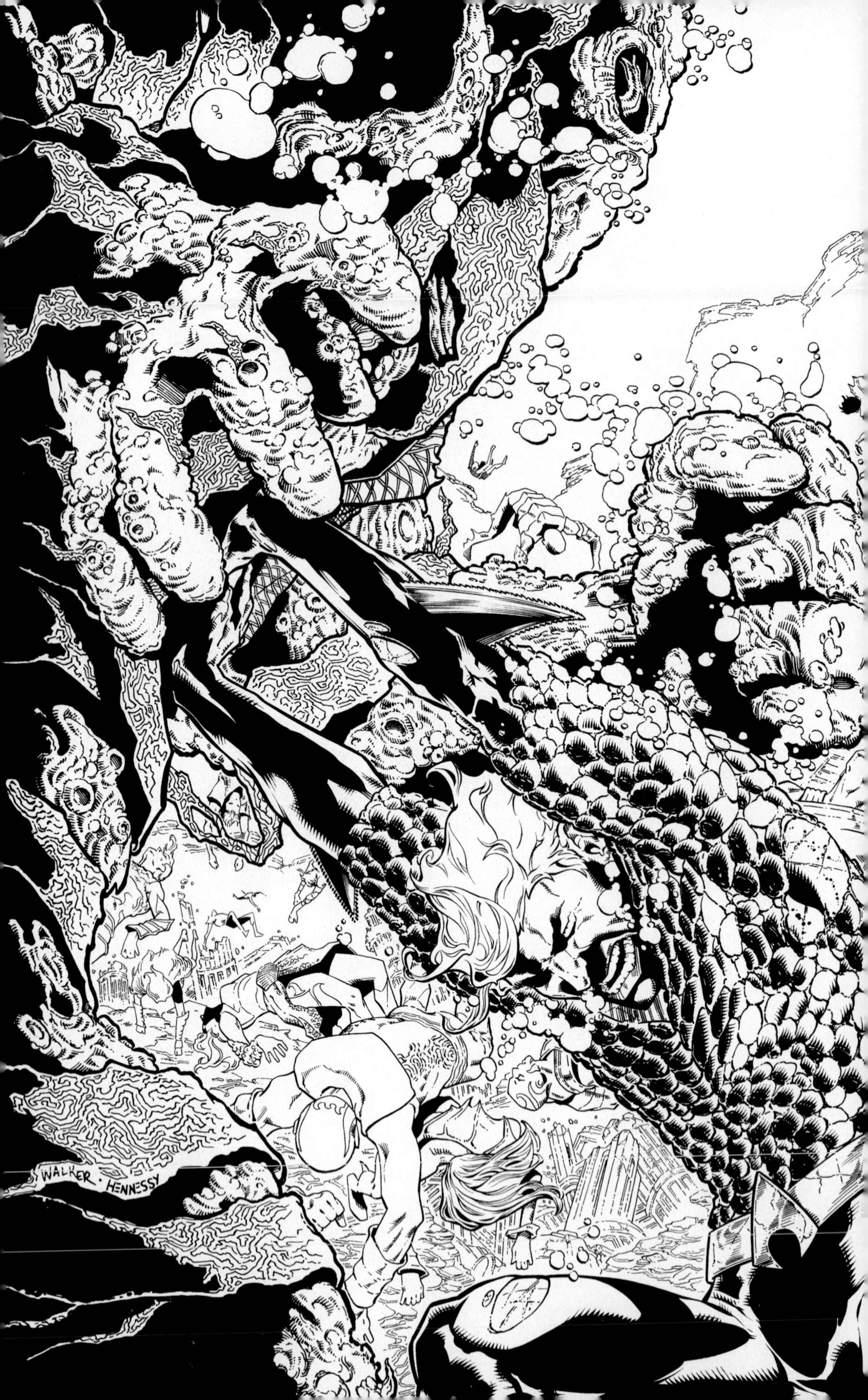
WALKER · HENNESSY

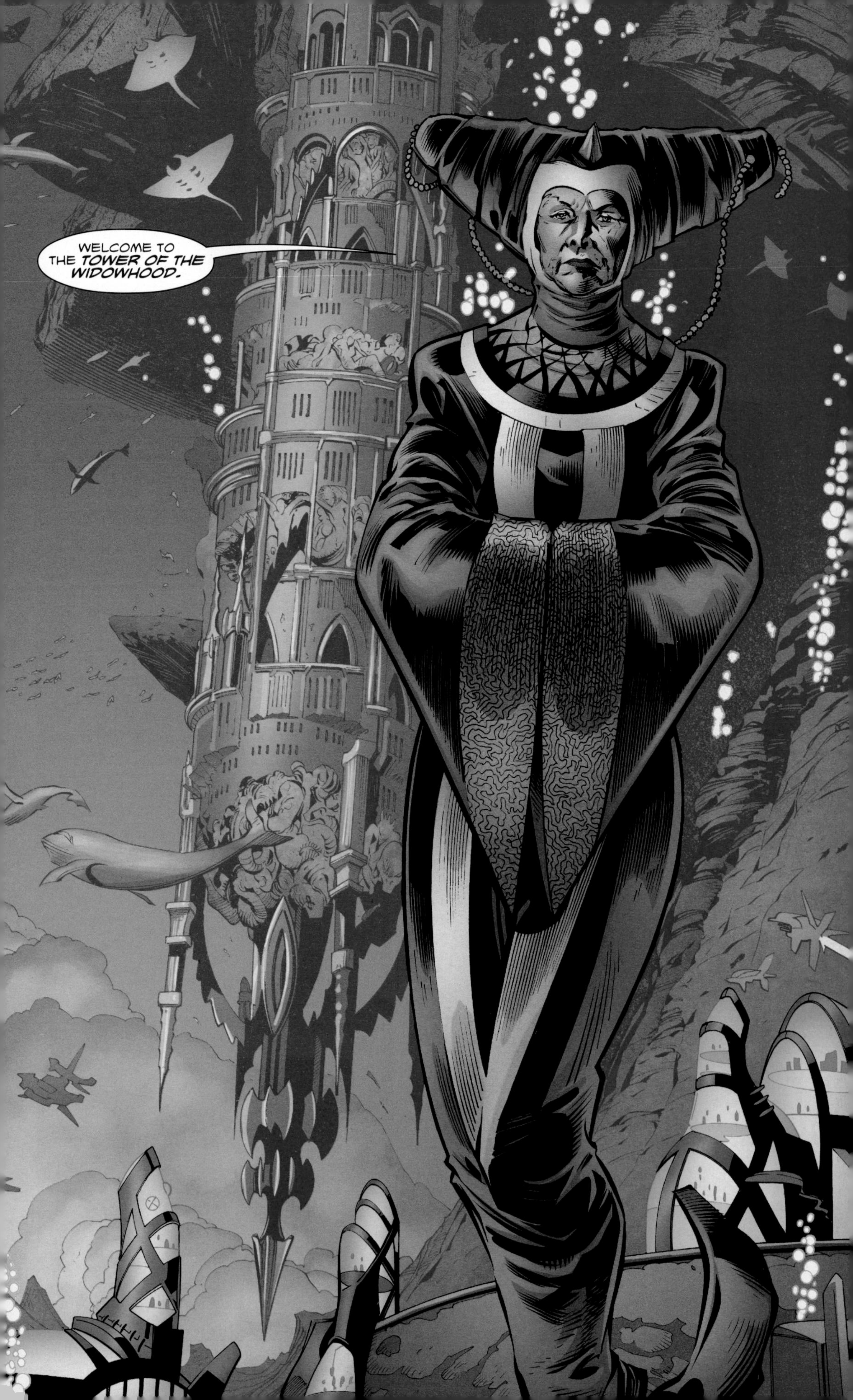
WELCOME TO THE *TOWER OF THE WIDOWHOOD*.

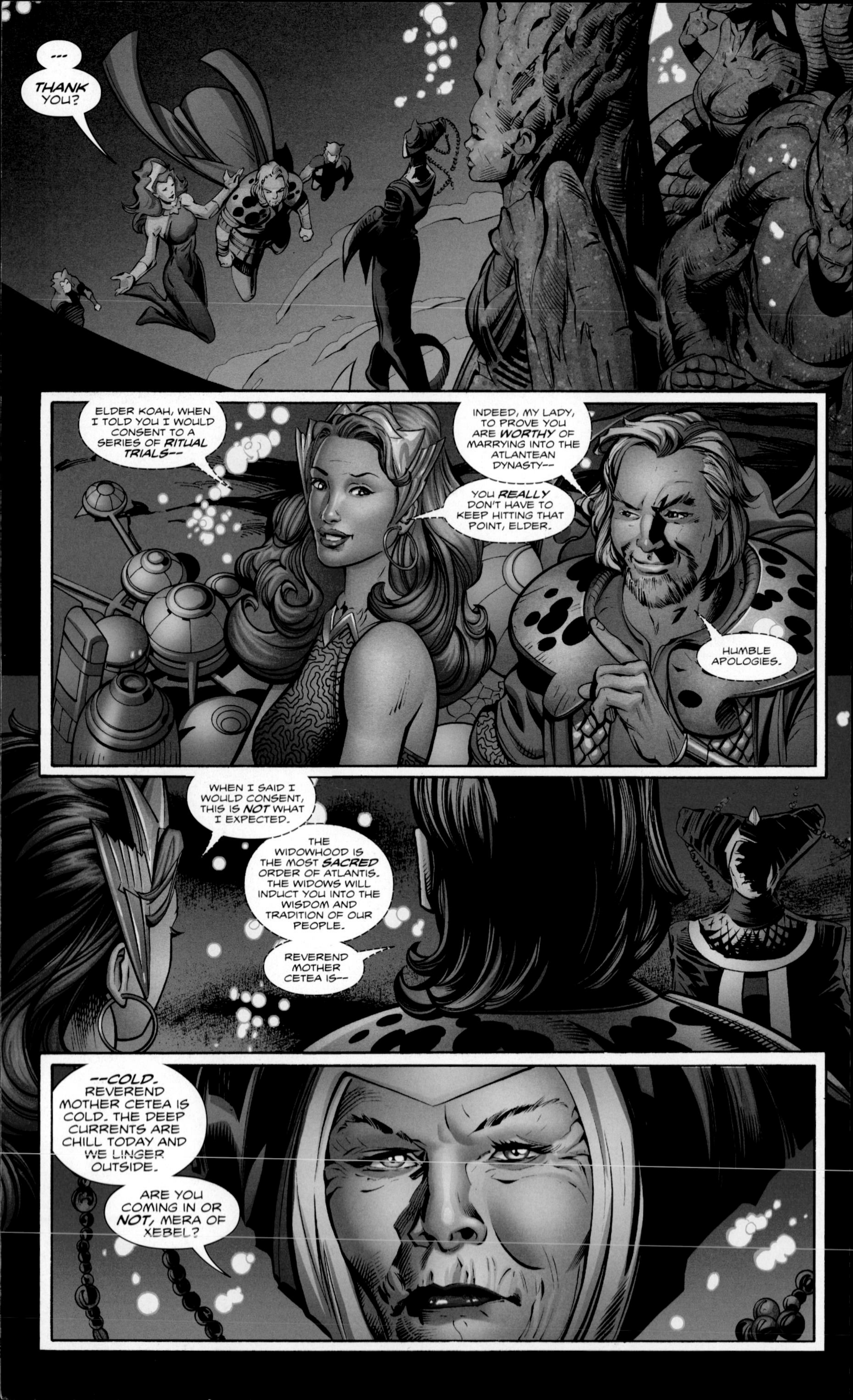

THANK YOU?
ELDER KOAH, WHEN I TOLD YOU I WOULD CONSENT TO A SERIES OF RITUAL TRIALS--
INDEED, MY LADY, TO PROVE YOU ARE WORTHY OF MARRYING INTO THE ATLANTEAN DYNASTY--
YOU REALLY DON'T HAVE TO KEEP HITTING THAT POINT, ELDER.
HUMBLE APOLOGIES.
WHEN I SAID I WOULD CONSENT, THIS IS NOT WHAT I EXPECTED.
THE WIDOWHOOD IS THE MOST SACRED ORDER OF ATLANTIS. THE WIDOWS WILL INDUCT YOU INTO THE WISDOM AND TRADITION OF OUR PEOPLE.
REVEREND MOTHER CETEA IS--
--COLD. REVEREND MOTHER CETEA IS COLD. THE DEEP CURRENTS ARE CHILL TODAY AND WE LINGER OUTSIDE.
ARE YOU COMING IN OR NOT, MERA OF XEBEL?

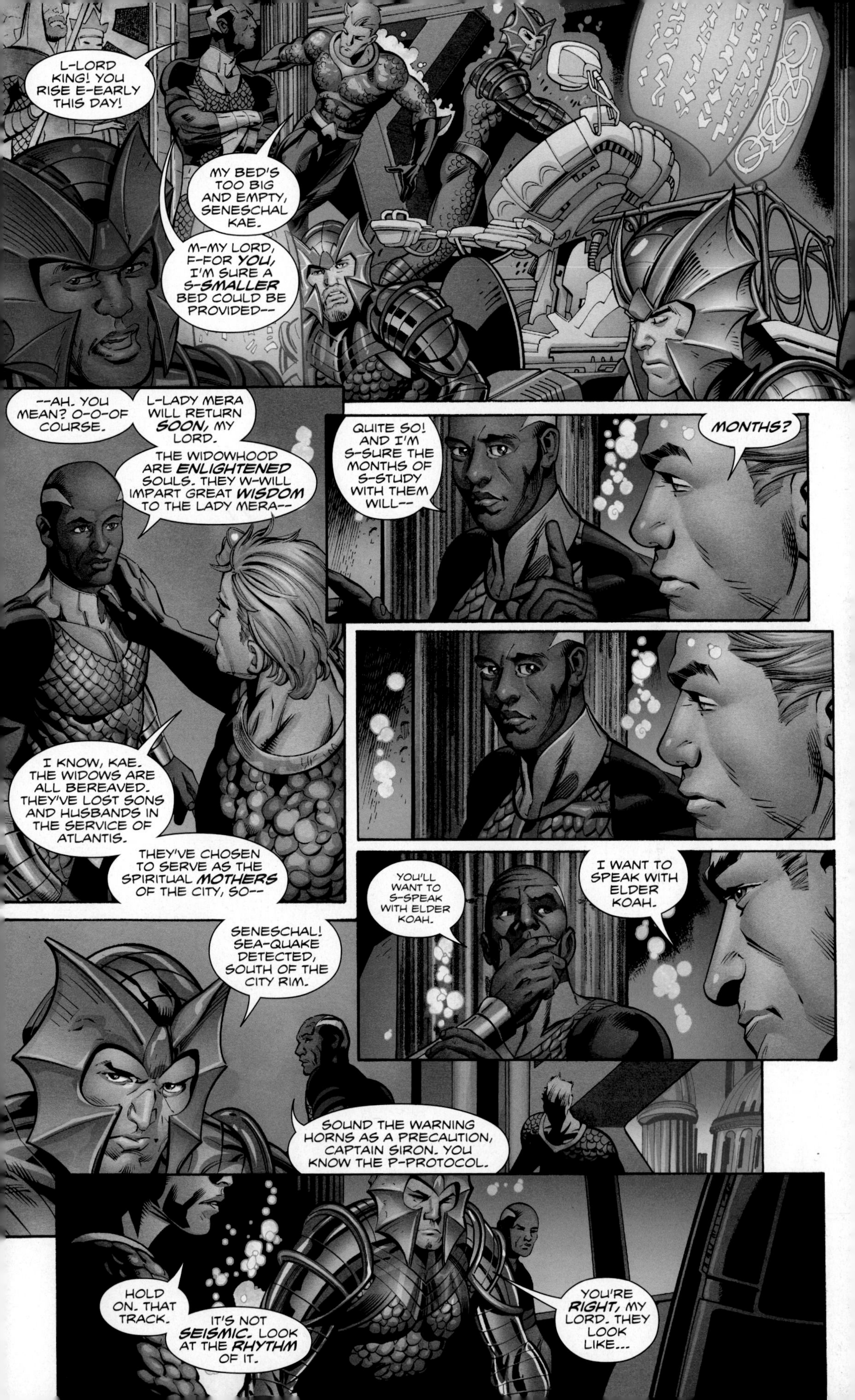

L-LORD KING! YOU RISE E-EARLY THIS DAY!
MY BED'S TOO BIG AND EMPTY, SENESCHAL KAE.
M-MY LORD, F-FOR YOU, I'M SURE A S-SMALLER BED COULD BE PROVIDED--
--AH. YOU MEAN? O-O-OF COURSE.
L-LADY MERA WILL RETURN SOON, MY LORD.
THE WIDOWHOOD ARE ENLIGHTENED SOULS. THEY W-WILL IMPART GREAT WISDOM TO THE LADY MERA--
I KNOW, KAE. THE WIDOWS ARE ALL BEREAVED. THEY'VE LOST SONS AND HUSBANDS IN THE SERVICE OF ATLANTIS.
THEY'VE CHOSEN TO SERVE AS THE SPIRITUAL MOTHERS OF THE CITY, SO--
QUITE SO! AND I'M S-SURE THE MONTHS OF S-STUDY WITH THEM WILL--
MONTHS?
YOU'LL WANT TO S-SPEAK WITH ELDER KOAH.
I WANT TO SPEAK WITH ELDER KOAH.
SENESCHAL! SEA-QUAKE DETECTED, SOUTH OF THE CITY RIM.
SOUND THE WARNING HORNS AS A PRECAUTION, CAPTAIN SIRON. YOU KNOW THE P-PROTOCOL.
HOLD ON. THAT TRACK.
IT'S NOT SEISMIC. LOOK AT THE RHYTHM OF IT.
YOU'RE RIGHT, MY LORD. THEY LOOK LIKE...

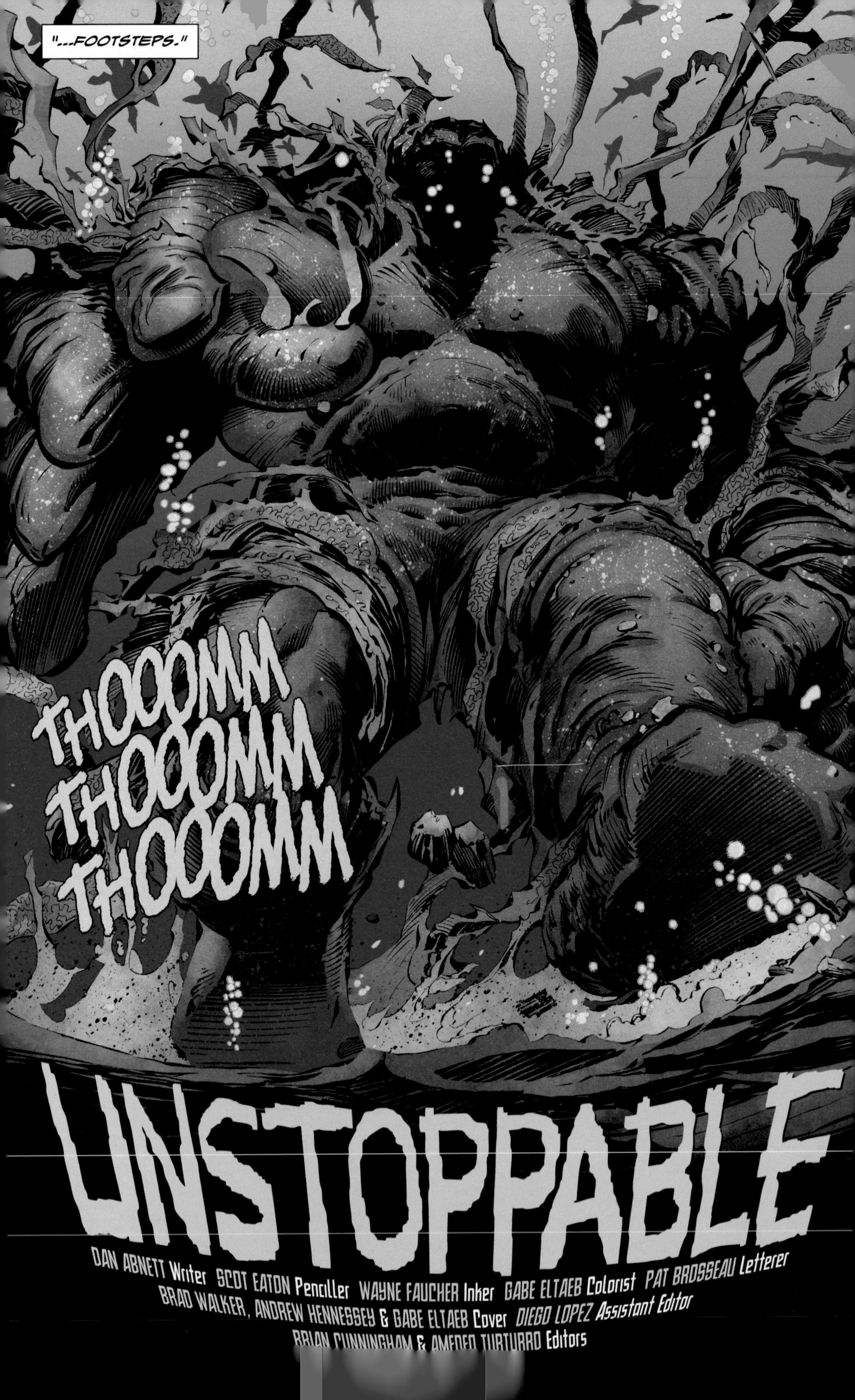
"...FOOTSTEPS."
THOOOMM THOOOMM THOOOMM
UNSTOPPABLE
DAN ABNETT Writer SCOT EATON Penciller WAYNE FAUCHER Inker GABE ELTAEB Colorist PAT BROSSEAU Letterer
BRAD WALKER, ANDREW HENNESSEY & GABE ELTAEB Cover DIEGO LOPEZ Assistant Editor
BRIAN CUNNINGHAM & AMEDEO TURTURRO Editors

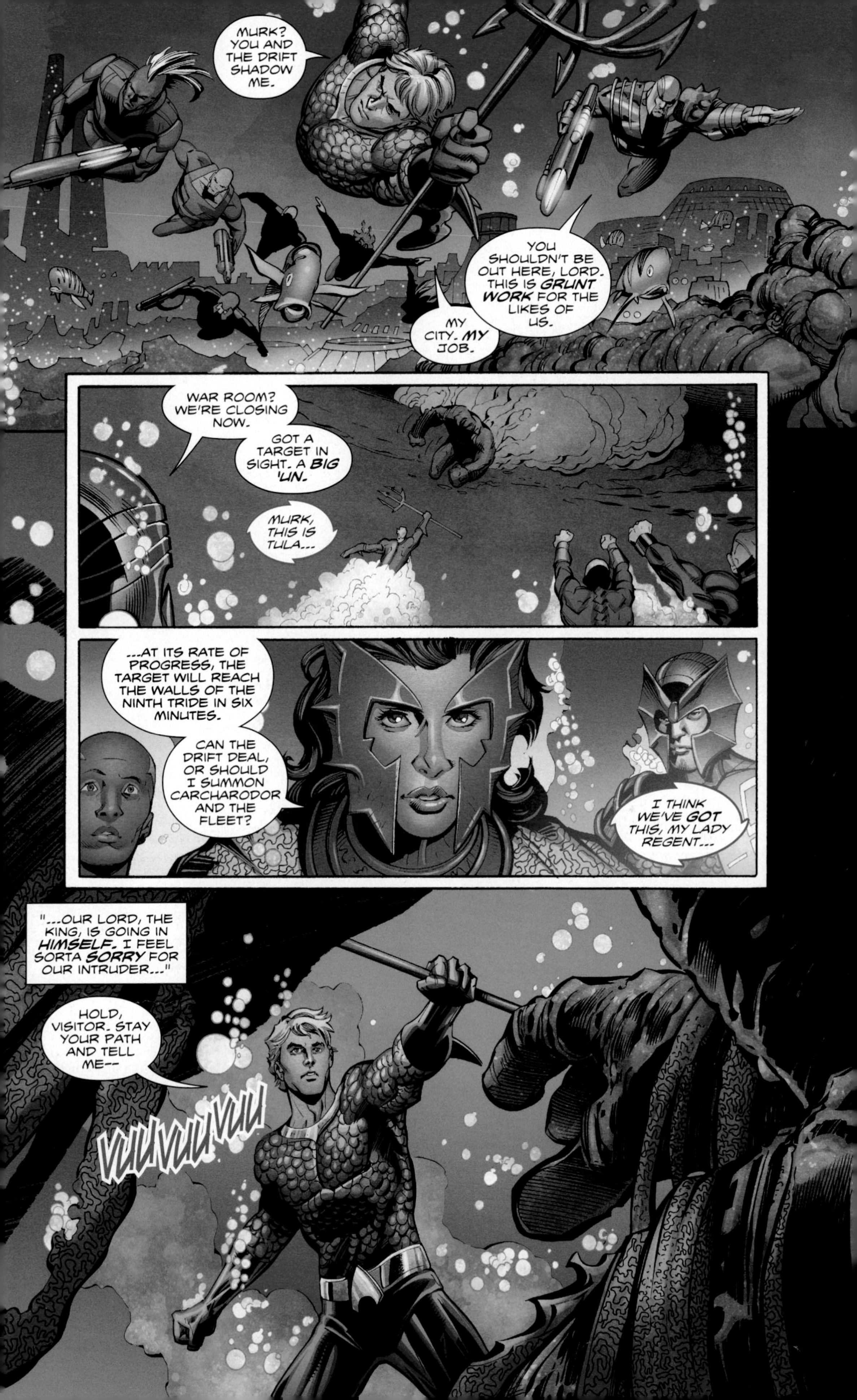

MURK? YOU AND THE DRIFT SHADOW ME.
YOU SHOULDN'T BE OUT HERE, LORD. THIS IS GRUNT WORK FOR THE LIKES OF US.
MY CITY. MY JOB.
WAR ROOM? WE'RE CLOSING NOW.
GOT A TARGET IN SIGHT. A BIG 'UN.
MURK, THIS IS TULA...
...AT ITS RATE OF PROGRESS, THE TARGET WILL REACH THE WALLS OF THE NINTH TRIDE IN SIX MINUTES.
CAN THE DRIFT DEAL, OR SHOULD I SUMMON CARCHARODOR AND THE FLEET?
I THINK WE'VE GOT THIS, MY LADY REGENT...
"...OUR LORD, THE KING, IS GOING IN HIMSELF. I FEEL SORTA SORRY FOR OUR INTRUDER..."
HOLD, VISITOR. STAY YOUR PATH AND TELL ME--
VUUVUUVUU

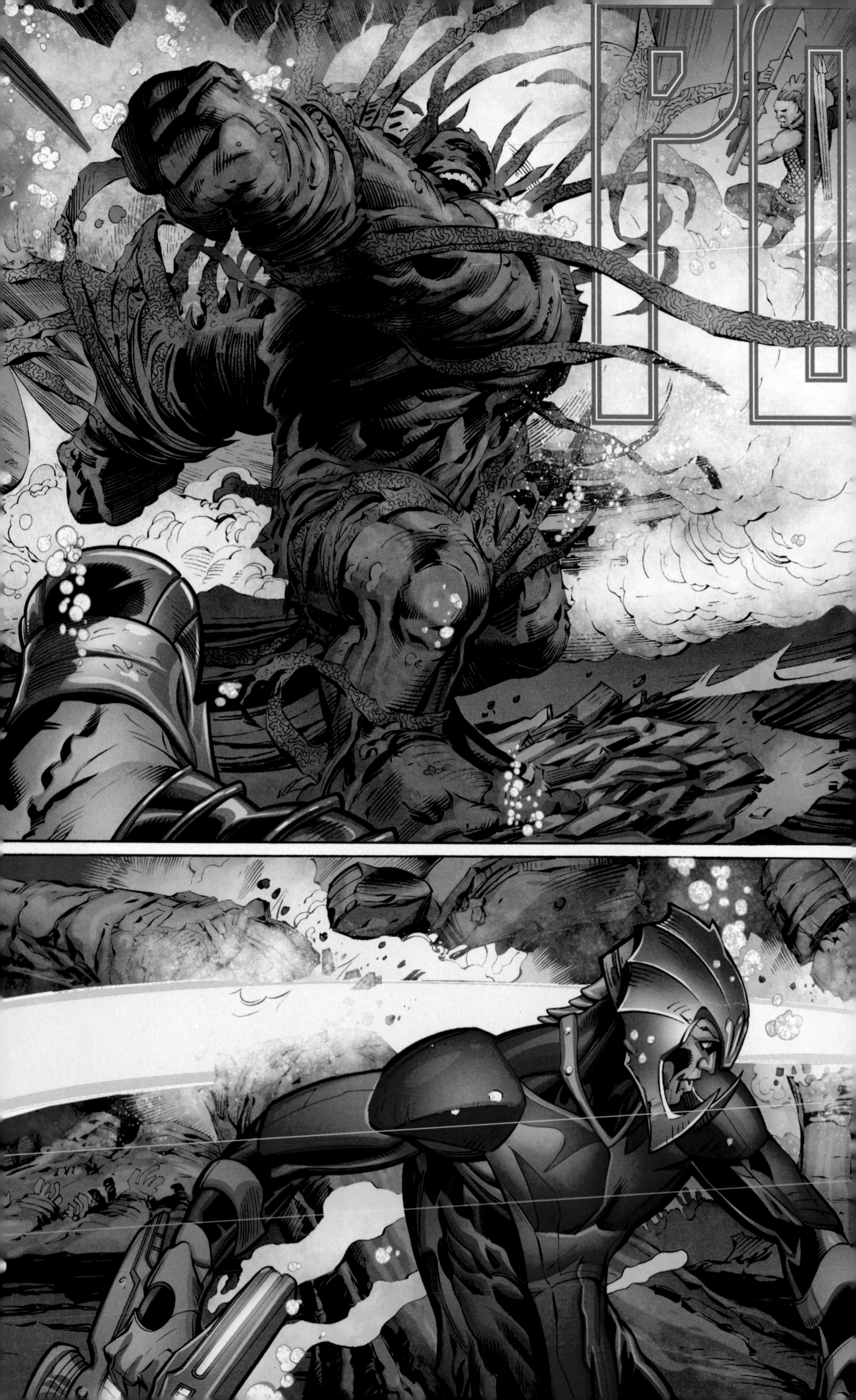

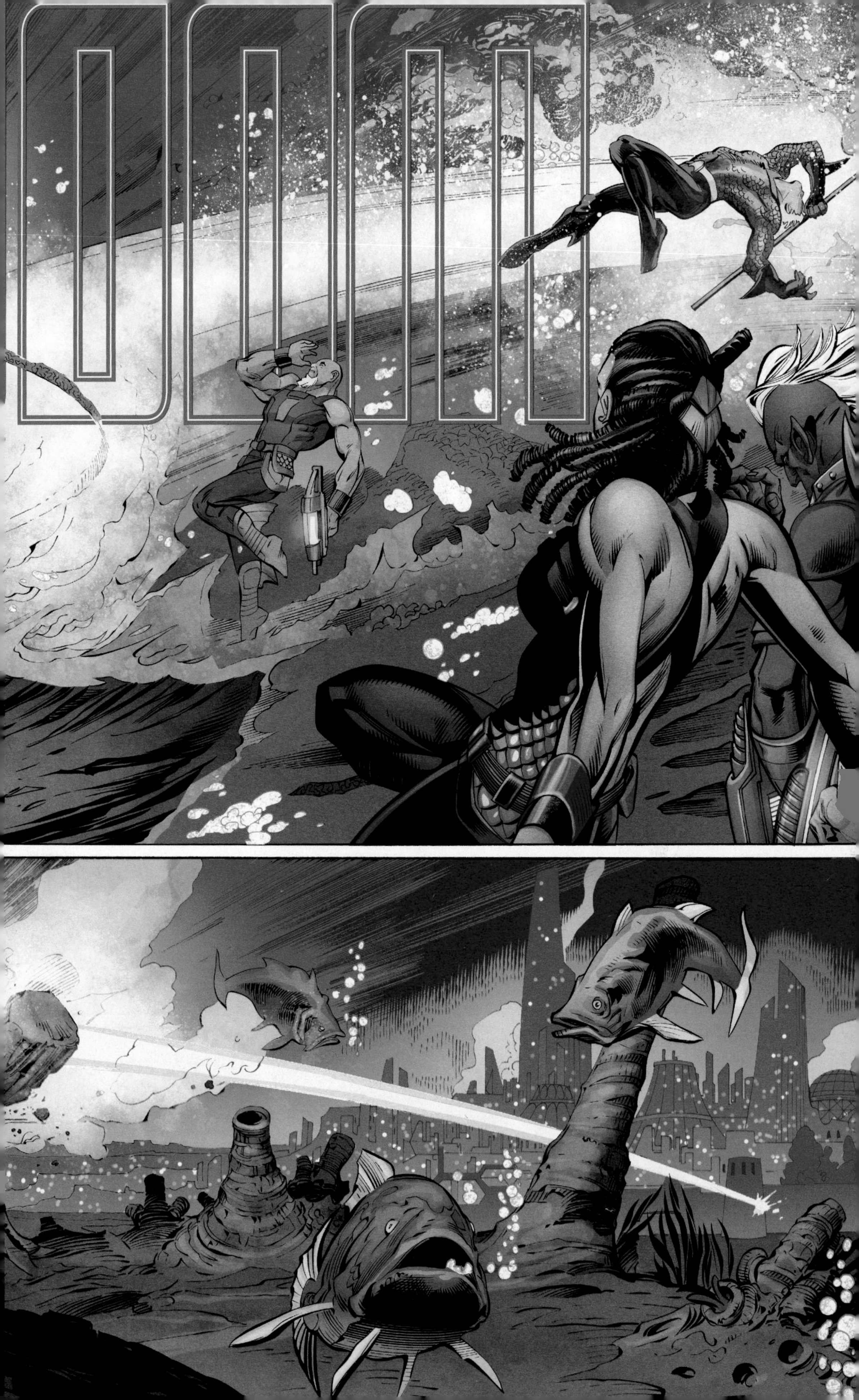

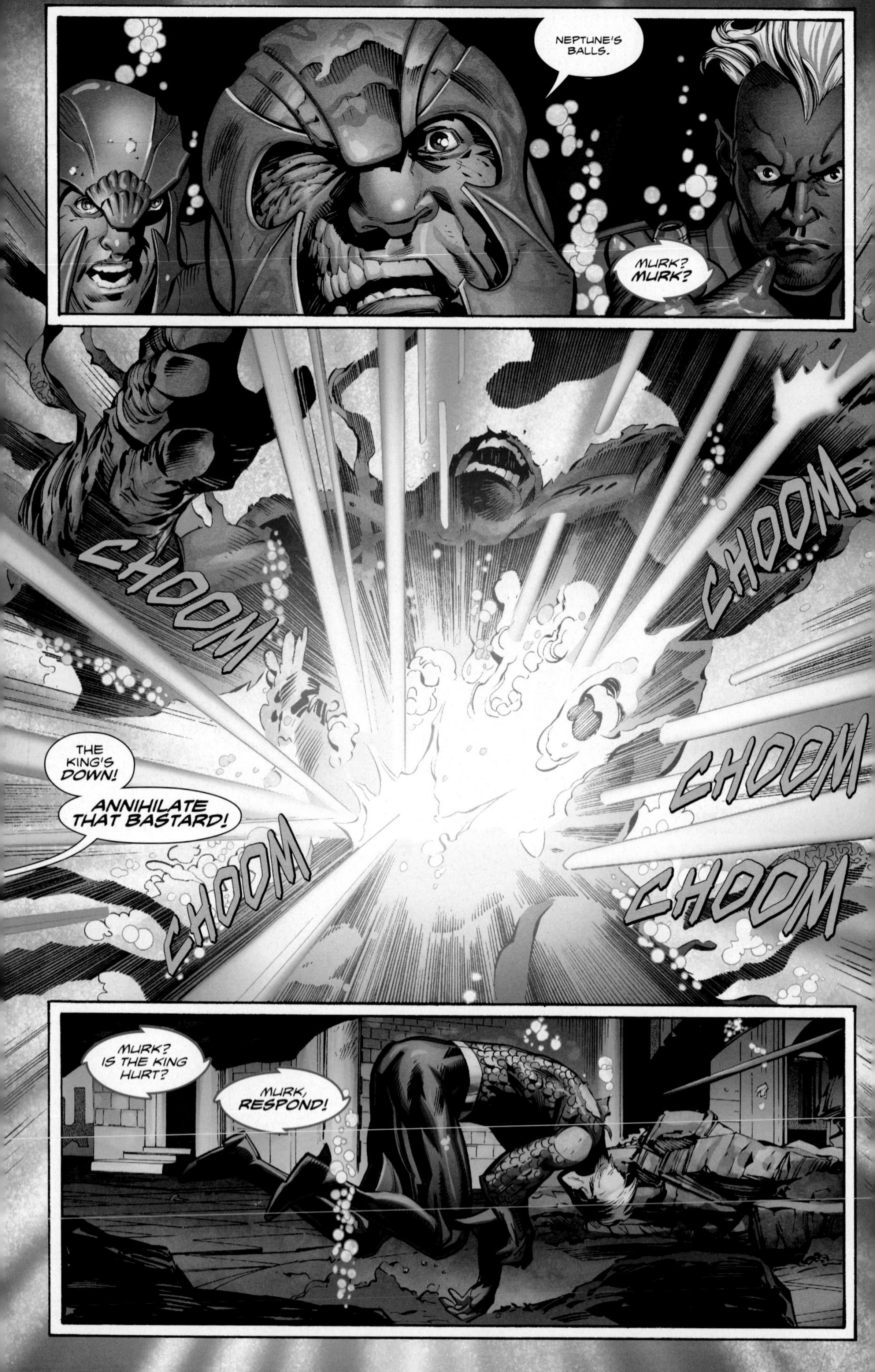
NEPTUNE'S BALLS.
MURK? MURK?
CHOOM
CHOOM
THE KING'S DOWN!
ANNIHILATE THAT BASTARD!
CHOOM
CHOOM
CHOOM
MURK? IS THE KING HURT?
MURK, RESPOND!

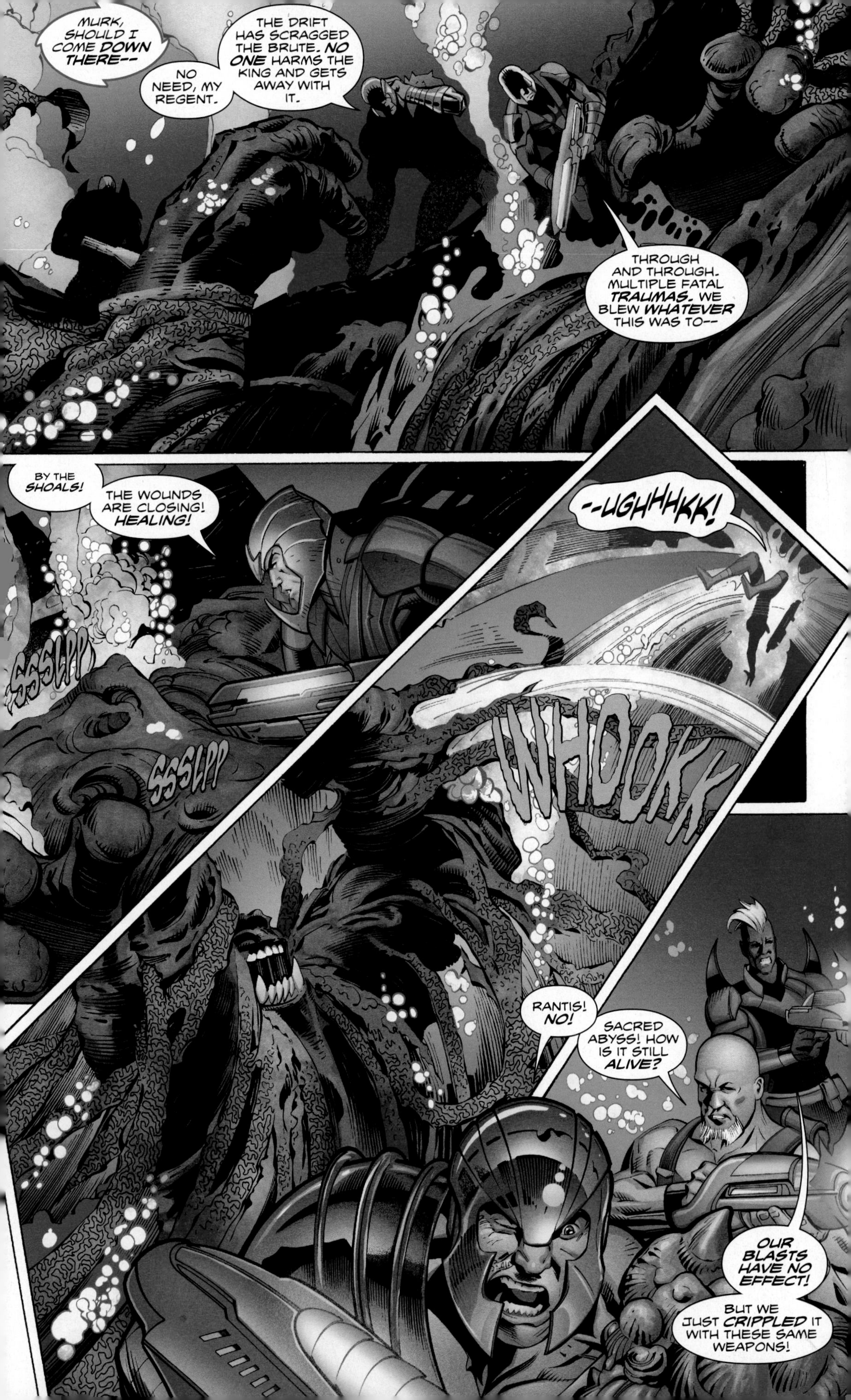
MURK, SHOULD I COME DOWN THERE--
NO NEED, MY REGENT.
THE DRIFT HAS SCRAGGED THE BRUTE. NO ONE HARMS THE KING AND GETS AWAY WITH IT.
THROUGH AND THROUGH. MULTIPLE FATAL TRAUMAS. WE BLEW WHATEVER THIS WAS TO--
BY THE SHOALS!
THE WOUNDS ARE CLOSING! HEALING!
SSSLPP
SSSLPP
--UGHHHKK!
WHOOKK
RANTIS! NO!
SACRED ABYSS! HOW IS IT STILL ALIVE?
OUR BLASTS HAVE NO EFFECT!
BUT WE JUST CRIPPLED IT WITH THESE SAME WEAPONS!

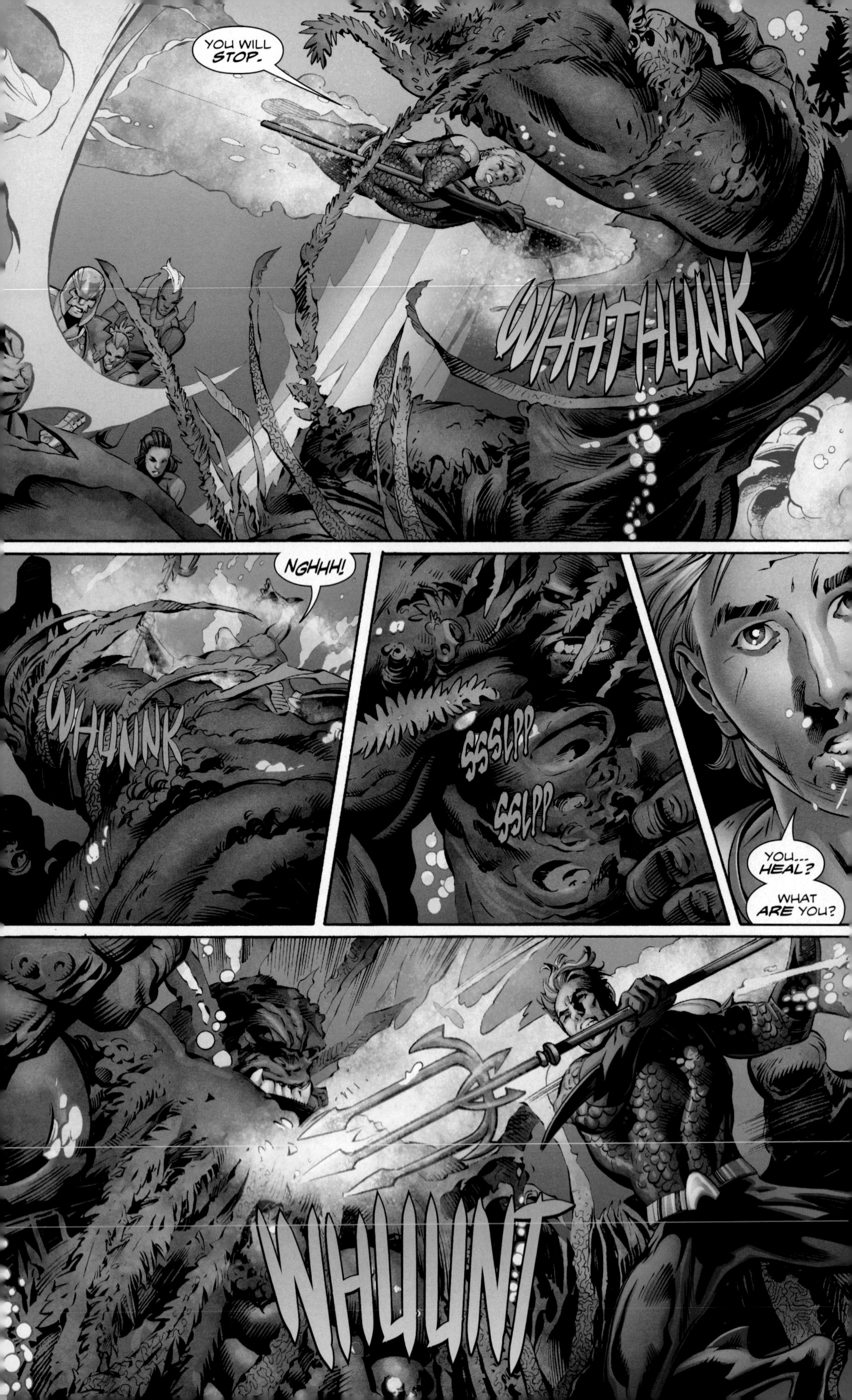
YOU WILL STOP.
WHHTHUNK
NGHHH!
WHUNNK
SSSLPP
SSLPP
YOU... HEAL?
WHAT ARE YOU?
WHUUNT

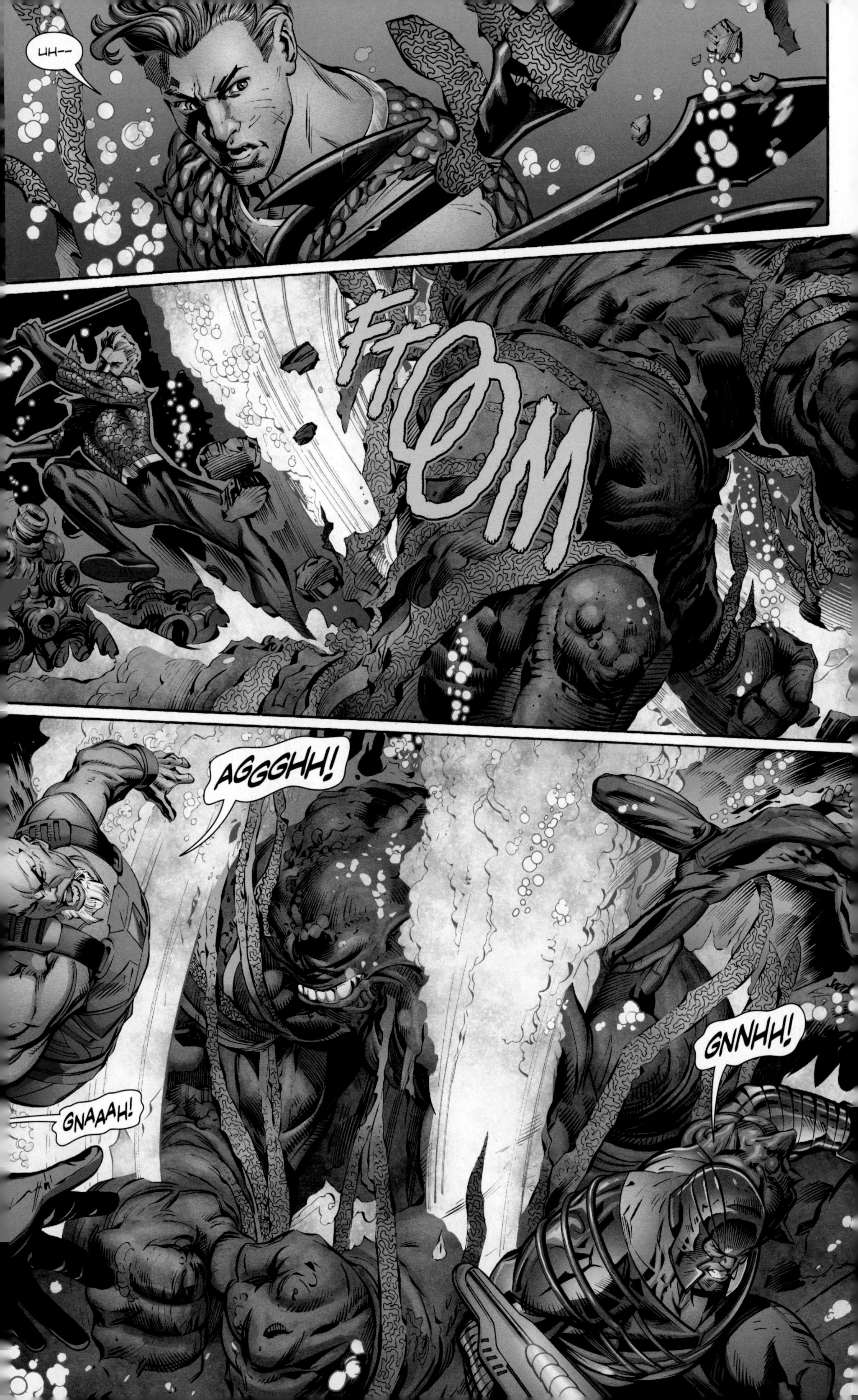
UH--
FTOOM
AGGGHH!
GNAAAH!
GNHH!

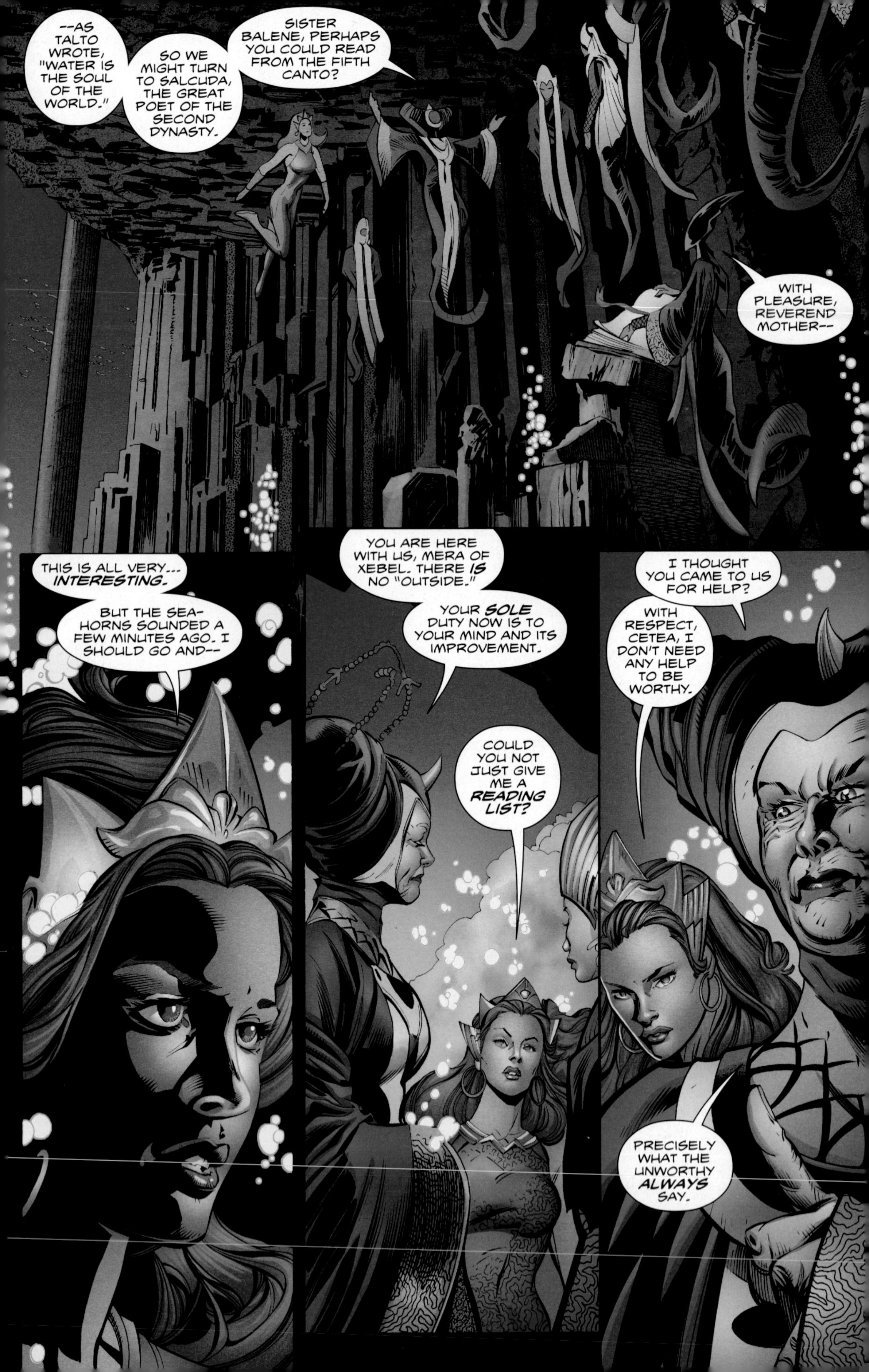
--AS TALTO WROTE, "WATER IS THE SOUL OF THE WORLD."
SO WE MIGHT TURN TO SALCUDA, THE GREAT POET OF THE SECOND DYNASTY.
SISTER BALENE, PERHAPS YOU COULD READ FROM THE FIFTH CANTO?
WITH PLEASURE, REVEREND MOTHER--
THIS IS ALL VERY... *INTERESTING.*
BUT THE SEA-HORNS SOUNDED A FEW MINUTES AGO. I SHOULD GO AND--
YOU ARE HERE WITH US, MERA OF XEBEL. THERE *IS* NO "OUTSIDE."
YOUR *SOLE* DUTY NOW IS TO YOUR MIND AND ITS IMPROVEMENT.
COULD YOU NOT JUST GIVE ME A *READING LIST?*
I THOUGHT YOU CAME TO US FOR HELP?
WITH RESPECT, CETEA, I DON'T NEED ANY HELP TO BE WORTHY.
PRECISELY WHAT THE UNWORTHY *ALWAYS* SAY.

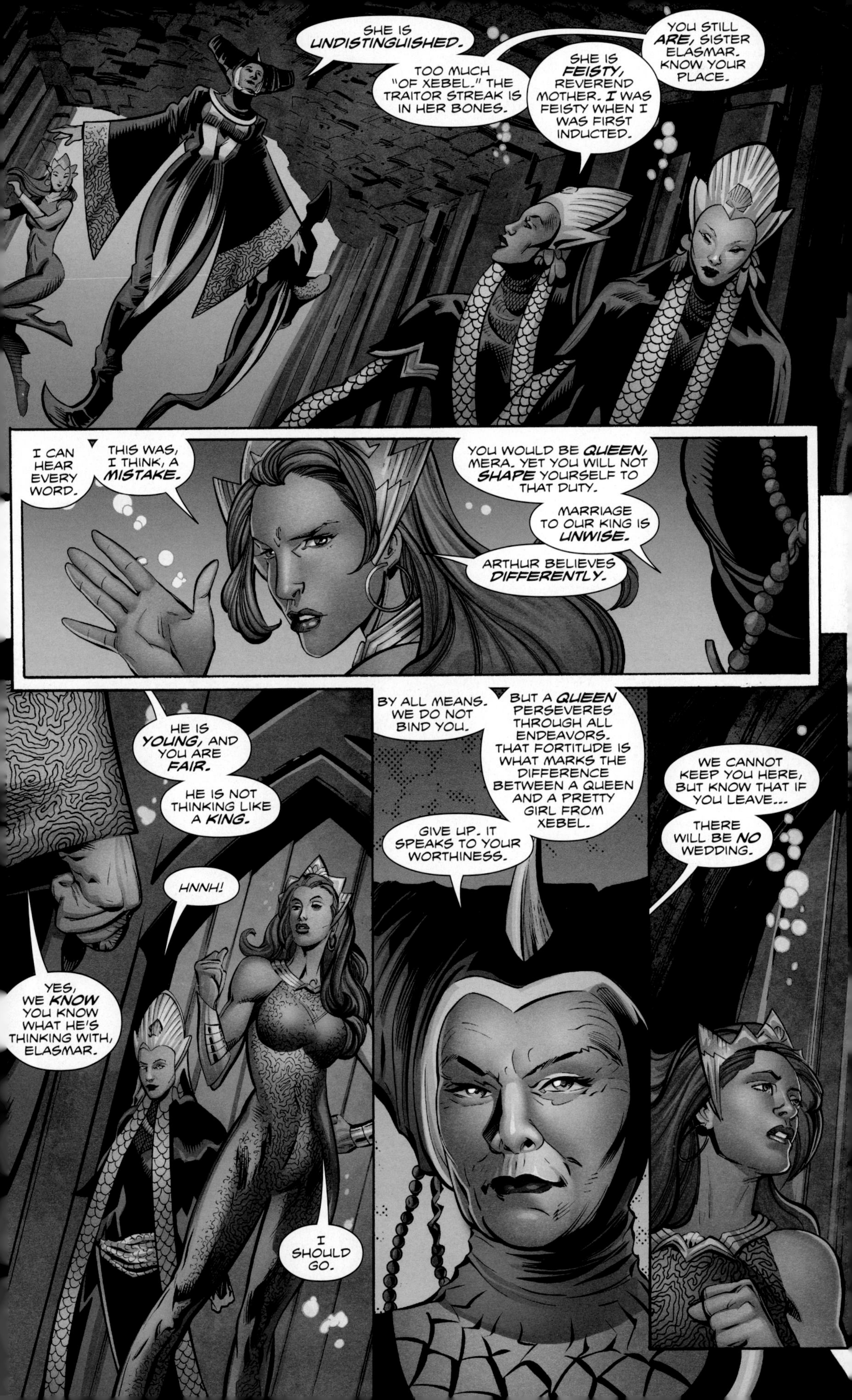

SHE IS UNDISTINGUISHED.
TOO MUCH "OF XEBEL." THE TRAITOR STREAK IS IN HER BONES.
SHE IS FEISTY, REVEREND MOTHER. I WAS FEISTY WHEN I WAS FIRST INDUCTED.
YOU STILL ARE, SISTER ELASMAR. KNOW YOUR PLACE.
I CAN HEAR EVERY WORD.
THIS WAS, I THINK, A MISTAKE.
YOU WOULD BE QUEEN, MERA. YET YOU WILL NOT SHAPE YOURSELF TO THAT DUTY.
MARRIAGE TO OUR KING IS UNWISE.
ARTHUR BELIEVES DIFFERENTLY.
HE IS YOUNG, AND YOU ARE FAIR.
HE IS NOT THINKING LIKE A KING.
HNNH!
YES, WE KNOW YOU KNOW WHAT HE'S THINKING WITH, ELASMAR.
I SHOULD GO.
BY ALL MEANS. WE DO NOT BIND YOU.
BUT A QUEEN PERSEVERES THROUGH ALL ENDEAVORS. THAT FORTITUDE IS WHAT MARKS THE DIFFERENCE BETWEEN A QUEEN AND A PRETTY GIRL FROM XEBEL.
GIVE UP. IT SPEAKS TO YOUR WORTHINESS.
WE CANNOT KEEP YOU HERE, BUT KNOW THAT IF YOU LEAVE...
THERE WILL BE NO WEDDING.

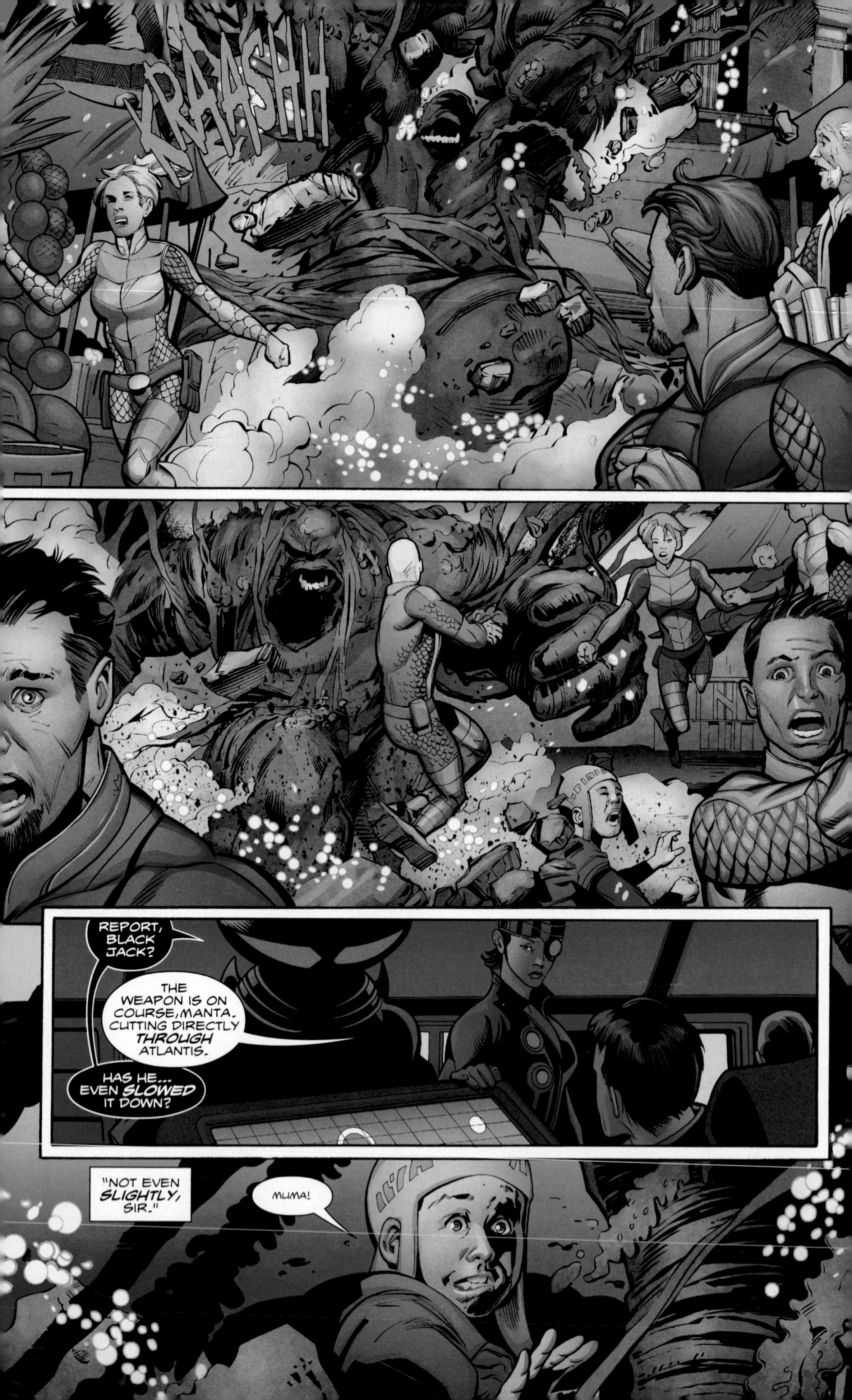
KRAASHH
REPORT, BLACK JACK?
THE WEAPON IS ON COURSE, MANTA. CUTTING DIRECTLY *THROUGH* ATLANTIS.
HAS HE... EVEN *SLOWED* IT DOWN?
"NOT EVEN *SLIGHTLY,* SIR."
MUMA!

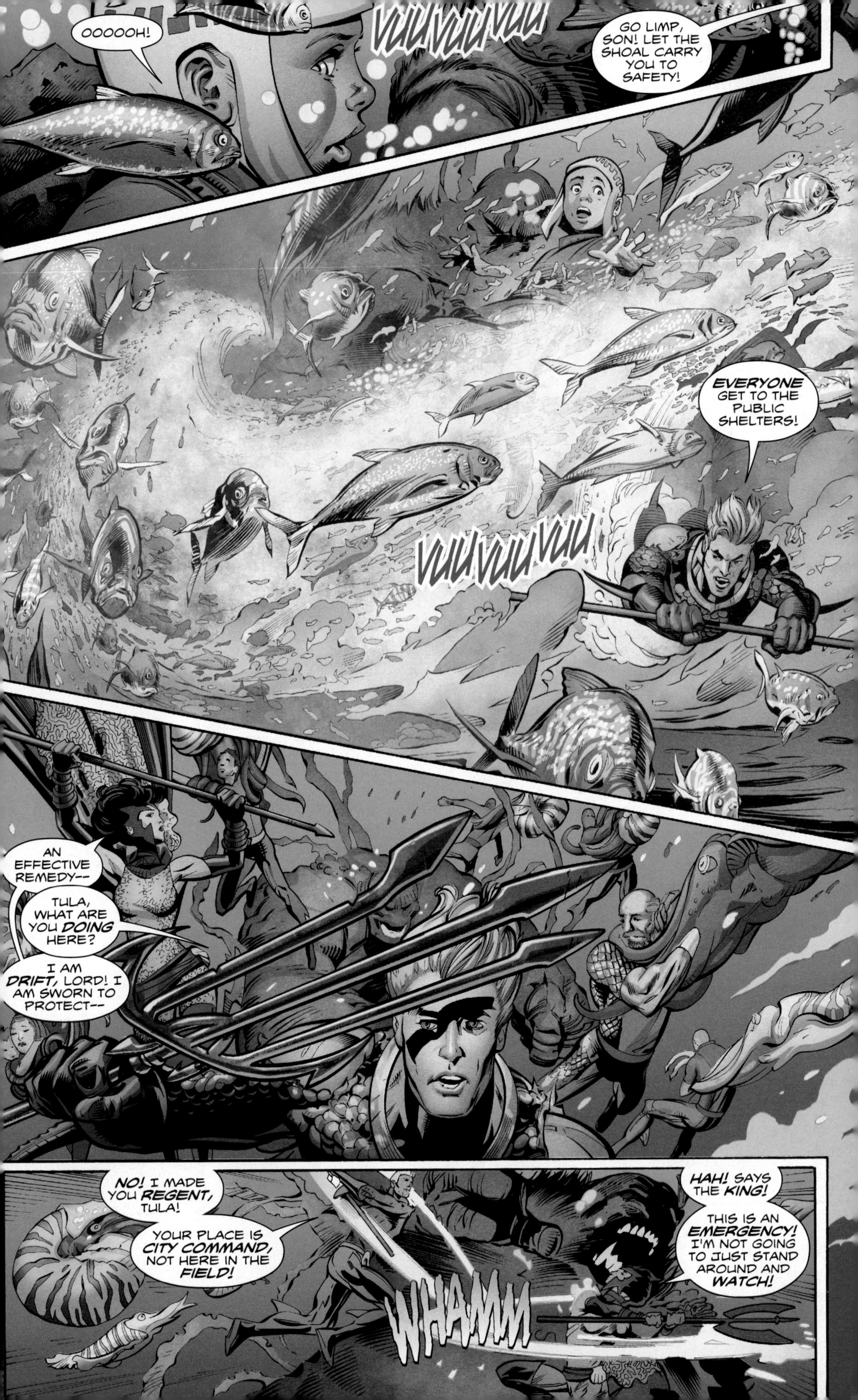
OOOOOH!
VUUVUUVUU
GO LIMP, SON! LET THE SHOAL CARRY YOU TO SAFETY!
EVERYONE GET TO THE PUBLIC SHELTERS!
VUUVUUVUU
AN EFFECTIVE REMEDY--
TULA, WHAT ARE YOU DOING HERE?
I AM DRIFT, LORD! I AM SWORN TO PROTECT--
NO! I MADE YOU REGENT, TULA!
YOUR PLACE IS CITY COMMAND, NOT HERE IN THE FIELD!
HAH! SAYS THE KING!
THIS IS AN EMERGENCY! I'M NOT GOING TO JUST STAND AROUND AND WATCH!
WHAMM

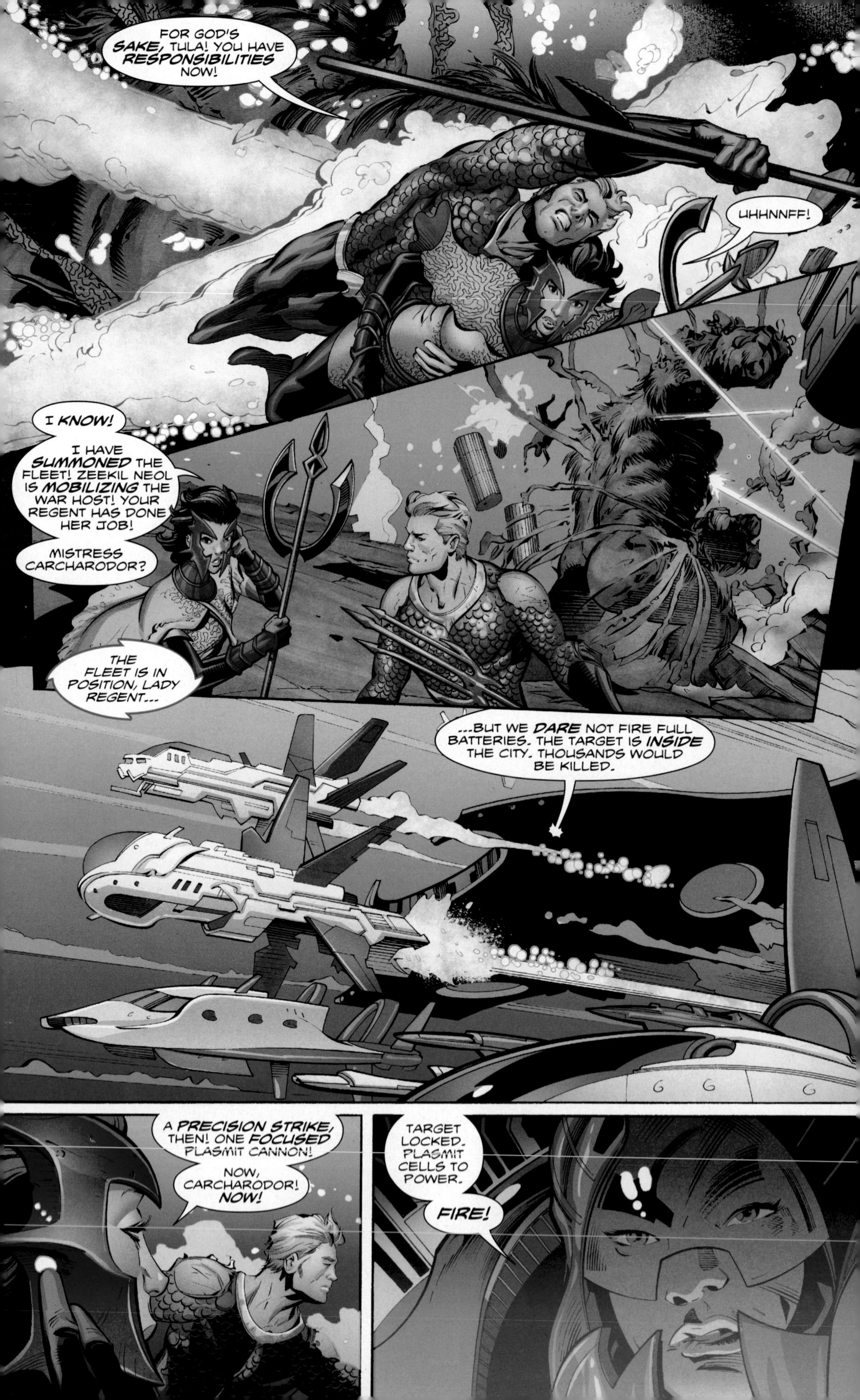
FOR GOD'S SAKE, TULA! YOU HAVE RESPONSIBILITIES NOW!
UHHNNFF!
I KNOW!
I HAVE SUMMONED THE FLEET! ZEEKIL NEOL IS MOBILIZING THE WAR HOST! YOUR REGENT HAS DONE HER JOB!
MISTRESS CARCHARODOR?
THE FLEET IS IN POSITION, LADY REGENT...
...BUT WE DARE NOT FIRE FULL BATTERIES. THE TARGET IS INSIDE THE CITY. THOUSANDS WOULD BE KILLED.
A PRECISION STRIKE, THEN! ONE FOCUSED PLASMIT CANNON!
NOW, CARCHARODOR! NOW!
TARGET LOCKED. PLASMIT CELLS TO POWER.
FIRE!

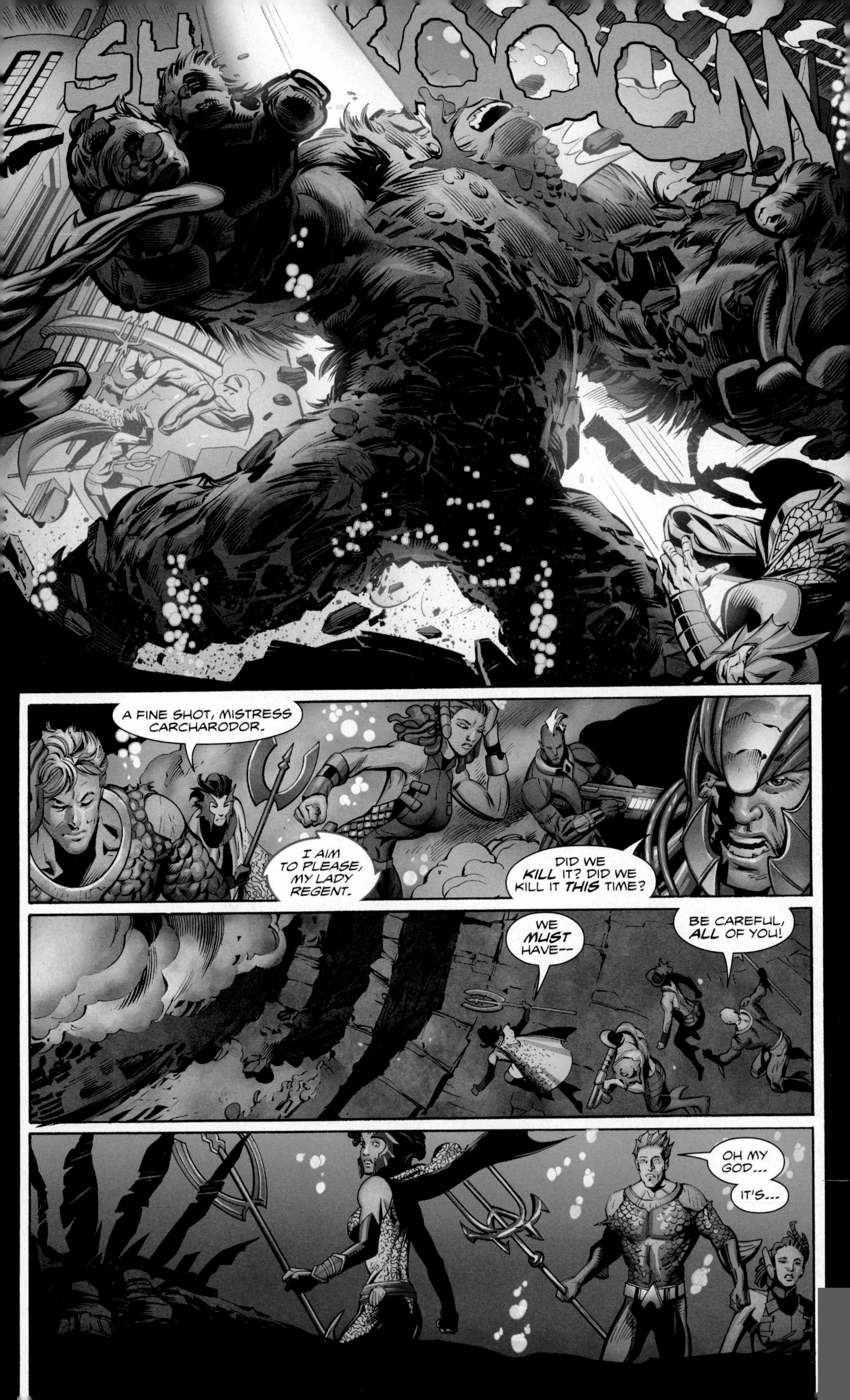
SHKOOOM!
A FINE SHOT, MISTRESS CARCHARODOR.
I AIM TO PLEASE, MY LADY REGENT.
DID WE KILL IT? DID WE KILL IT THIS TIME?
WE MUST HAVE--
BE CAREFUL, ALL OF YOU!
OH MY GOD---
IT'S---

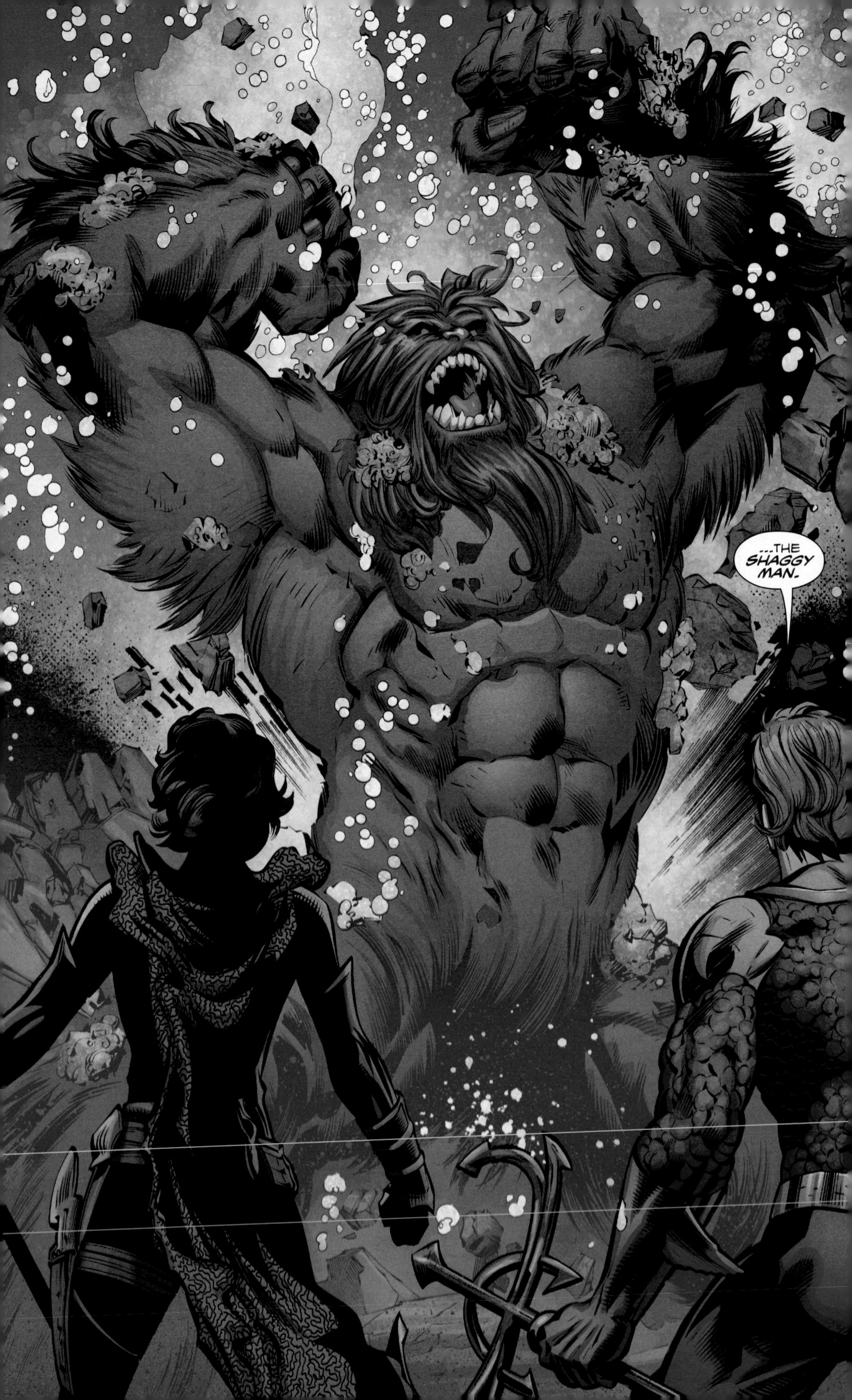
...THE SHAGGY MAN.

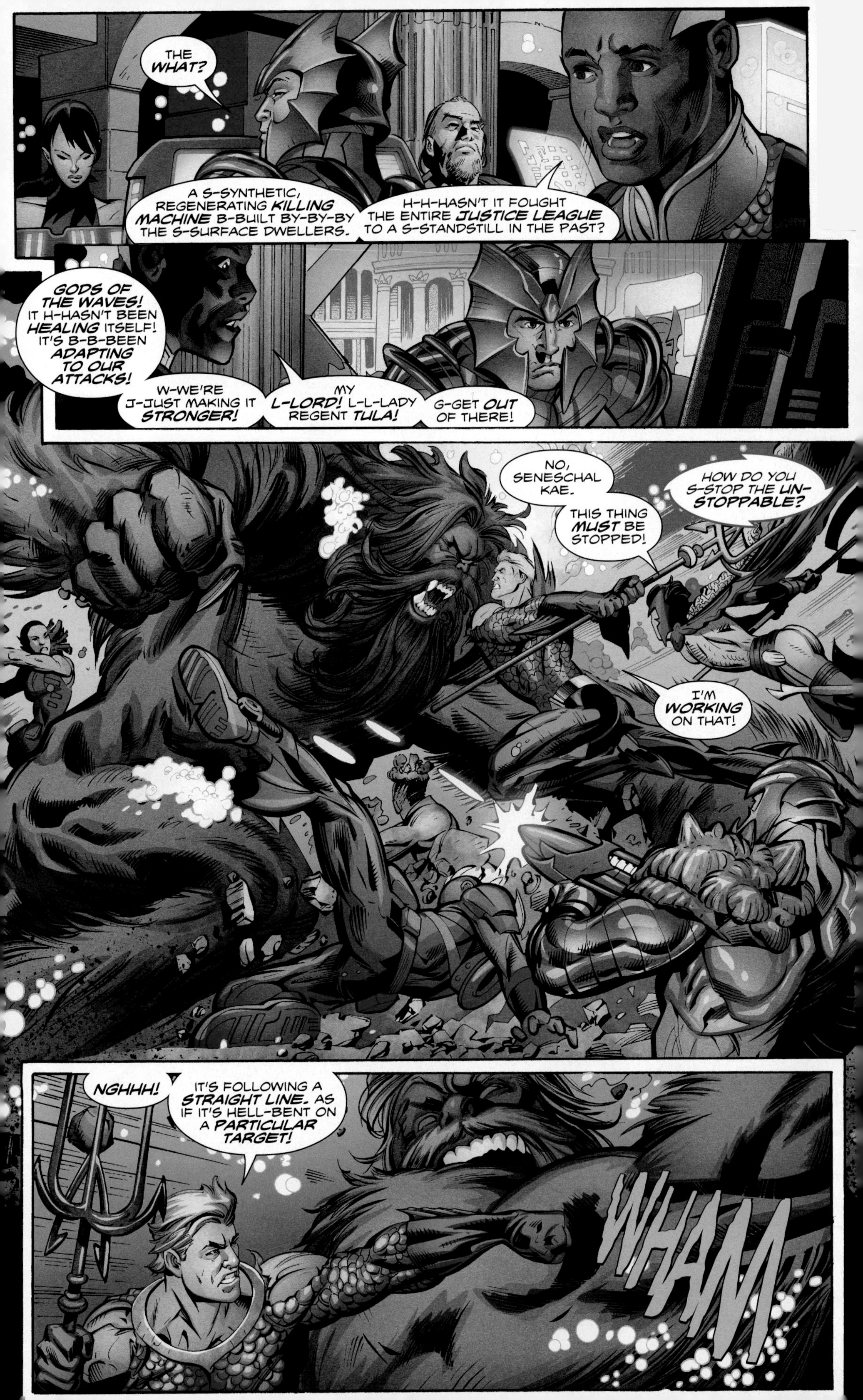
THE WHAT?
A S-SYNTHETIC, REGENERATING KILLING MACHINE B-BUILT BY-BY-BY THE S-SURFACE DWELLERS.
H-H-HASN'T IT FOUGHT THE ENTIRE JUSTICE LEAGUE TO A S-STANDSTILL IN THE PAST?
GODS OF THE WAVES! IT H-HASN'T BEEN HEALING ITSELF! IT'S B-B-BEEN ADAPTING TO OUR ATTACKS!
W-WE'RE J-JUST MAKING IT STRONGER!
MY L-LORD! L-L-LADY REGENT TULA!
G-GET OUT OF THERE!
NO, SENESCHAL KAE.
THIS THING MUST BE STOPPED!
HOW DO YOU S-STOP THE UN-STOPPABLE?
I'M WORKING ON THAT!
NGHHH!
IT'S FOLLOWING A STRAIGHT LINE. AS IF IT'S HELL-BENT ON A PARTICULAR TARGET!
WHAM

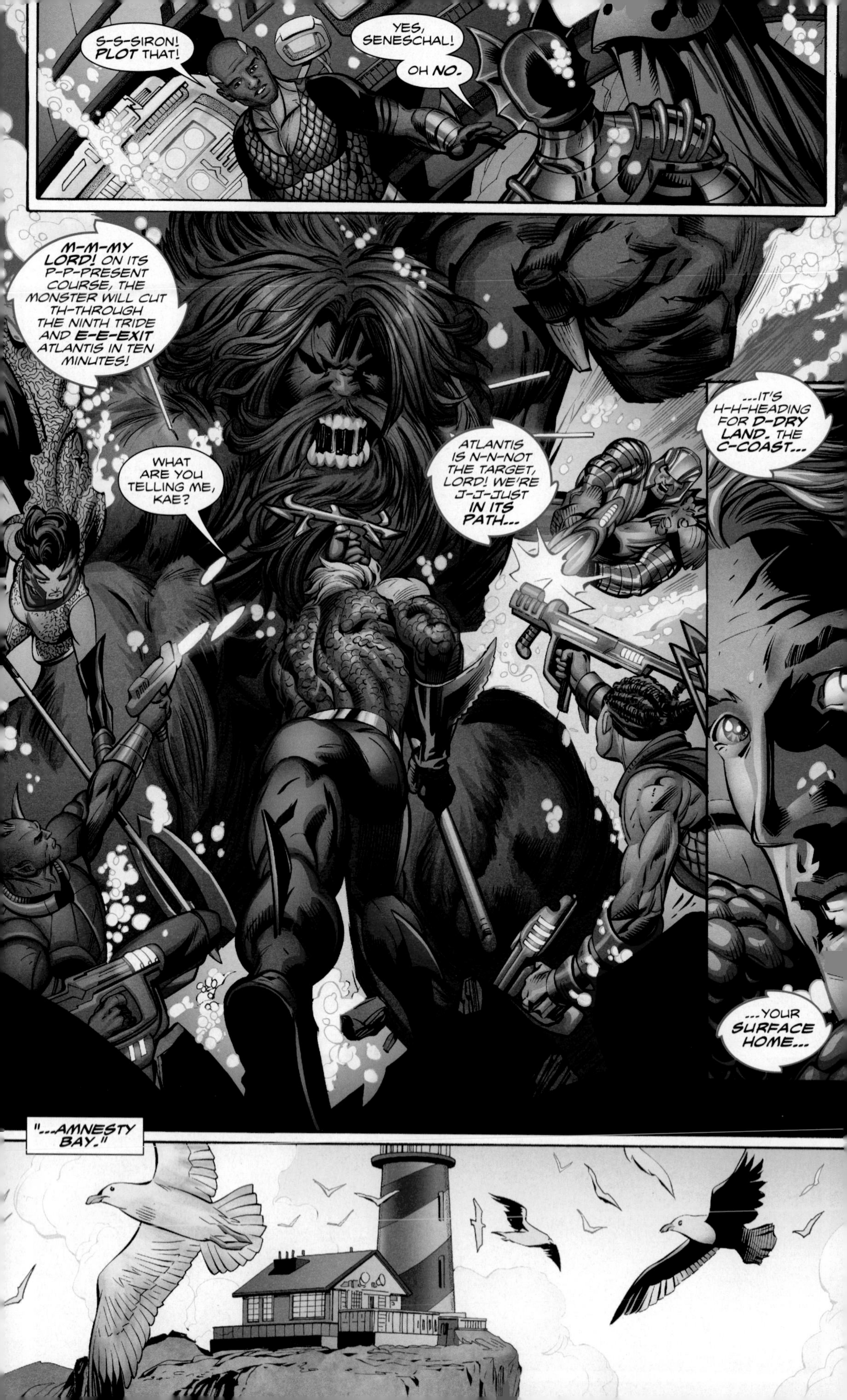
S-S-SIRON! PLOT THAT!
YES, SENESCHAL!
OH NO.
M-M-MY LORD! ON ITS P-P-PRESENT COURSE, THE MONSTER WILL CUT TH-THROUGH THE NINTH TRIDE AND E-E-EXIT ATLANTIS IN TEN MINUTES!
WHAT ARE YOU TELLING ME, KAE?
ATLANTIS IS N-N-NOT THE TARGET, LORD! WE'RE J-J-JUST IN ITS PATH...
...IT'S H-H-HEADING FOR D-DRY LAND. THE C-COAST...
...YOUR SURFACE HOME...
"...AMNESTY BAY."

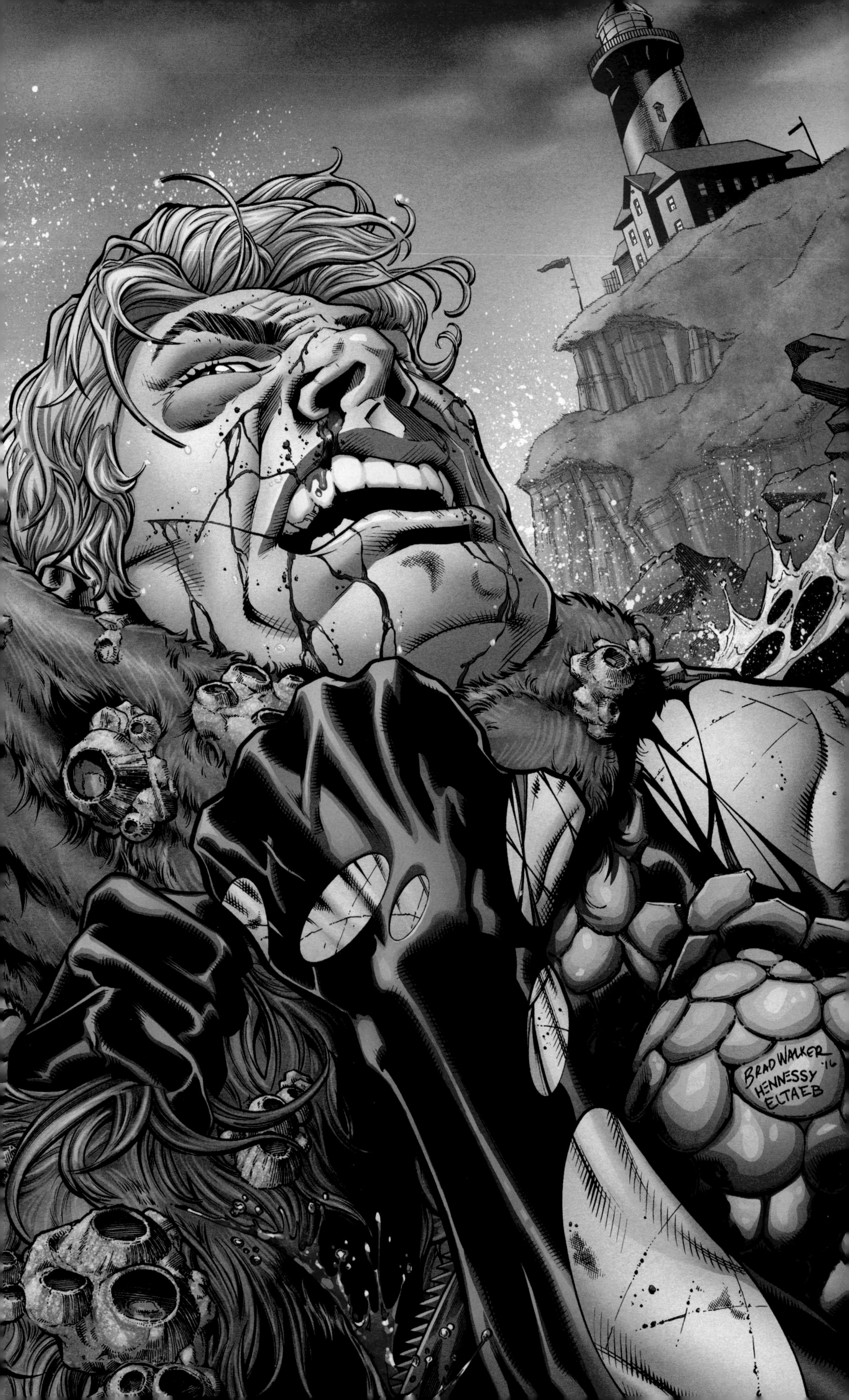
BRAD WALKER '16
HENNESSY
ELTAEB

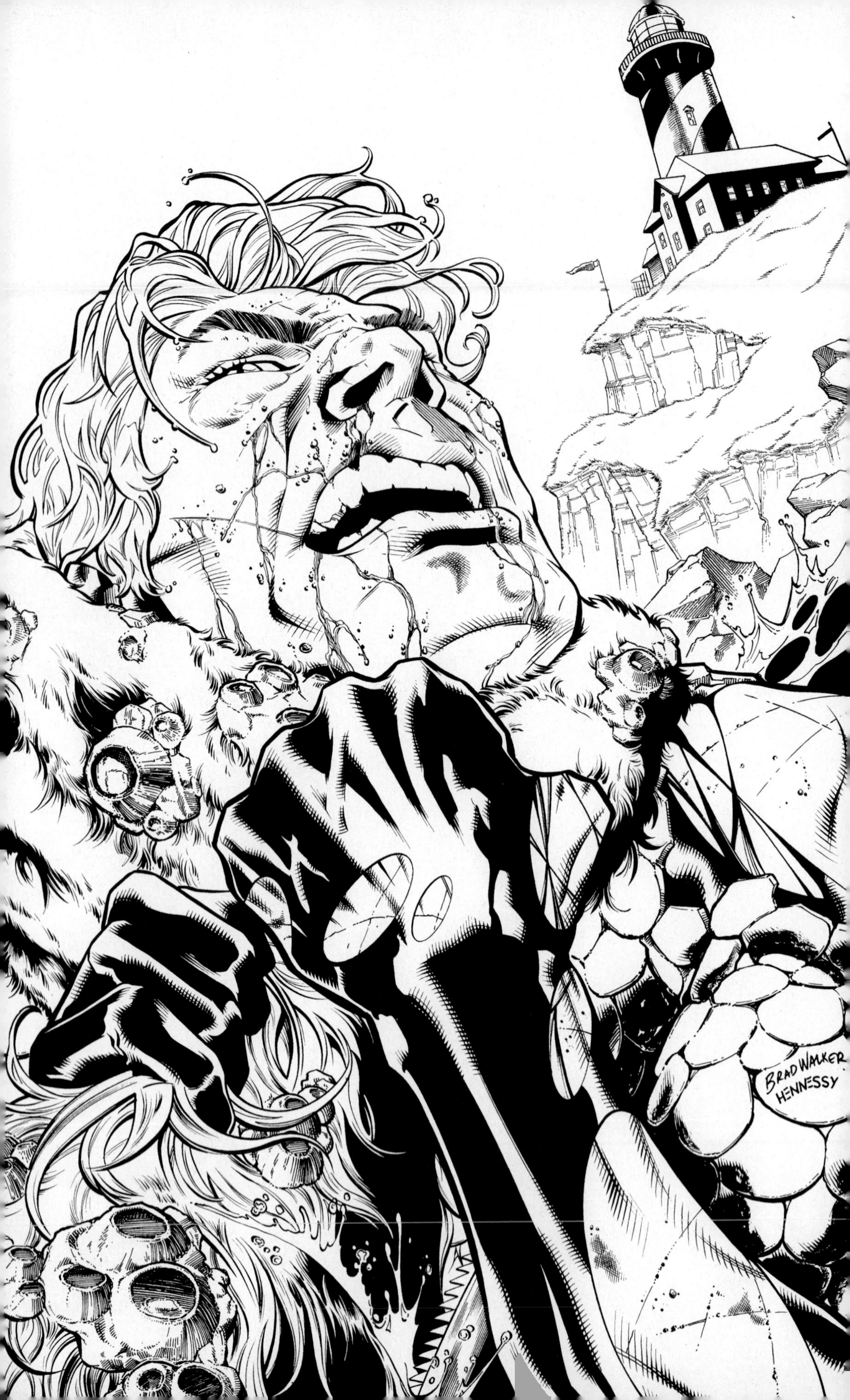
BRAD WALKER
HENNESSY

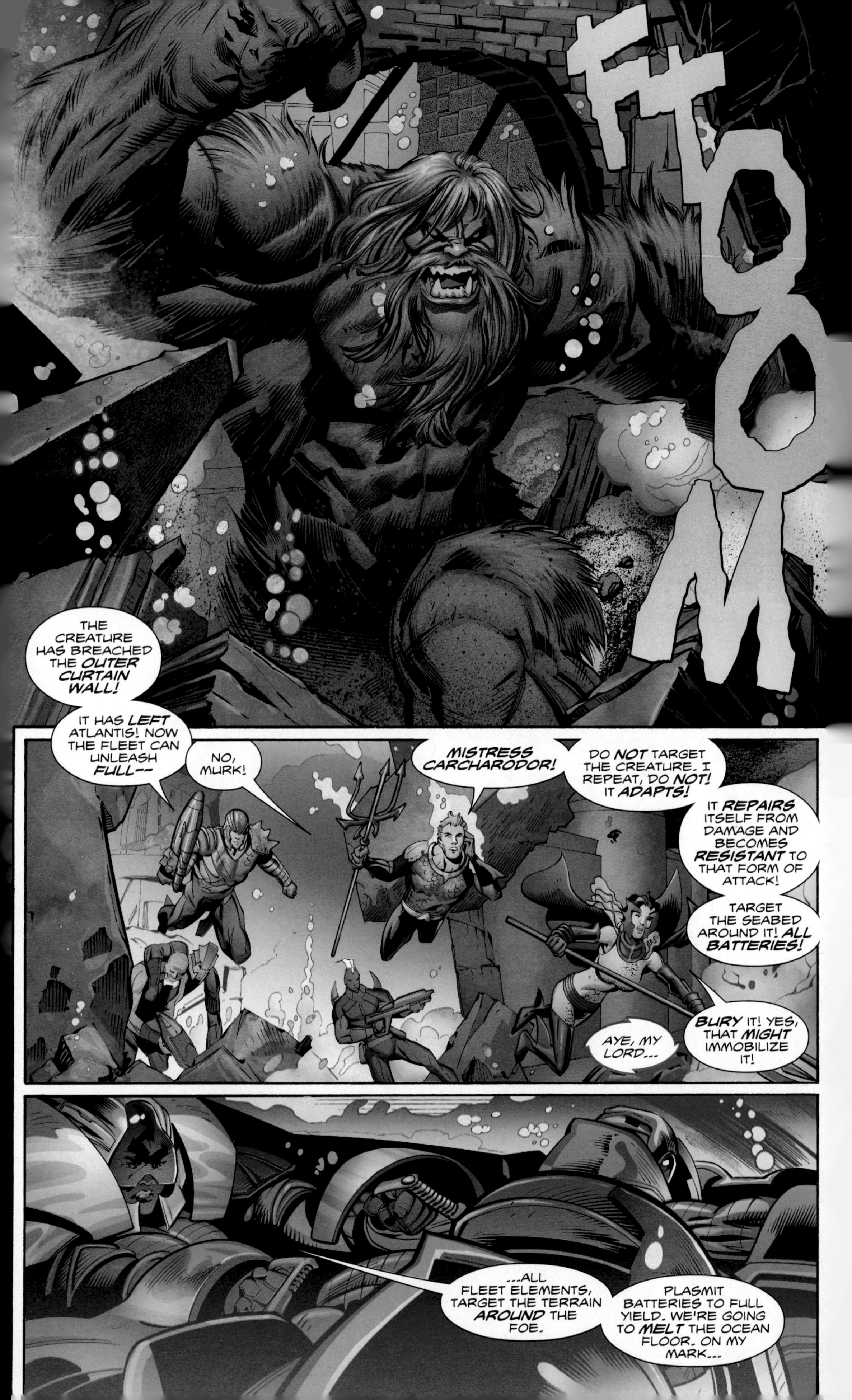
FTOOOM
THE CREATURE HAS BREACHED THE OUTER CURTAIN WALL!
IT HAS LEFT ATLANTIS! NOW THE FLEET CAN UNLEASH FULL--
NO, MURK!
MISTRESS CARCHARODOR!
DO NOT TARGET THE CREATURE. I REPEAT, DO NOT! IT ADAPTS!
IT REPAIRS ITSELF FROM DAMAGE AND BECOMES RESISTANT TO THAT FORM OF ATTACK!
TARGET THE SEABED AROUND IT! ALL BATTERIES!
BURY IT! YES, THAT MIGHT IMMOBILIZE IT!
AYE, MY LORD...
...ALL FLEET ELEMENTS, TARGET THE TERRAIN AROUND THE FOE.
PLASMIT BATTERIES TO FULL YIELD. WE'RE GOING TO MELT THE OCEAN FLOOR. ON MY MARK...

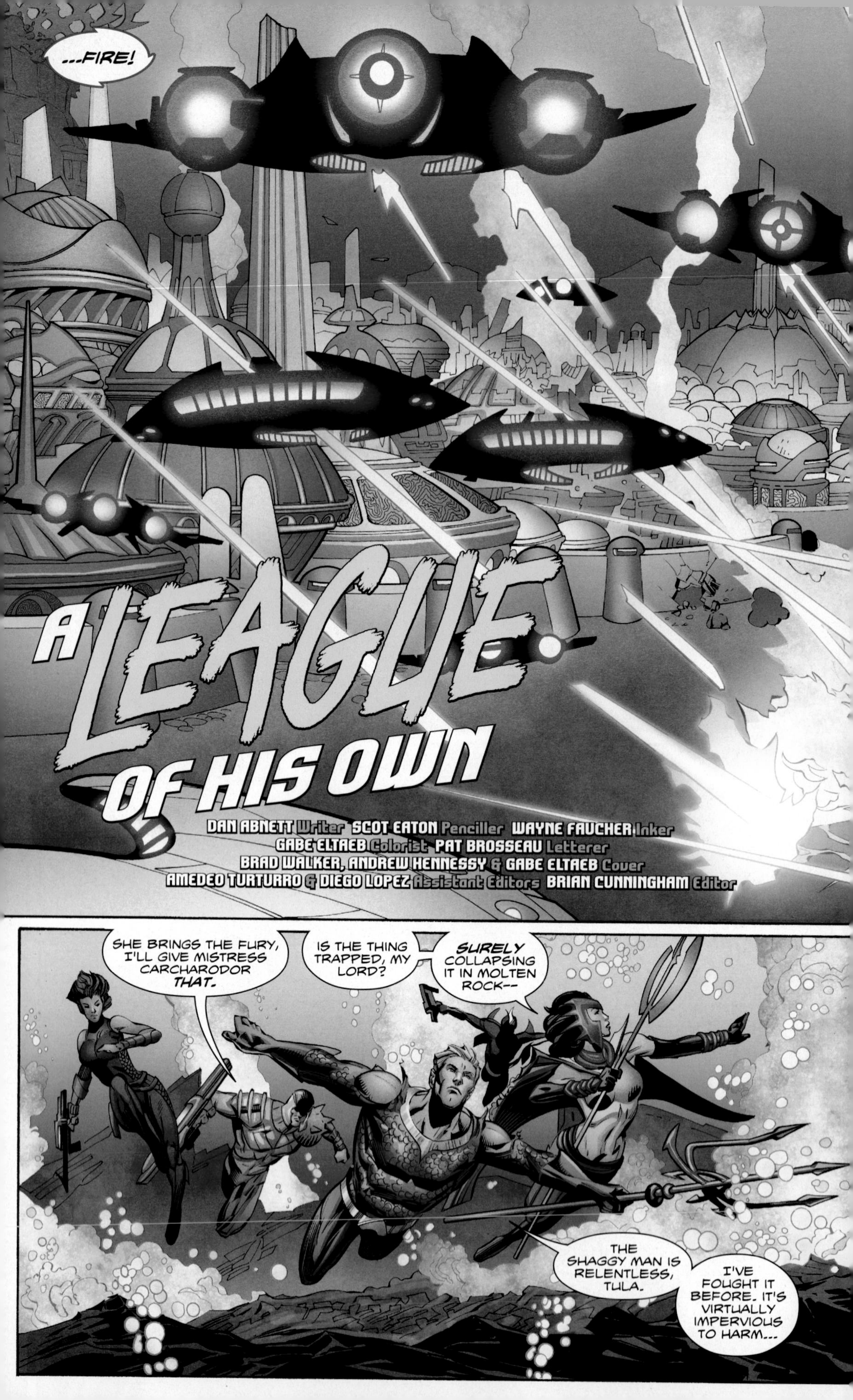
...FIRE!
A LEAGUE OF HIS OWN
DAN ABNETT Writer SCOT EATON Penciller WAYNE FAUCHER Inker
GABE ELTAEB Colorist PAT BROSSEAU Letterer
BRAD WALKER, ANDREW HENNESSY & GABE ELTAEB Cover
AMEDEO TURTURRO & DIEGO LOPEZ Assistant Editors BRIAN CUNNINGHAM Editor
SHE BRINGS THE FURY, I'LL GIVE MISTRESS CARCHARODOR *THAT*.
IS THE THING TRAPPED, MY LORD?
SURELY COLLAPSING IT IN MOLTEN ROCK--
THE SHAGGY MAN IS RELENTLESS, TULA.
I'VE FOUGHT IT BEFORE. IT'S VIRTUALLY IMPERVIOUS TO HARM...

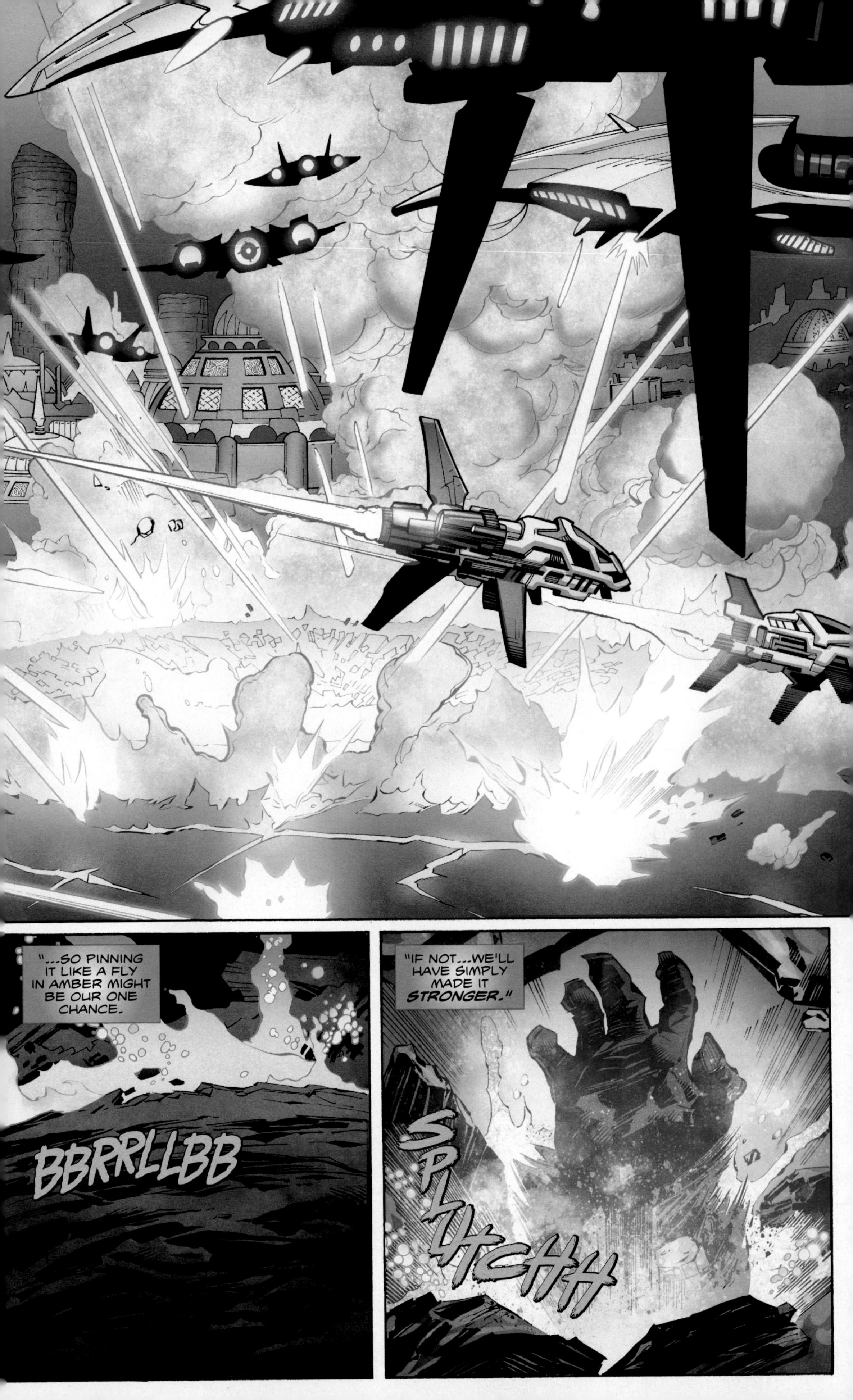
"...SO PINNING IT LIKE A FLY IN AMBER MIGHT BE OUR ONE CHANCE.
BBRRRLLBB
"IF NOT...WE'LL HAVE SIMPLY MADE IT STRONGER."
SPLUTCHH

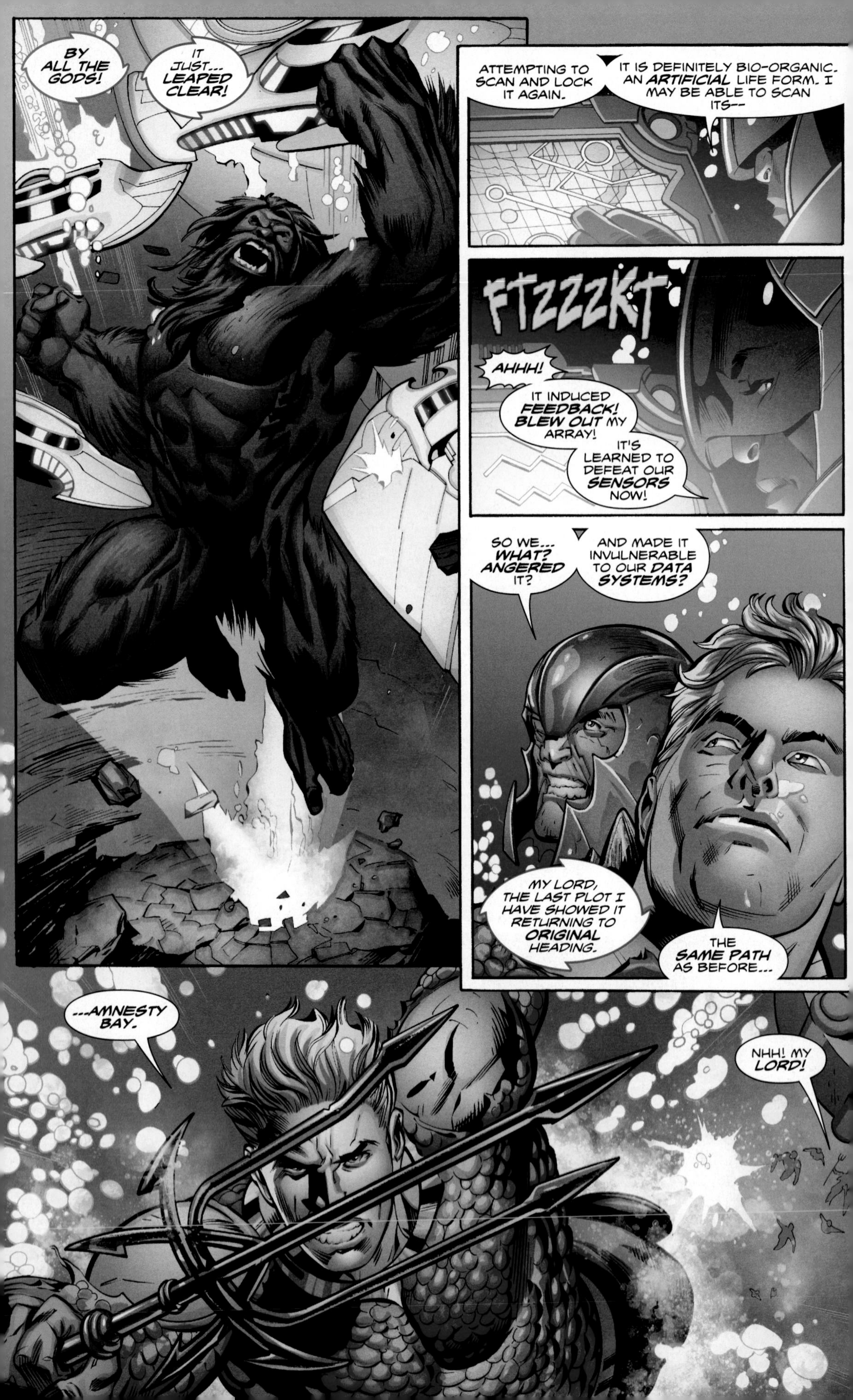
BY ALL THE GODS!
IT JUST... LEAPED CLEAR!
ATTEMPTING TO SCAN AND LOCK IT AGAIN.
IT IS DEFINITELY BIO-ORGANIC. AN ARTIFICIAL LIFE FORM. I MAY BE ABLE TO SCAN ITS--
FTZZZKT
AHHH!
IT INDUCED FEEDBACK! BLEW OUT MY ARRAY!
IT'S LEARNED TO DEFEAT OUR SENSORS NOW!
SO WE... WHAT? ANGERED IT?
AND MADE IT INVULNERABLE TO OUR DATA SYSTEMS?
MY LORD, THE LAST PLOT I HAVE SHOWED IT RETURNING TO ORIGINAL HEADING.
THE SAME PATH AS BEFORE...
...AMNESTY BAY.
NHH! MY LORD!

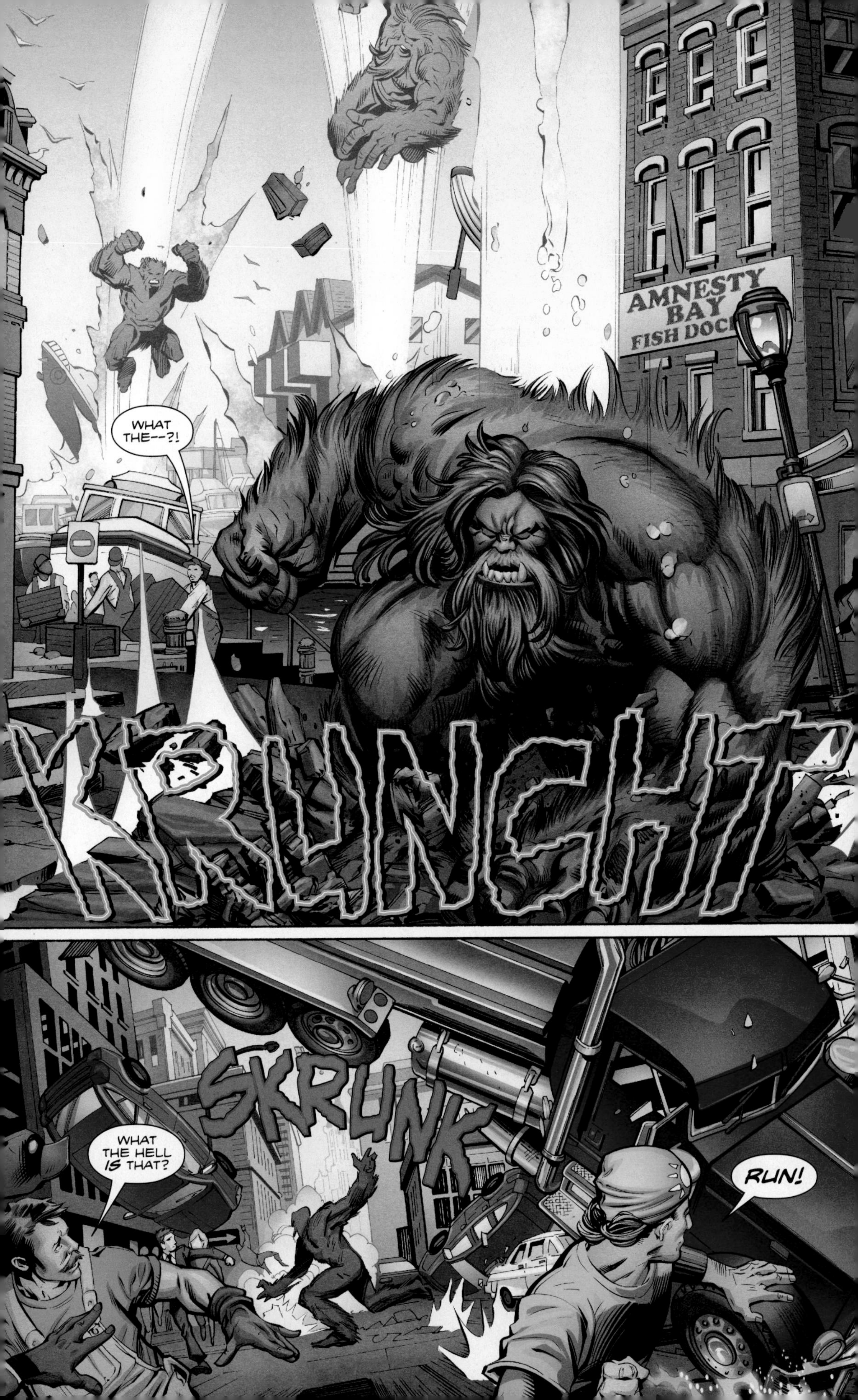
AMNESTY
BAY
FISH DOCK
WHAT THE--?!
KRUNCH!
SKRUNK
WHAT THE HELL IS THAT?
RUN!

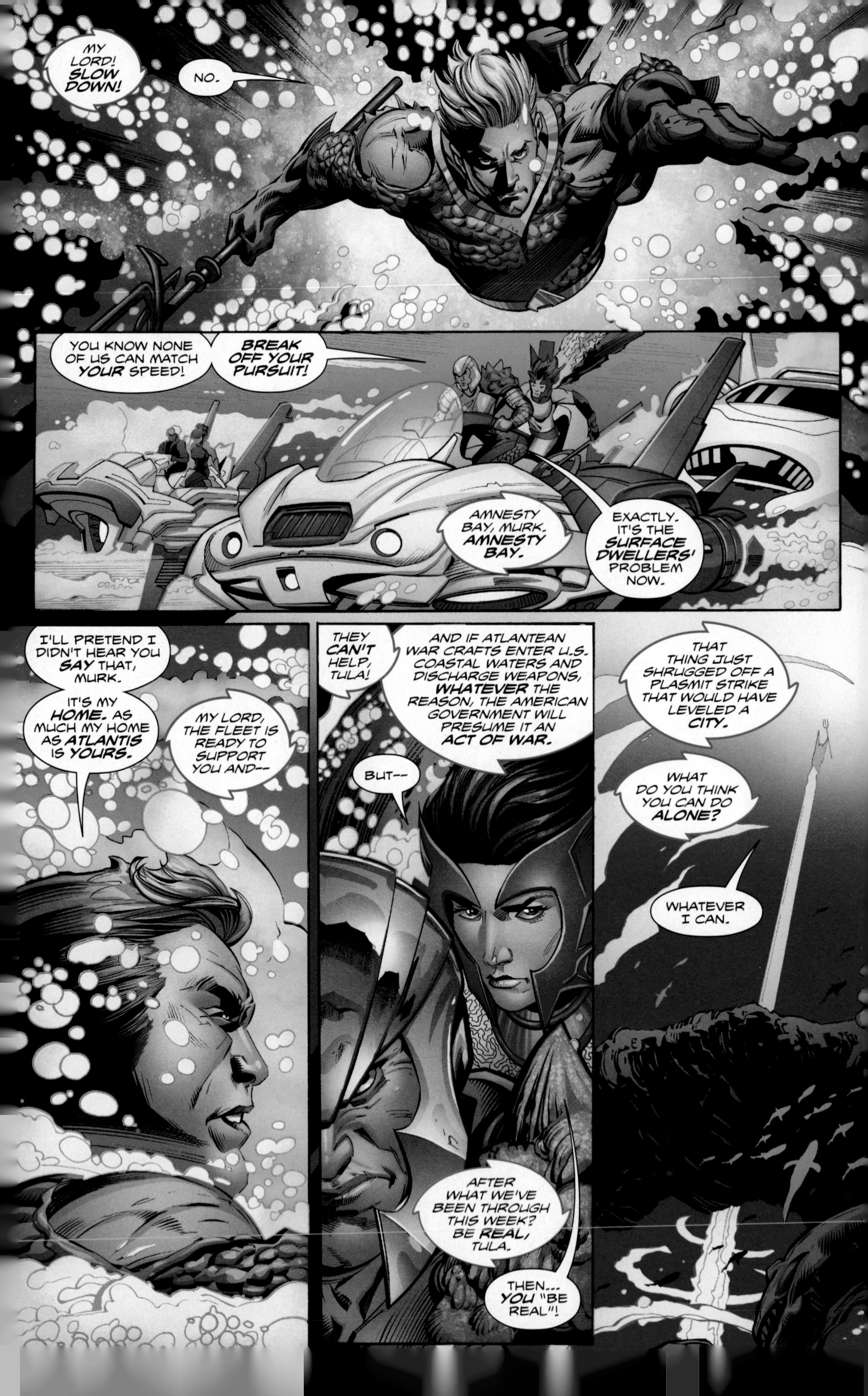
MY LORD! SLOW DOWN!
NO.
YOU KNOW NONE OF US CAN MATCH YOUR SPEED!
BREAK OFF YOUR PURSUIT!
AMNESTY BAY, MURK. AMNESTY BAY.
EXACTLY. IT'S THE SURFACE DWELLERS' PROBLEM NOW.
I'LL PRETEND I DIDN'T HEAR YOU SAY THAT, MURK.
IT'S MY HOME. AS MUCH MY HOME AS ATLANTIS IS YOURS.
MY LORD, THE FLEET IS READY TO SUPPORT YOU AND--
THEY CAN'T HELP, TULA!
AND IF ATLANTEAN WAR CRAFTS ENTER U.S. COASTAL WATERS AND DISCHARGE WEAPONS, WHATEVER THE REASON, THE AMERICAN GOVERNMENT WILL PRESUME IT AN ACT OF WAR.
BUT--
AFTER WHAT WE'VE BEEN THROUGH THIS WEEK? BE REAL, TULA.
THEN... YOU "BE REAL"!
THAT THING JUST SHRUGGED OFF A PLASMIT STRIKE THAT WOULD HAVE LEVELED A CITY.
WHAT DO YOU THINK YOU CAN DO ALONE?
WHATEVER I CAN.

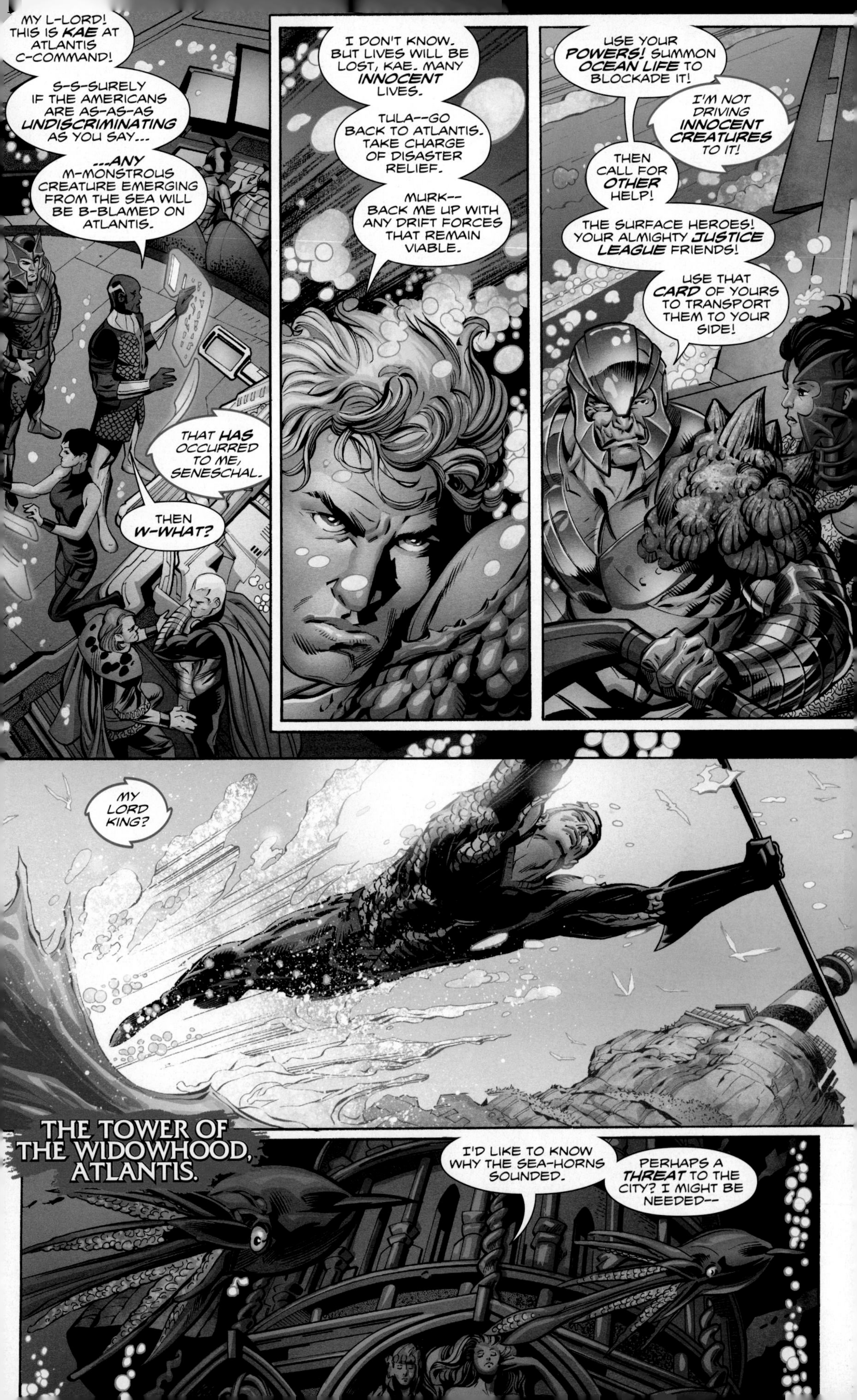

MY L-LORD! THIS IS KAE AT ATLANTIS C-COMMAND!
S-S-SURELY IF THE AMERICANS ARE AS-AS-AS UNDISCRIMINATING AS YOU SAY...
...ANY M-MONSTROUS CREATURE EMERGING FROM THE SEA WILL BE B-BLAMED ON ATLANTIS.
THAT HAS OCCURRED TO ME, SENESCHAL.
THEN W-WHAT?
I DON'T KNOW. BUT LIVES WILL BE LOST, KAE. MANY INNOCENT LIVES.
TULA--GO BACK TO ATLANTIS. TAKE CHARGE OF DISASTER RELIEF.
MURK--BACK ME UP WITH ANY DRIFT FORCES THAT REMAIN VIABLE.
USE YOUR POWERS! SUMMON OCEAN LIFE TO BLOCKADE IT!
I'M NOT DRIVING INNOCENT CREATURES TO IT!
THEN CALL FOR OTHER HELP!
THE SURFACE HEROES! YOUR ALMIGHTY JUSTICE LEAGUE FRIENDS!
USE THAT CARD OF YOURS TO TRANSPORT THEM TO YOUR SIDE!
MY LORD KING?
THE TOWER OF THE WIDOWHOOD, ATLANTIS.
I'D LIKE TO KNOW WHY THE SEA-HORNS SOUNDED.
PERHAPS A THREAT TO THE CITY? I MIGHT BE NEEDED--

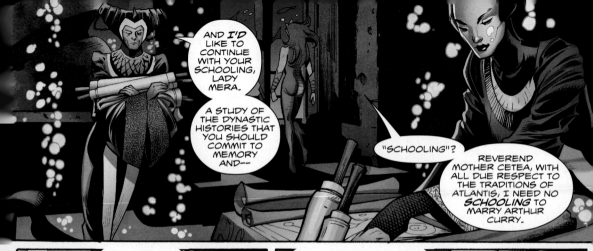

AND **I'D** LIKE TO CONTINUE WITH YOUR SCHOOLING, LADY MERA.

A STUDY OF THE DYNASTIC HISTORIES THAT YOU SHOULD COMMIT TO MEMORY AND--

"SCHOOLING"? REVEREND MOTHER CETEA, WITH ALL DUE RESPECT TO THE TRADITIONS OF ATLANTIS, I NEED NO **SCHOOLING** TO MARRY ARTHUR CURRY.

HE IS KING OF ATLANTIS, LADY. ARE YOU **FIT** TO BE QUEEN?

I BOTH UNDERSTAND AND **SUPPORT** ARTHUR'S LEADERSHIP OF THE REALM.

HE SEEKS **PEACE.** TO ALIGN OUR LOST CIVILIZATION MORE FAVORABLY WITH THE NATIONS OF THE SURFACE.

TO DISPEL **FEAR.**

AND DURING YOUR RECENT DIPLOMATIC DEALINGS WITH WASHINGTON, IT WAS YOU WHO RESORTED TO VIOLENCE.

AGAINST **HIS** EXPRESS WISHES.

IT WAS **NECESSARY!** WE WERE ON THE BRINK OF **WAR**--

ANYWAY, HOW DO YOU **KNOW** THAT?

THE WIDOWHOOD WATCHES OVER ATLANTIS AS THOUGH IT WERE OUR CHILD.

WE NURTURE IT. WE PROTECT ITS TRADITIONS. WE ADMINISTER TO ITS SPIRITUAL HEALTH.

AND WE MONITOR **ALL** INTELLIGENCE REPORTS.

OFFICIALLY?

OF COURSE. YOU DIDN'T KNOW THAT?

I **WOULDN'T,** I'M NOT QUEEN YET.

ARTHUR'S TASK IS FORMIDABLE.

ALREADY, TO DEFUSE WAR BETWEEN US AND THE SURFACE, HE HAS CLASHED WITH SUPERMAN.

ALSO IN THE REPORTS.

THE JUSTICE LEAGUE WERE HIS **FRIENDS.** TRUE AND LOYAL.

HE FEARS HE **CANNOT** CALL ON THEM NOW.

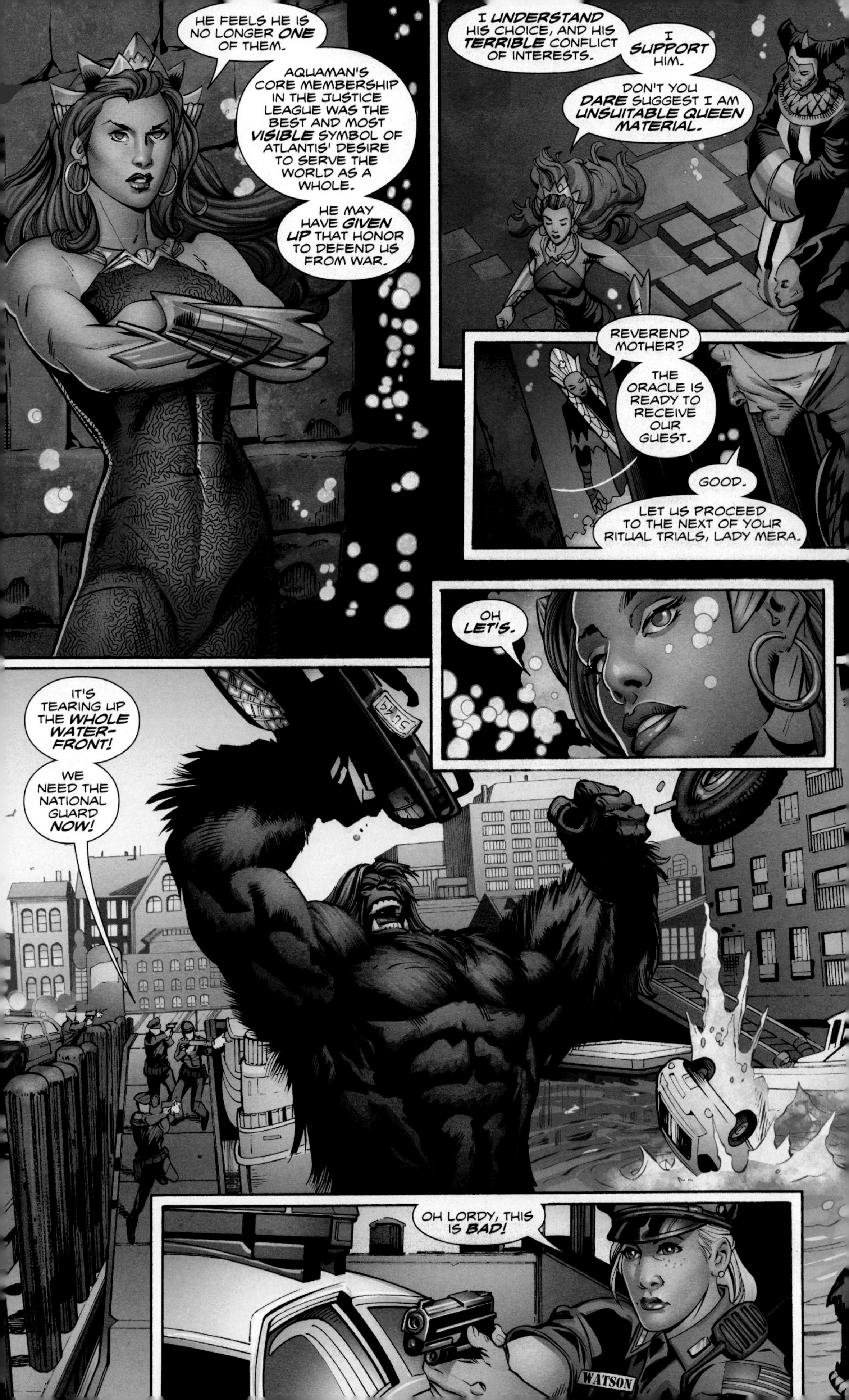
HE FEELS HE IS NO LONGER ONE OF THEM.
AQUAMAN'S CORE MEMBERSHIP IN THE JUSTICE LEAGUE WAS THE BEST AND MOST VISIBLE SYMBOL OF ATLANTIS' DESIRE TO SERVE THE WORLD AS A WHOLE.
HE MAY HAVE GIVEN UP THAT HONOR TO DEFEND US FROM WAR.
I UNDERSTAND HIS CHOICE, AND HIS TERRIBLE CONFLICT OF INTERESTS.
I SUPPORT HIM.
DON'T YOU DARE SUGGEST I AM UNSUITABLE QUEEN MATERIAL.
REVEREND MOTHER?
THE ORACLE IS READY TO RECEIVE OUR GUEST.
GOOD.
LET US PROCEED TO THE NEXT OF YOUR RITUAL TRIALS, LADY MERA.
OH LET'S.
IT'S TEARING UP THE WHOLE WATER-FRONT!
WE NEED THE NATIONAL GUARD NOW!
OH LORDY, THIS IS BAD!
WATSON

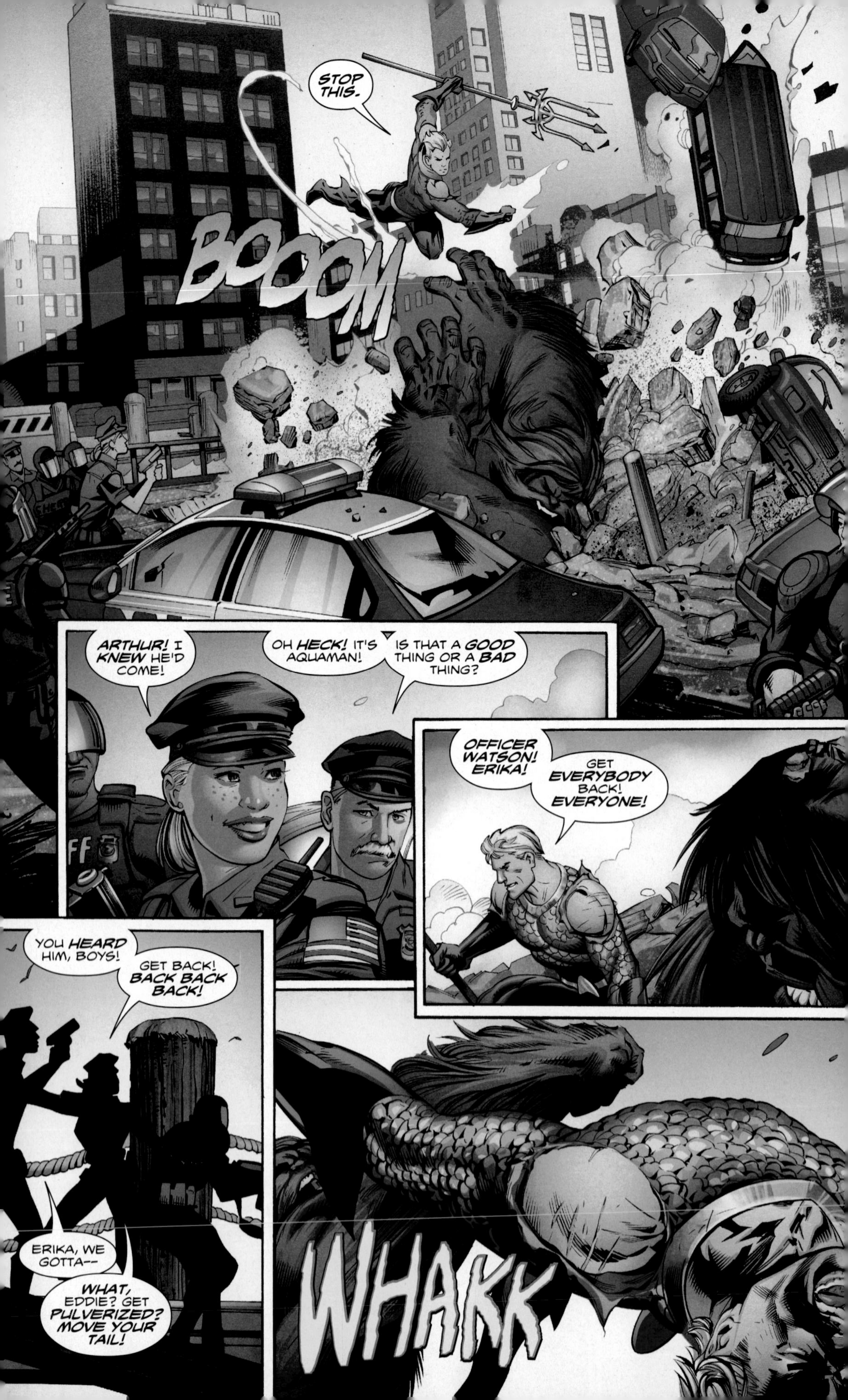
STOP THIS.
BOOOM
ARTHUR! I KNEW HE'D COME!
OH HECK! IT'S AQUAMAN!
IS THAT A GOOD THING OR A BAD THING?
OFFICER WATSON! ERIKA!
GET EVERYBODY BACK! EVERYONE!
YOU HEARD HIM, BOYS!
GET BACK! BACK BACK BACK!
ERIKA, WE GOTTA--
WHAT, EDDIE? GET PULVERIZED? MOVE YOUR TAIL!
WHAKK

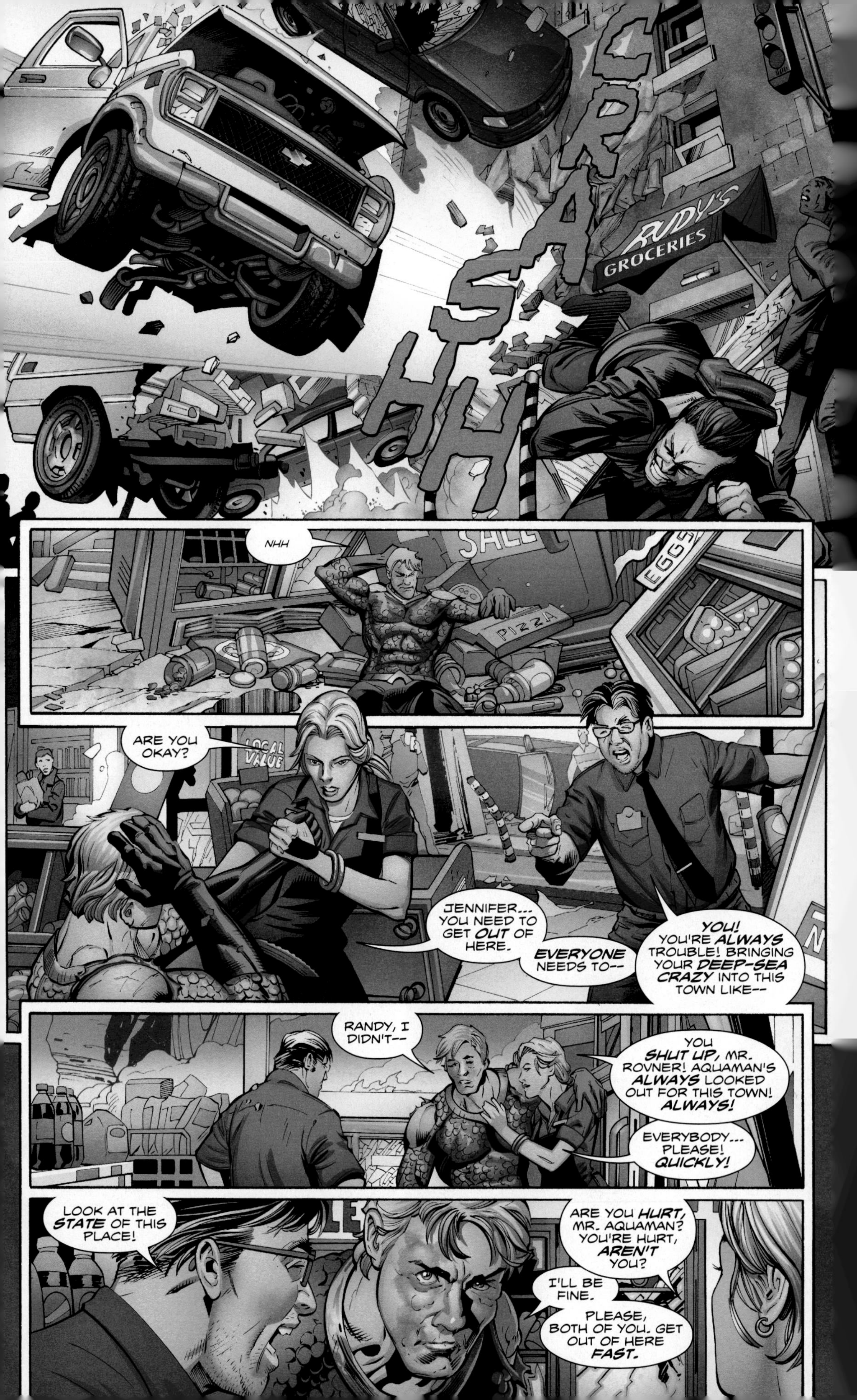
CRASHHH
RUDY'S GROCERIES
NHH
SALE
EGGS
PIZZA
ARE YOU OKAY?
LOCAL VALUE
JENNIFER... YOU NEED TO GET OUT OF HERE.
EVERYONE NEEDS TO--
YOU! YOU'RE ALWAYS TROUBLE! BRINGING YOUR DEEP-SEA CRAZY INTO THIS TOWN LIKE--
RANDY, I DIDN'T--
YOU SHUT UP, MR. ROVNER! AQUAMAN'S ALWAYS LOOKED OUT FOR THIS TOWN! ALWAYS!
EVERYBODY... PLEASE! QUICKLY!
LOOK AT THE STATE OF THIS PLACE!
ARE YOU HURT, MR. AQUAMAN? YOU'RE HURT, AREN'T YOU?
I'LL BE FINE.
PLEASE, BOTH OF YOU. GET OUT OF HERE FAST.

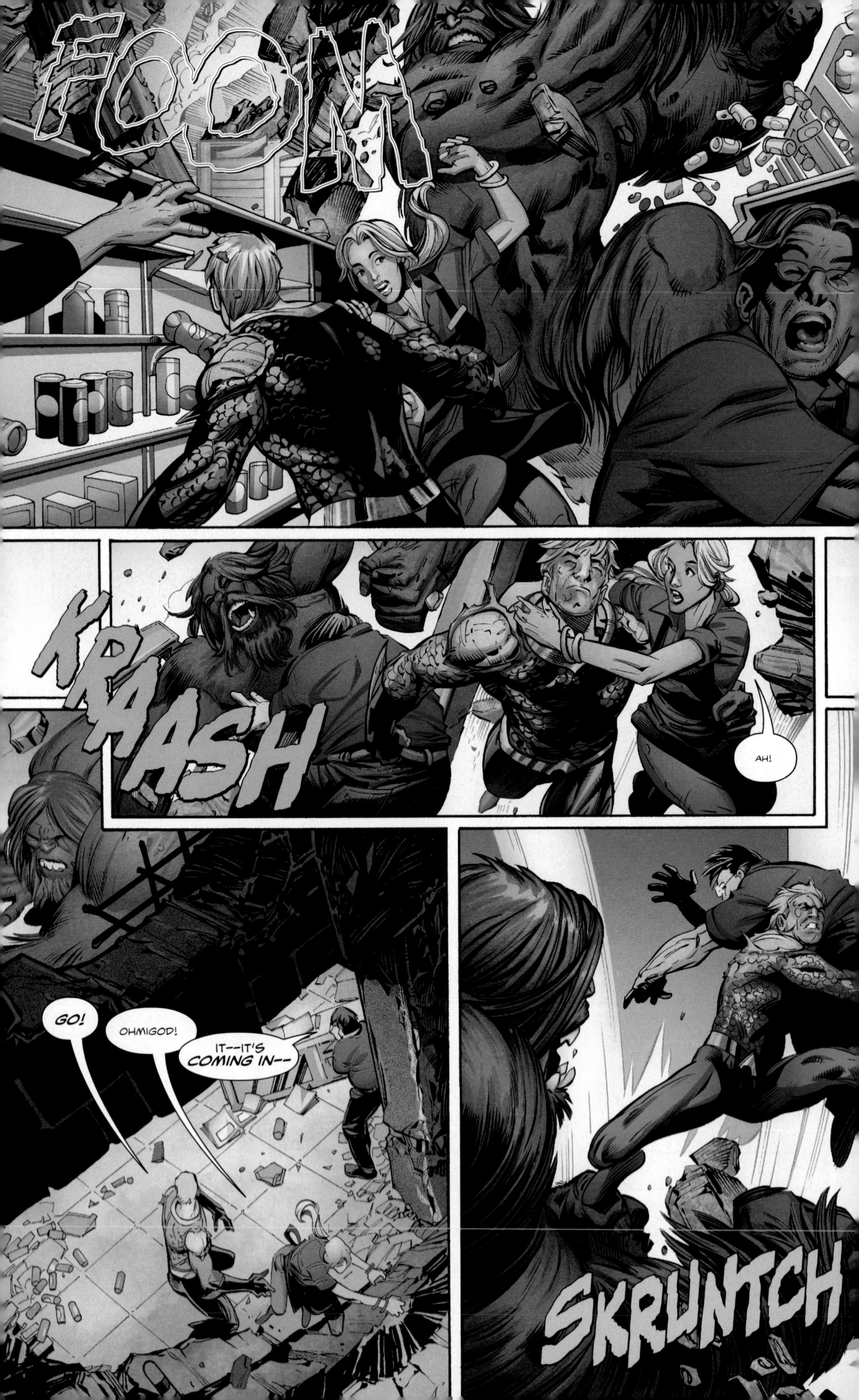
FOOM
KRAASH
AH!
GO!
OHMIGOD!
IT--IT'S COMING IN--
SKRUNTCH

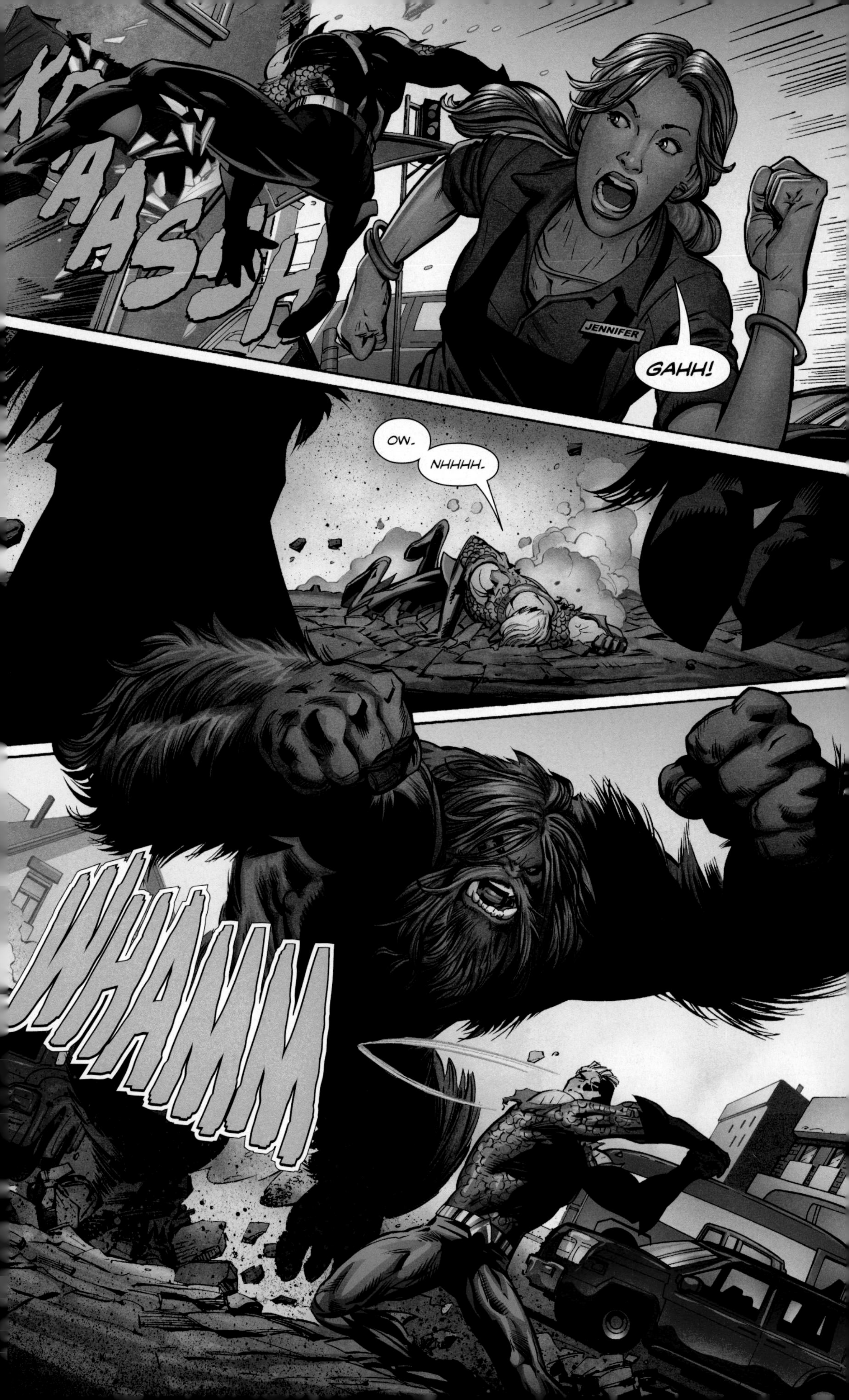
JENNIFER
GAHH!
OW-
NHHHH-
WHAMM

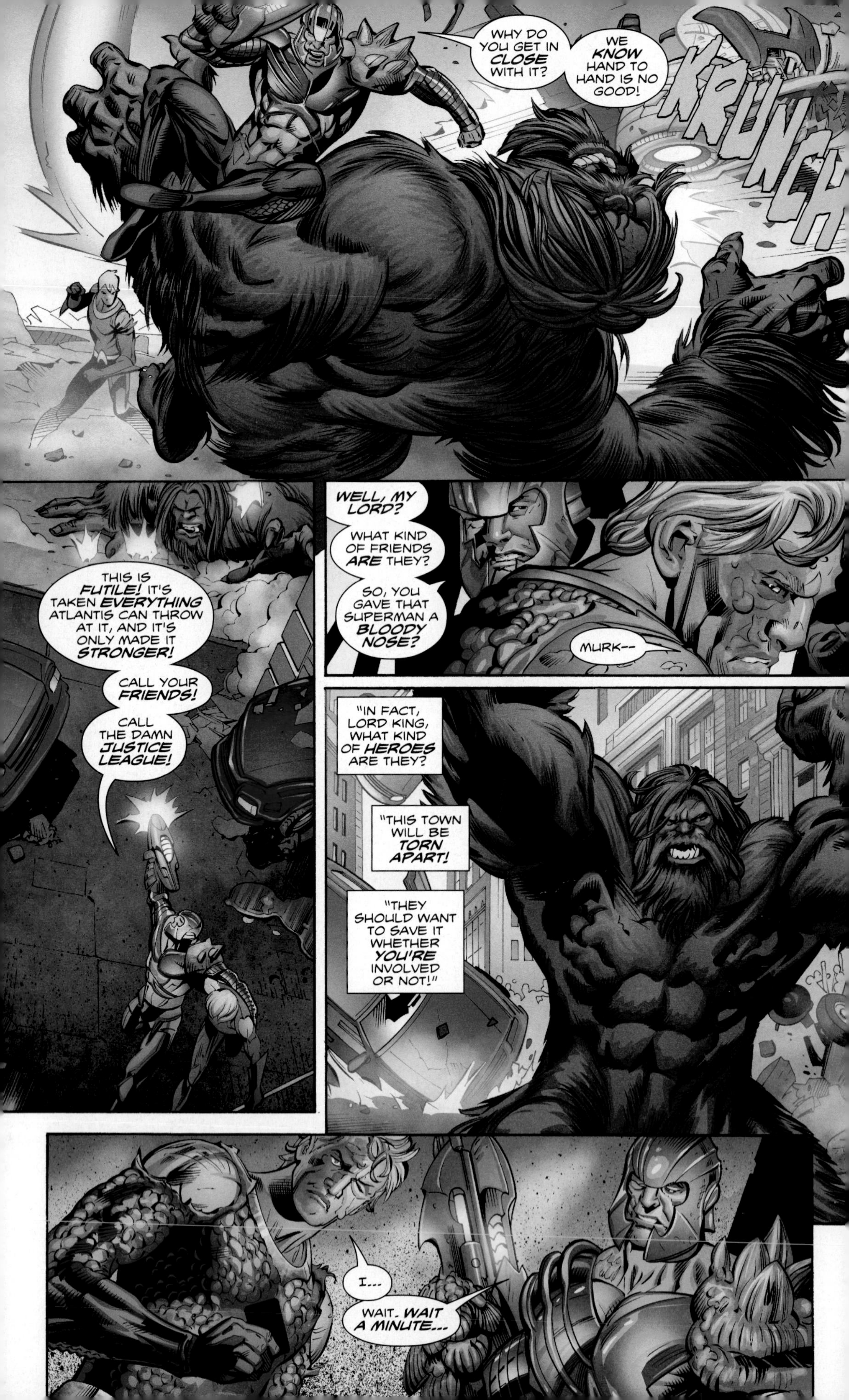

WHY DO YOU GET IN CLOSE WITH IT?
WE KNOW HAND TO HAND IS NO GOOD!
KRUNCH
THIS IS FUTILE! IT'S TAKEN EVERYTHING ATLANTIS CAN THROW AT IT, AND IT'S ONLY MADE IT STRONGER!
CALL YOUR FRIENDS!
CALL THE DAMN JUSTICE LEAGUE!
WELL, MY LORD?
WHAT KIND OF FRIENDS ARE THEY?
SO, YOU GAVE THAT SUPERMAN A BLOODY NOSE?
MURK--
"IN FACT, LORD KING, WHAT KIND OF HEROES ARE THEY?
"THIS TOWN WILL BE TORN APART!
"THEY SHOULD WANT TO SAVE IT WHETHER YOU'RE INVOLVED OR NOT!"
I...
WAIT. WAIT A MINUTE...

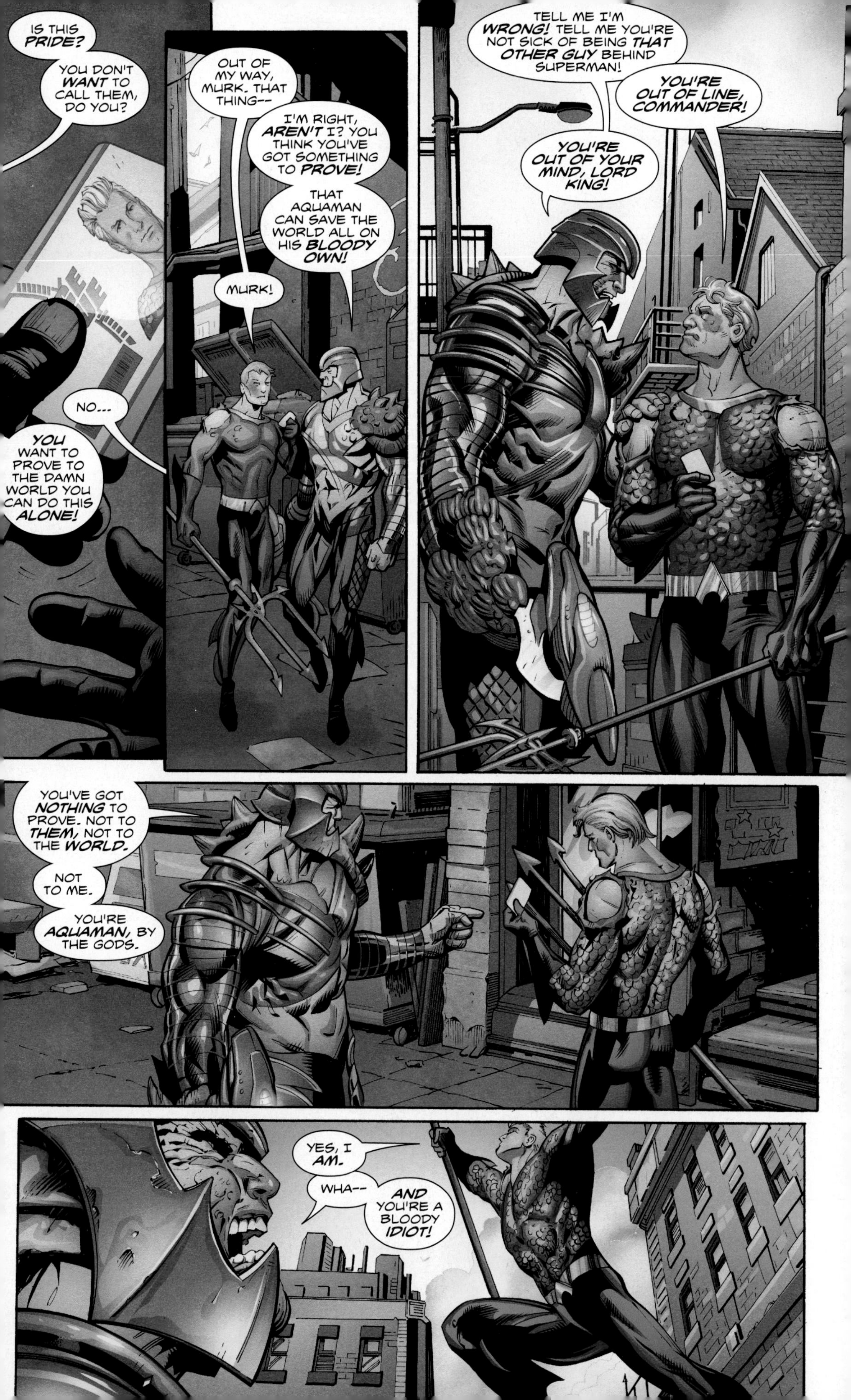

IS THIS PRIDE?
YOU DON'T WANT TO CALL THEM, DO YOU?
OUT OF MY WAY, MURK. THAT THING--
I'M RIGHT, AREN'T I? YOU THINK YOU'VE GOT SOMETHING TO PROVE!
THAT AQUAMAN CAN SAVE THE WORLD ALL ON HIS BLOODY OWN!
MURK!
NO...
YOU WANT TO PROVE TO THE DAMN WORLD YOU CAN DO THIS ALONE!
TELL ME I'M WRONG! TELL ME YOU'RE NOT SICK OF BEING THAT OTHER GUY BEHIND SUPERMAN!
YOU'RE OUT OF LINE, COMMANDER!
YOU'RE OUT OF YOUR MIND, LORD KING!
YOU'VE GOT NOTHING TO PROVE. NOT TO THEM, NOT TO THE WORLD.
NOT TO ME.
YOU'RE AQUAMAN, BY THE GODS.
YES, I AM.
WHA--
AND YOU'RE A BLOODY IDIOT!

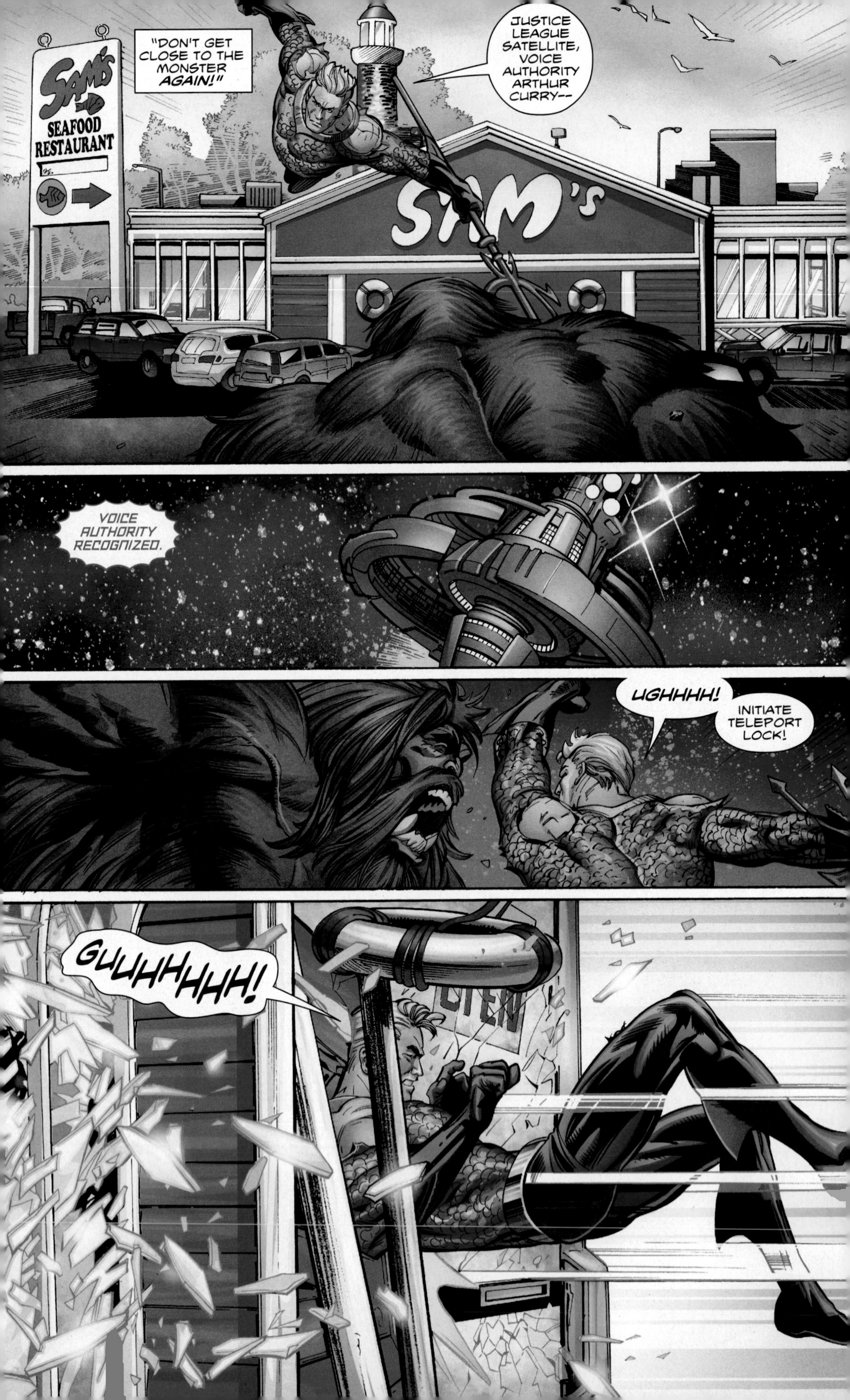
SAM'S
SEAFOOD RESTAURANT
"DON'T GET CLOSE TO THE MONSTER AGAIN!"
JUSTICE LEAGUE SATELLITE, VOICE AUTHORITY ARTHUR CURRY--
SAM'S
VOICE AUTHORITY RECOGNIZED.
UGHHHH!
INITIATE TELEPORT LOCK!
GUUHHHHH!

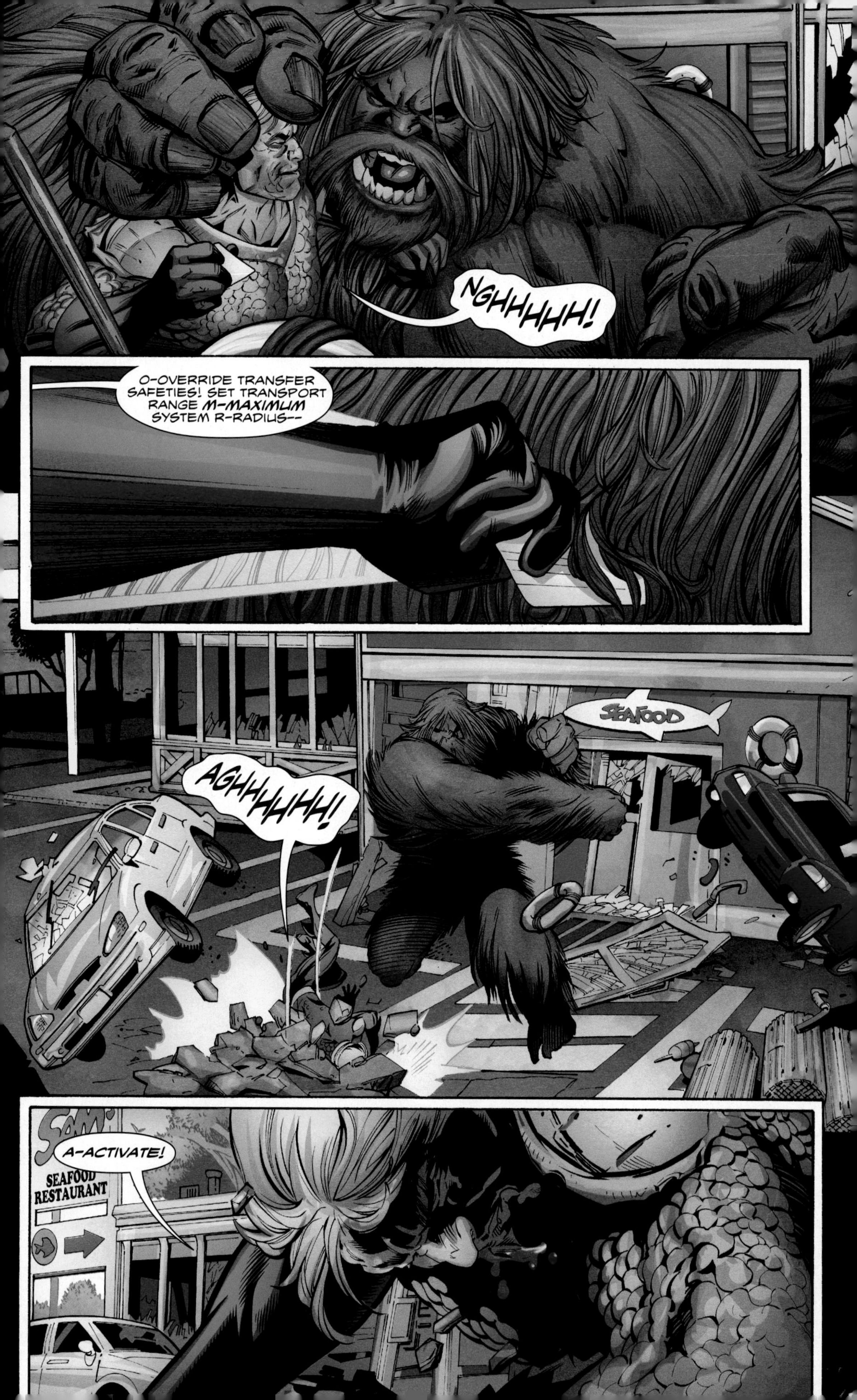
NGHHHHH!
O-OVERRIDE TRANSFER SAFETIES! SET TRANSPORT RANGE M-MAXIMUM SYSTEM R-RADIUS--
SEAFOOD
AGHHHHHH!
A-ACTIVATE!
SEAFOOD RESTAURANT

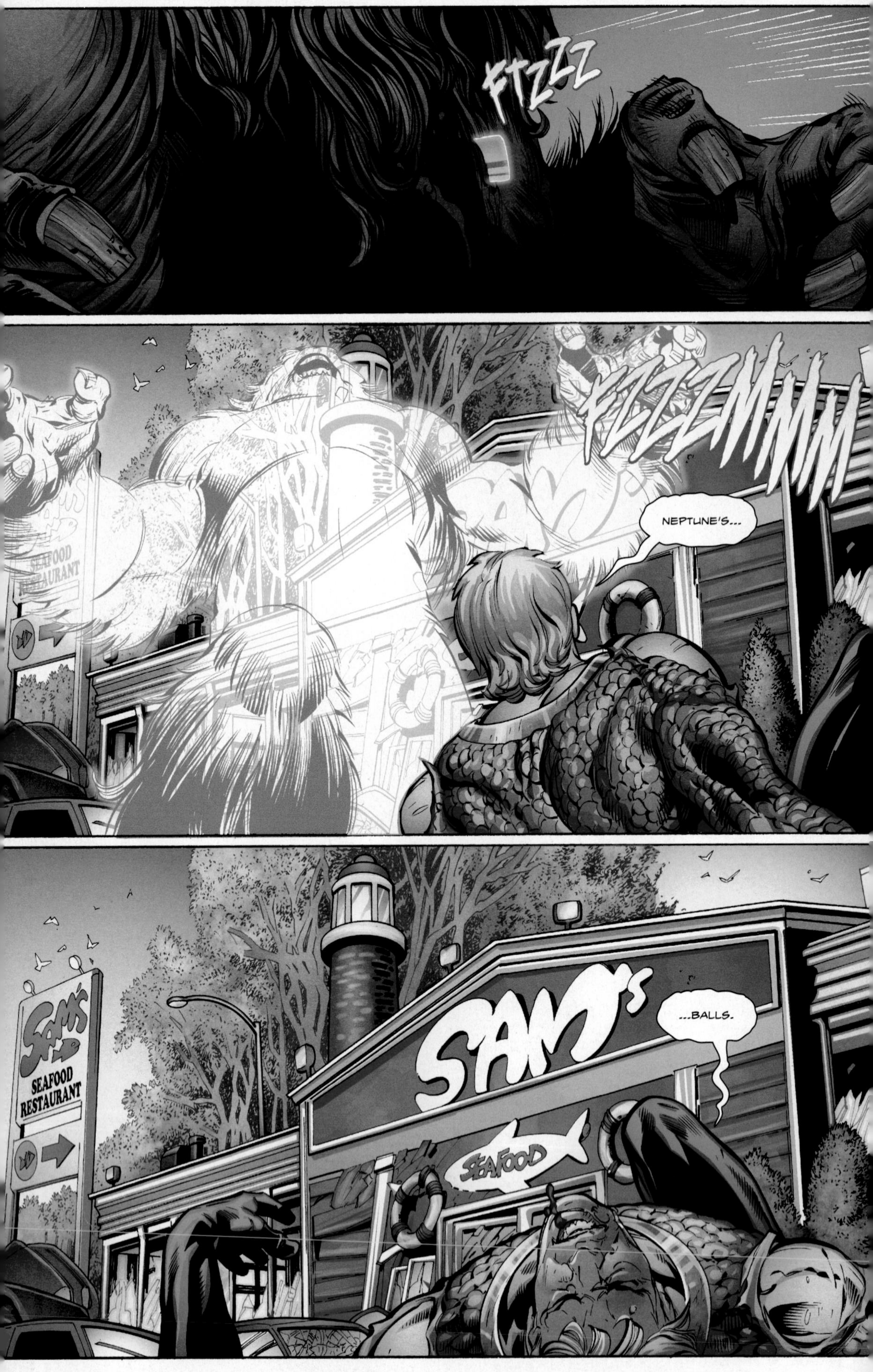
FTZZZ
FZZZMMMM
NEPTUNE'S...
SAM'S
SEAFOOD
RESTAURANT
...BALLS.
SEAFOOD

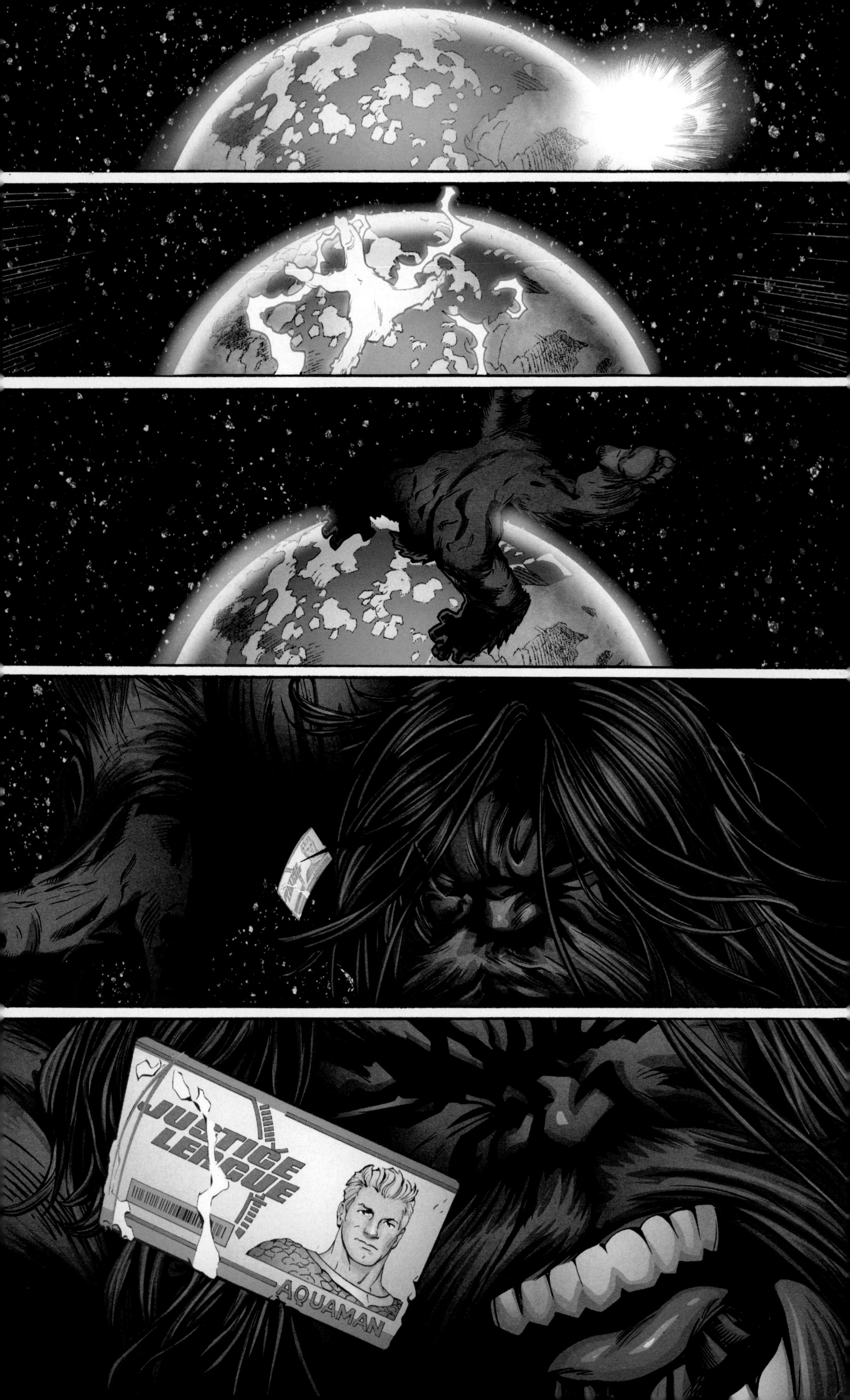
JUSTICE LEAGUE
AQUAMAN

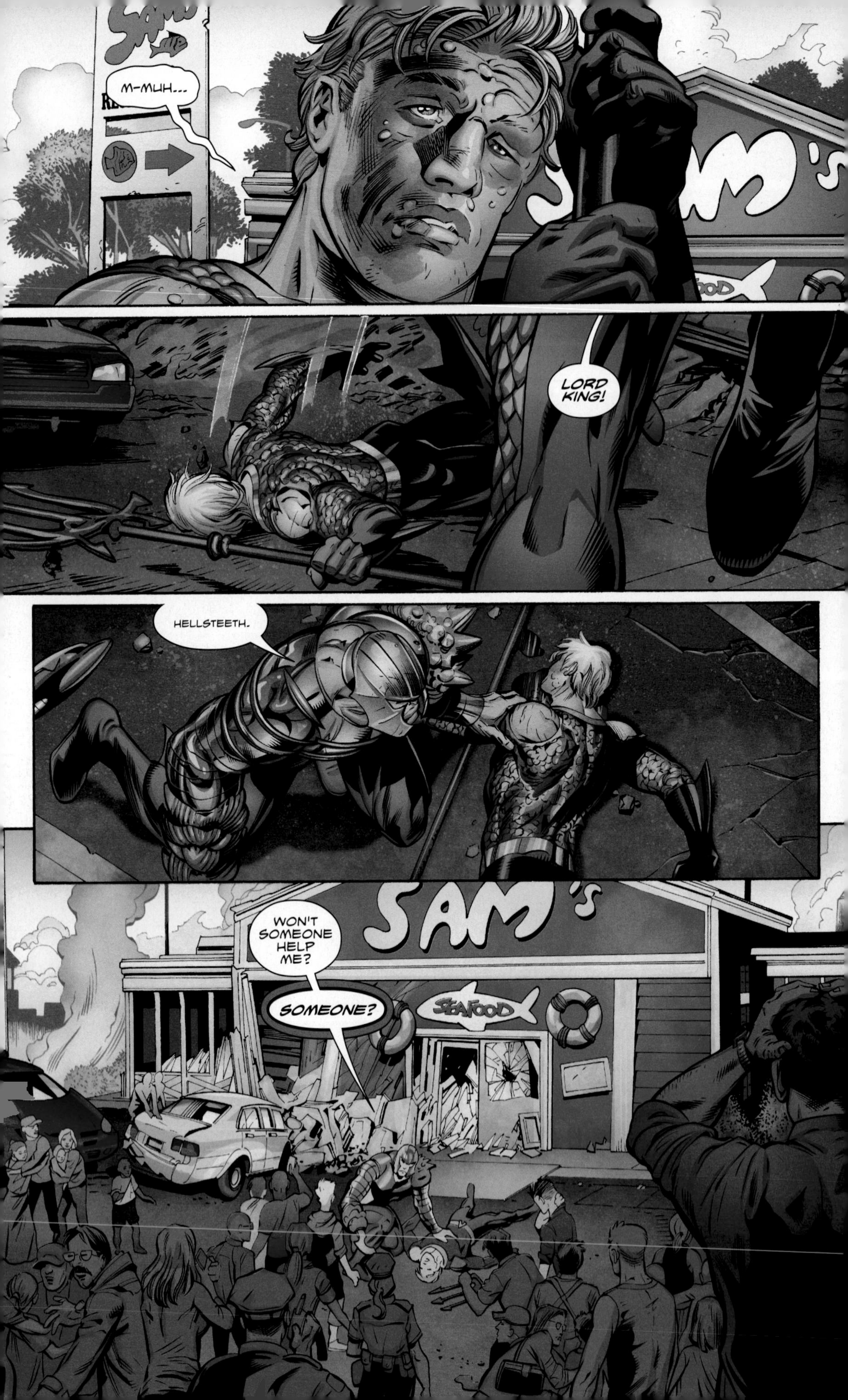

M-MUH...
LORD KING!
HELLSTEETH.
SAM'S
WON'T SOMEONE HELP ME?
SOMEONE?
SEAFOOD

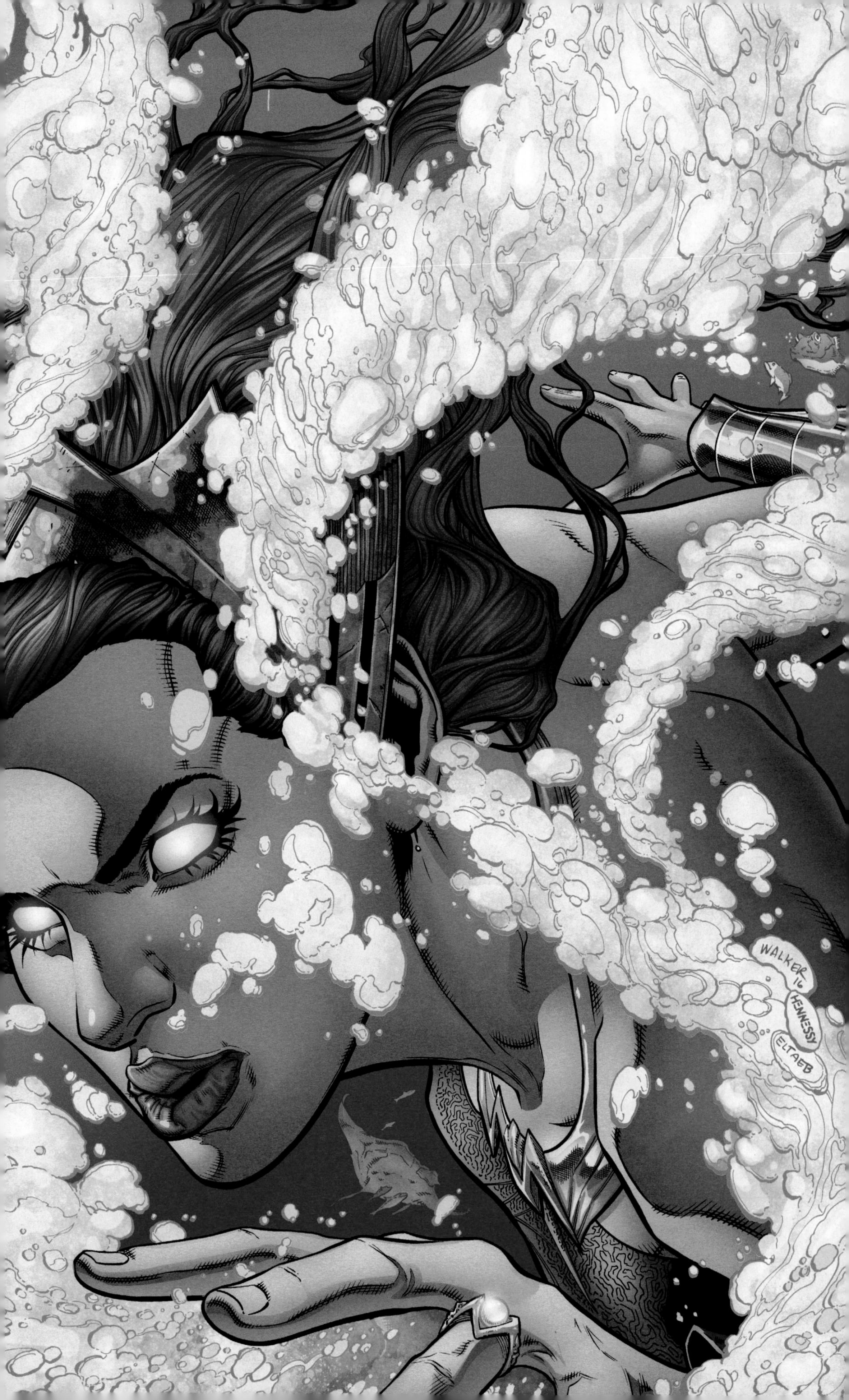
WALKER 16
HENNESSY
ELTAEB

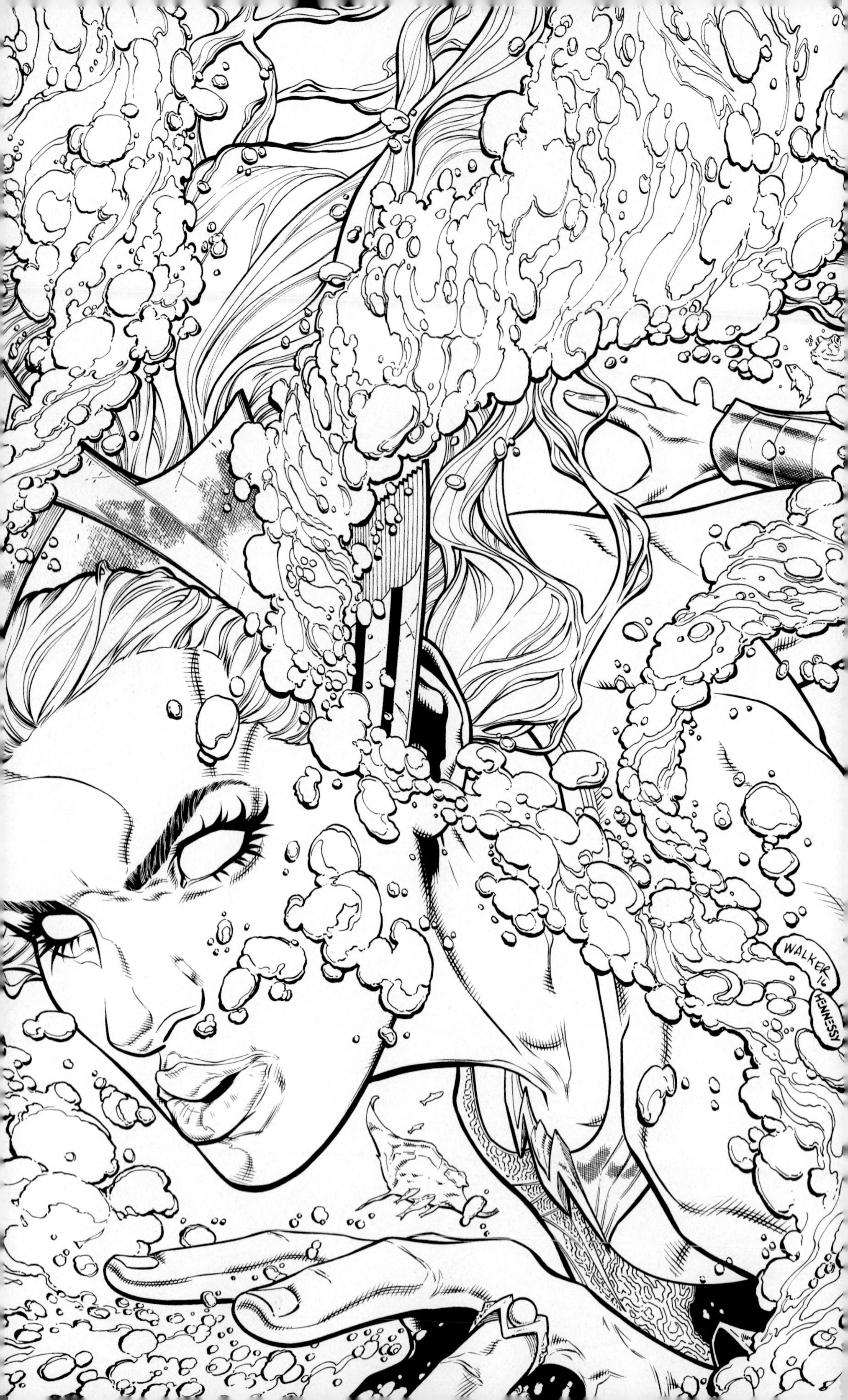
WALKER '16
HENNESSY

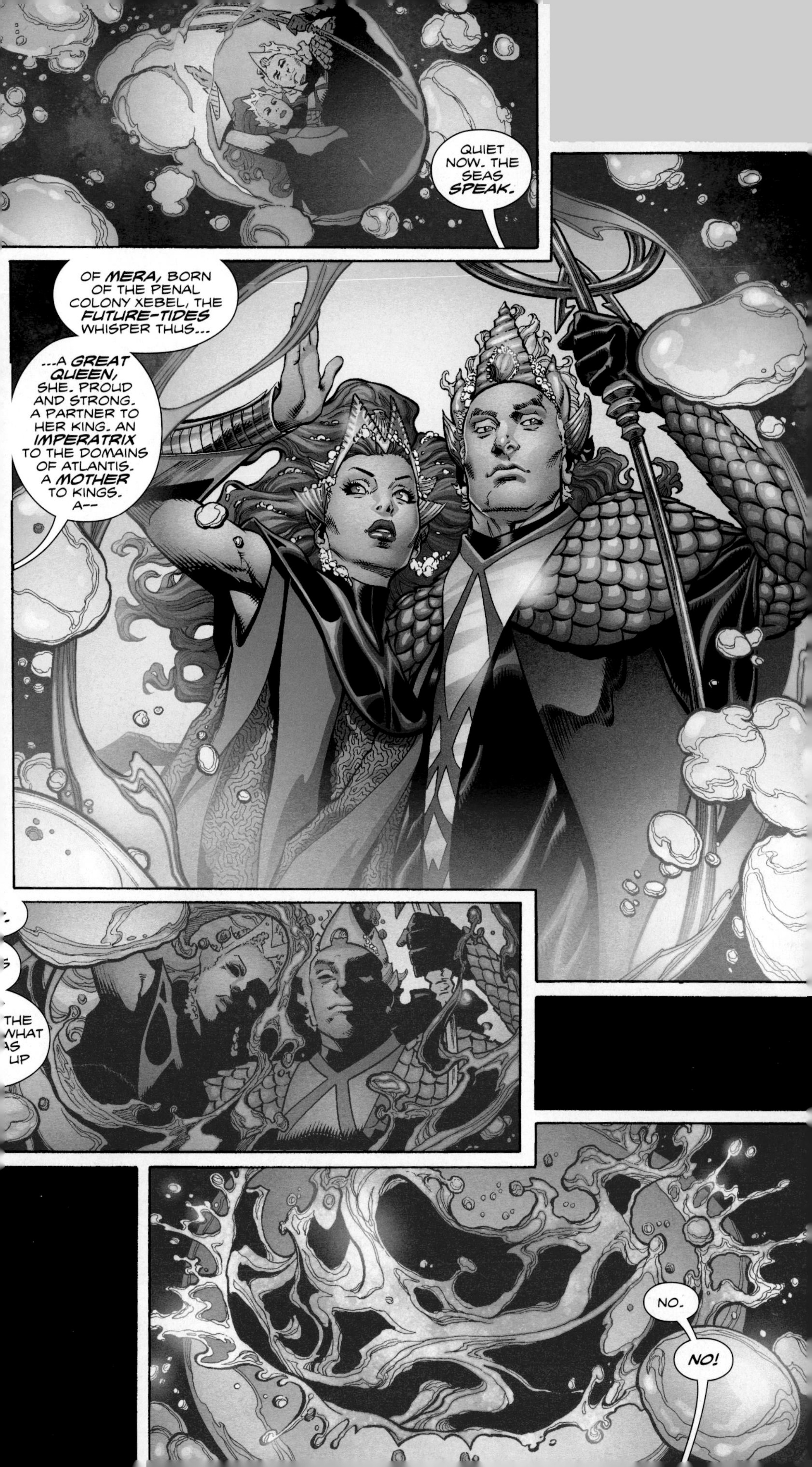
QUIET NOW. THE SEAS SPEAK.
OF MERA, BORN OF THE PENAL COLONY XEBEL, THE FUTURE-TIDES WHISPER THUS...
...A GREAT QUEEN, SHE. PROUD AND STRONG. A PARTNER TO HER KING. AN IMPERATRIX TO THE DOMAINS OF ATLANTIS. A MOTHER TO KINGS. A--
NO.
NO!

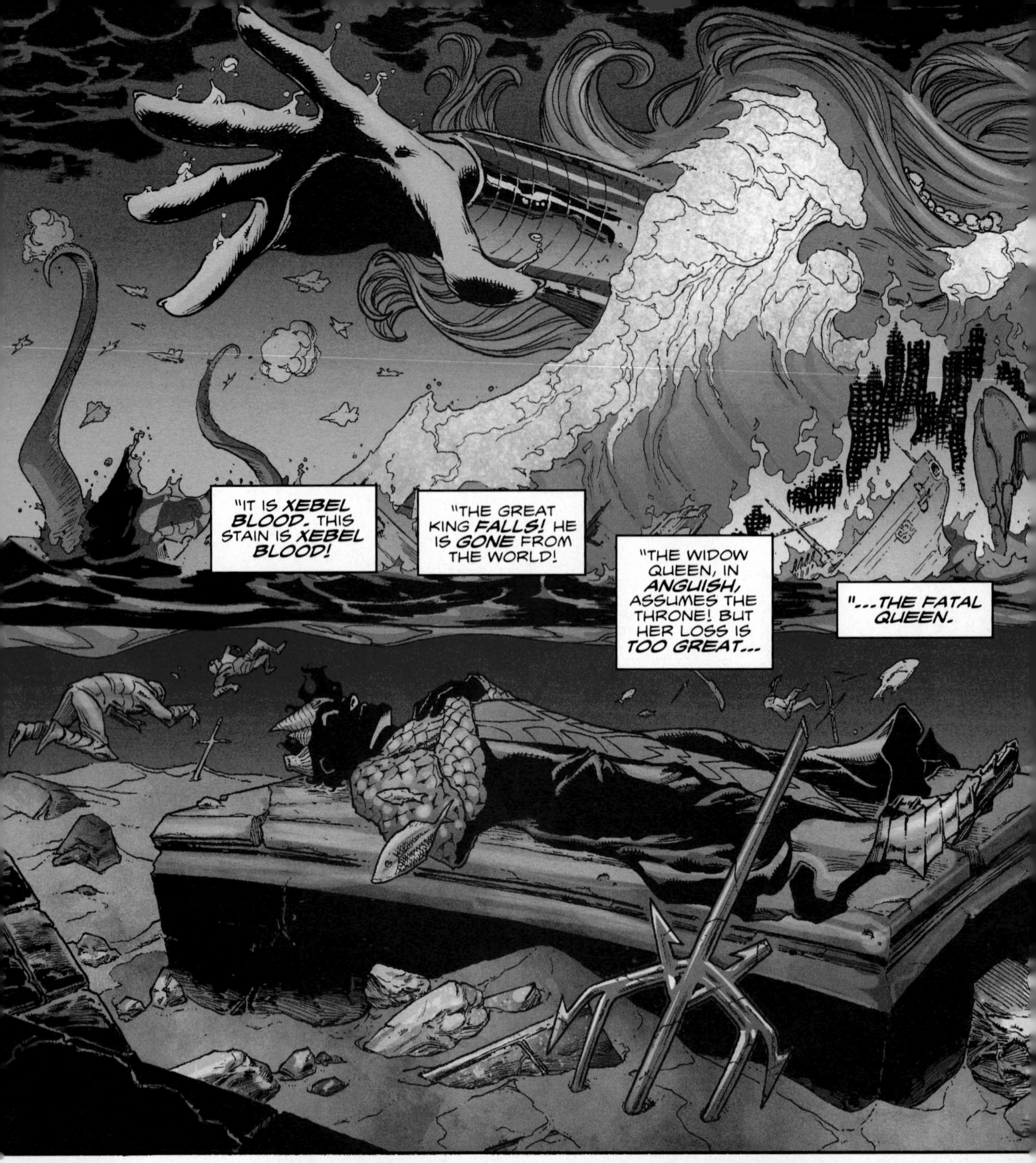
"IT IS XEBEL BLOOD. THIS STAIN IS XEBEL BLOOD!
"THE GREAT KING FALLS! HE IS GONE FROM THE WORLD!
"THE WIDOW QUEEN, IN ANGUISH, ASSUMES THE THRONE! BUT HER LOSS IS TOO GREAT...
"...THE FATAL QUEEN.

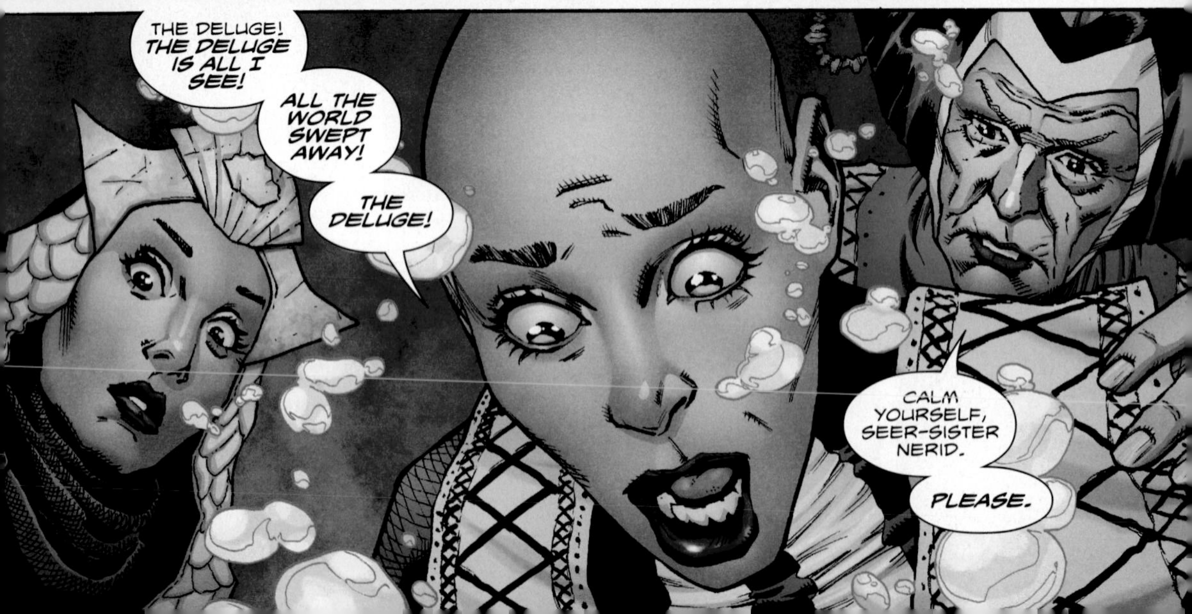
THE DELUGE! THE DELUGE IS ALL I SEE!
ALL THE WORLD SWEPT AWAY!
THE DELUGE!
CALM YOURSELF, SEER-SISTER NERID.
PLEASE.

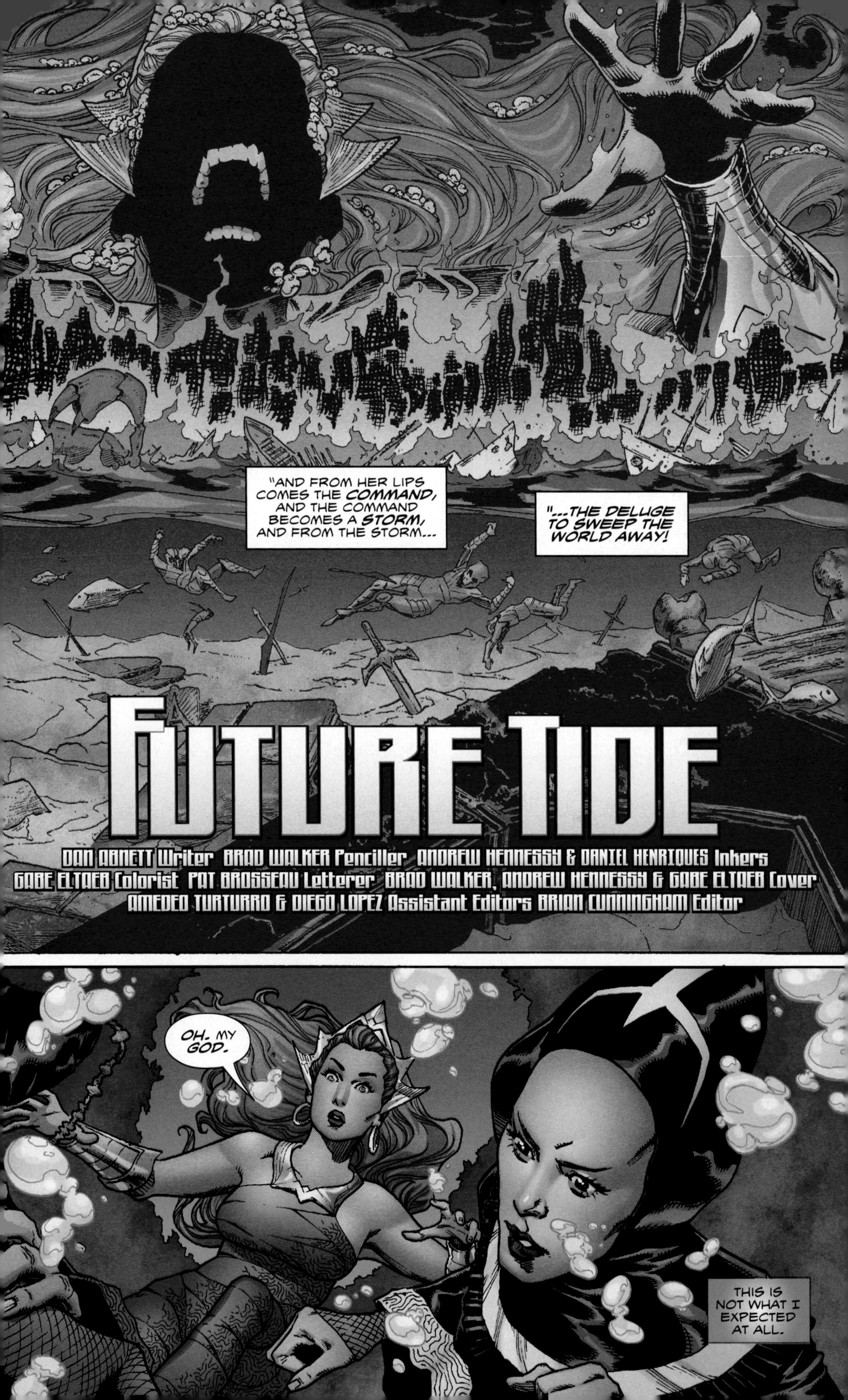
"AND FROM HER LIPS COMES THE COMMAND, AND THE COMMAND BECOMES A STORM, AND FROM THE STORM...
"...THE DELUGE TO SWEEP THE WORLD AWAY!
FUTURE TIDE
DAN ABNETT Writer BRAD WALKER Penciller ANDREW HENNESSY & DANIEL HENRIQUES Inkers
GABE ELTAEB Colorist PAT BROSSEAU Letterer BRAD WALKER, ANDREW HENNESSY & GABE ELTAEB Cover
AMEDEO TURTURRO & DIEGO LOPEZ Assistant Editors BRIAN CUNNINGHAM Editor
OH. MY GOD.
THIS IS NOT WHAT I EXPECTED AT ALL.

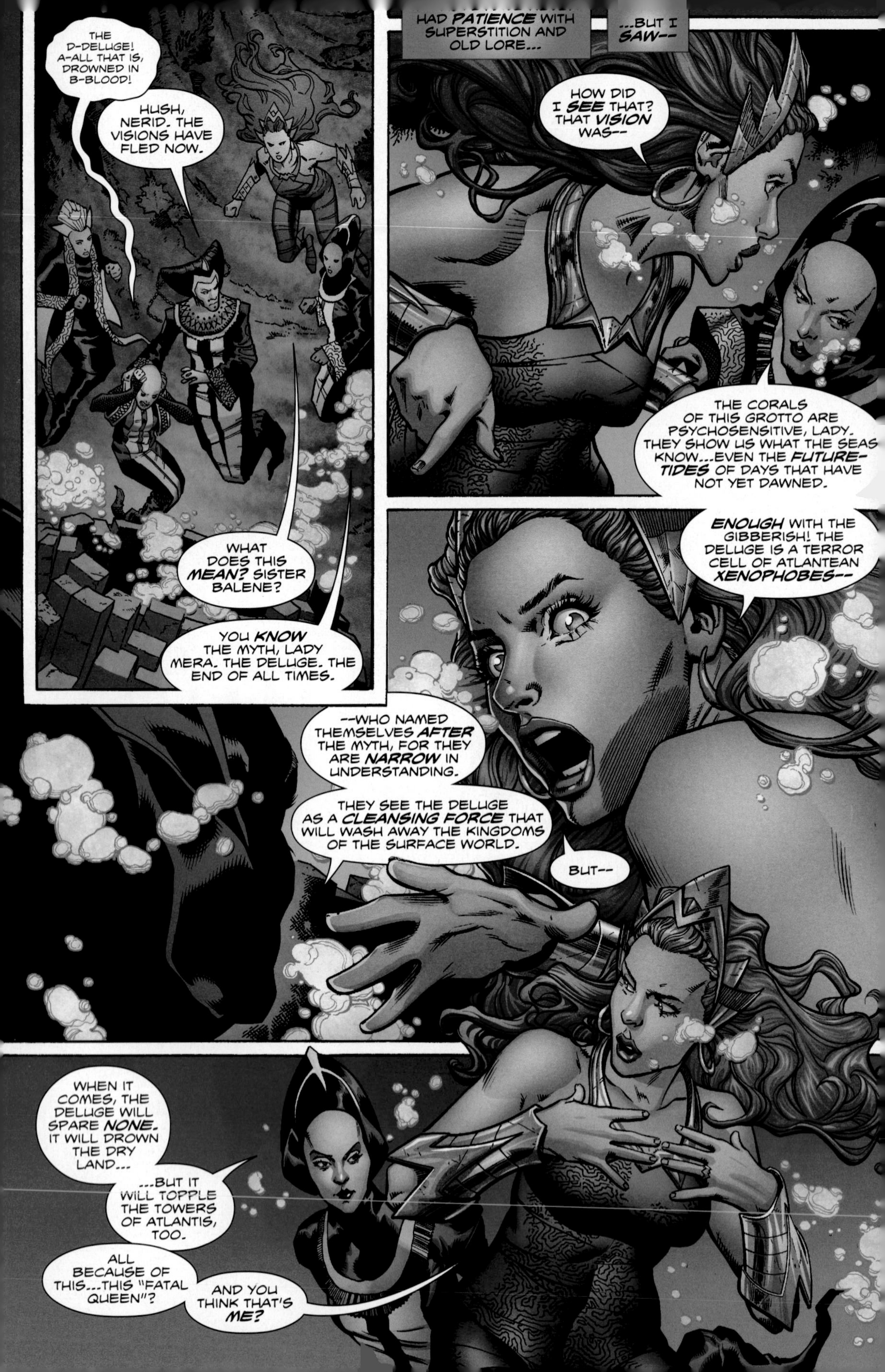
HAD PATIENCE WITH SUPERSTITION AND OLD LORE...
...BUT I SAW--
THE D-DELUGE! A-ALL THAT IS, DROWNED IN B-BLOOD!
HUSH, NERID. THE VISIONS HAVE FLED NOW.
WHAT DOES THIS MEAN? SISTER BALENE?
YOU KNOW THE MYTH, LADY MERA. THE DELUGE. THE END OF ALL TIMES.
HOW DID I SEE THAT? THAT VISION WAS--
THE CORALS OF THIS GROTTO ARE PSYCHOSENSITIVE, LADY. THEY SHOW US WHAT THE SEAS KNOW...EVEN THE FUTURE-TIDES OF DAYS THAT HAVE NOT YET DAWNED.
ENOUGH WITH THE GIBBERISH! THE DELUGE IS A TERROR CELL OF ATLANTEAN XENOPHOBES--
--WHO NAMED THEMSELVES AFTER THE MYTH, FOR THEY ARE NARROW IN UNDERSTANDING.
THEY SEE THE DELUGE AS A CLEANSING FORCE THAT WILL WASH AWAY THE KINGDOMS OF THE SURFACE WORLD.
BUT--
WHEN IT COMES, THE DELUGE WILL SPARE NONE. IT WILL DROWN THE DRY LAND...
...BUT IT WILL TOPPLE THE TOWERS OF ATLANTIS, TOO.
ALL BECAUSE OF THIS...THIS "FATAL QUEEN"?
AND YOU THINK THAT'S ME?

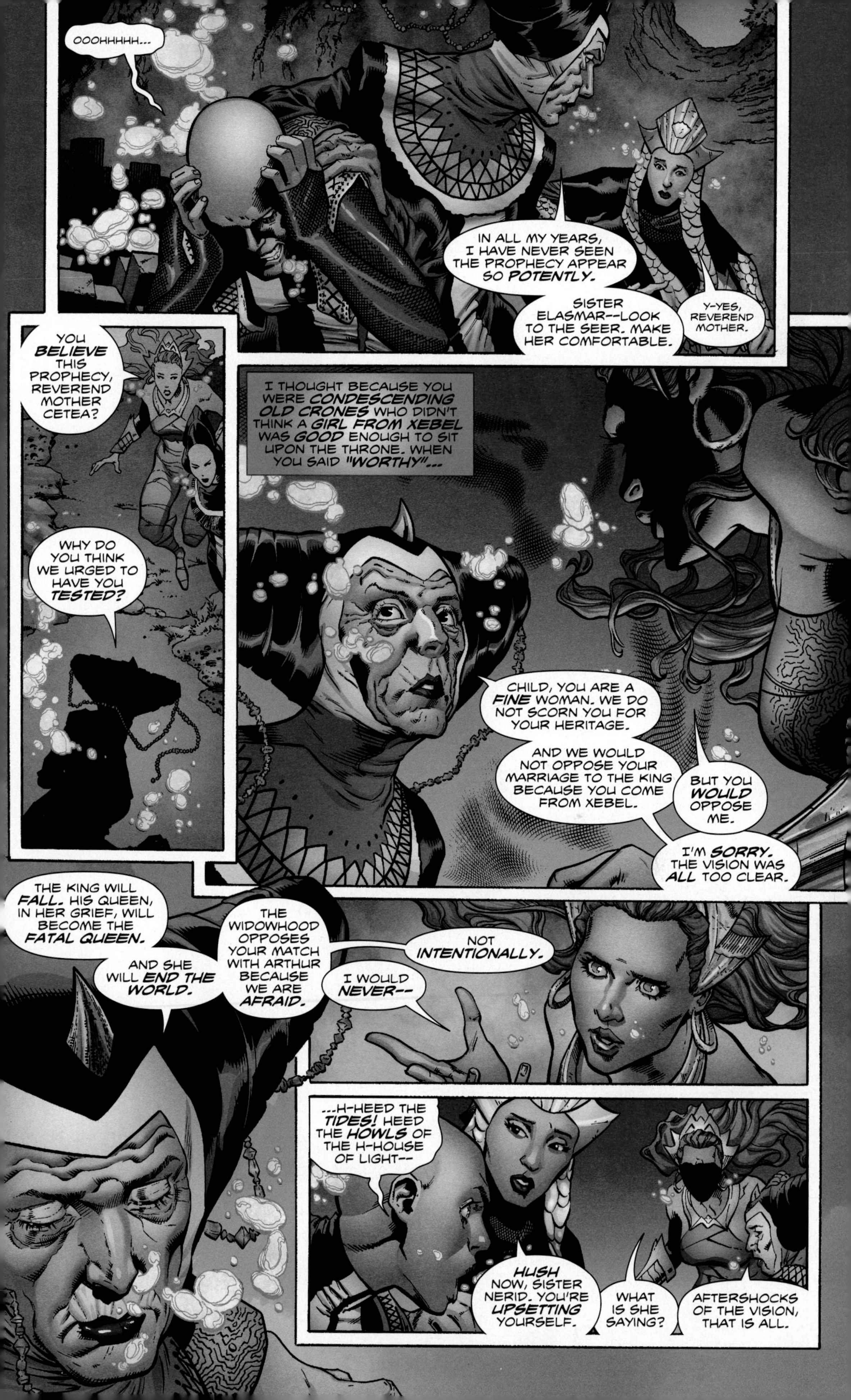
OOOHHHHH...
IN ALL MY YEARS, I HAVE NEVER SEEN THE PROPHECY APPEAR SO POTENTLY.
SISTER ELASMAR--LOOK TO THE SEER. MAKE HER COMFORTABLE.
Y-YES, REVEREND MOTHER.
YOU BELIEVE THIS PROPHECY, REVEREND MOTHER CETEA?
WHY DO YOU THINK WE URGED TO HAVE YOU TESTED?
I THOUGHT BECAUSE YOU WERE CONDESCENDING OLD CRONES WHO DIDN'T THINK A GIRL FROM XEBEL WAS GOOD ENOUGH TO SIT UPON THE THRONE. WHEN YOU SAID "WORTHY"...
CHILD, YOU ARE A FINE WOMAN. WE DO NOT SCORN YOU FOR YOUR HERITAGE.
AND WE WOULD NOT OPPOSE YOUR MARRIAGE TO THE KING BECAUSE YOU COME FROM XEBEL.
BUT YOU WOULD OPPOSE ME.
I'M SORRY. THE VISION WAS ALL TOO CLEAR.
THE KING WILL FALL. HIS QUEEN, IN HER GRIEF, WILL BECOME THE FATAL QUEEN.
AND SHE WILL END THE WORLD.
THE WIDOWHOOD OPPOSES YOUR MATCH WITH ARTHUR BECAUSE WE ARE AFRAID.
I WOULD NEVER--
NOT INTENTIONALLY.
...H-HEED THE TIDES! HEED THE HOWLS OF THE H-HOUSE OF LIGHT--
HUSH NOW, SISTER NERID. YOU'RE UPSETTING YOURSELF.
WHAT IS SHE SAYING?
AFTERSHOCKS OF THE VISION, THAT IS ALL.

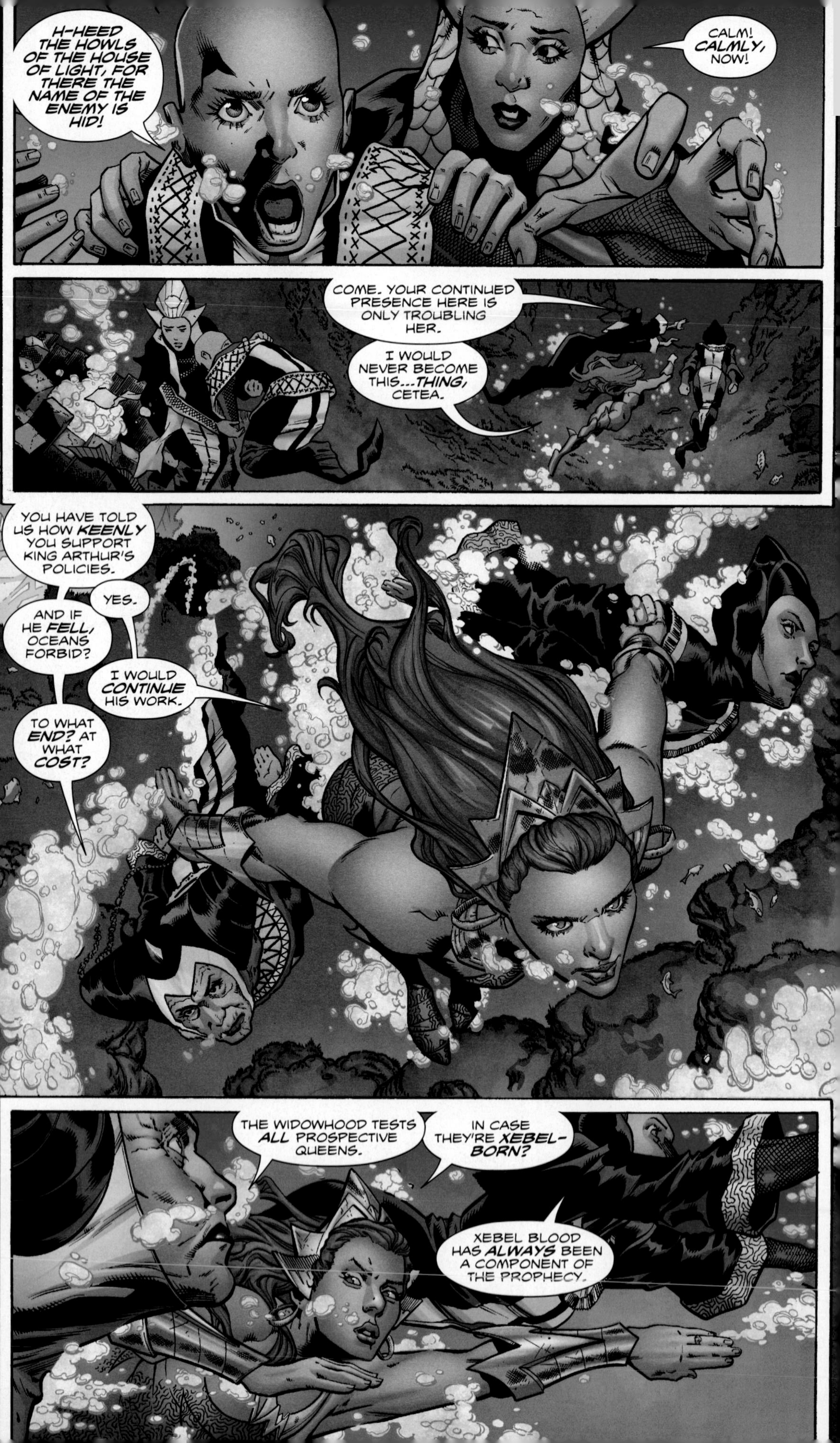
H-HEED THE HOWLS OF THE HOUSE OF LIGHT, FOR THERE THE NAME OF THE ENEMY IS HID!
CALM! CALMLY, NOW!
COME. YOUR CONTINUED PRESENCE HERE IS ONLY TROUBLING HER.
I WOULD NEVER BECOME THIS...THING, CETEA.
YOU HAVE TOLD US HOW KEENLY YOU SUPPORT KING ARTHUR'S POLICIES.
YES.
AND IF HE FELL, OCEANS FORBID?
I WOULD CONTINUE HIS WORK.
TO WHAT END? AT WHAT COST?
THE WIDOWHOOD TESTS ALL PROSPECTIVE QUEENS.
IN CASE THEY'RE XEBEL-BORN?
XEBEL BLOOD HAS ALWAYS BEEN A COMPONENT OF THE PROPHECY.

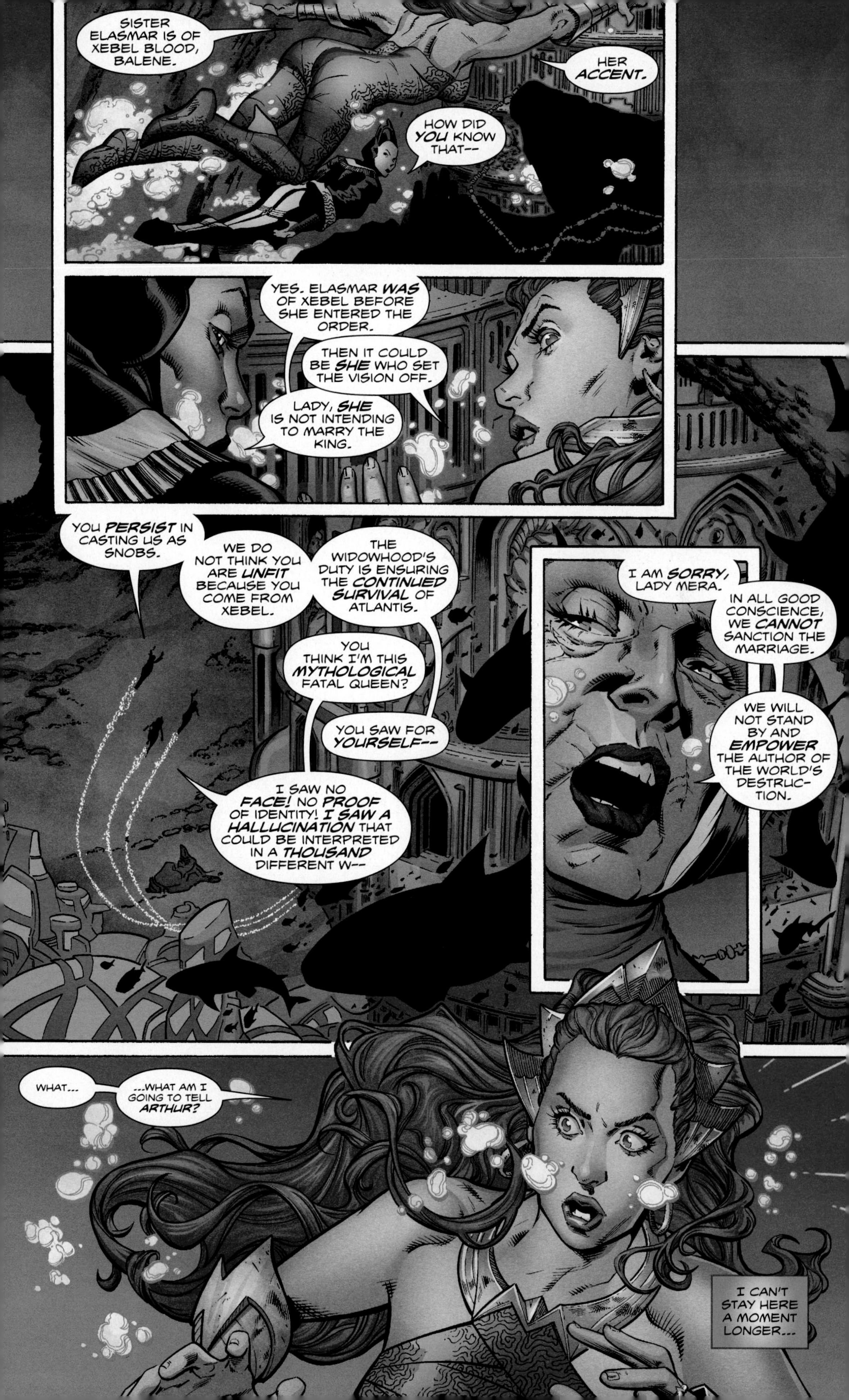

SISTER ELASMAR IS OF XEBEL BLOOD, BALENE.
HER ACCENT.
HOW DID YOU KNOW THAT--
YES. ELASMAR WAS OF XEBEL BEFORE SHE ENTERED THE ORDER.
THEN IT COULD BE SHE WHO SET THE VISION OFF.
LADY, SHE IS NOT INTENDING TO MARRY THE KING.
YOU PERSIST IN CASTING US AS SNOBS.
WE DO NOT THINK YOU ARE UNFIT BECAUSE YOU COME FROM XEBEL.
THE WIDOWHOOD'S DUTY IS ENSURING THE CONTINUED SURVIVAL OF ATLANTIS.
YOU THINK I'M THIS MYTHOLOGICAL FATAL QUEEN?
YOU SAW FOR YOURSELF--
I SAW NO FACE! NO PROOF OF IDENTITY! I SAW A HALLUCINATION THAT COULD BE INTERPRETED IN A THOUSAND DIFFERENT W--
I AM SORRY, LADY MERA.
IN ALL GOOD CONSCIENCE, WE CANNOT SANCTION THE MARRIAGE.
WE WILL NOT STAND BY AND EMPOWER THE AUTHOR OF THE WORLD'S DESTRUCTION.
WHAT...
...WHAT AM I GOING TO TELL ARTHUR?
I CAN'T STAY HERE A MOMENT LONGER...

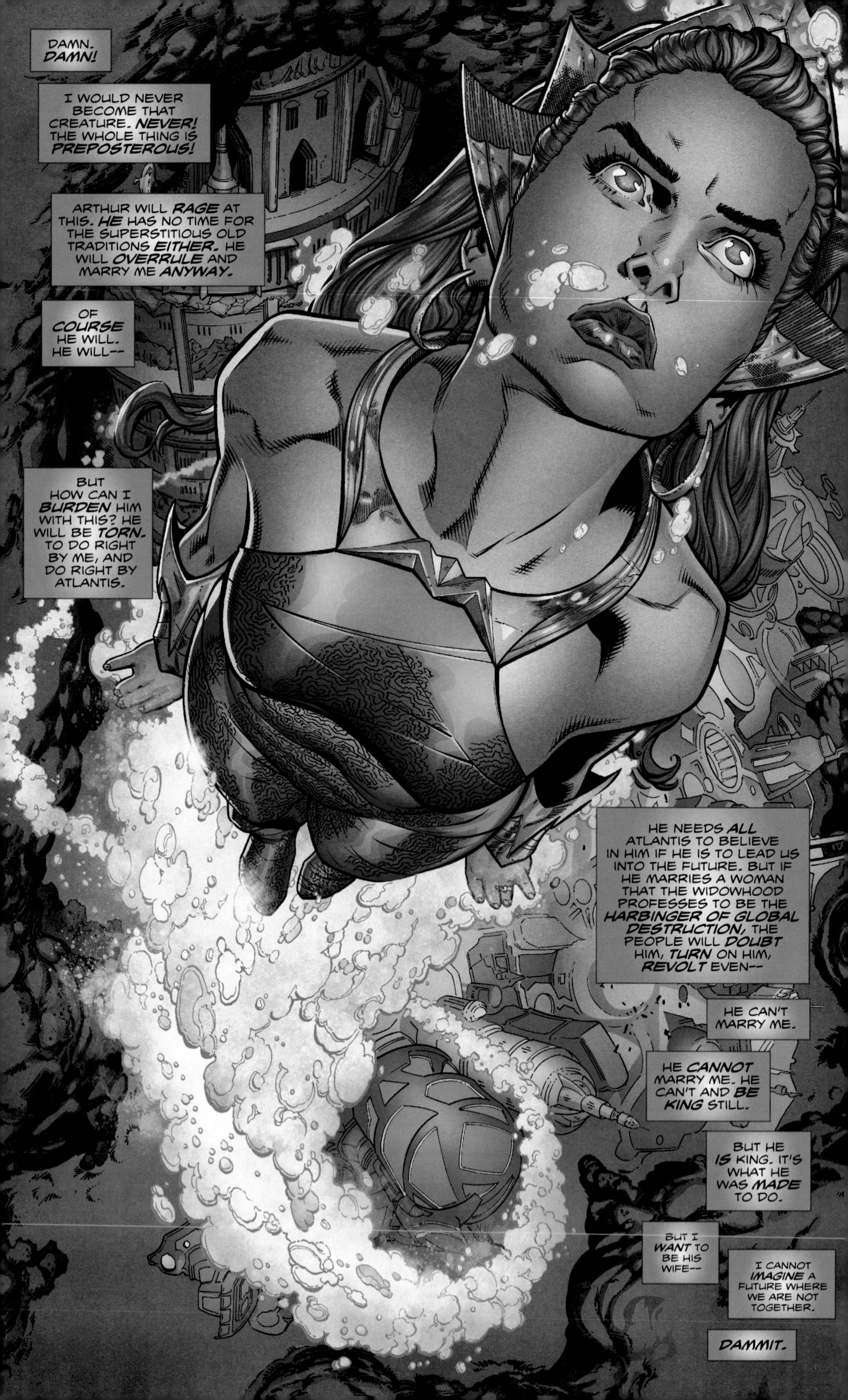
DAMN. DAMN!
I WOULD NEVER BECOME THAT CREATURE. NEVER! THE WHOLE THING IS PREPOSTEROUS!
ARTHUR WILL RAGE AT THIS. HE HAS NO TIME FOR THE SUPERSTITIOUS OLD TRADITIONS EITHER. HE WILL OVERRULE AND MARRY ME ANYWAY.
OF COURSE HE WILL. HE WILL--
BUT HOW CAN I BURDEN HIM WITH THIS? HE WILL BE TORN. TO DO RIGHT BY ME, AND DO RIGHT BY ATLANTIS.
HE NEEDS ALL ATLANTIS TO BELIEVE IN HIM IF HE IS TO LEAD US INTO THE FUTURE. BUT IF HE MARRIES A WOMAN THAT THE WIDOWHOOD PROFESSES TO BE THE HARBINGER OF GLOBAL DESTRUCTION, THE PEOPLE WILL DOUBT HIM, TURN ON HIM, REVOLT EVEN--
HE CAN'T MARRY ME.
HE CANNOT MARRY ME. HE CAN'T AND BE KING STILL.
BUT HE IS KING. IT'S WHAT HE WAS MADE TO DO.
BUT I WANT TO BE HIS WIFE--
I CANNOT IMAGINE A FUTURE WHERE WE ARE NOT TOGETHER.
DAMMIT.

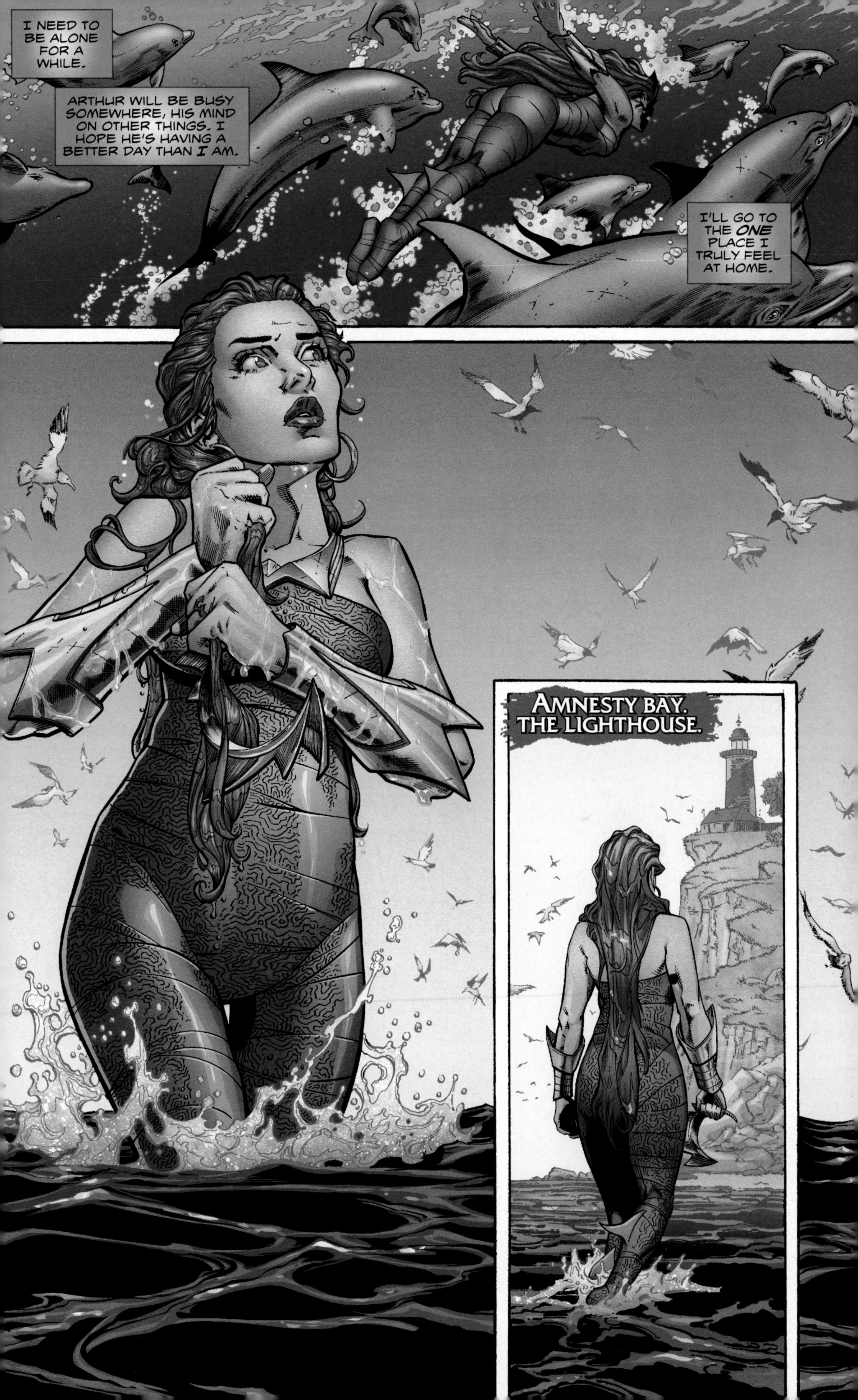
I NEED TO BE ALONE FOR A WHILE.
ARTHUR WILL BE BUSY SOMEWHERE, HIS MIND ON OTHER THINGS. I HOPE HE'S HAVING A BETTER DAY THAN I AM.
I'LL GO TO THE ONE PLACE I TRULY FEEL AT HOME.
AMNESTY BAY. THE LIGHTHOUSE.

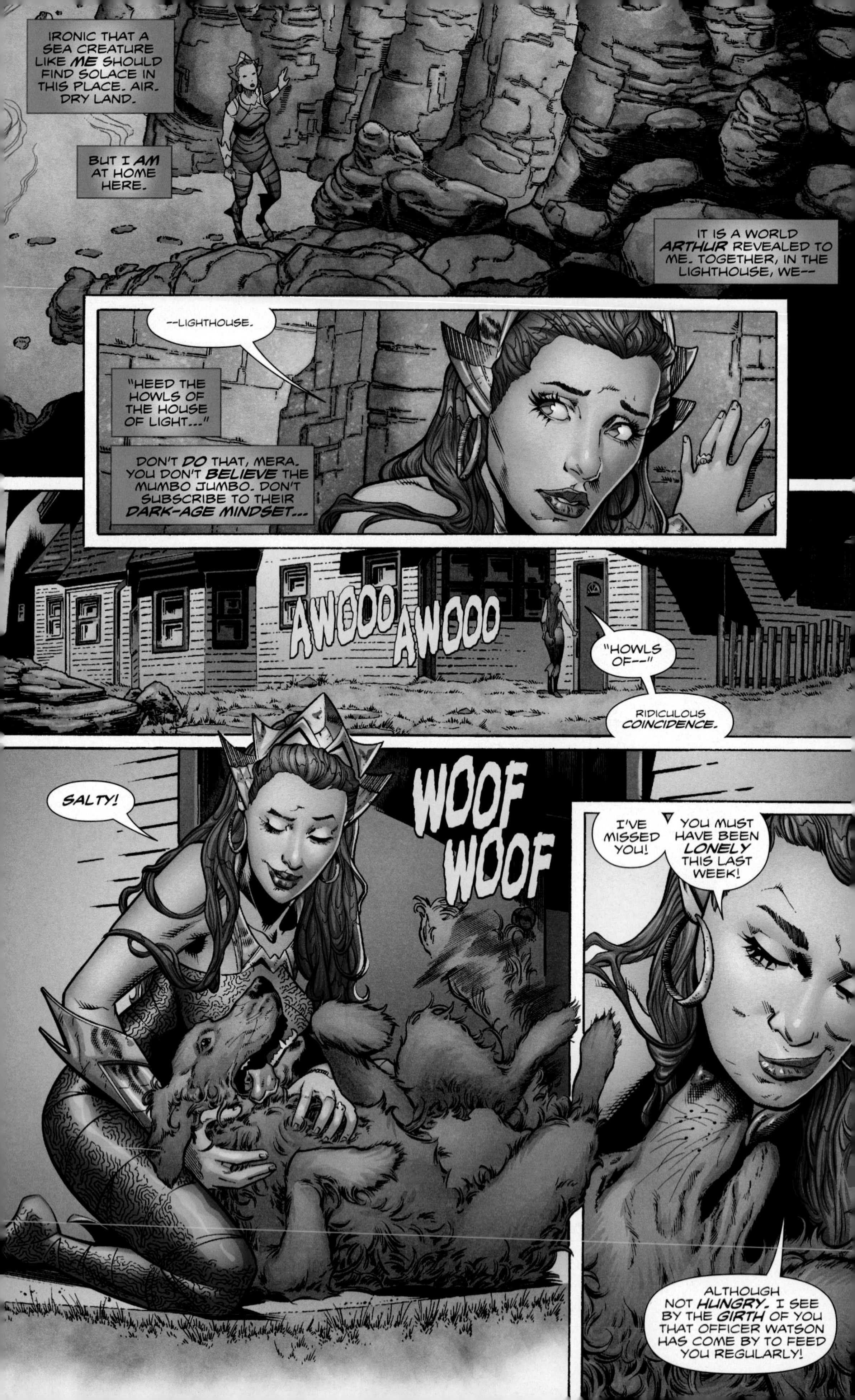
IRONIC THAT A SEA CREATURE LIKE ME SHOULD FIND SOLACE IN THIS PLACE. AIR. DRY LAND.
BUT I AM AT HOME HERE.
IT IS A WORLD ARTHUR REVEALED TO ME. TOGETHER, IN THE LIGHTHOUSE, WE--
--LIGHTHOUSE.
"HEED THE HOWLS OF THE HOUSE OF LIGHT..."
DON'T DO THAT, MERA. YOU DON'T BELIEVE THE MUMBO JUMBO. DON'T SUBSCRIBE TO THEIR DARK-AGE MINDSET...
AWOOO AWOOO
"HOWLS OF--"
RIDICULOUS COINCIDENCE.
SALTY!
WOOF WOOF
I'VE MISSED YOU!
YOU MUST HAVE BEEN LONELY THIS LAST WEEK!
ALTHOUGH NOT HUNGRY. I SEE BY THE GIRTH OF YOU THAT OFFICER WATSON HAS COME BY TO FEED YOU REGULARLY!

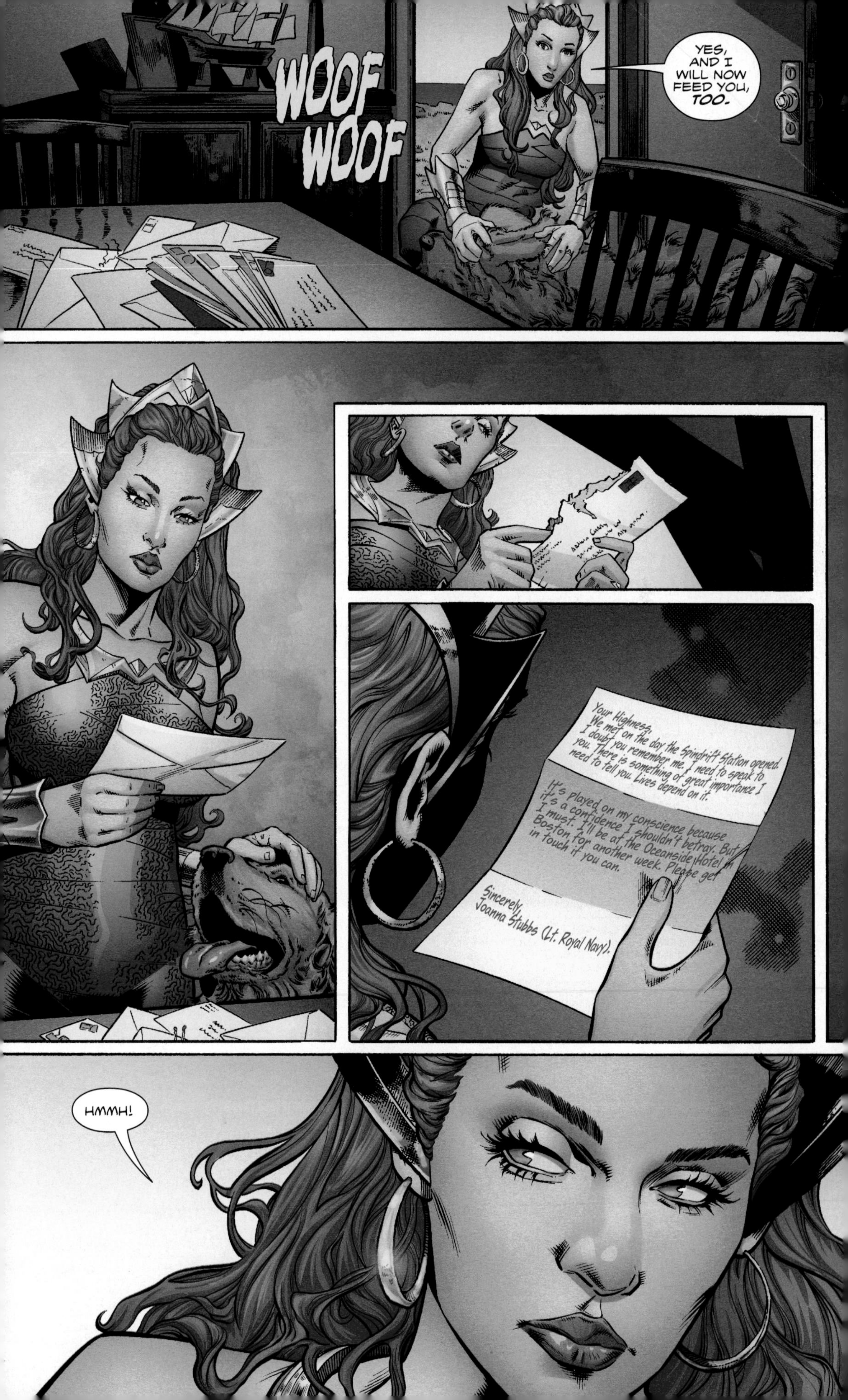
WOOF
WOOF
YES, AND I WILL NOW FEED YOU, TOO.
Your Highness,
We met on the day the Spindrift Station opened. I doubt you remember me. I need to speak to you. There is something of great importance I need to tell you. Lives depend on it.
It's played on my conscience because it's a confidence I shouldn't betray. But I must. I'll be at the Oceanside Hotel in Boston, for another week. Please get in touch if you can.
Sincerely,
Joanna Stubbs (Lt. Royal Navy).
HMMH!

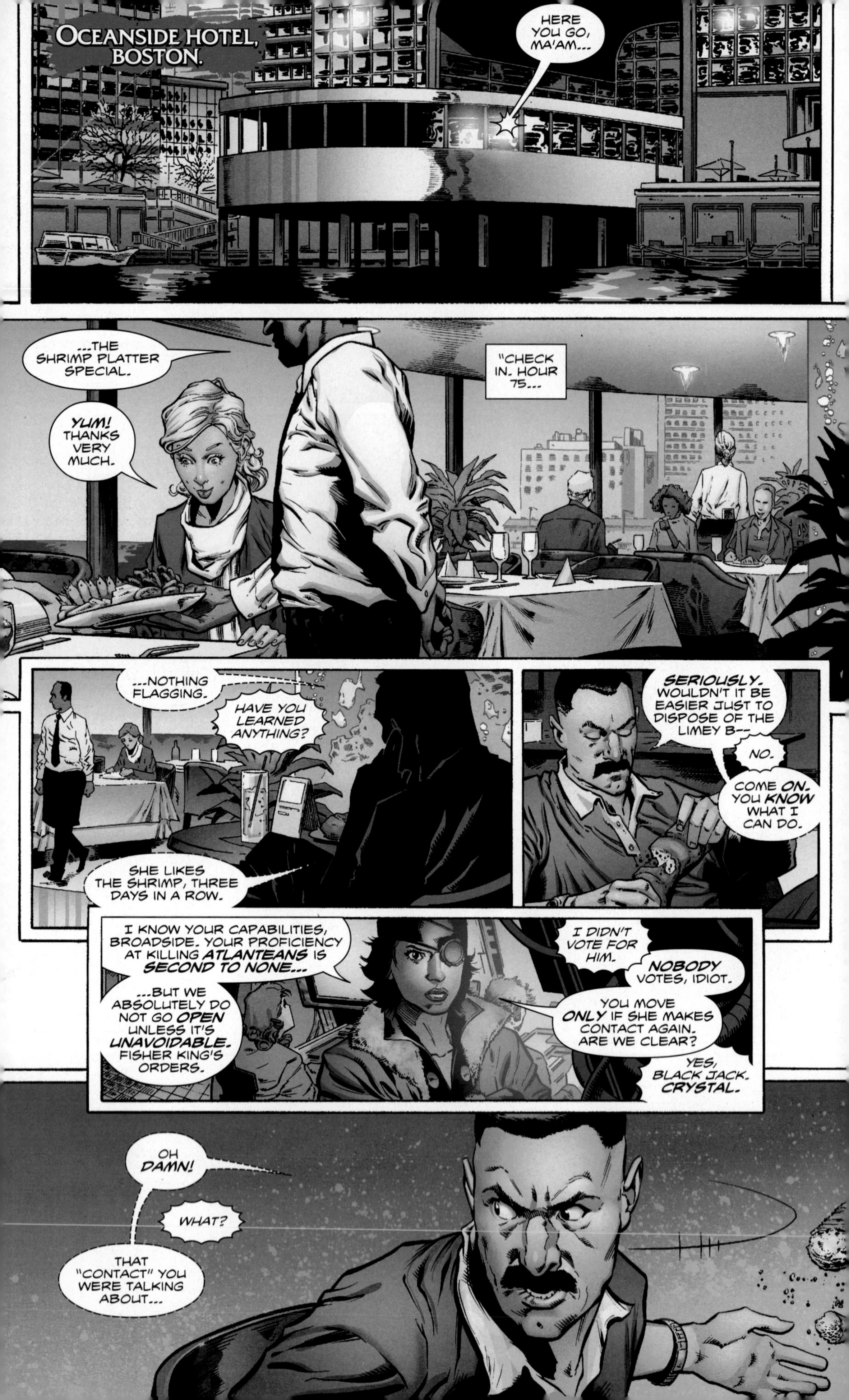
OCEANSIDE HOTEL, BOSTON.
HERE YOU GO, MA'AM...
...THE SHRIMP PLATTER SPECIAL.
"CHECK IN. HOUR 75...
YUM! THANKS VERY MUCH.
...NOTHING FLAGGING.
HAVE YOU LEARNED ANYTHING?
SHE LIKES THE SHRIMP, THREE DAYS IN A ROW.
SERIOUSLY. WOULDN'T IT BE EASIER JUST TO DISPOSE OF THE LIMEY B--
NO.
COME ON. YOU KNOW WHAT I CAN DO.
I KNOW YOUR CAPABILITIES, BROADSIDE. YOUR PROFICIENCY AT KILLING ATLANTEANS IS SECOND TO NONE...
...BUT WE ABSOLUTELY DO NOT GO OPEN UNLESS IT'S UNAVOIDABLE. FISHER KING'S ORDERS.
I DIDN'T VOTE FOR HIM.
NOBODY VOTES, IDIOT.
YOU MOVE ONLY IF SHE MAKES CONTACT AGAIN. ARE WE CLEAR?
YES, BLACK JACK. CRYSTAL.
OH DAMN!
WHAT?
THAT "CONTACT" YOU WERE TALKING ABOUT...

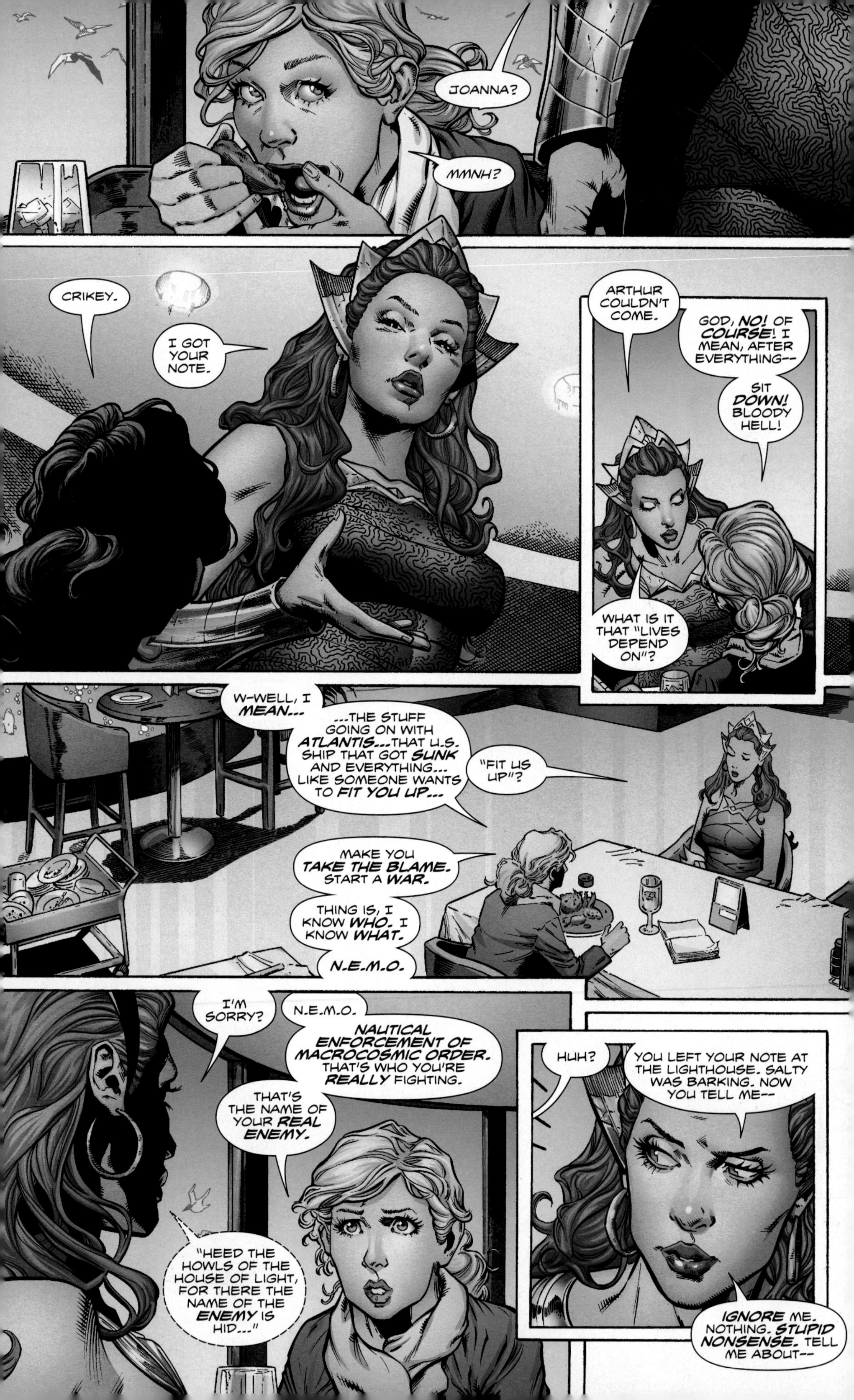
JOANNA?
MMNH?
CRIKEY.
I GOT YOUR NOTE.
ARTHUR COULDN'T COME.
GOD, NO! OF COURSE! I MEAN, AFTER EVERYTHING--
SIT DOWN! BLOODY HELL!
WHAT IS IT THAT "LIVES DEPEND ON"?
W-WELL, I MEAN...
...THE STUFF GOING ON WITH ATLANTIS...THAT U.S. SHIP THAT GOT SUNK AND EVERYTHING... LIKE SOMEONE WANTS TO FIT YOU UP...
"FIT US UP"?
MAKE YOU TAKE THE BLAME. START A WAR.
THING IS, I KNOW WHO. I KNOW WHAT.
N.E.M.O.
I'M SORRY?
N.E.M.O.
NAUTICAL ENFORCEMENT OF MACROCOSMIC ORDER. THAT'S WHO YOU'RE REALLY FIGHTING.
THAT'S THE NAME OF YOUR REAL ENEMY.
"HEED THE HOWLS OF THE HOUSE OF LIGHT, FOR THERE THE NAME OF THE ENEMY IS HID..."
HUH?
YOU LEFT YOUR NOTE AT THE LIGHTHOUSE. SALTY WAS BARKING. NOW YOU TELL ME--
IGNORE ME. NOTHING. STUPID NONSENSE. TELL ME ABOUT--

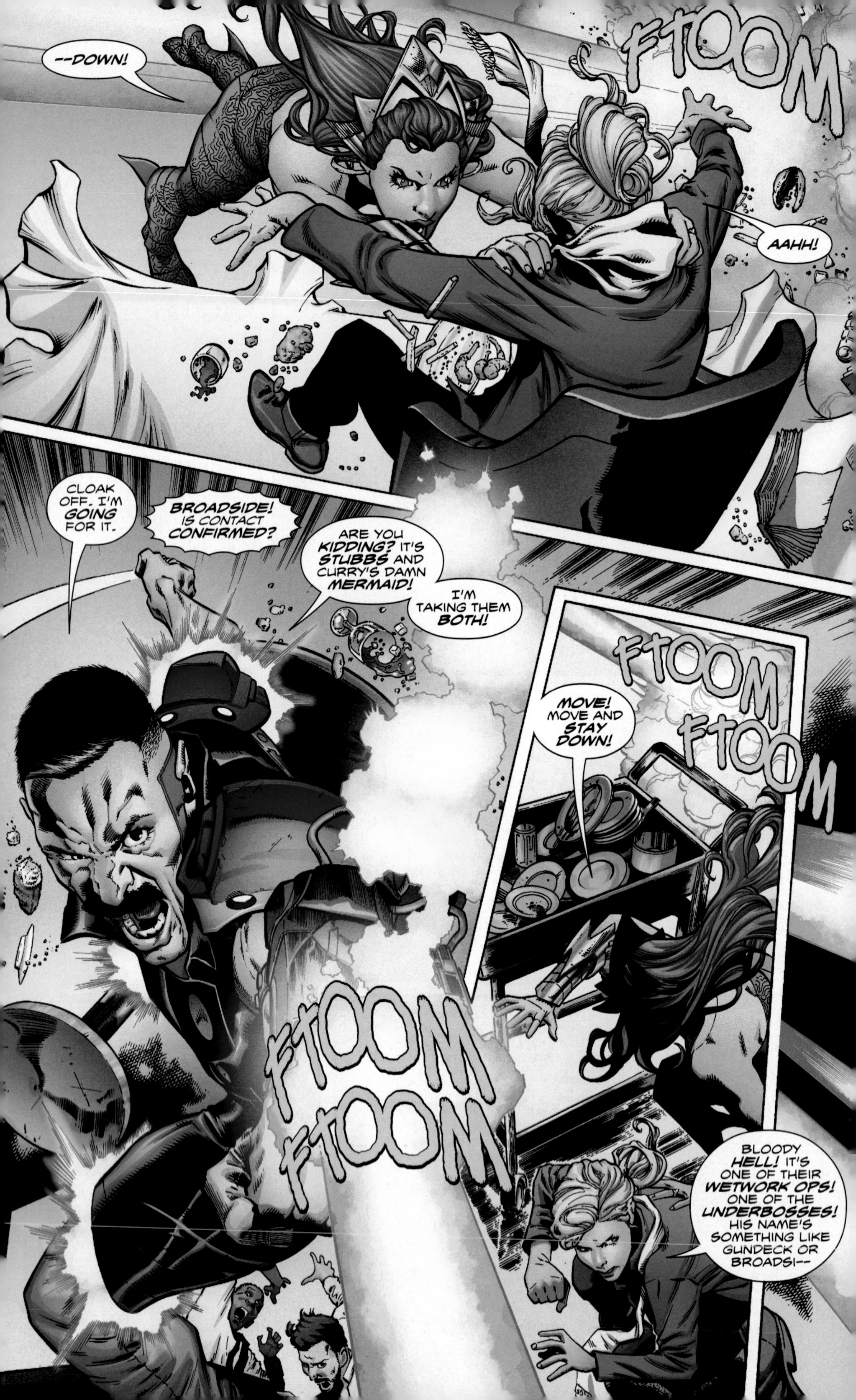
--DOWN!
FTOOM
AAHH!
CLOAK OFF. I'M GOING FOR IT.
BROADSIDE! IS CONTACT CONFIRMED?
ARE YOU KIDDING? IT'S STUBBS AND CURRY'S DAMN MERMAID!
I'M TAKING THEM BOTH!
FTOOM
FTOOM
MOVE! MOVE AND STAY DOWN!
FTOOM
FTOOM
BLOODY HELL! IT'S ONE OF THEIR WETWORK OPS! ONE OF THE UNDERBOSSES! HIS NAME'S SOMETHING LIKE GUNDECK OR BROADSI--

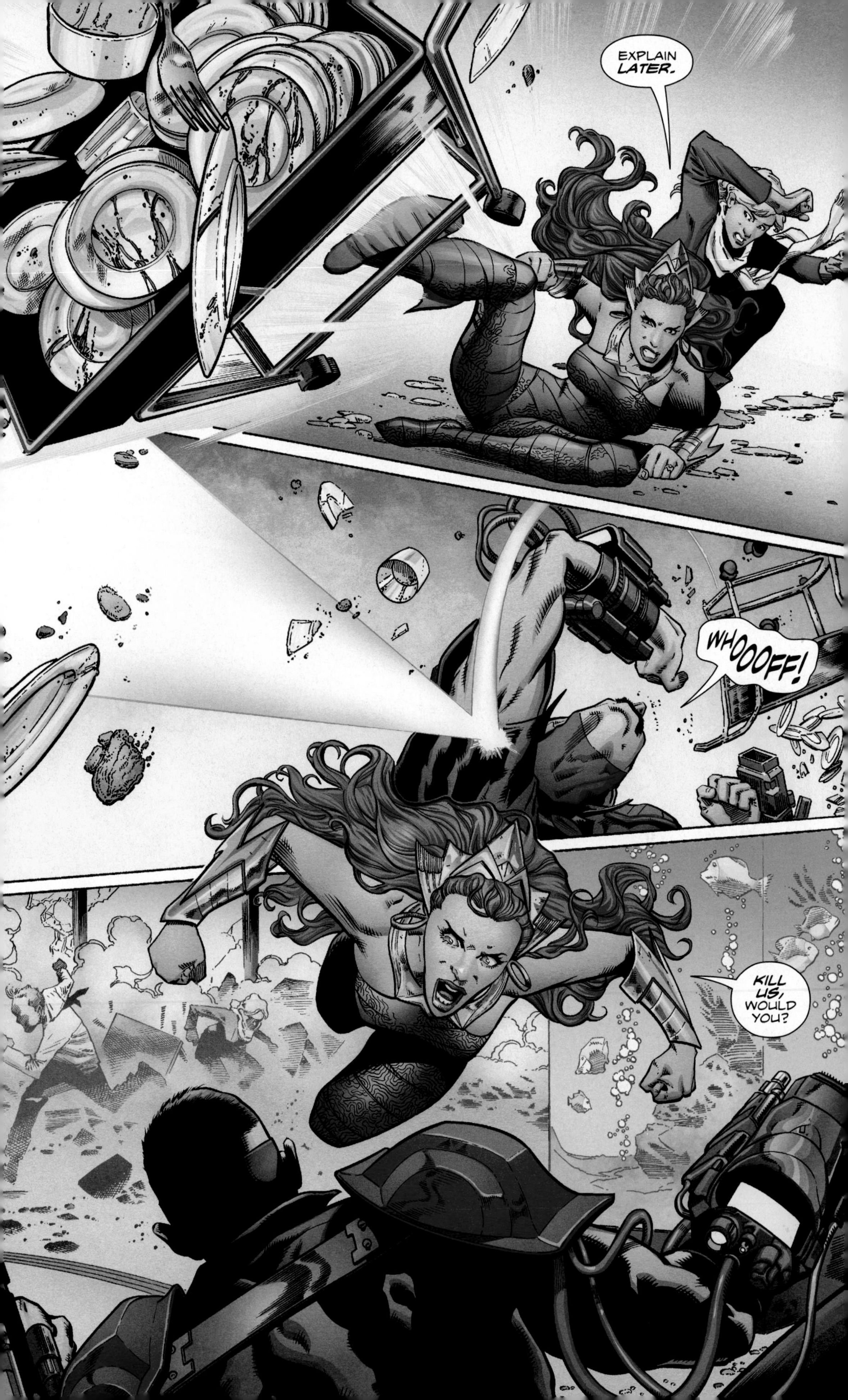
EXPLAIN LATER.
WHOOOFF!
KILL US, WOULD YOU?

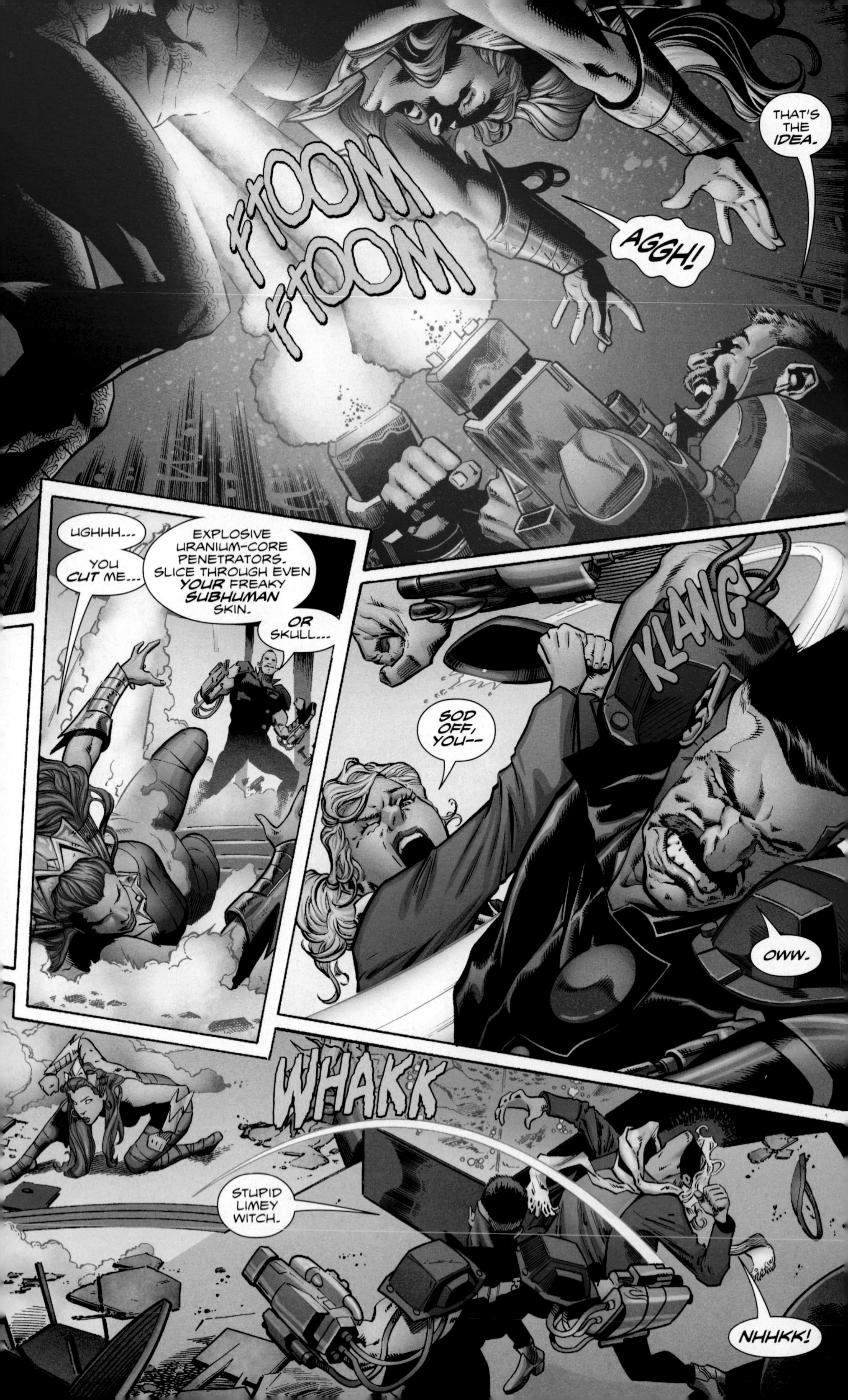
THAT'S THE IDEA.
FTOOM FTOOM
AGGH!
UGHHH...
YOU CUT ME...
EXPLOSIVE URANIUM-CORE PENETRATORS. SLICE THROUGH EVEN YOUR FREAKY SUBHUMAN SKIN.
OR SKULL...
KLANG
SOD OFF, YOU--
OWW.
WHAKK
STUPID LIMEY WITCH.
NHHKK!

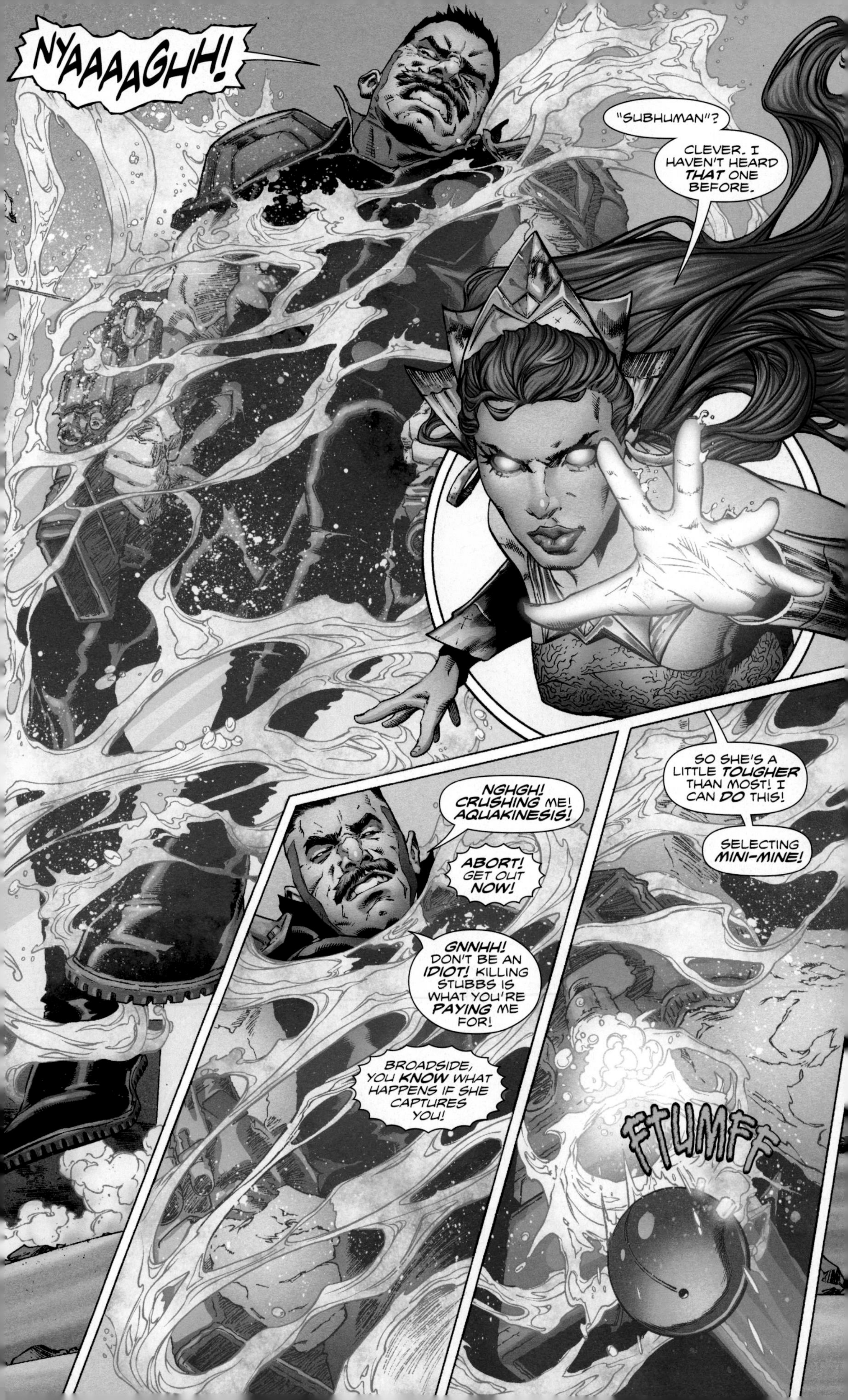
NYAAAAGHH!
"SUBHUMAN"?
CLEVER. I HAVEN'T HEARD THAT ONE BEFORE.
NGHGH! CRUSHING ME! AQUAKINESIS!
ABORT! GET OUT NOW!
GNNHH! DON'T BE AN IDIOT! KILLING STUBBS IS WHAT YOU'RE PAYING ME FOR!
BROADSIDE, YOU KNOW WHAT HAPPENS IF SHE CAPTURES YOU!
SO SHE'S A LITTLE TOUGHER THAN MOST! I CAN DO THIS!
SELECTING MINI-MINE!
FTUMFF

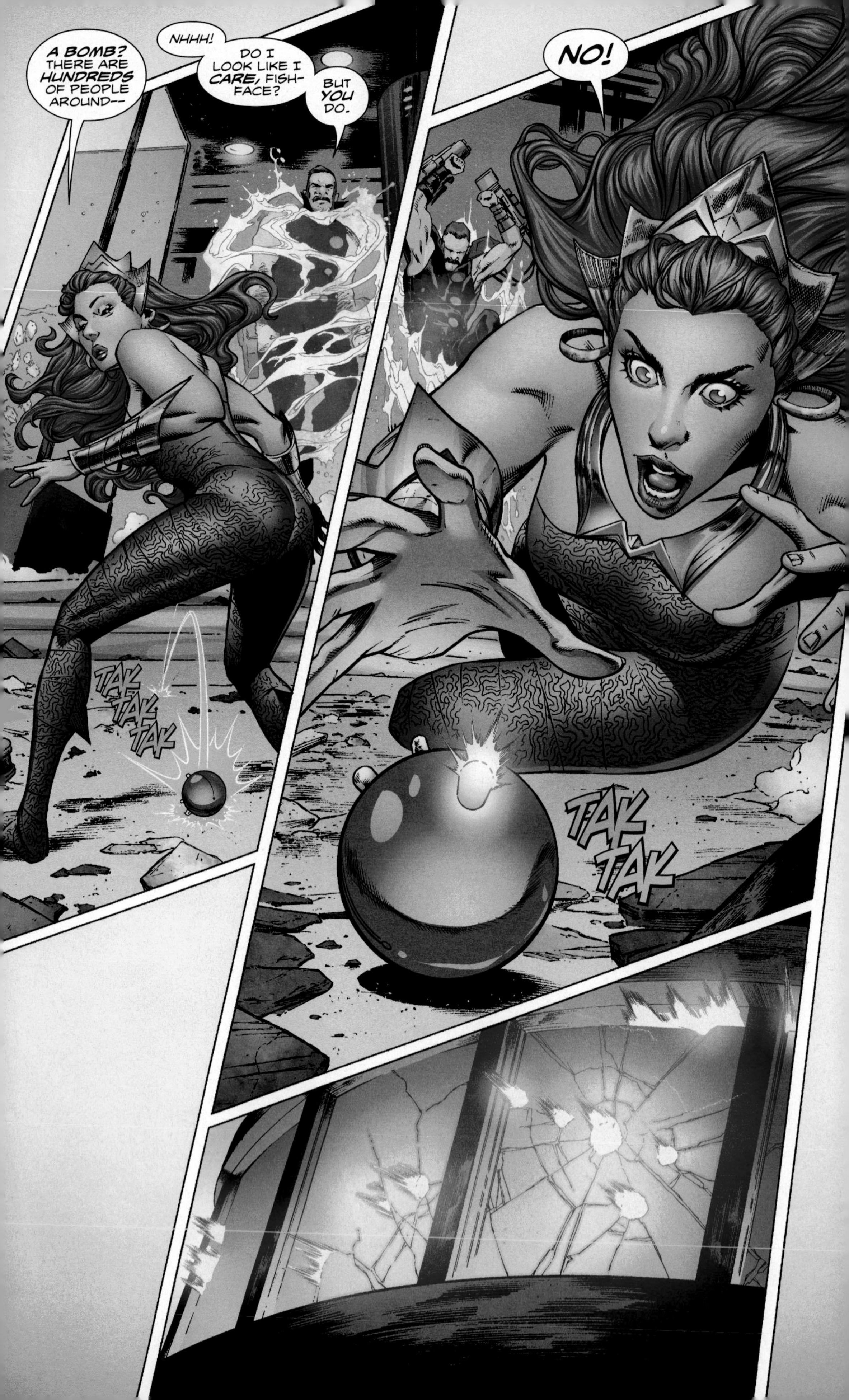
A BOMB? THERE ARE HUNDREDS OF PEOPLE AROUND--
NHHH!
DO I LOOK LIKE I CARE, FISH-FACE?
BUT YOU DO.
TAK TAK TAK
NO!
TAK TAK

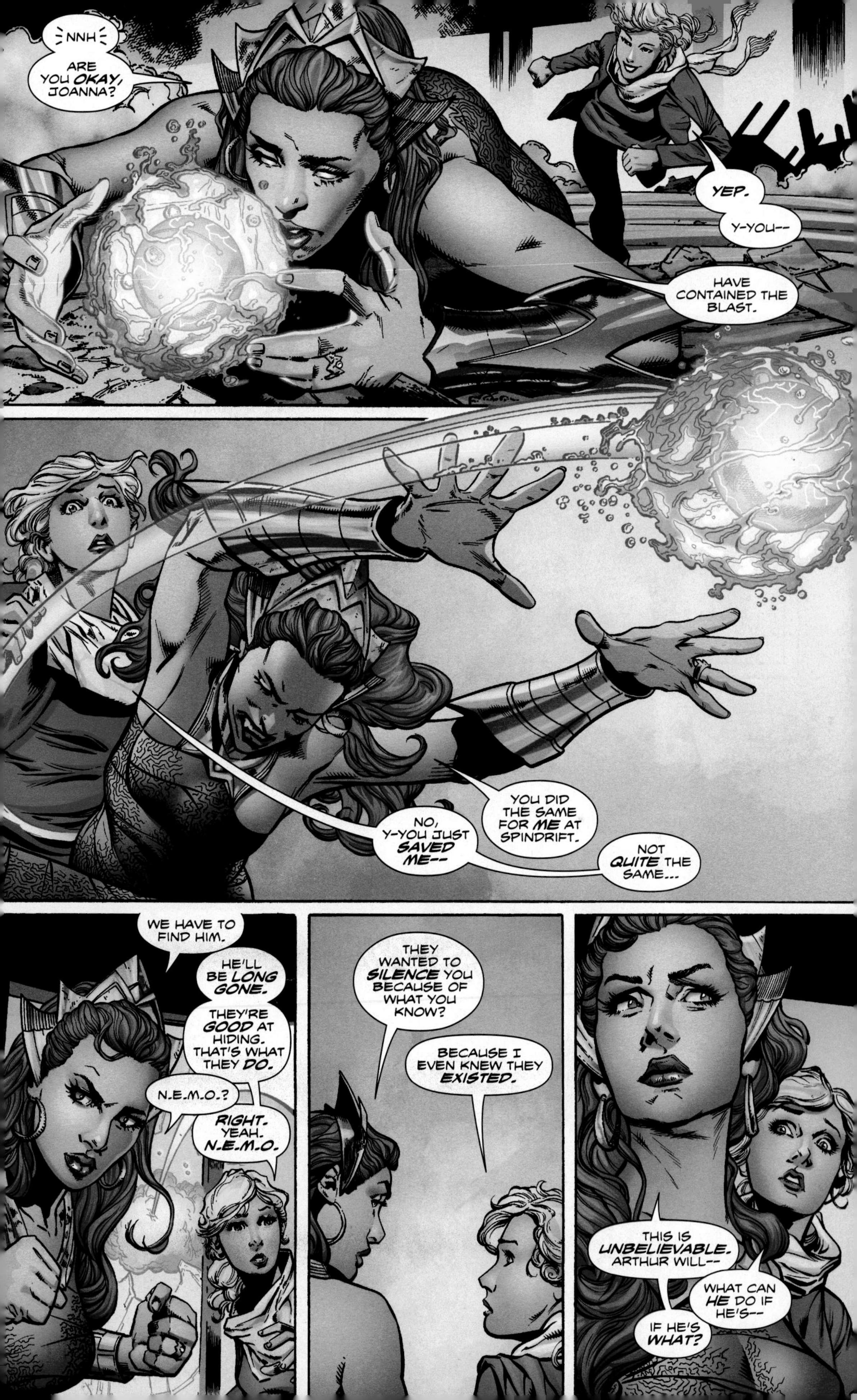
NNH
ARE YOU OKAY, JOANNA?
YEP.
Y-YOU--
HAVE CONTAINED THE BLAST.
YOU DID THE SAME FOR ME AT SPINDRIFT.
NO, Y-YOU JUST SAVED ME--
NOT QUITE THE SAME...
WE HAVE TO FIND HIM.
HE'LL BE LONG GONE.
THEY'RE GOOD AT HIDING. THAT'S WHAT THEY DO.
N.E.M.O.?
RIGHT. YEAH. N.E.M.O.
THEY WANTED TO SILENCE YOU BECAUSE OF WHAT YOU KNOW?
BECAUSE I EVEN KNEW THEY EXISTED.
THIS IS UNBELIEVABLE. ARTHUR WILL--
WHAT CAN HE DO IF HE'S--
IF HE'S WHAT?

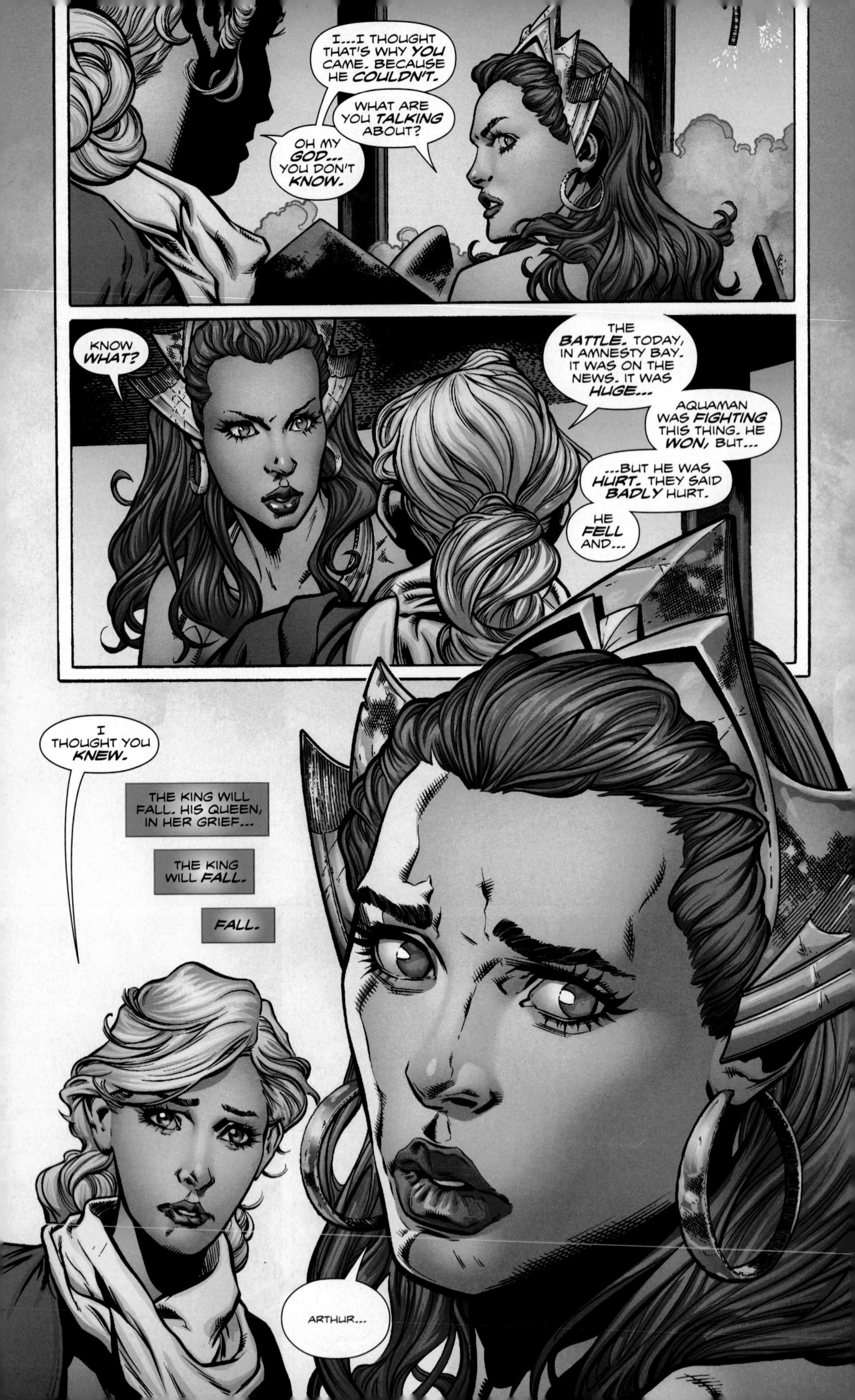
I...I THOUGHT THAT'S WHY YOU CAME. BECAUSE HE COULDN'T.
WHAT ARE YOU TALKING ABOUT?
OH MY GOD... YOU DON'T KNOW.
KNOW WHAT?
THE BATTLE. TODAY, IN AMNESTY BAY. IT WAS ON THE NEWS. IT WAS HUGE...
AQUAMAN WAS FIGHTING THIS THING. HE WON, BUT...
...BUT HE WAS HURT. THEY SAID BADLY HURT.
HE FELL AND...
I THOUGHT YOU KNEW.
THE KING WILL FALL. HIS QUEEN, IN HER GRIEF...
THE KING WILL FALL.
FALL.
ARTHUR...

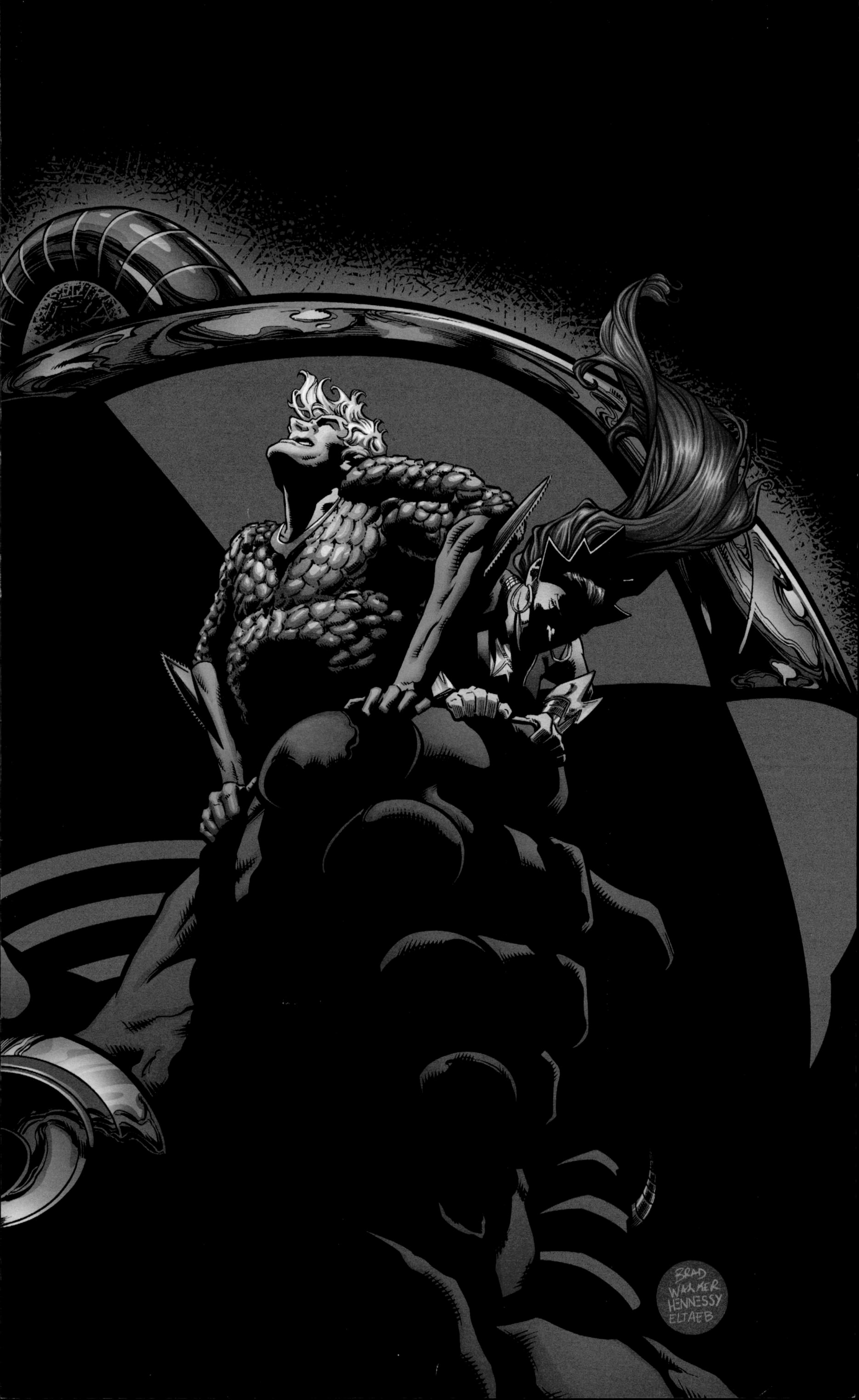
BRAD
WALKER
HENNESSY
ELTAEB

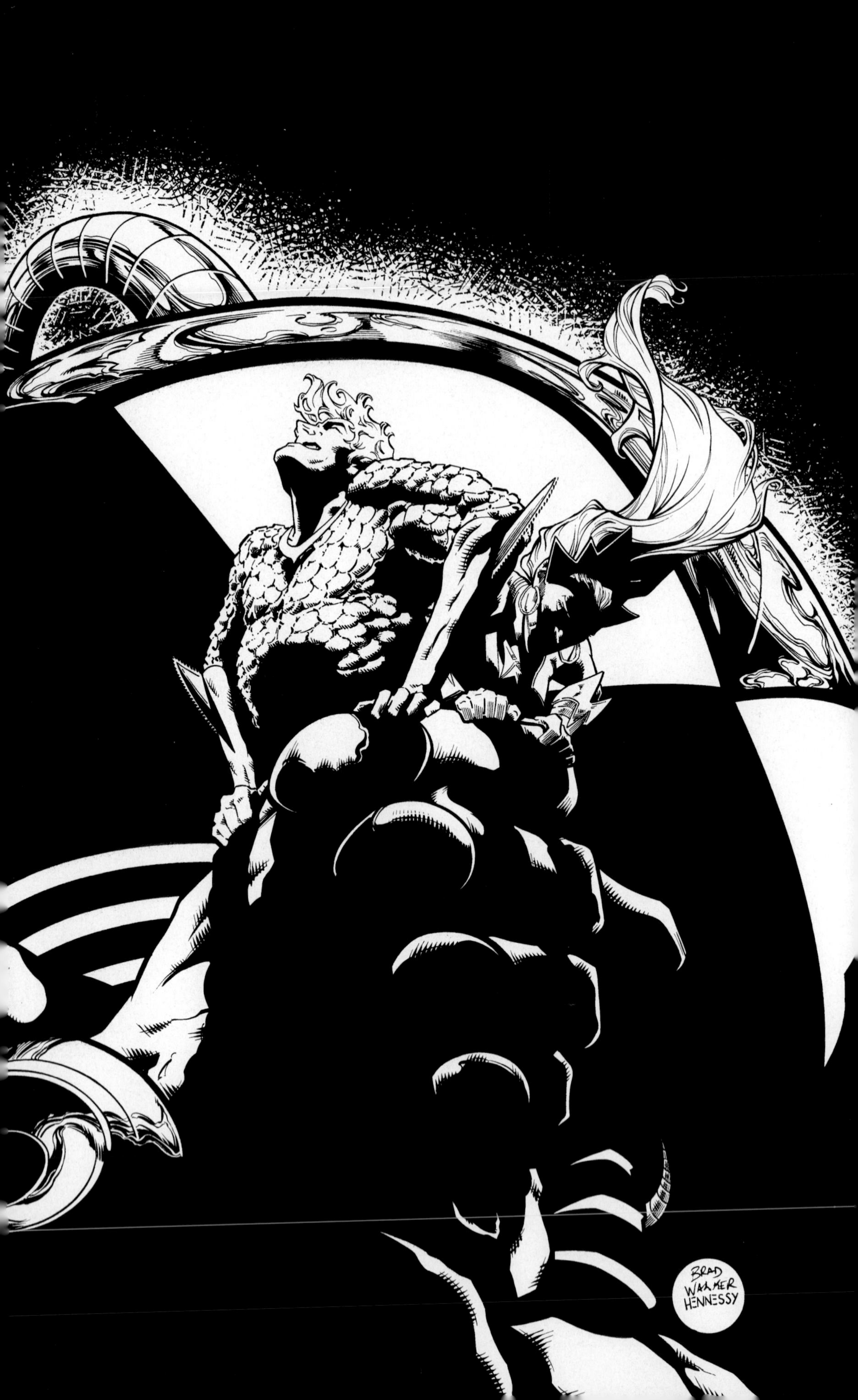
BRAD
WALKER
HENNESSY

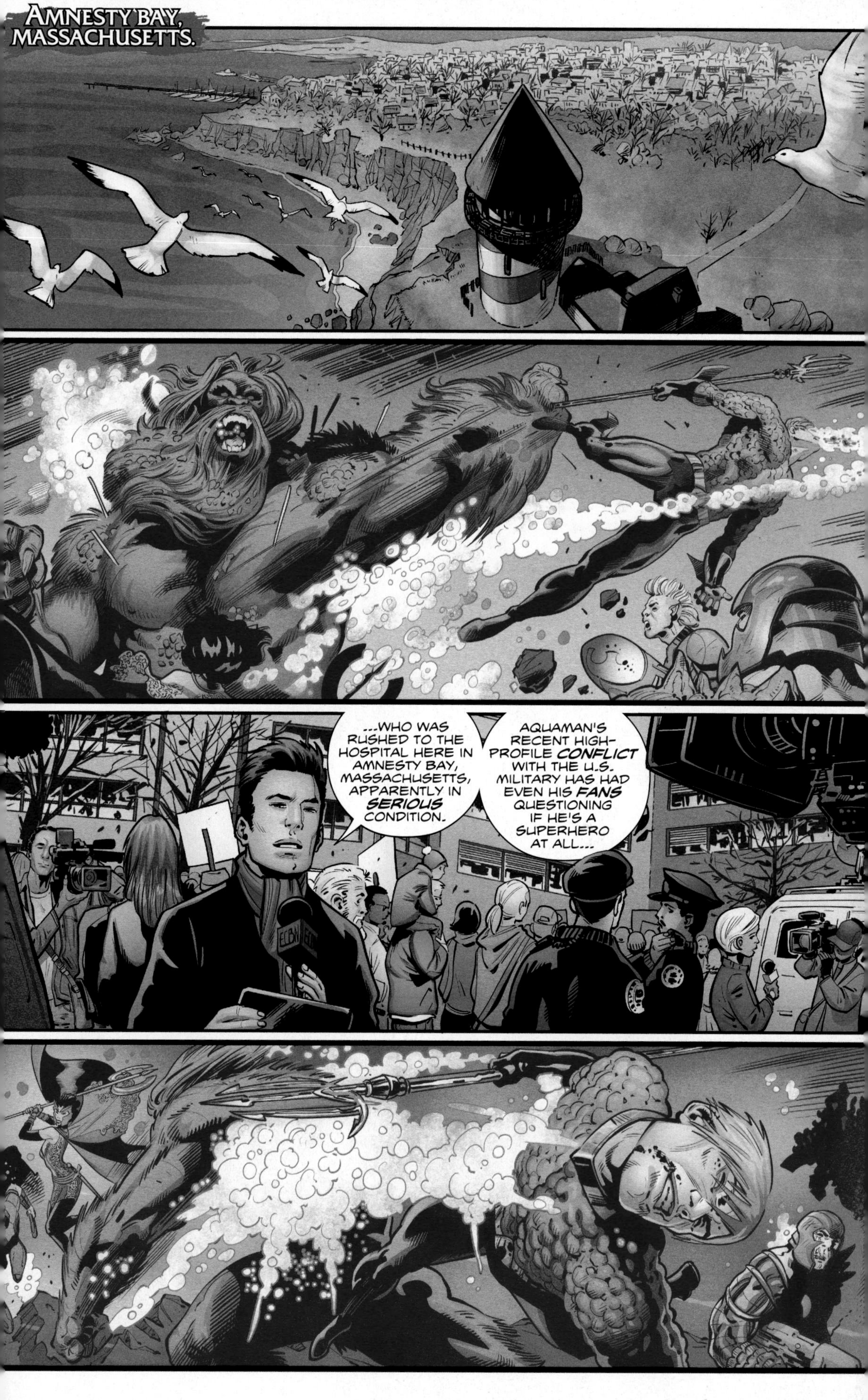
AMNESTY BAY, MASSACHUSETTS.
...WHO WAS RUSHED TO THE HOSPITAL HERE IN AMNESTY BAY, MASSACHUSETTS, APPARENTLY IN SERIOUS CONDITION.
AQUAMAN'S RECENT HIGH-PROFILE CONFLICT WITH THE U.S. MILITARY HAS HAD EVEN HIS FANS QUESTIONING IF HE'S A SUPERHERO AT ALL...

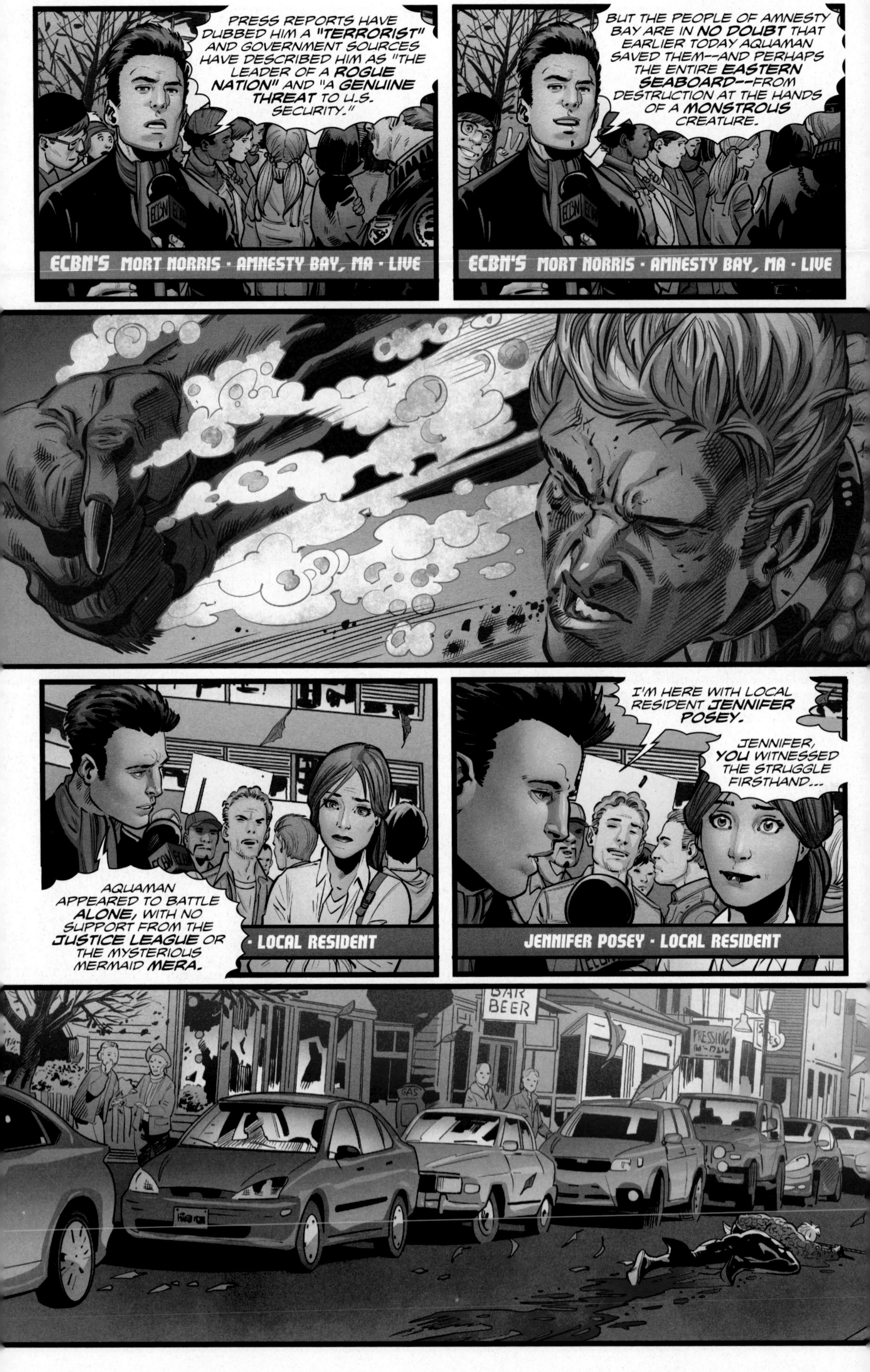
PRESS REPORTS HAVE DUBBED HIM A "TERRORIST" AND GOVERNMENT SOURCES HAVE DESCRIBED HIM AS "THE LEADER OF A ROGUE NATION" AND "A GENUINE THREAT TO U.S. SECURITY."
ECBN
ECBN'S MORT NORRIS · AMNESTY BAY, MA · LIVE
BUT THE PEOPLE OF AMNESTY BAY ARE IN NO DOUBT THAT EARLIER TODAY AQUAMAN SAVED THEM--AND PERHAPS THE ENTIRE EASTERN SEABOARD--FROM DESTRUCTION AT THE HANDS OF A MONSTROUS CREATURE.
ECBN
ECBN'S MORT NORRIS · AMNESTY BAY, MA · LIVE
AQUAMAN APPEARED TO BATTLE ALONE, WITH NO SUPPORT FROM THE JUSTICE LEAGUE OR THE MYSTERIOUS MERMAID MERA.
· LOCAL RESIDENT
I'M HERE WITH LOCAL RESIDENT JENNIFER POSEY.
JENNIFER, YOU WITNESSED THE STRUGGLE FIRSTHAND...
JENNIFER POSEY · LOCAL RESIDENT
BAR BEER
PRESSING

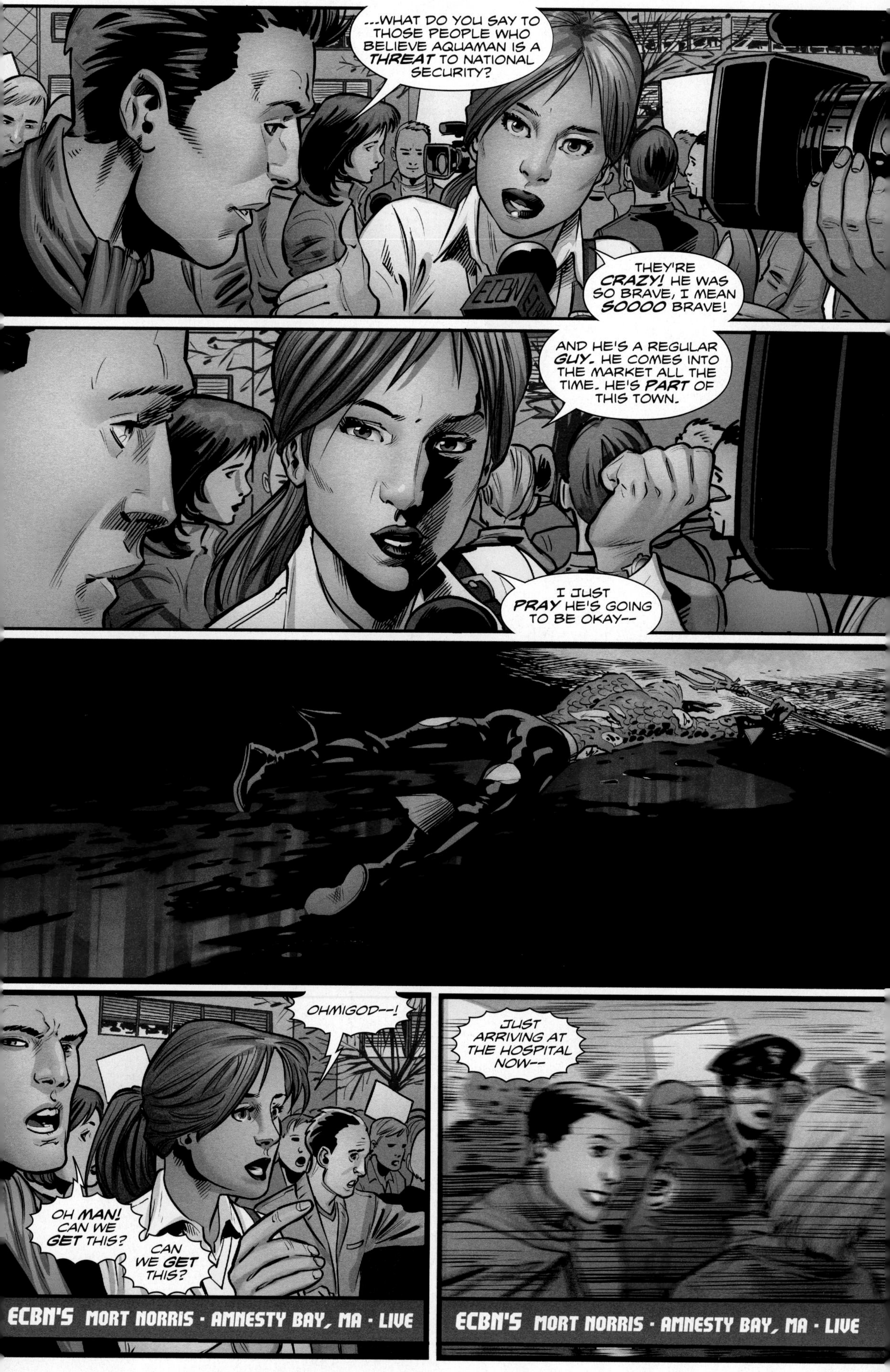

---WHAT DO YOU SAY TO THOSE PEOPLE WHO BELIEVE AQUAMAN IS A THREAT TO NATIONAL SECURITY?
THEY'RE CRAZY! HE WAS SO BRAVE, I MEAN SOOOO BRAVE!
ECBN
AND HE'S A REGULAR GUY. HE COMES INTO THE MARKET ALL THE TIME. HE'S PART OF THIS TOWN.
I JUST PRAY HE'S GOING TO BE OKAY--
OHMIGOD--!
OH MAN! CAN WE GET THIS?
CAN WE GET THIS?
ECBN'S MORT NORRIS · AMNESTY BAY, MA · LIVE
JUST ARRIVING AT THE HOSPITAL NOW--
ECBN'S MORT NORRIS · AMNESTY BAY, MA · LIVE

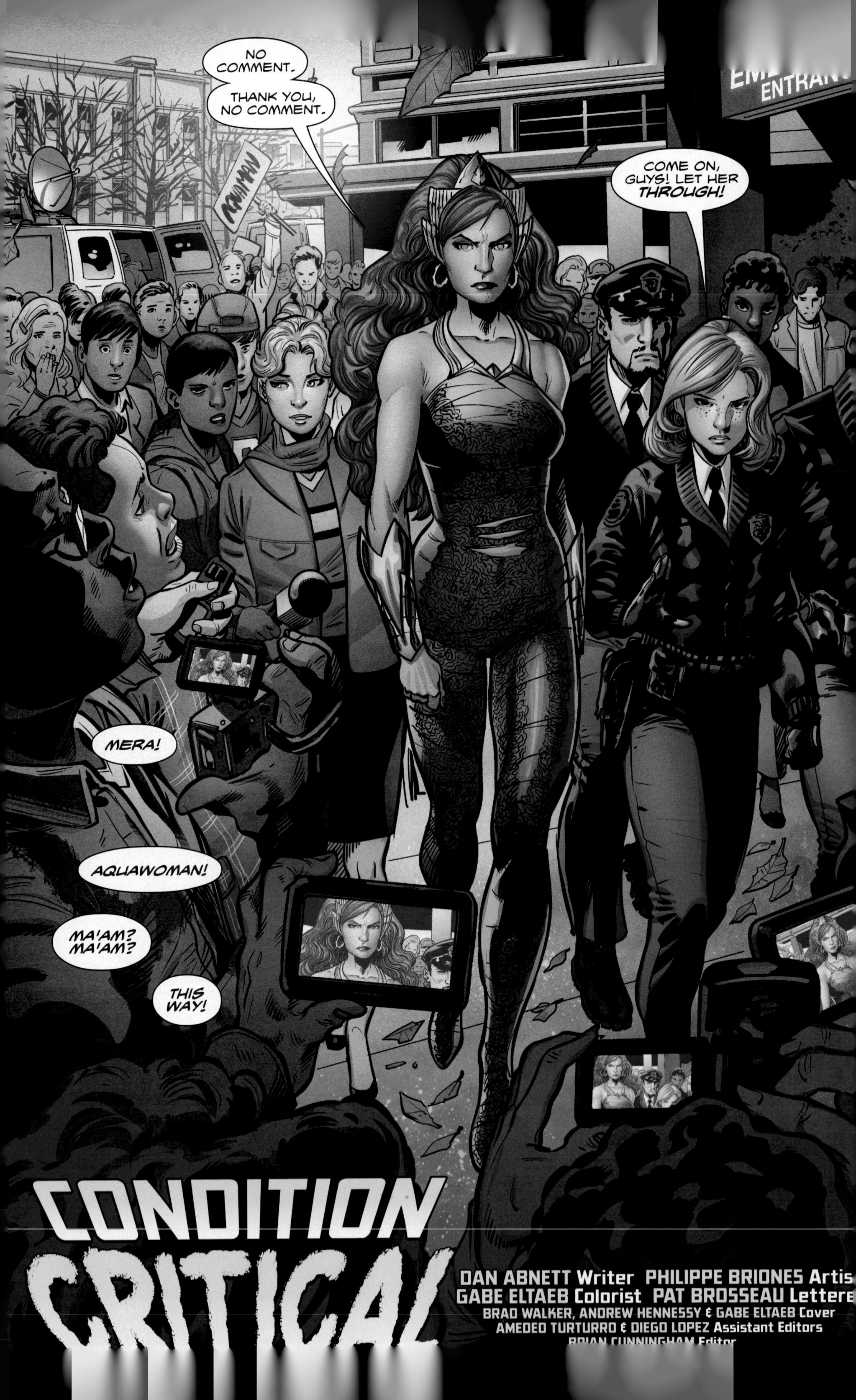
NO COMMENT.
THANK YOU, NO COMMENT.
COME ON, GUYS! LET HER THROUGH!
MERA!
AQUAWOMAN!
MA'AM? MA'AM?
THIS WAY!
CONDITION CRITICAL
DAN ABNETT Writer PHILIPPE BRIONES Artis
GABE ELTAEB Colorist PAT BROSSEAU Lettere
BRAD WALKER, ANDREW HENNESSY & GABE ELTAEB Cover
AMEDEO TURTURRO & DIEGO LOPEZ Assistant Editors

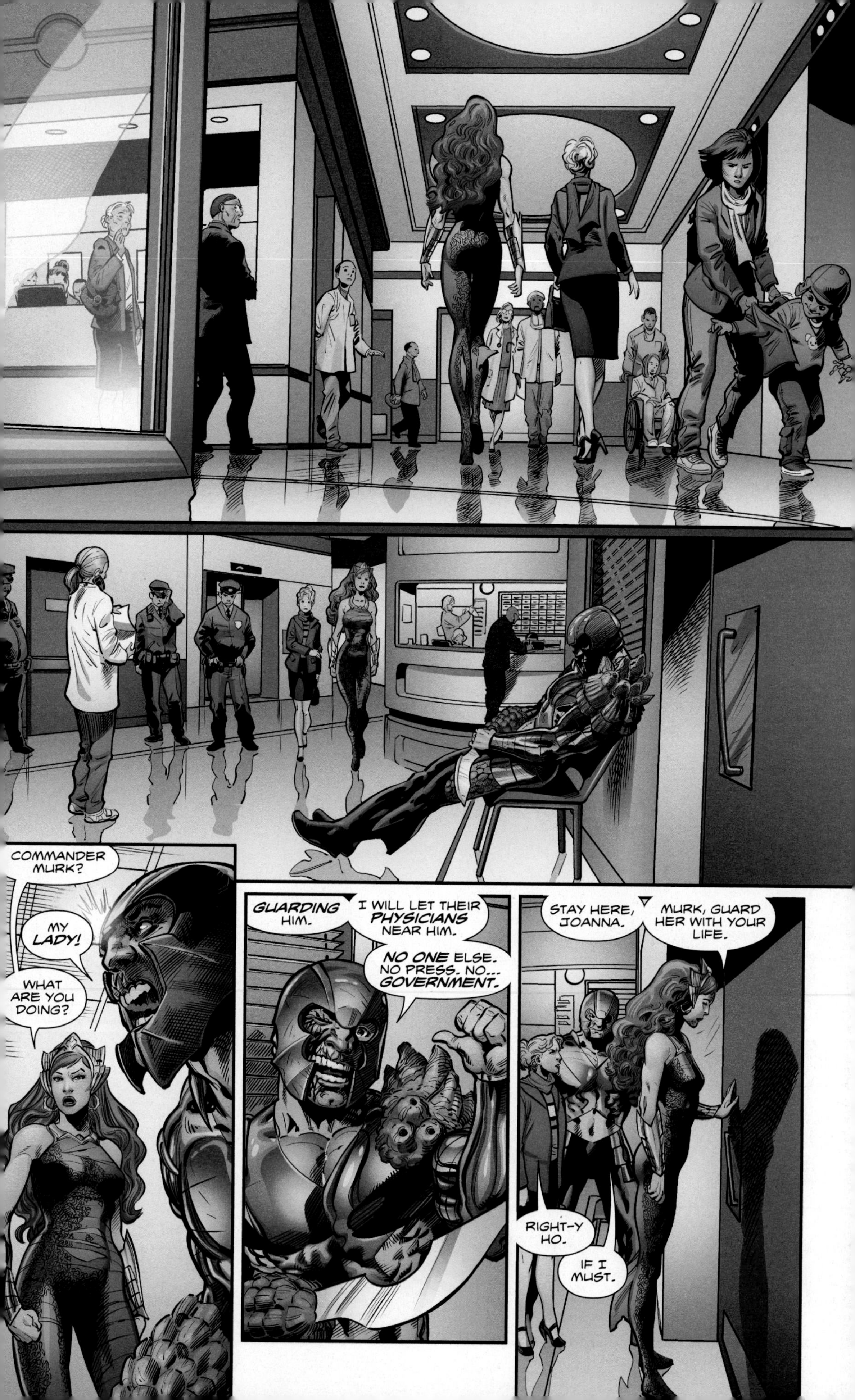
COMMANDER MURK?
MY *LADY!*
WHAT ARE YOU DOING?
GUARDING HIM.
I WILL LET THEIR *PHYSICIANS* NEAR HIM.
NO ONE ELSE. NO PRESS. NO... *GOVERNMENT.*
STAY HERE, JOANNA.
MURK, GUARD HER WITH YOUR LIFE.
RIGHT-Y HO.
IF I MUST.

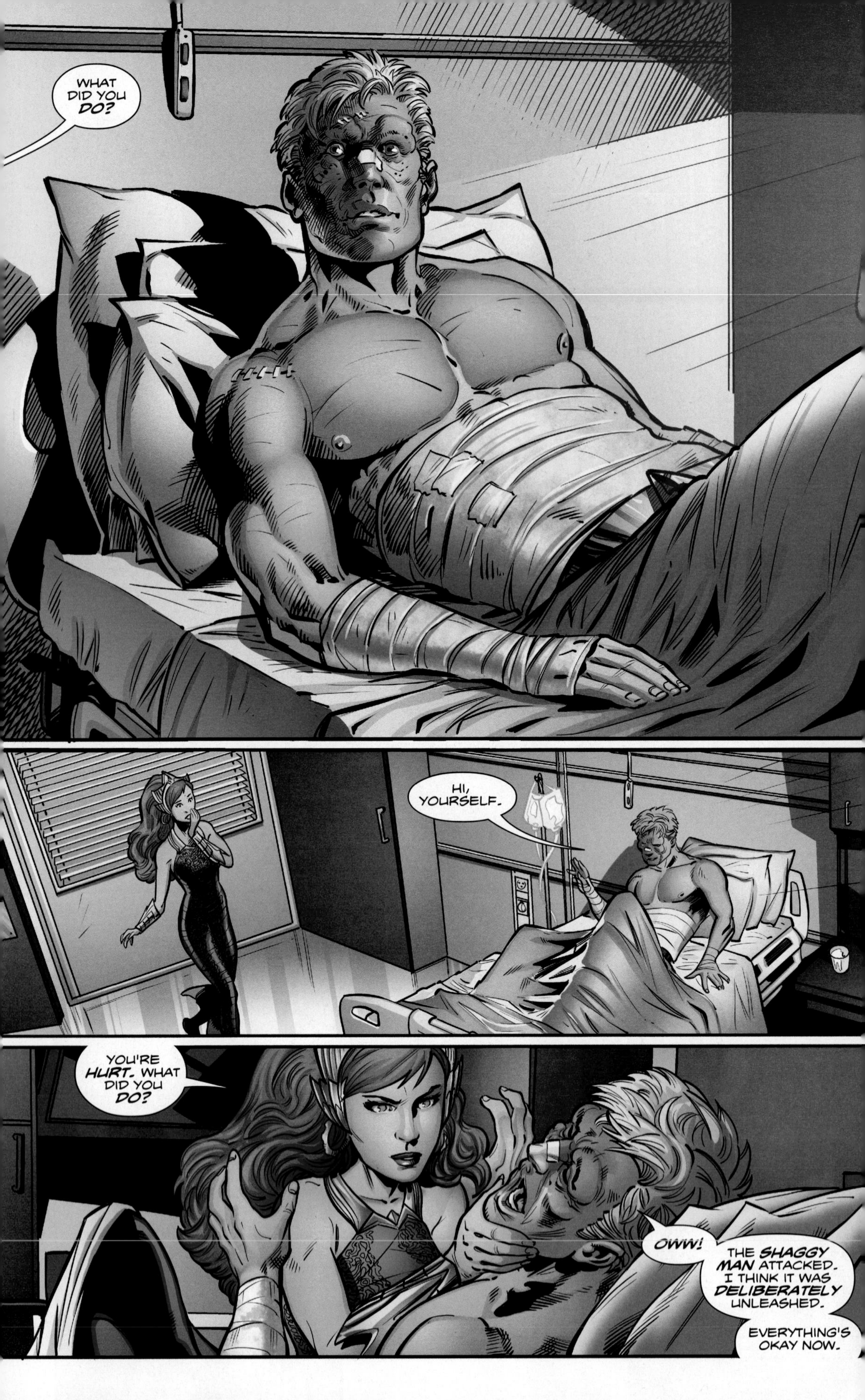
WHAT DID YOU DO?
HI, YOURSELF.
YOU'RE HURT. WHAT DID YOU DO?
OWW!
THE SHAGGY MAN ATTACKED. I THINK IT WAS DELIBERATELY UNLEASHED.
EVERYTHING'S OKAY NOW.

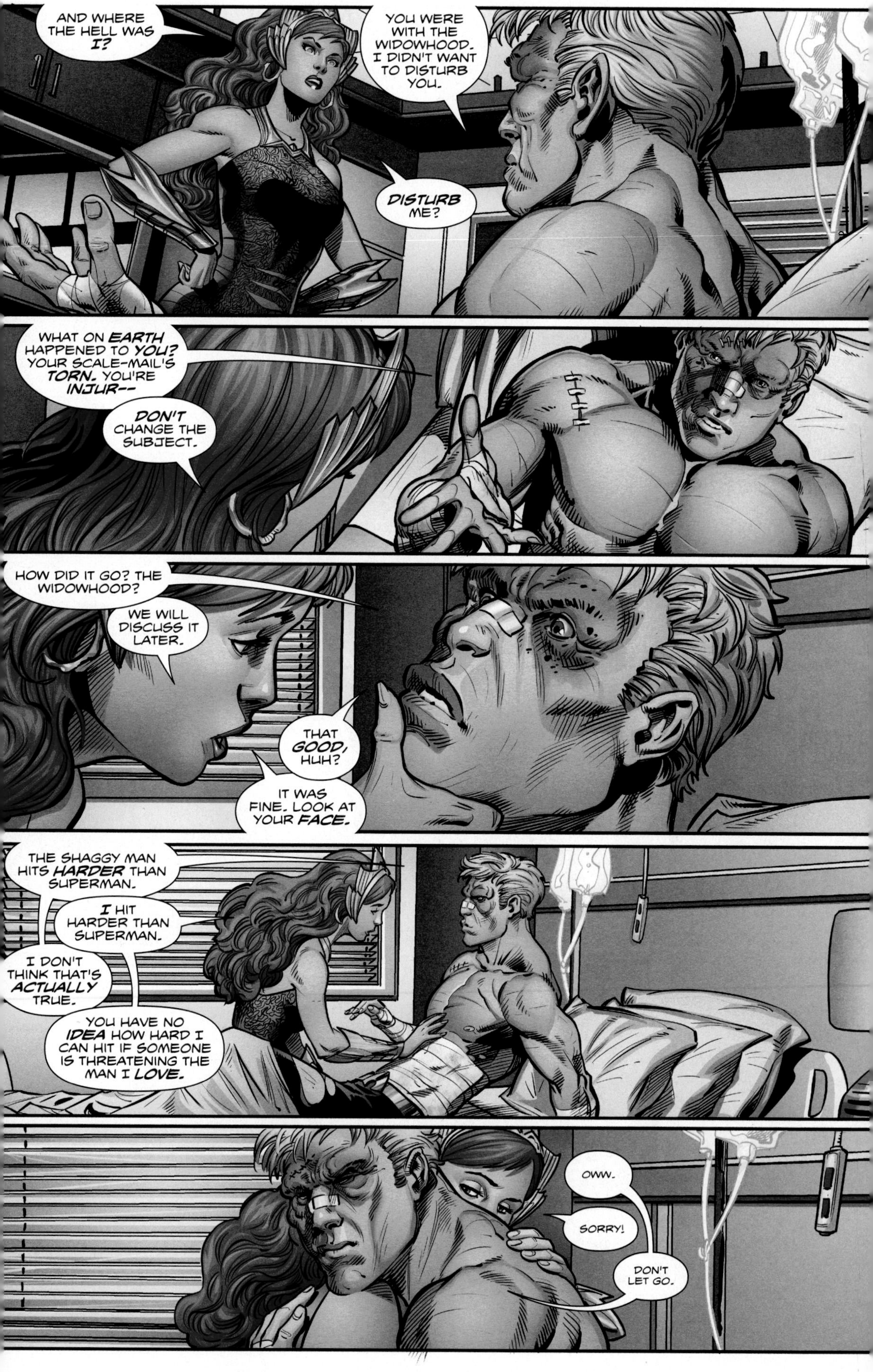
AND WHERE THE HELL WAS *I?*
YOU WERE WITH THE WIDOWHOOD. I DIDN'T WANT TO DISTURB YOU.
DISTURB ME?
WHAT ON *EARTH* HAPPENED TO *YOU?* YOUR SCALE-MAIL'S *TORN.* YOU'RE *INJUR--*
DON'T CHANGE THE SUBJECT.
HOW DID IT GO? THE WIDOWHOOD?
WE WILL DISCUSS IT LATER.
THAT *GOOD,* HUH?
IT WAS FINE. LOOK AT YOUR *FACE.*
THE SHAGGY MAN HITS *HARDER* THAN SUPERMAN.
I HIT HARDER THAN SUPERMAN.
I DON'T THINK THAT'S *ACTUALLY* TRUE.
YOU HAVE NO *IDEA* HOW HARD I CAN HIT IF SOMEONE IS THREATENING THE MAN I *LOVE.*
OWW.
SORRY!
DON'T LET GO.

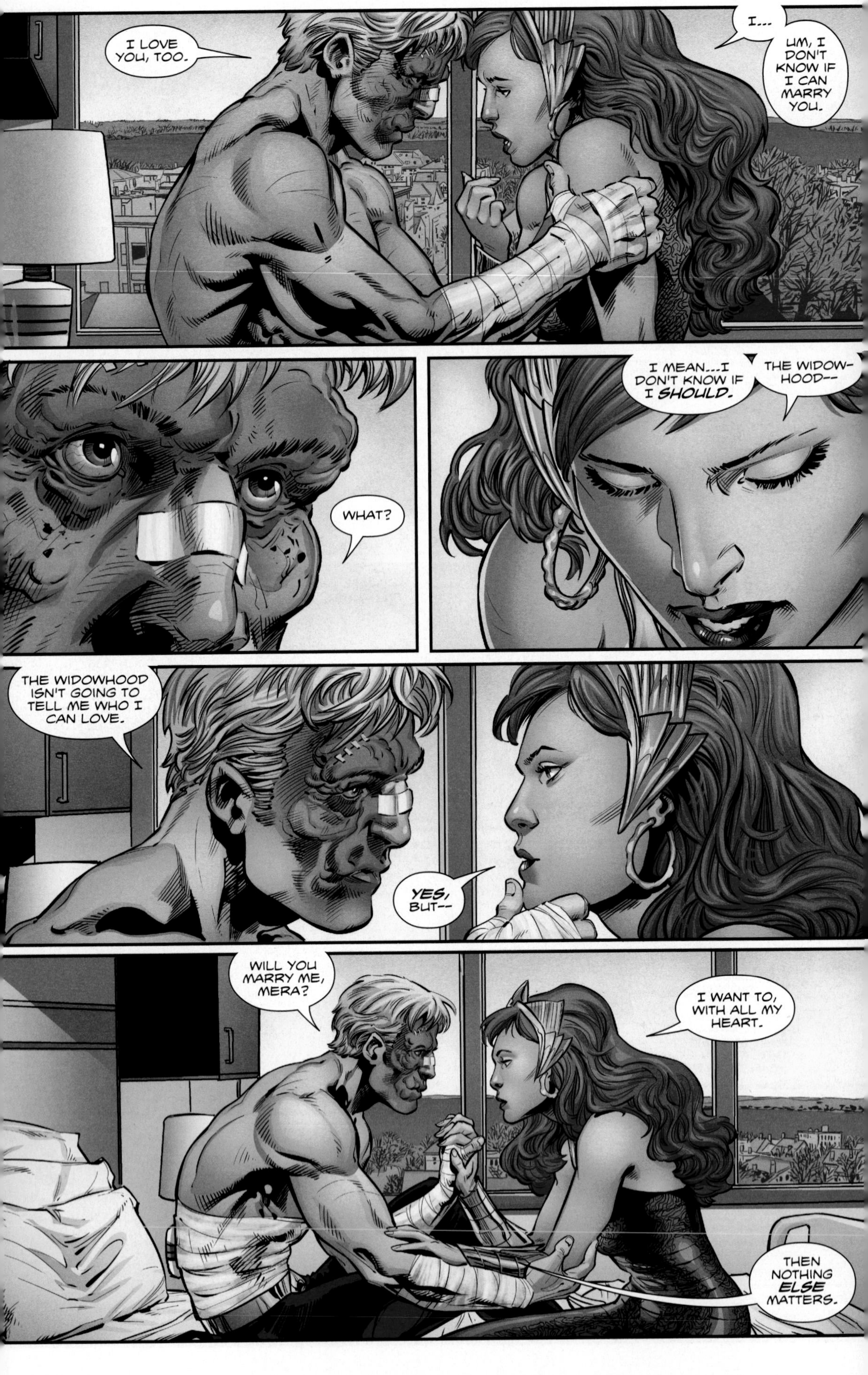
I LOVE YOU, TOO.
I...
UM, I DON'T KNOW IF I CAN MARRY YOU.
WHAT?
I MEAN...I DON'T KNOW IF I SHOULD.
THE WIDOW-HOOD--
THE WIDOWHOOD ISN'T GOING TO TELL ME WHO I CAN LOVE.
YES, BUT--
WILL YOU MARRY ME, MERA?
I WANT TO, WITH ALL MY HEART.
THEN NOTHING ELSE MATTERS.

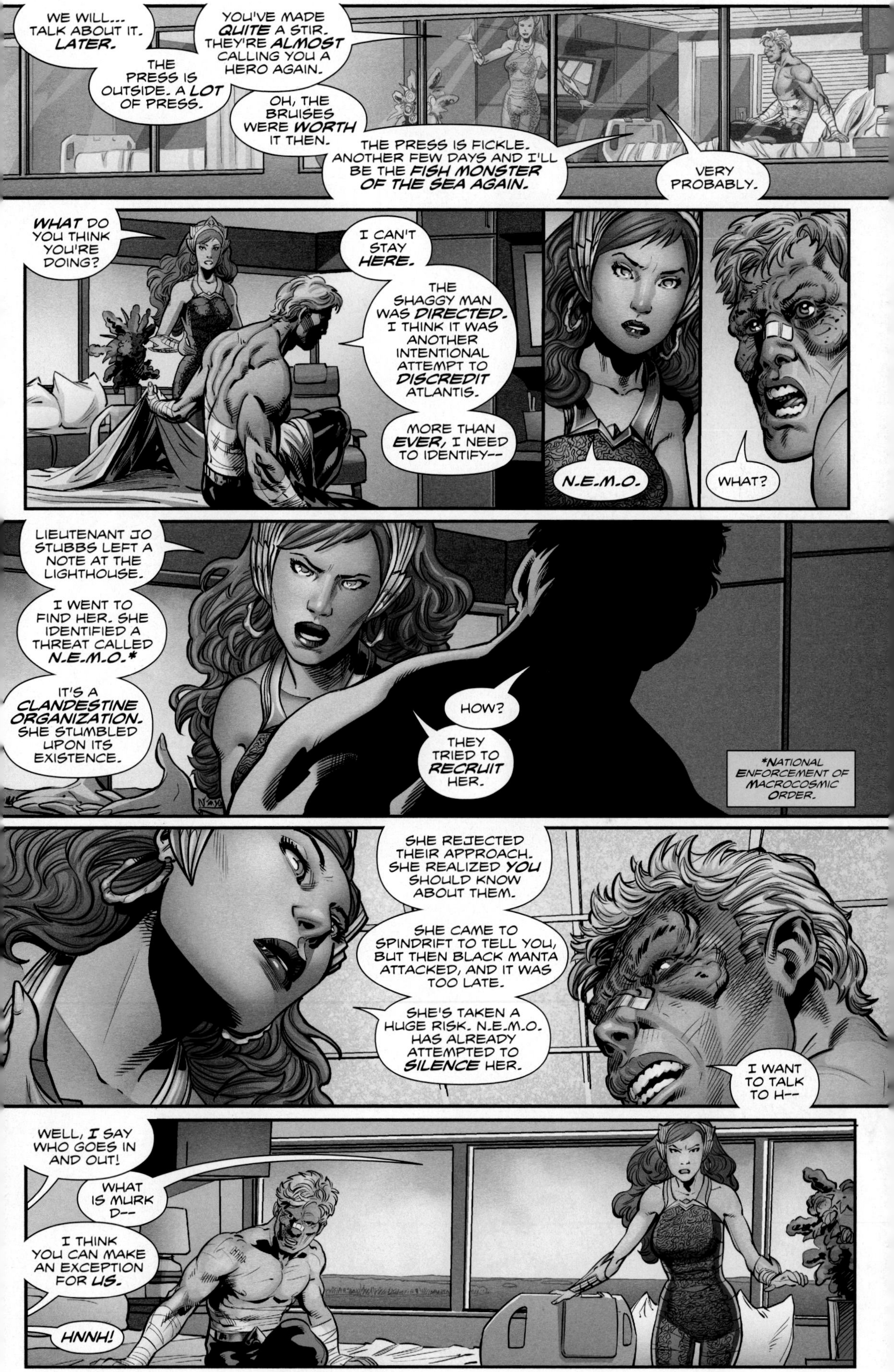

WE WILL... TALK ABOUT IT. LATER.
THE PRESS IS OUTSIDE. A LOT OF PRESS.
YOU'VE MADE QUITE A STIR. THEY'RE ALMOST CALLING YOU A HERO AGAIN.
OH, THE BRUISES WERE WORTH IT THEN.
THE PRESS IS FICKLE. ANOTHER FEW DAYS AND I'LL BE THE FISH MONSTER OF THE SEA AGAIN.
VERY PROBABLY.
WHAT DO YOU THINK YOU'RE DOING?
I CAN'T STAY HERE.
THE SHAGGY MAN WAS DIRECTED. I THINK IT WAS ANOTHER INTENTIONAL ATTEMPT TO DISCREDIT ATLANTIS.
MORE THAN EVER, I NEED TO IDENTIFY--
N.E.M.O.
WHAT?
LIEUTENANT JO STUBBS LEFT A NOTE AT THE LIGHTHOUSE.
I WENT TO FIND HER. SHE IDENTIFIED A THREAT CALLED N.E.M.O.*
IT'S A CLANDESTINE ORGANIZATION. SHE STUMBLED UPON ITS EXISTENCE.
HOW?
THEY TRIED TO RECRUIT HER.
*NATIONAL ENFORCEMENT OF MACROCOSMIC ORDER.
SHE REJECTED THEIR APPROACH. SHE REALIZED YOU SHOULD KNOW ABOUT THEM.
SHE CAME TO SPINDRIFT TO TELL YOU, BUT THEN BLACK MANTA ATTACKED, AND IT WAS TOO LATE.
SHE'S TAKEN A HUGE RISK. N.E.M.O. HAS ALREADY ATTEMPTED TO SILENCE HER.
I WANT TO TALK TO H--
WELL, I SAY WHO GOES IN AND OUT!
WHAT IS MURK D--
I THINK YOU CAN MAKE AN EXCEPTION FOR US.
HNNH!

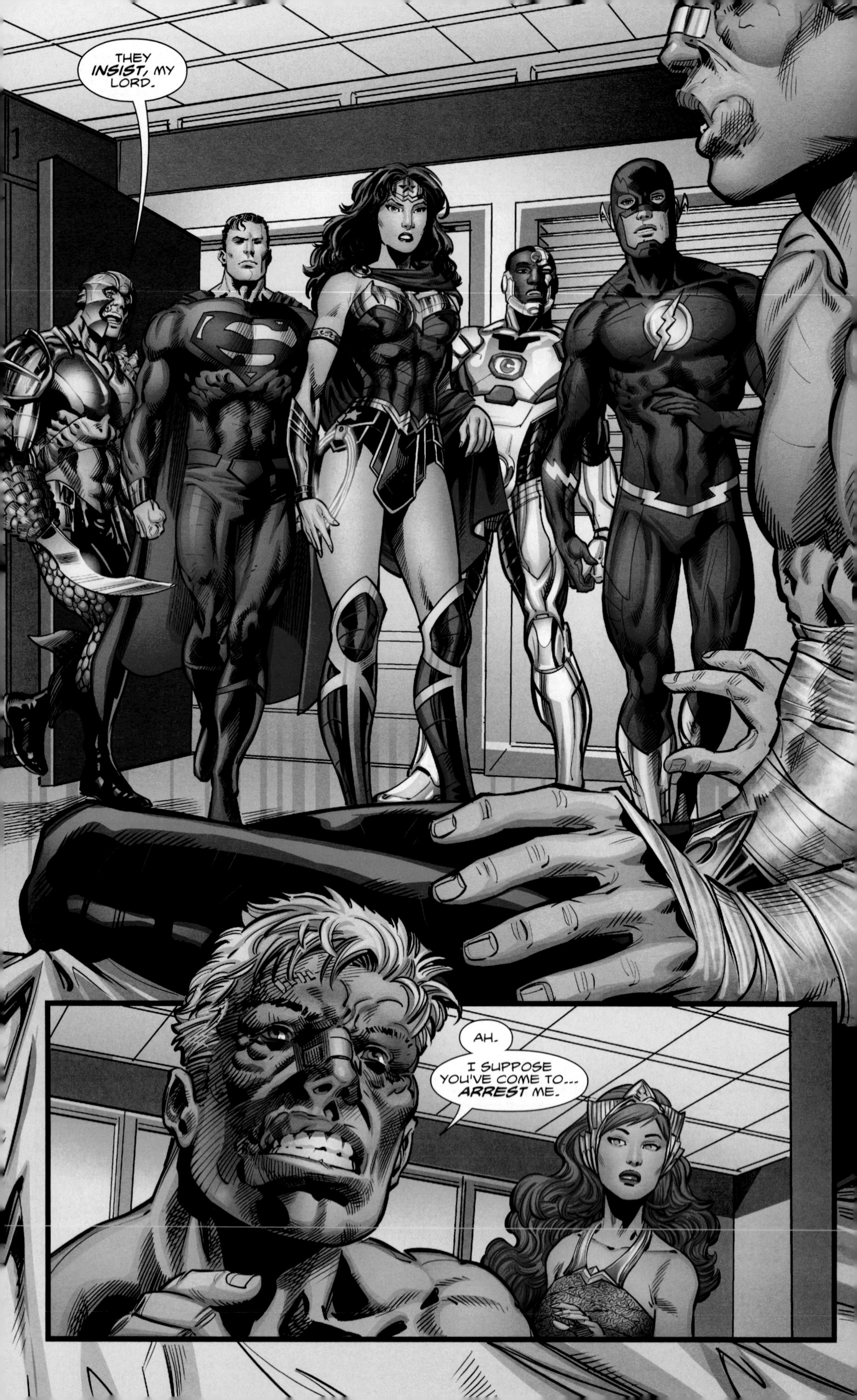
THEY INSIST, MY LORD.
AH.
I SUPPOSE YOU'VE COME TO... ARREST ME.

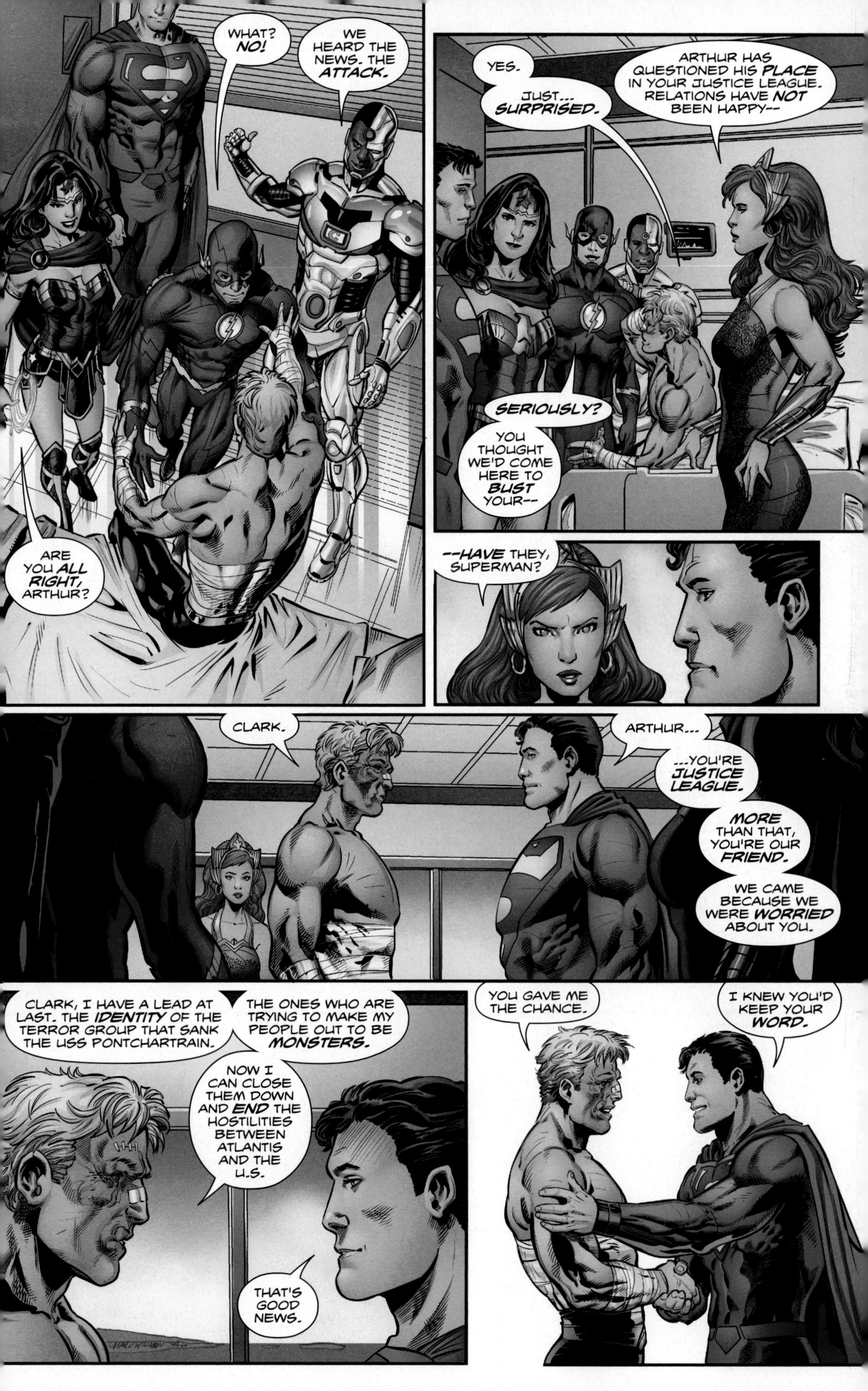
WHAT? NO!
WE HEARD THE NEWS. THE ATTACK.
ARE YOU ALL RIGHT, ARTHUR?
YES.
JUST... SURPRISED.
ARTHUR HAS QUESTIONED HIS PLACE IN YOUR JUSTICE LEAGUE. RELATIONS HAVE NOT BEEN HAPPY--
SERIOUSLY?
YOU THOUGHT WE'D COME HERE TO BUST YOUR--
--HAVE THEY, SUPERMAN?
CLARK.
ARTHUR...
...YOU'RE JUSTICE LEAGUE.
MORE THAN THAT, YOU'RE OUR FRIEND.
WE CAME BECAUSE WE WERE WORRIED ABOUT YOU.
CLARK, I HAVE A LEAD AT LAST. THE IDENTITY OF THE TERROR GROUP THAT SANK THE USS PONTCHARTRAIN.
THE ONES WHO ARE TRYING TO MAKE MY PEOPLE OUT TO BE MONSTERS.
NOW I CAN CLOSE THEM DOWN AND END THE HOSTILITIES BETWEEN ATLANTIS AND THE U.S.
THAT'S GOOD NEWS.
YOU GAVE ME THE CHANCE.
I KNEW YOU'D KEEP YOUR WORD.

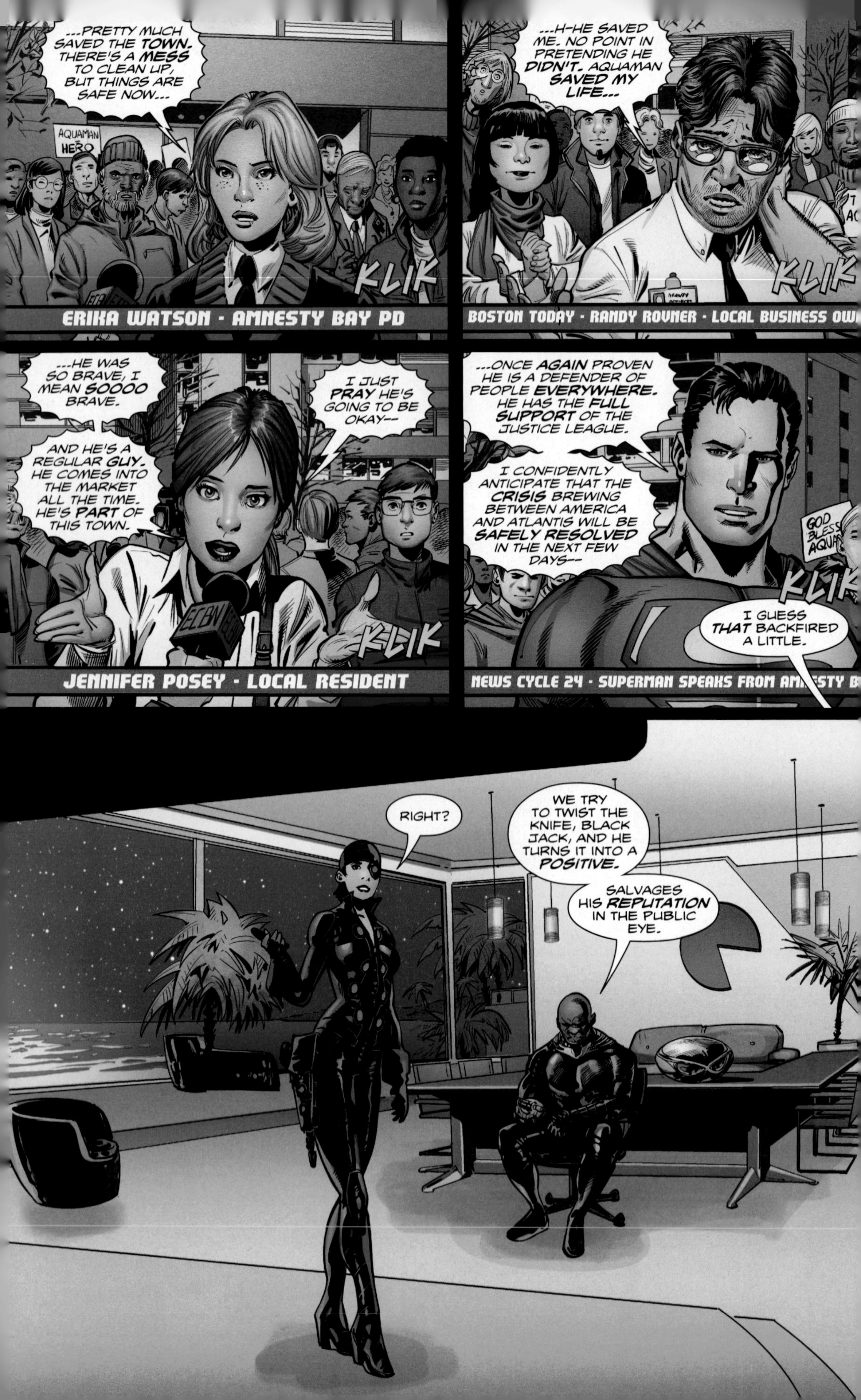

...PRETTY MUCH SAVED THE TOWN. THERE'S A MESS TO CLEAN UP, BUT THINGS ARE SAFE NOW...
AQUAMAN HERO
KLIK
ERIKA WATSON - AMNESTY BAY PD
...H-HE SAVED ME. NO POINT IN PRETENDING HE DIDN'T. AQUAMAN SAVED MY LIFE...
KLIK
BOSTON TODAY - RANDY ROVNER - LOCAL BUSINESS OW
...HE WAS SO BRAVE, I MEAN SOOOO BRAVE.
AND HE'S A REGULAR GUY. HE COMES INTO THE MARKET ALL THE TIME. HE'S PART OF THIS TOWN.
I JUST PRAY HE'S GOING TO BE OKAY--
KLIK
JENNIFER POSEY - LOCAL RESIDENT
...ONCE AGAIN PROVEN HE IS A DEFENDER OF PEOPLE EVERYWHERE. HE HAS THE FULL SUPPORT OF THE JUSTICE LEAGUE.
I CONFIDENTLY ANTICIPATE THAT THE CRISIS BREWING BETWEEN AMERICA AND ATLANTIS WILL BE SAFELY RESOLVED IN THE NEXT FEW DAYS--
KLIK
I GUESS THAT BACKFIRED A LITTLE.
NEWS CYCLE 24 - SUPERMAN SPEAKS FROM AMNESTY B
RIGHT?
WE TRY TO TWIST THE KNIFE, BLACK JACK, AND HE TURNS IT INTO A POSITIVE.
SALVAGES HIS REPUTATION IN THE PUBLIC EYE.

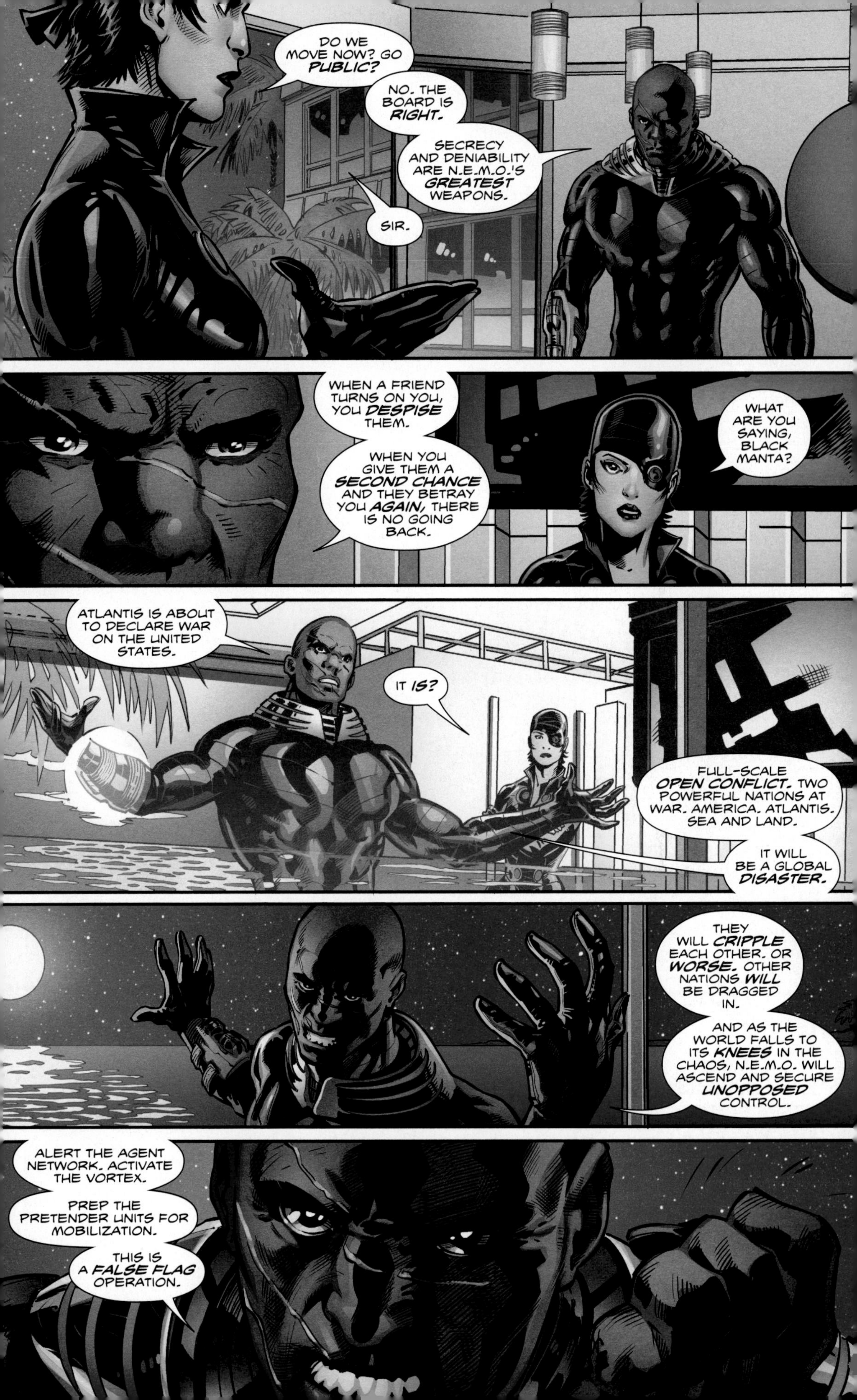
DO WE MOVE NOW? GO PUBLIC?
NO. THE BOARD IS RIGHT.
SECRECY AND DENIABILITY ARE N.E.M.O.'S GREATEST WEAPONS.
SIR.
WHEN A FRIEND TURNS ON YOU, YOU DESPISE THEM.
WHEN YOU GIVE THEM A SECOND CHANCE AND THEY BETRAY YOU AGAIN, THERE IS NO GOING BACK.
WHAT ARE YOU SAYING, BLACK MANTA?
ATLANTIS IS ABOUT TO DECLARE WAR ON THE UNITED STATES.
IT IS?
FULL-SCALE OPEN CONFLICT. TWO POWERFUL NATIONS AT WAR. AMERICA. ATLANTIS. SEA AND LAND.
IT WILL BE A GLOBAL DISASTER.
THEY WILL CRIPPLE EACH OTHER. OR WORSE. OTHER NATIONS WILL BE DRAGGED IN.
AND AS THE WORLD FALLS TO ITS KNEES IN THE CHAOS, N.E.M.O. WILL ASCEND AND SECURE UNOPPOSED CONTROL.
ALERT THE AGENT NETWORK. ACTIVATE THE VORTEX.
PREP THE PRETENDER UNITS FOR MOBILIZATION.
THIS IS A FALSE FLAG OPERATION.

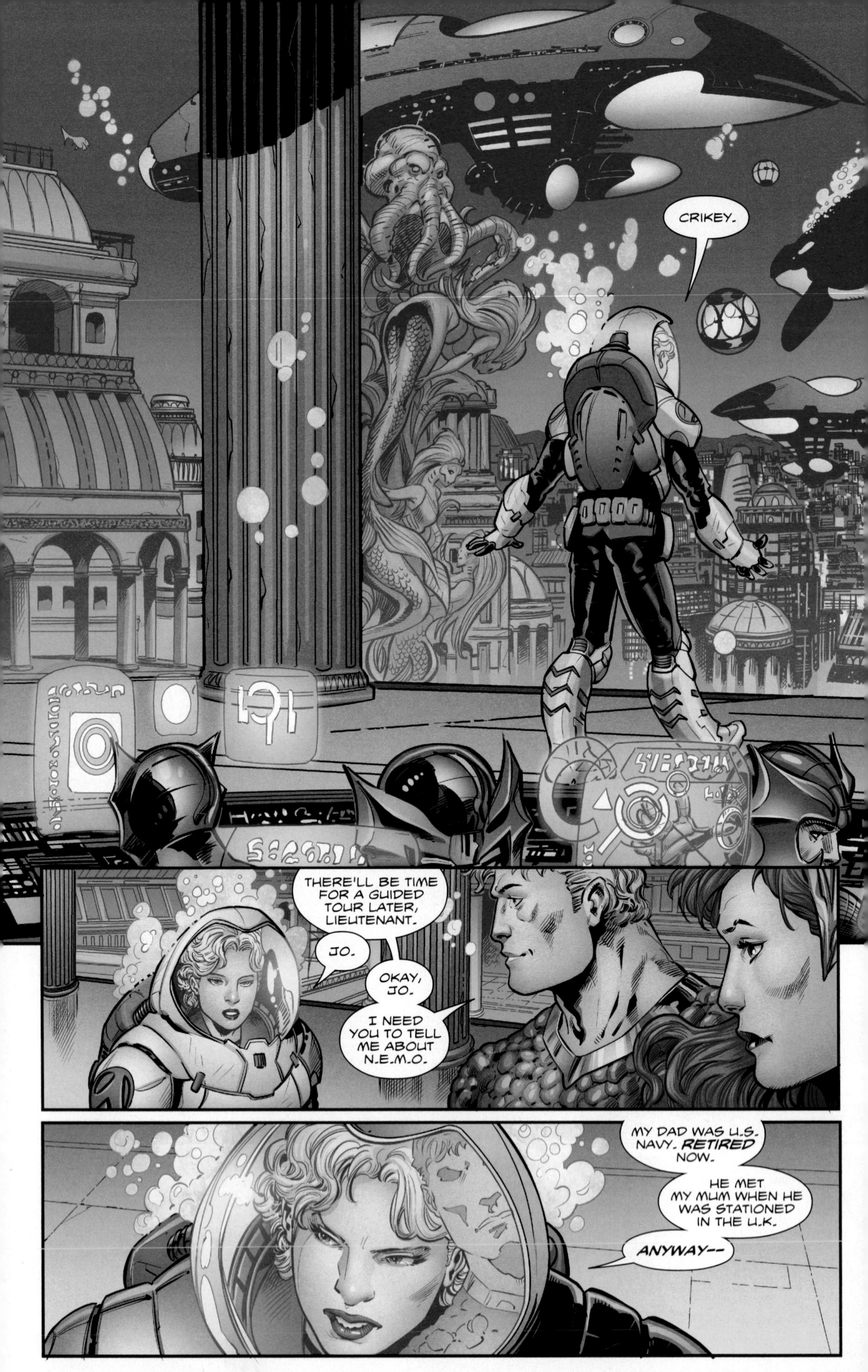
CRIKEY.
THERE'LL BE TIME FOR A GUIDED TOUR LATER, LIEUTENANT.
JO.
OKAY, JO.
I NEED YOU TO TELL ME ABOUT N.E.M.O.
MY DAD WAS U.S. NAVY. RETIRED NOW.
HE MET MY MUM WHEN HE WAS STATIONED IN THE U.K.
ANYWAY--

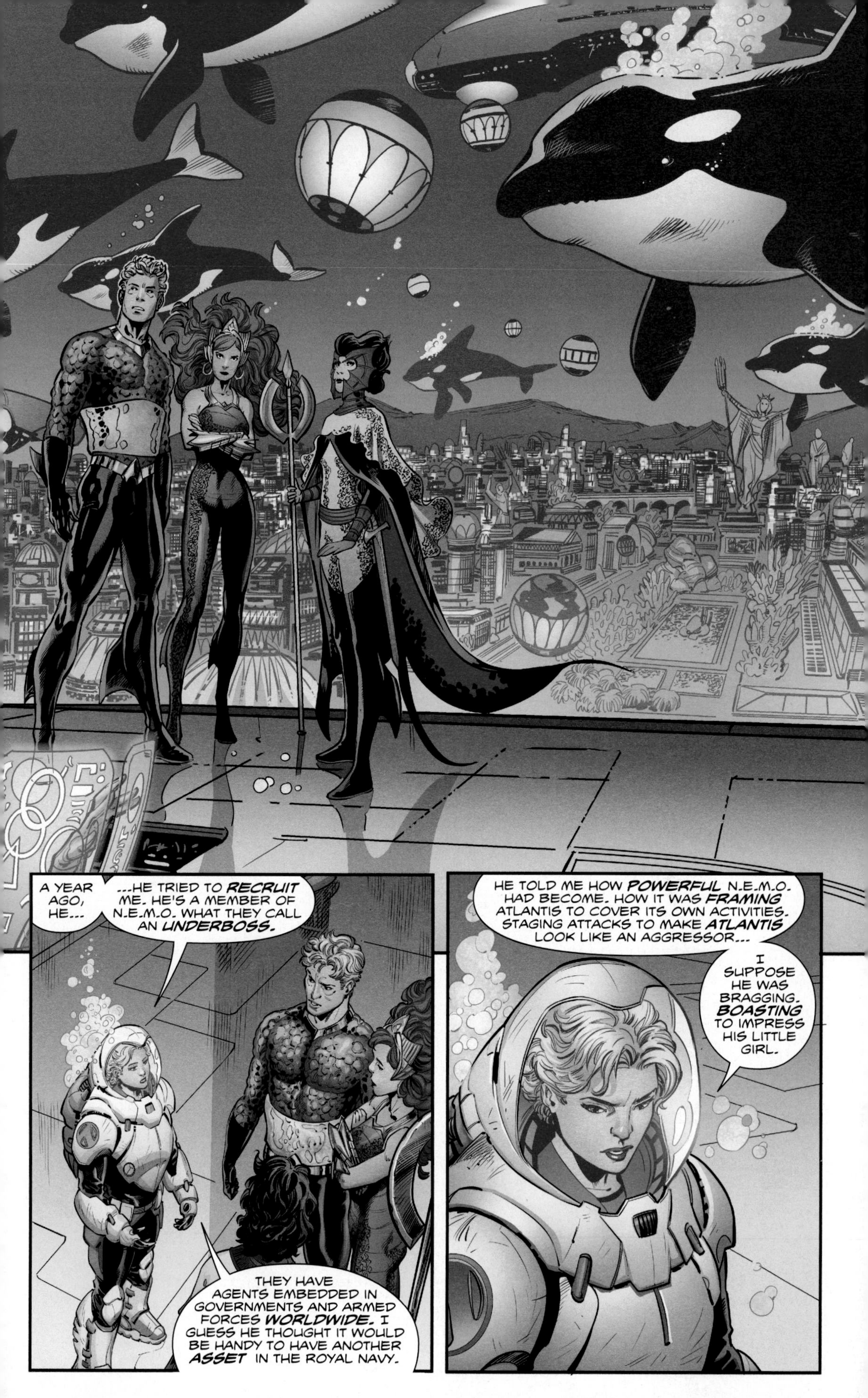
A YEAR AGO, HE...
...HE TRIED TO RECRUIT ME. HE'S A MEMBER OF N.E.M.O. WHAT THEY CALL AN UNDERBOSS.
THEY HAVE AGENTS EMBEDDED IN GOVERNMENTS AND ARMED FORCES WORLDWIDE. I GUESS HE THOUGHT IT WOULD BE HANDY TO HAVE ANOTHER ASSET IN THE ROYAL NAVY.
HE TOLD ME HOW POWERFUL N.E.M.O. HAD BECOME. HOW IT WAS FRAMING ATLANTIS TO COVER ITS OWN ACTIVITIES. STAGING ATTACKS TO MAKE ATLANTIS LOOK LIKE AN AGGRESSOR...
I SUPPOSE HE WAS BRAGGING. BOASTING TO IMPRESS HIS LITTLE GIRL.

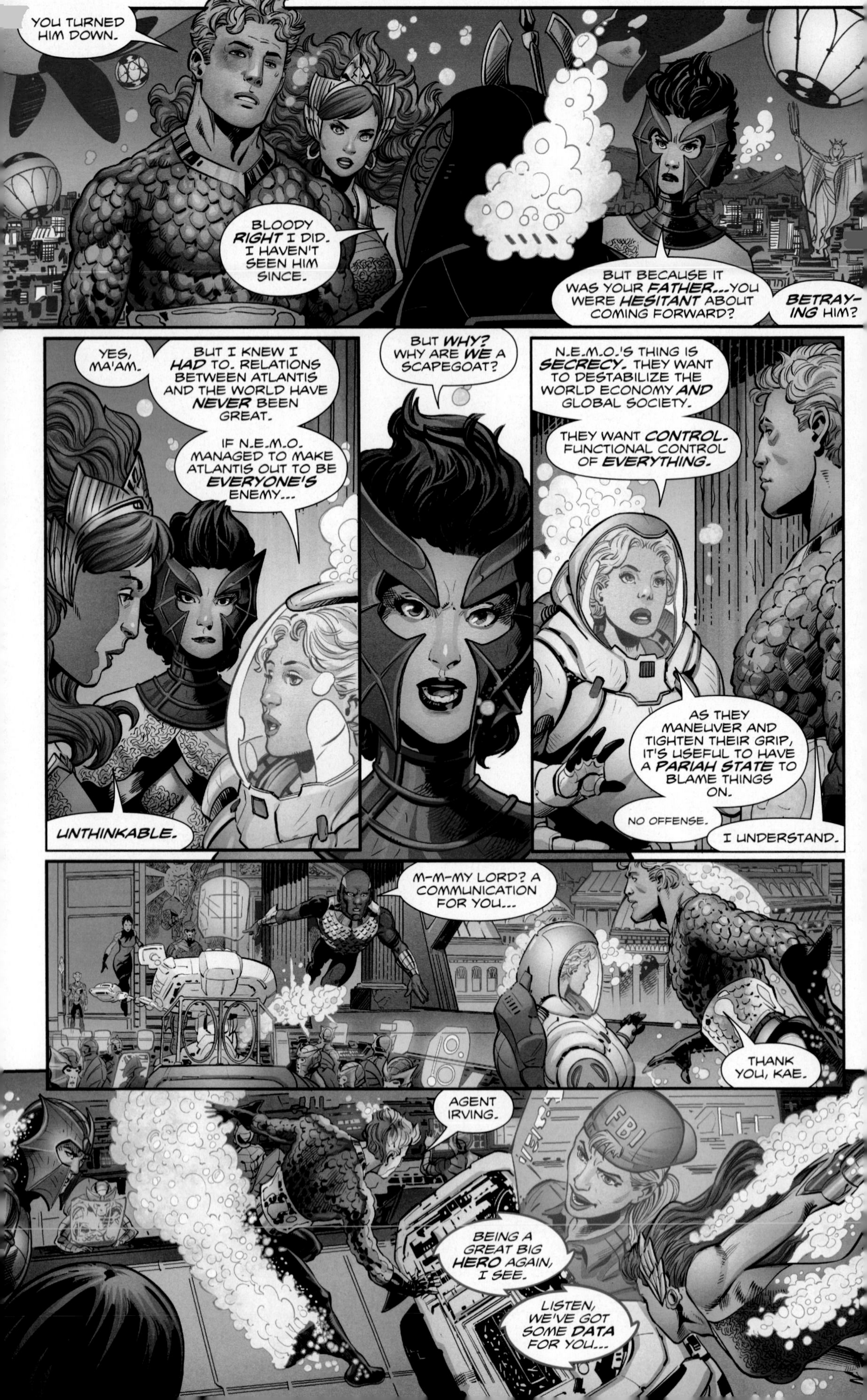
YOU TURNED HIM DOWN.
BLOODY RIGHT I DID. I HAVEN'T SEEN HIM SINCE.
BUT BECAUSE IT WAS YOUR FATHER...YOU WERE HESITANT ABOUT COMING FORWARD?
BETRAYING HIM?
YES, MA'AM.
BUT I KNEW I HAD TO. RELATIONS BETWEEN ATLANTIS AND THE WORLD HAVE NEVER BEEN GREAT.
IF N.E.M.O. MANAGED TO MAKE ATLANTIS OUT TO BE EVERYONE'S ENEMY...
UNTHINKABLE.
BUT WHY? WHY ARE WE A SCAPEGOAT?
N.E.M.O.'S THING IS SECRECY. THEY WANT TO DESTABILIZE THE WORLD ECONOMY AND GLOBAL SOCIETY.
THEY WANT CONTROL. FUNCTIONAL CONTROL OF EVERYTHING.
AS THEY MANEUVER AND TIGHTEN THEIR GRIP, IT'S USEFUL TO HAVE A PARIAH STATE TO BLAME THINGS ON.
NO OFFENSE.
I UNDERSTAND.
M-M-MY LORD? A COMMUNICATION FOR YOU...
THANK YOU, KAE.
AGENT IRVING.
FBI
BEING A GREAT BIG HERO AGAIN, I SEE.
LISTEN, WE'VE GOT SOME DATA FOR YOU...

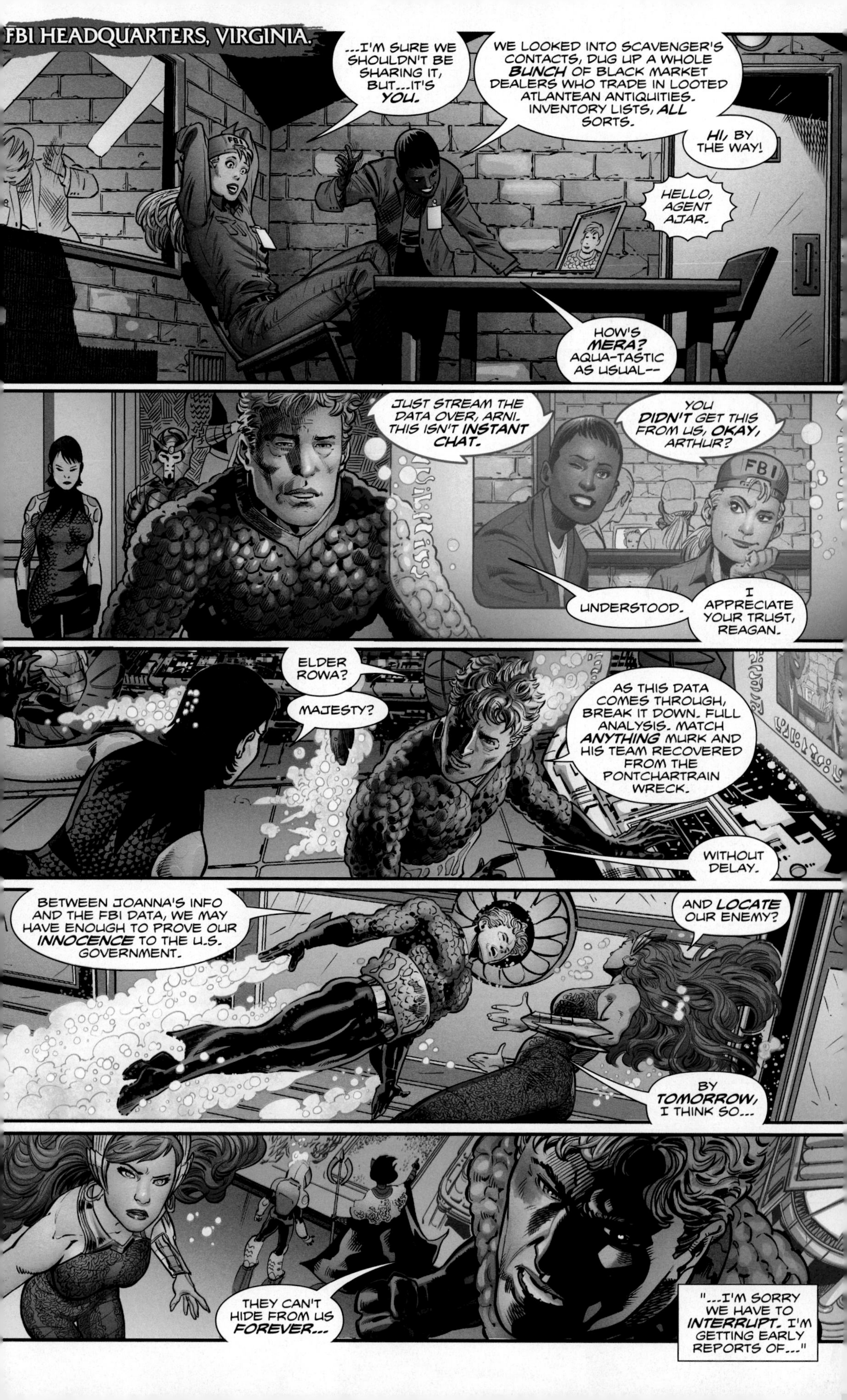
FBI HEADQUARTERS, VIRGINIA.
...I'M SURE WE SHOULDN'T BE SHARING IT, BUT...IT'S YOU.
WE LOOKED INTO SCAVENGER'S CONTACTS, DUG UP A WHOLE BUNCH OF BLACK MARKET DEALERS WHO TRADE IN LOOTED ATLANTEAN ANTIQUITIES. INVENTORY LISTS, ALL SORTS.
HI, BY THE WAY!
HELLO, AGENT AJAR.
HOW'S MERA? AQUA-TASTIC AS USUAL--
JUST STREAM THE DATA OVER, ARNI. THIS ISN'T INSTANT CHAT.
YOU DIDN'T GET THIS FROM US, OKAY, ARTHUR?
UNDERSTOOD.
I APPRECIATE YOUR TRUST, REAGAN.
ELDER ROWA?
MAJESTY?
AS THIS DATA COMES THROUGH, BREAK IT DOWN. FULL ANALYSIS. MATCH ANYTHING MURK AND HIS TEAM RECOVERED FROM THE PONTCHARTRAIN WRECK.
WITHOUT DELAY.
BETWEEN JOANNA'S INFO AND THE FBI DATA, WE MAY HAVE ENOUGH TO PROVE OUR INNOCENCE TO THE U.S. GOVERNMENT.
AND LOCATE OUR ENEMY?
BY TOMORROW, I THINK SO...
THEY CAN'T HIDE FROM US FOREVER...
"...I'M SORRY WE HAVE TO INTERRUPT. I'M GETTING EARLY REPORTS OF..."

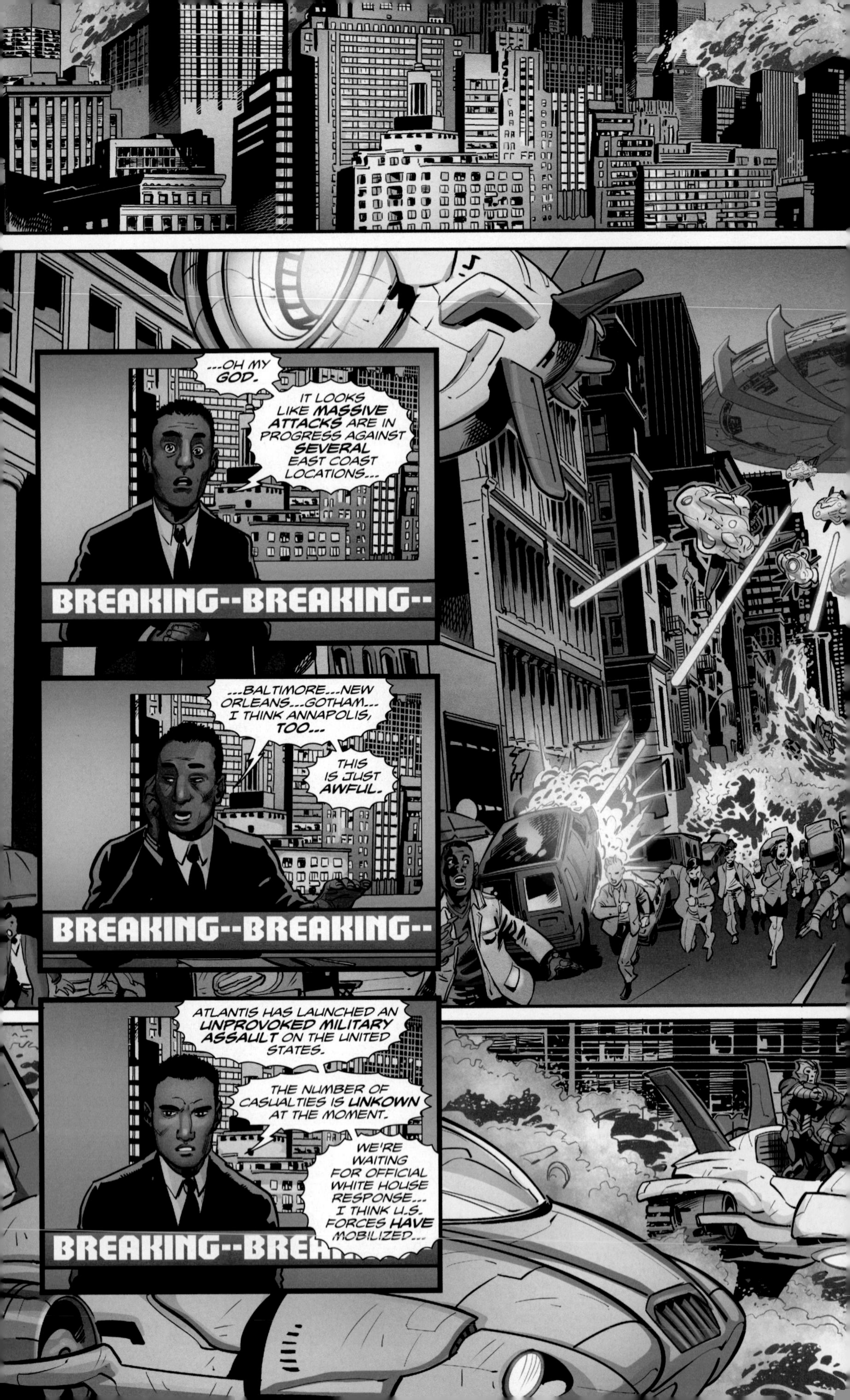
...OH MY GOD.
IT LOOKS LIKE MASSIVE ATTACKS ARE IN PROGRESS AGAINST SEVERAL EAST COAST LOCATIONS...
BREAKING--BREAKING--
...BALTIMORE...NEW ORLEANS...GOTHAM... I THINK ANNAPOLIS, TOO...
THIS IS JUST AWFUL.
BREAKING--BREAKING--
ATLANTIS HAS LAUNCHED AN UNPROVOKED MILITARY ASSAULT ON THE UNITED STATES.
THE NUMBER OF CASUALTIES IS UNKOWN AT THE MOMENT.
WE'RE WAITING FOR OFFICIAL WHITE HOUSE RESPONSE... I THINK U.S. FORCES HAVE MOBILIZED...
BREAKING--BREA

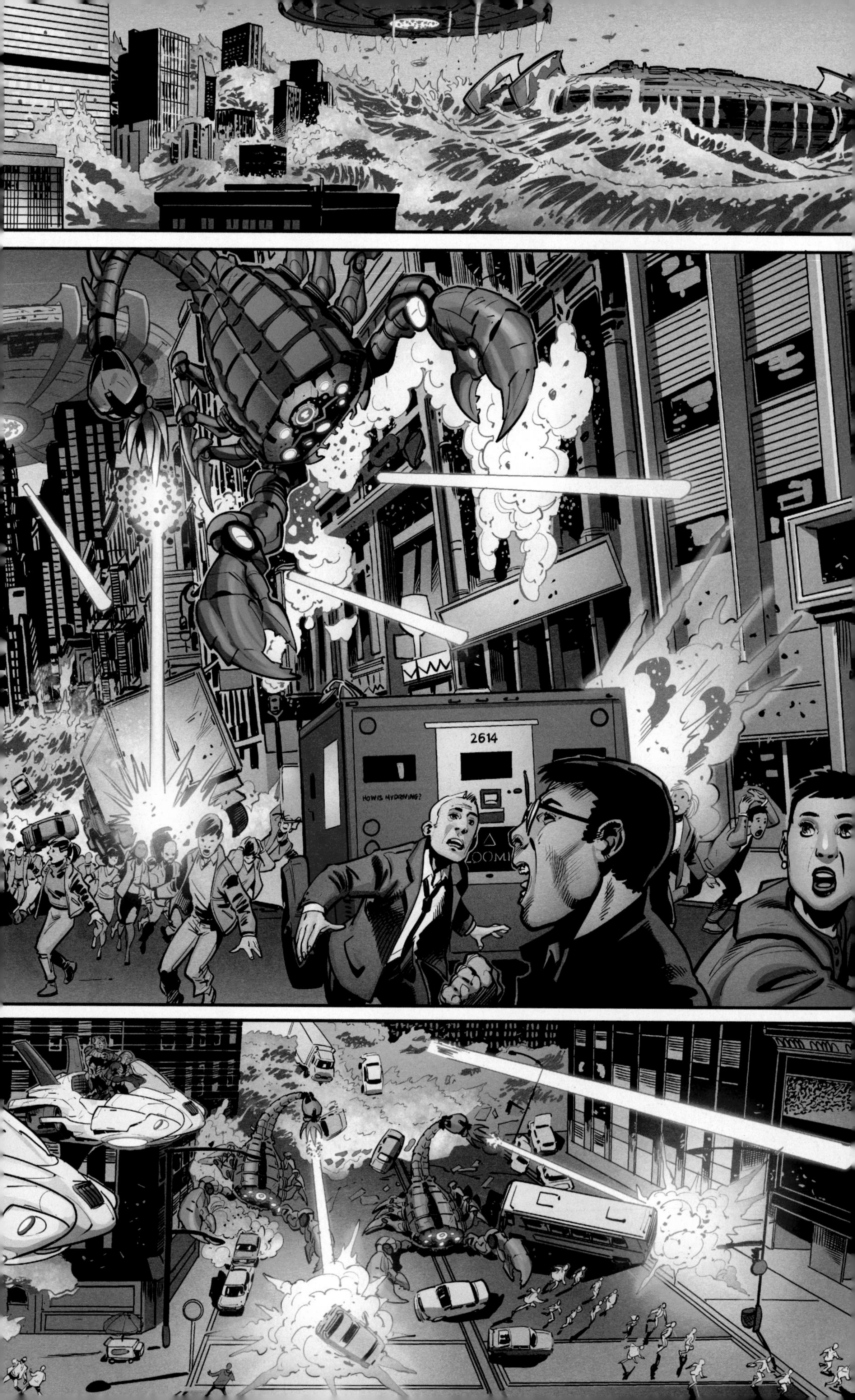
2614
HOW IS MY DRIVING?

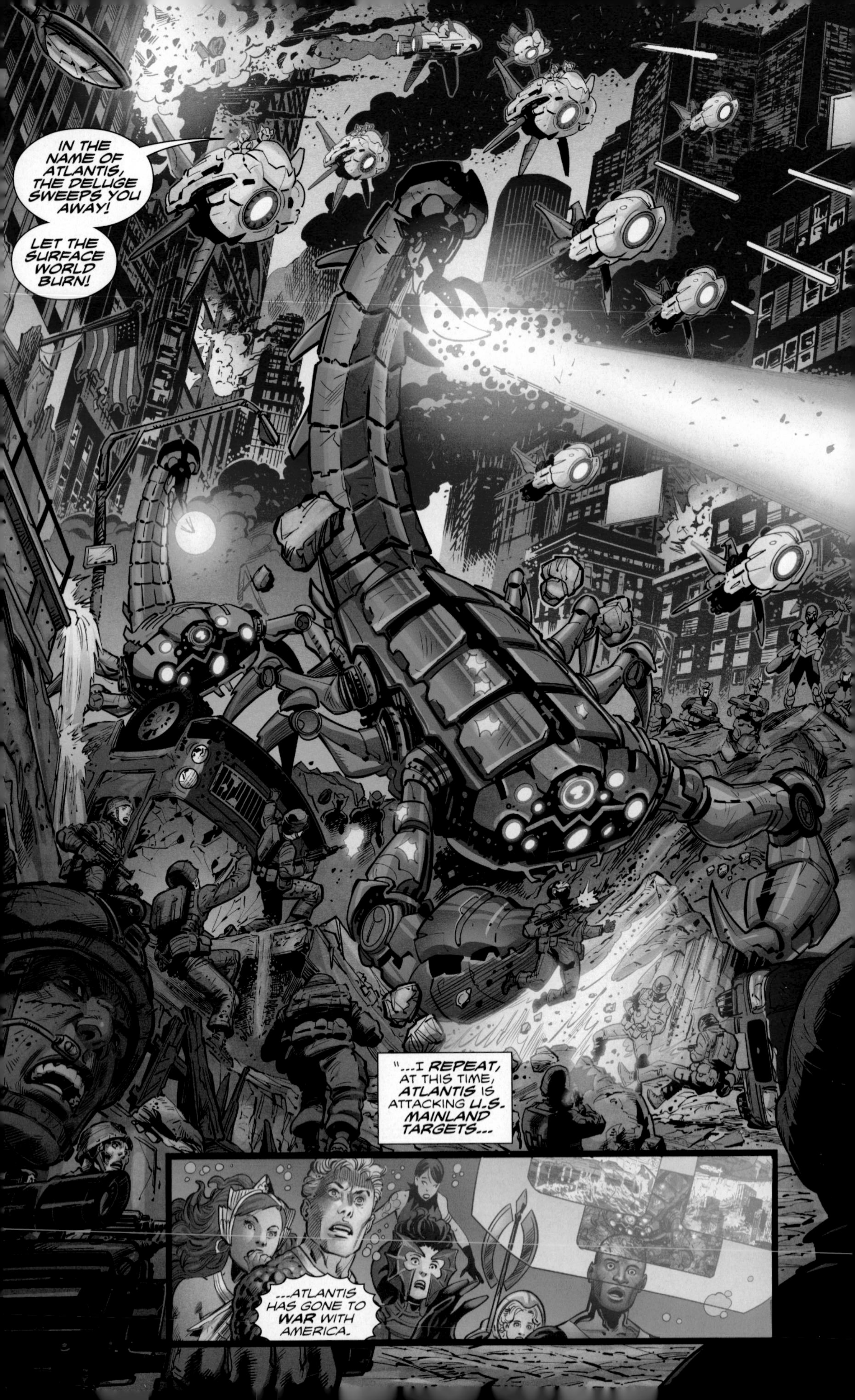
IN THE NAME OF ATLANTIS, THE DELUGE SWEEPS YOU AWAY!
LET THE SURFACE WORLD BURN!
"...I REPEAT, AT THIS TIME, ATLANTIS IS ATTACKING U.S. MAINLAND TARGETS...
...ATLANTIS HAS GONE TO WAR WITH AMERICA.

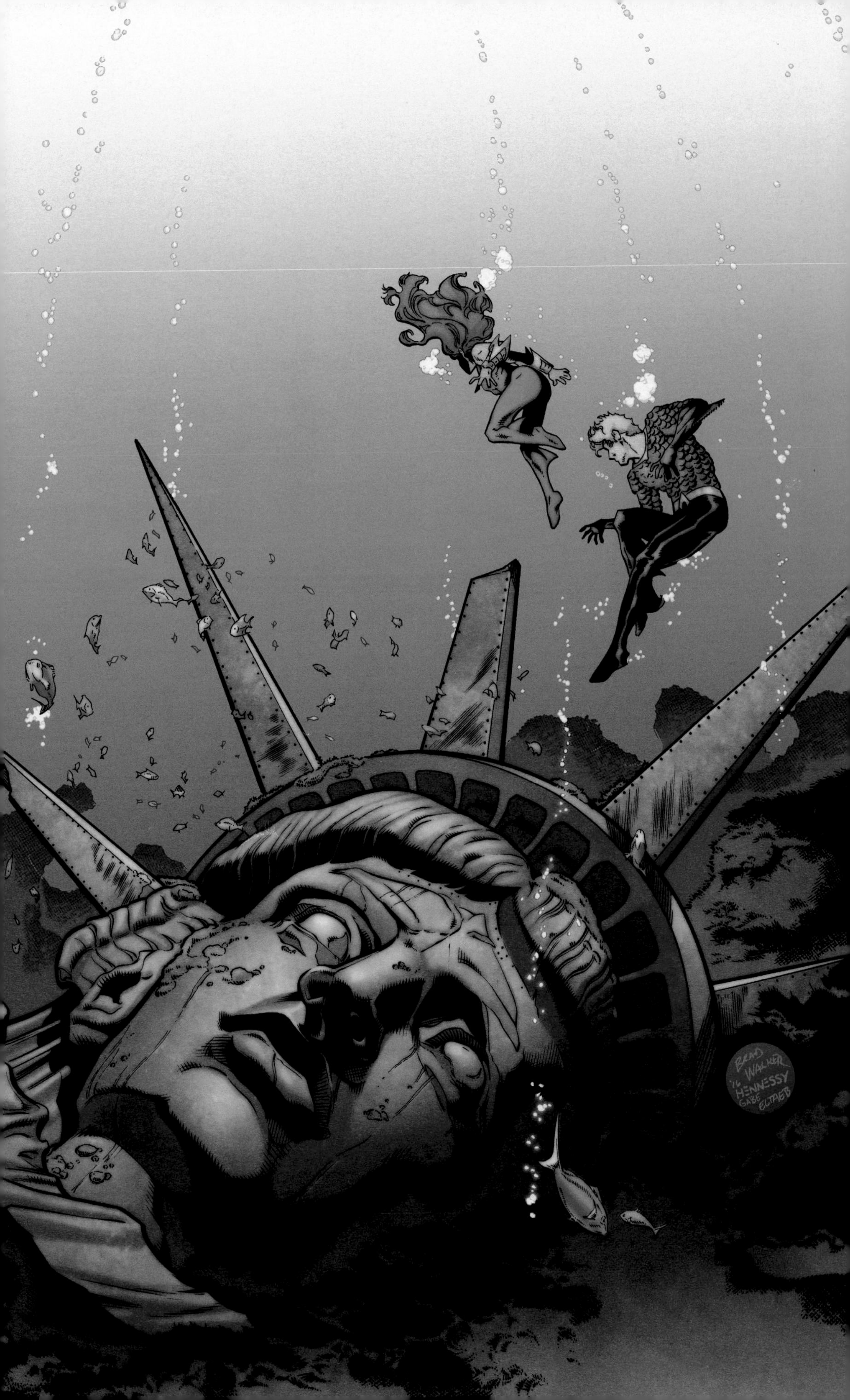
BRAD WALKER '16
HENNESSY
GABE ELTAEB

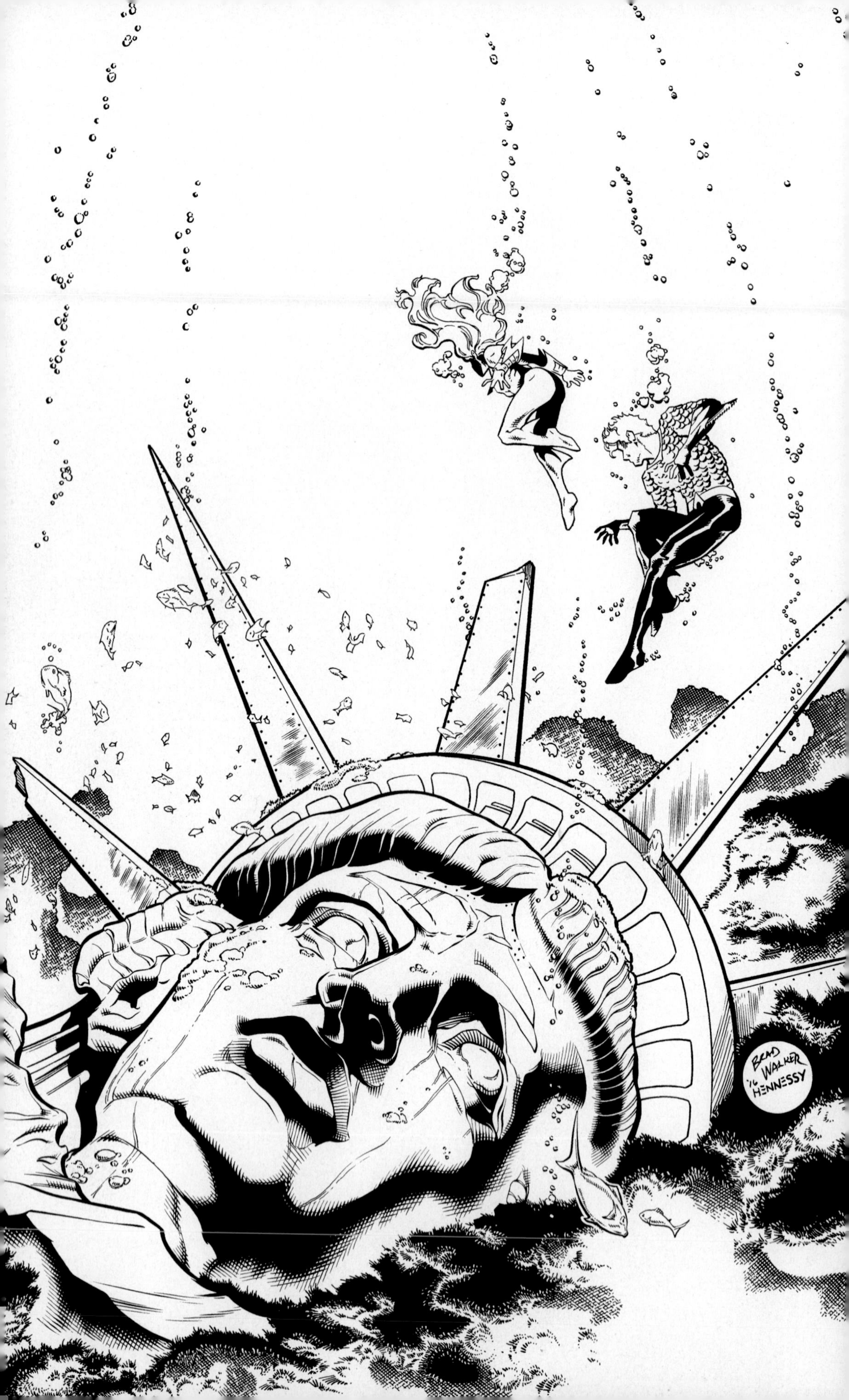
BRAD WALKER '16 HENNESSY

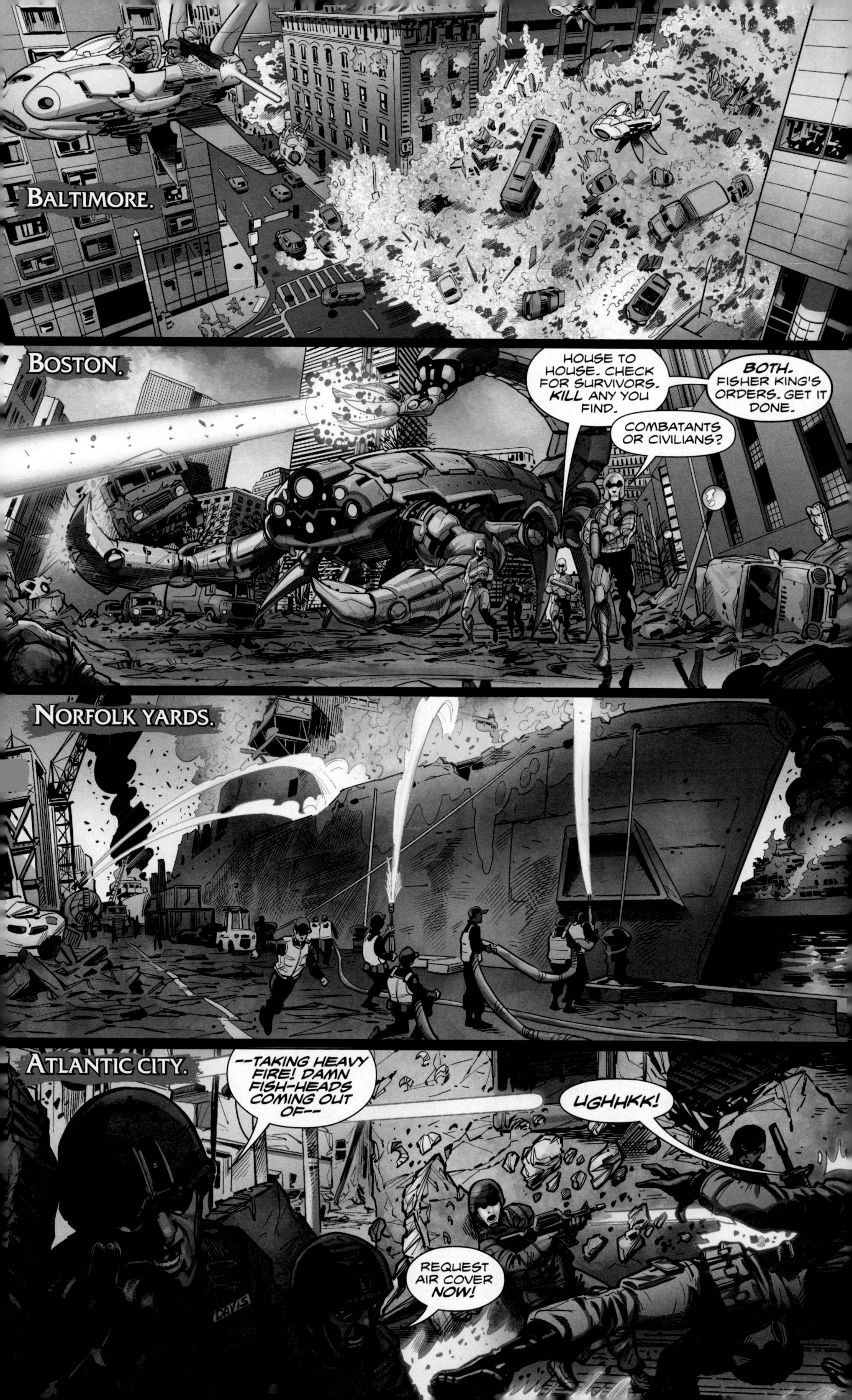
BALTIMORE.
BOSTON.
HOUSE TO HOUSE. CHECK FOR SURVIVORS. KILL ANY YOU FIND.
COMBATANTS OR CIVILIANS?
BOTH. FISHER KING'S ORDERS. GET IT DONE.
NORFOLK YARDS.
ATLANTIC CITY.
--TAKING HEAVY FIRE! DAMN FISH-HEADS COMING OUT OF--
UGHHKK!
REQUEST AIR COVER NOW!
DAVIS

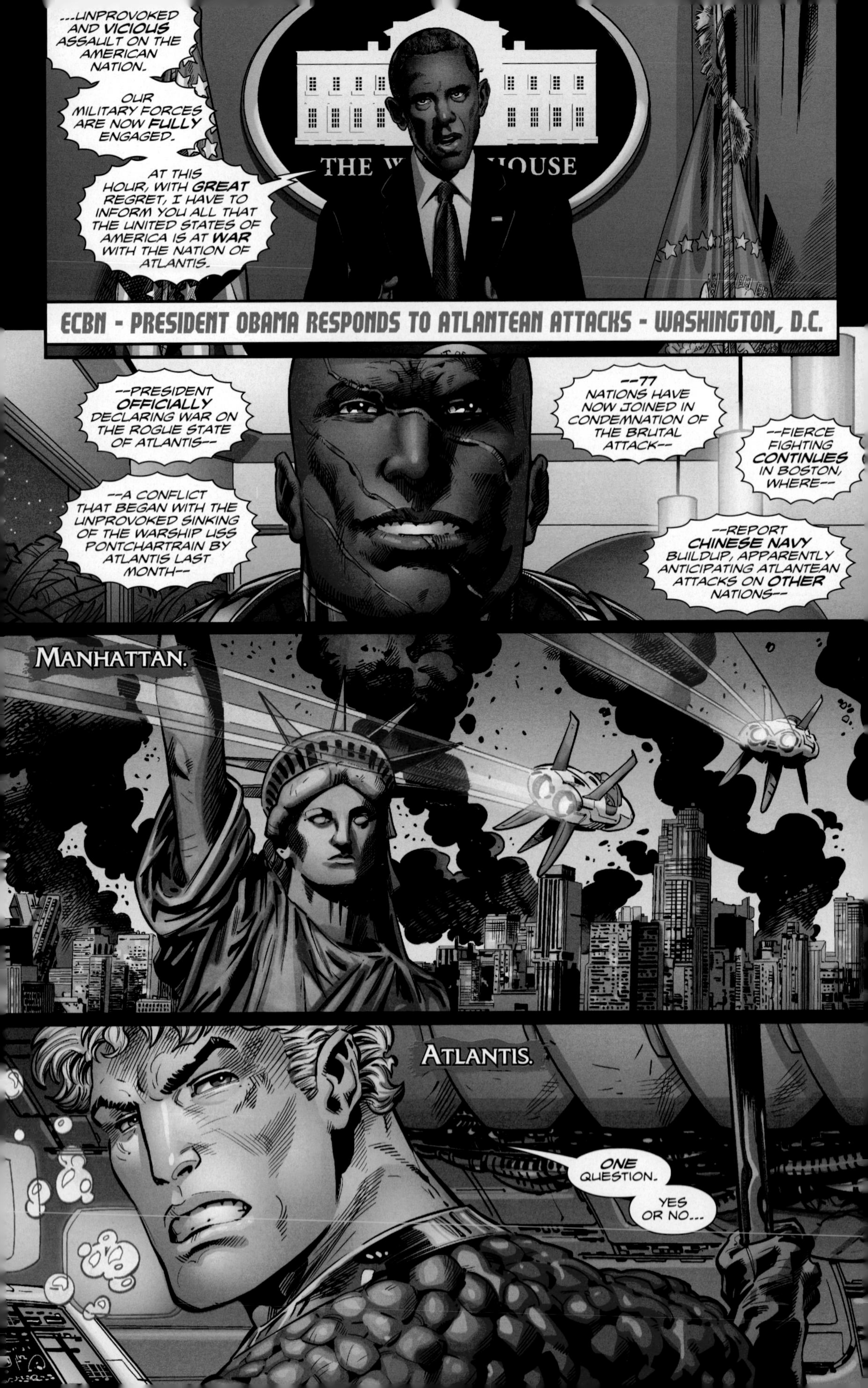

...UNPROVOKED AND VICIOUS ASSAULT ON THE AMERICAN NATION.
OUR MILITARY FORCES ARE NOW FULLY ENGAGED.
AT THIS HOUR, WITH GREAT REGRET, I HAVE TO INFORM YOU ALL THAT THE UNITED STATES OF AMERICA IS AT WAR WITH THE NATION OF ATLANTIS.
ECBN - PRESIDENT OBAMA RESPONDS TO ATLANTEAN ATTACKS - WASHINGTON, D.C.
--PRESIDENT OFFICIALLY DECLARING WAR ON THE ROGUE STATE OF ATLANTIS--
--A CONFLICT THAT BEGAN WITH THE UNPROVOKED SINKING OF THE WARSHIP USS PONTCHARTRAIN BY ATLANTIS LAST MONTH--
--77 NATIONS HAVE NOW JOINED IN CONDEMNATION OF THE BRUTAL ATTACK--
--FIERCE FIGHTING CONTINUES IN BOSTON, WHERE--
--REPORT CHINESE NAVY BUILDUP, APPARENTLY ANTICIPATING ATLANTEAN ATTACKS ON OTHER NATIONS--
MANHATTAN.
ATLANTIS.
ONE QUESTION.
YES OR NO...

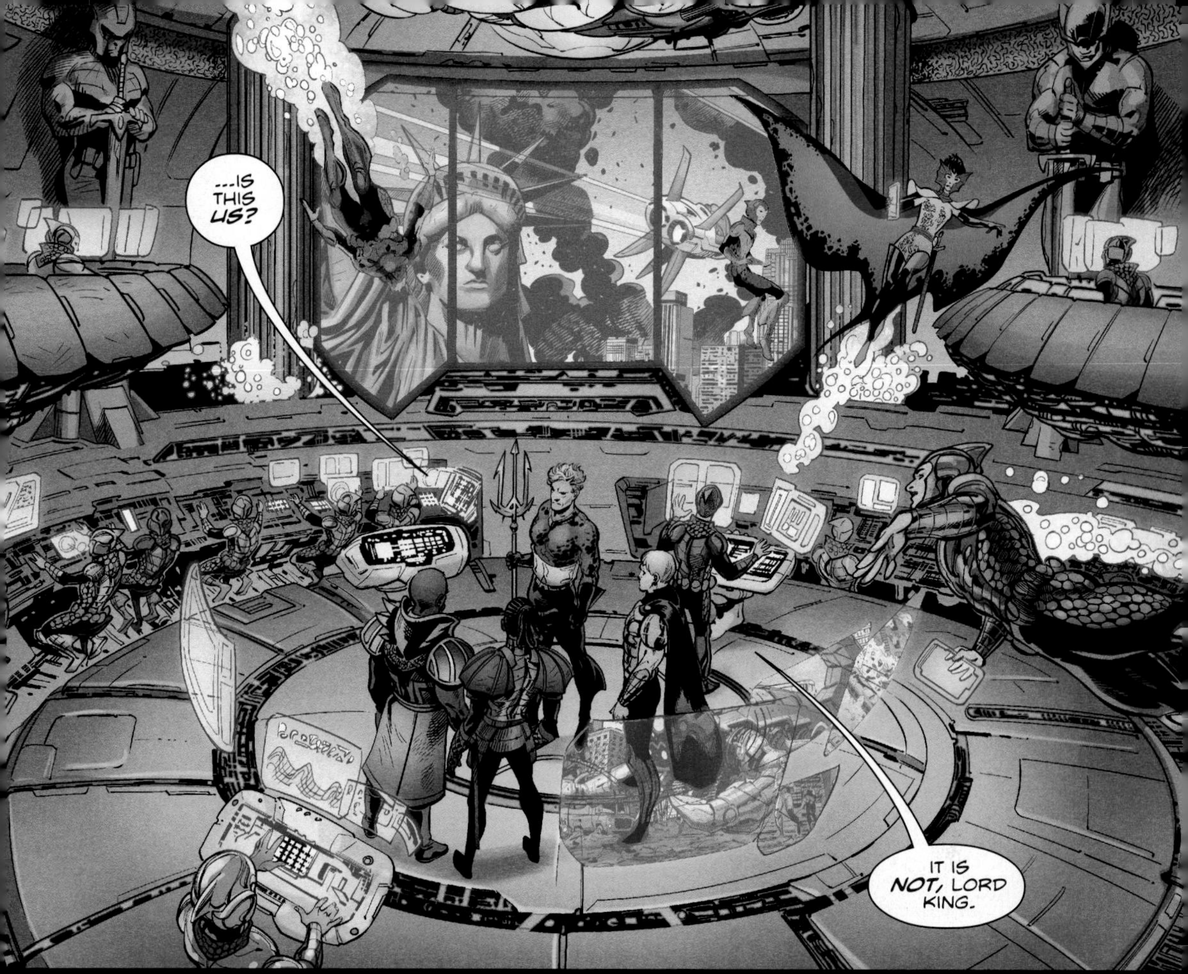
...IS THIS US?
IT IS NOT, LORD KING.

THE DELUGE ACT ONE

DAN ABNETT WRITER
PHILIPPE BRIONES ARTIST
GABE ELTAEB COLORIST
PAT BROSSEAU LETTERER

BRAD WALKER, ANDREW HENNESSY & GABE ELTAEB COVER
AMEDEO TURTURRO & DIEGO LOPEZ ASSISTANT EDITORS
BRIAN CUNNINGHAM EDITOR

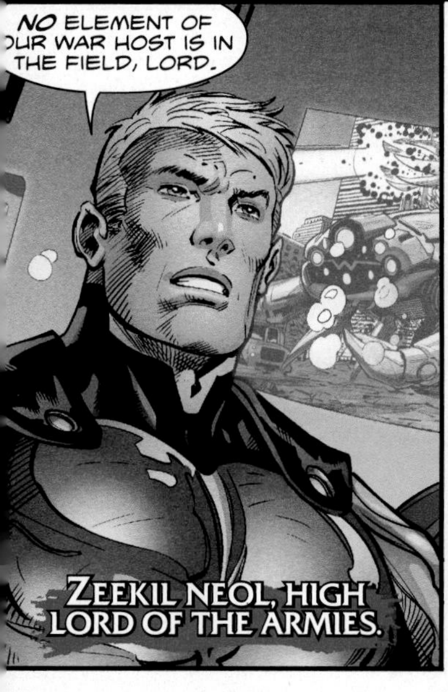
NO ELEMENT OF OUR WAR HOST IS IN THE FIELD, LORD.
ZEEKIL NEOL, HIGH LORD OF THE ARMIES.

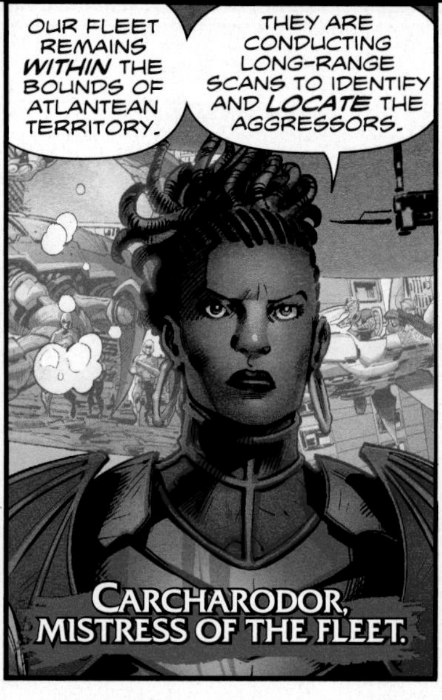
OUR FLEET REMAINS WITHIN THE BOUNDS OF ATLANTEAN TERRITORY.
THEY ARE CONDUCTING LONG-RANGE SCANS TO IDENTIFY AND LOCATE THE AGGRESSORS.
CARCHARODOR, MISTRESS OF THE FLEET.

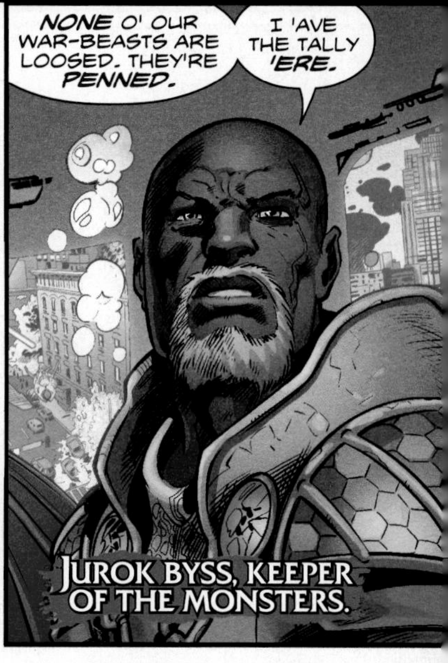
NONE O' OUR WAR-BEASTS ARE LOOSED. THEY'RE PENNED.
I 'AVE THE TALLY 'ERE.
JUROK BYSS, KEEPER OF THE MONSTERS.

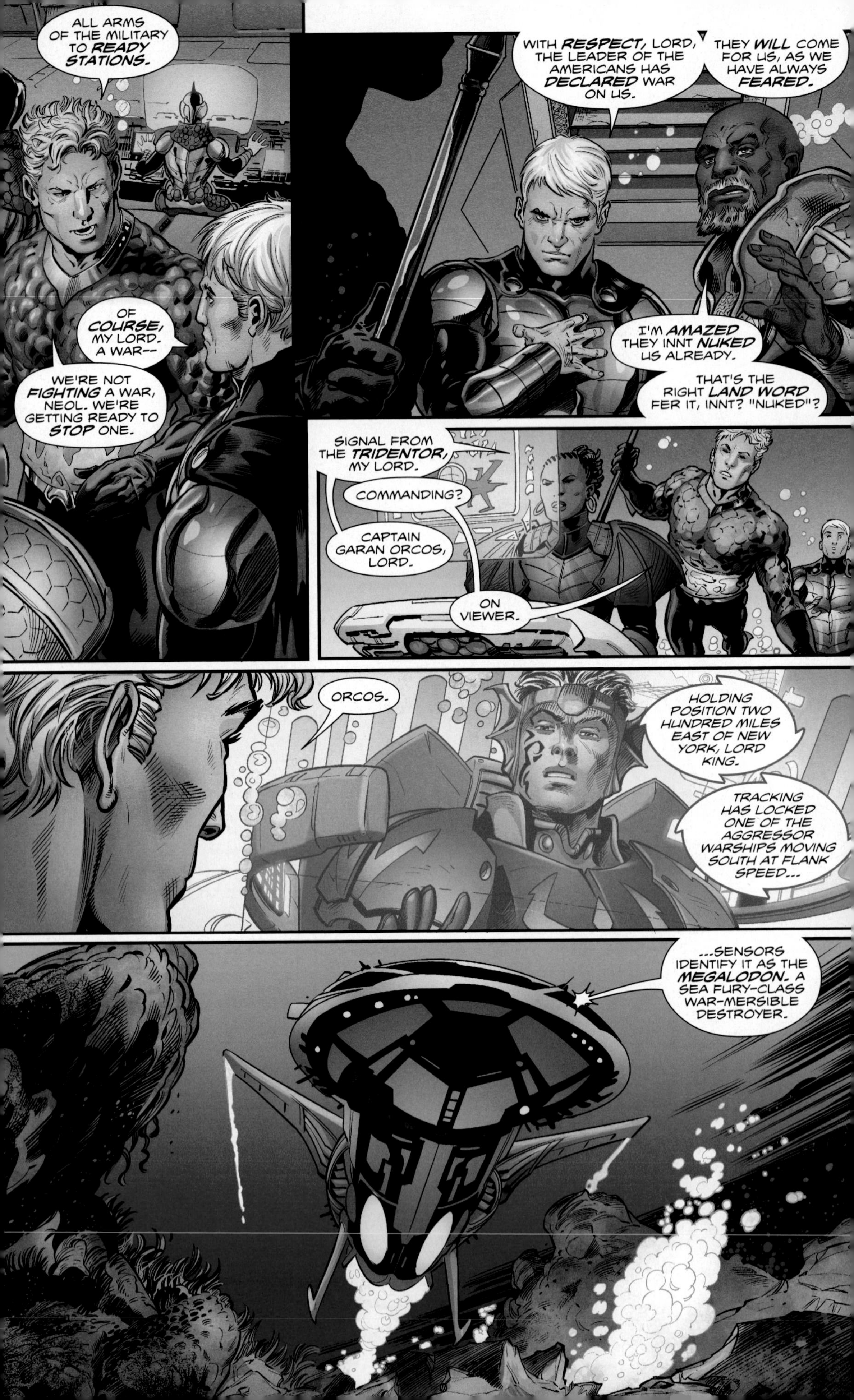
ALL ARMS OF THE MILITARY TO READY STATIONS.
OF COURSE, MY LORD. A WAR--
WE'RE NOT FIGHTING A WAR, NEOL. WE'RE GETTING READY TO STOP ONE.
WITH RESPECT, LORD, THE LEADER OF THE AMERICANS HAS DECLARED WAR ON US.
THEY WILL COME FOR US, AS WE HAVE ALWAYS FEARED.
I'M AMAZED THEY INNT NUKED US ALREADY.
THAT'S THE RIGHT LAND WORD FER IT, INNT? "NUKED"?
SIGNAL FROM THE TRIDENTOR, MY LORD.
COMMANDING?
CAPTAIN GARAN ORCOS, LORD.
ON VIEWER.
ORCOS.
HOLDING POSITION TWO HUNDRED MILES EAST OF NEW YORK, LORD KING.
TRACKING HAS LOCKED ONE OF THE AGGRESSOR WARSHIPS MOVING SOUTH AT FLANK SPEED...
...SENSORS IDENTIFY IT AS THE MEGALODON. A SEA FURY-CLASS WAR-MERSIBLE DESTROYER.

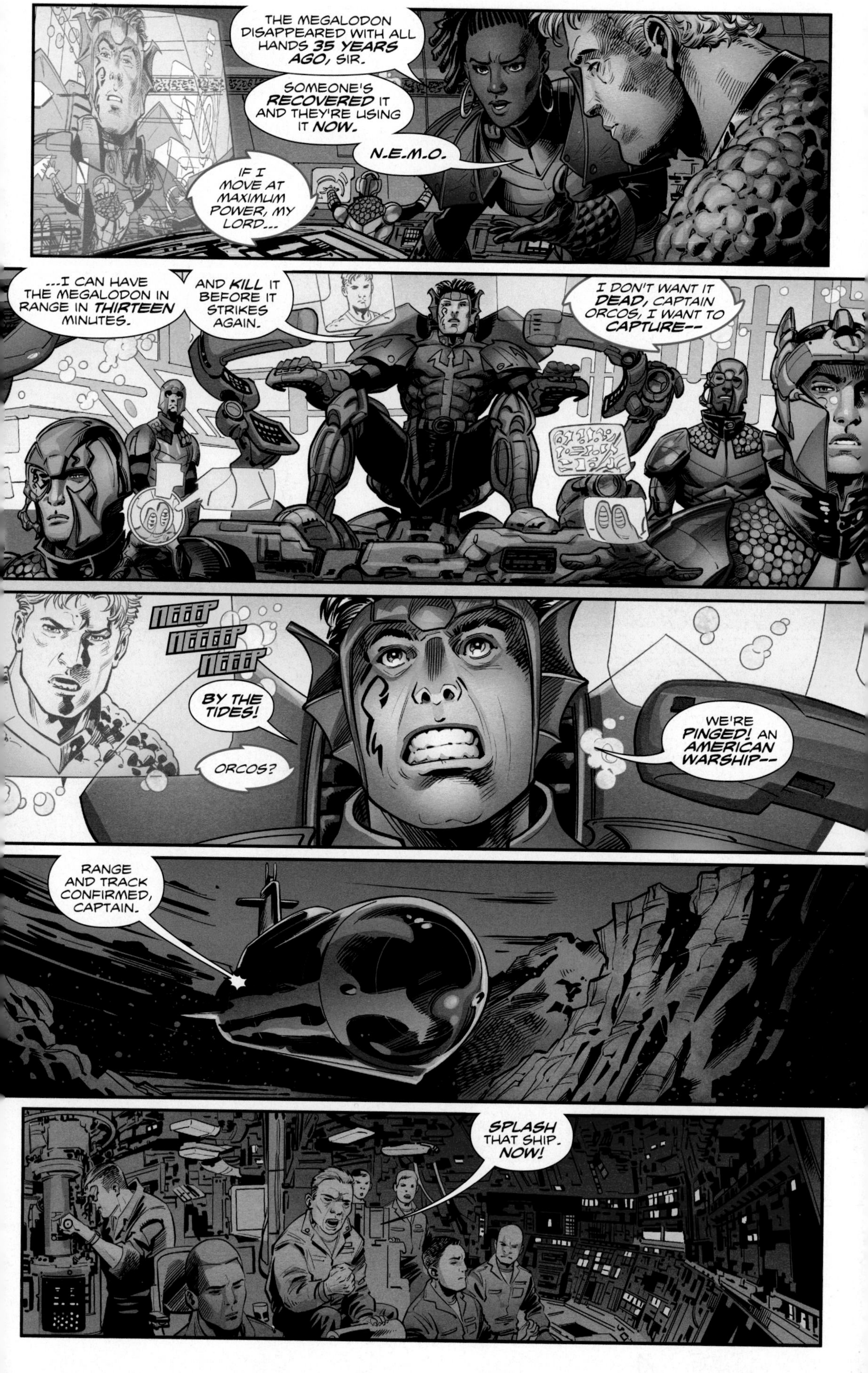
THE MEGALODON DISAPPEARED WITH ALL HANDS 35 YEARS AGO, SIR.
SOMEONE'S RECOVERED IT AND THEY'RE USING IT NOW.
N.E.M.O.
IF I MOVE AT MAXIMUM POWER, MY LORD...
...I CAN HAVE THE MEGALODON IN RANGE IN THIRTEEN MINUTES.
AND KILL IT BEFORE IT STRIKES AGAIN.
I DON'T WANT IT DEAD, CAPTAIN ORCOS, I WANT TO CAPTURE--
NEEEP NEEEP NEEEP
BY THE TIDES!
ORCOS?
WE'RE PINGED! AN AMERICAN WARSHIP--
RANGE AND TRACK CONFIRMED, CAPTAIN.
SPLASH THAT SHIP. NOW!

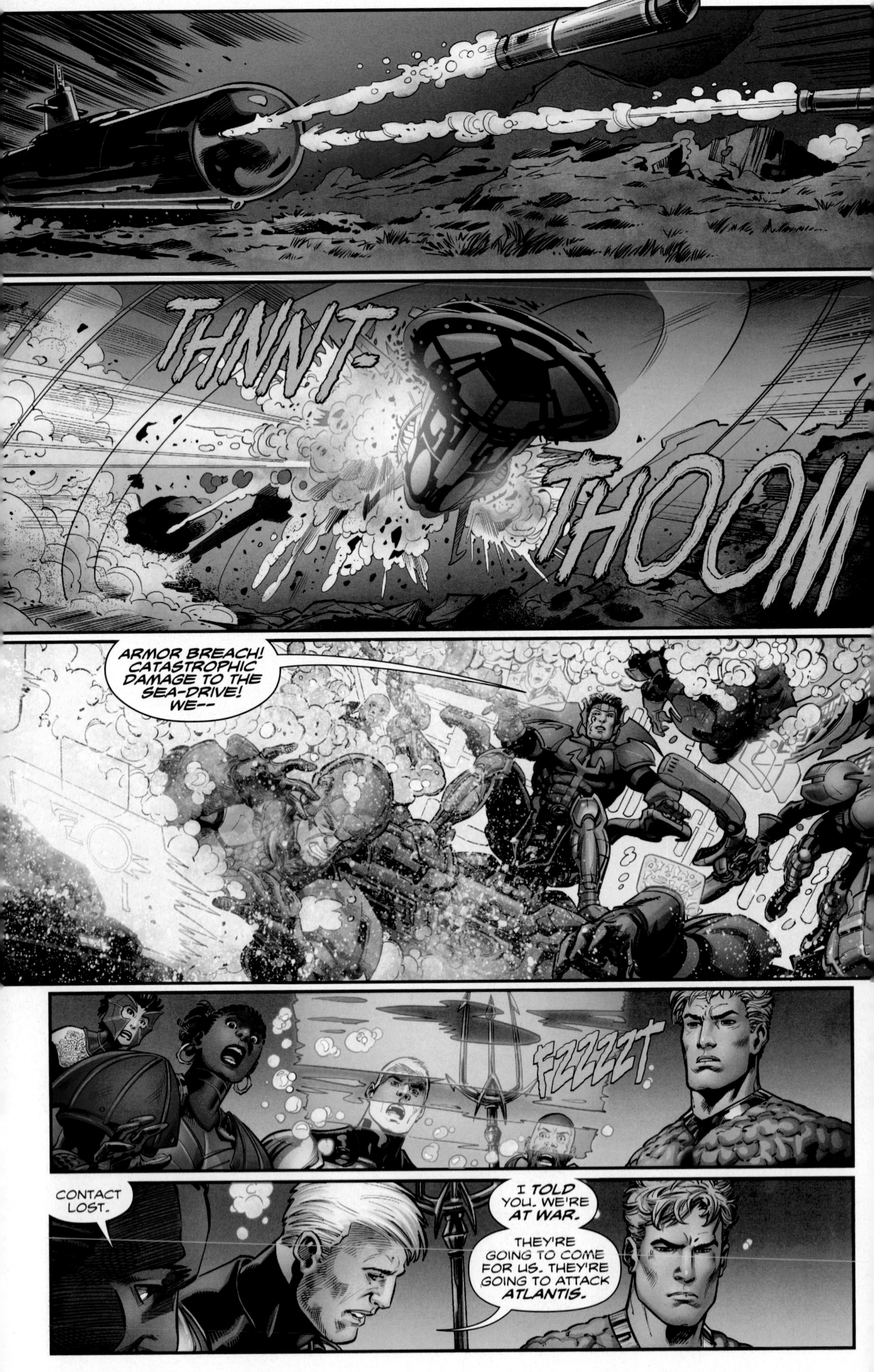
THNNT-
THOOM
ARMOR BREACH! CATASTROPHIC DAMAGE TO THE SEA-DRIVE! WE--
FZZZZT
CONTACT LOST.
I TOLD YOU. WE'RE AT WAR.
THEY'RE GOING TO COME FOR US. THEY'RE GOING TO ATTACK ATLANTIS.

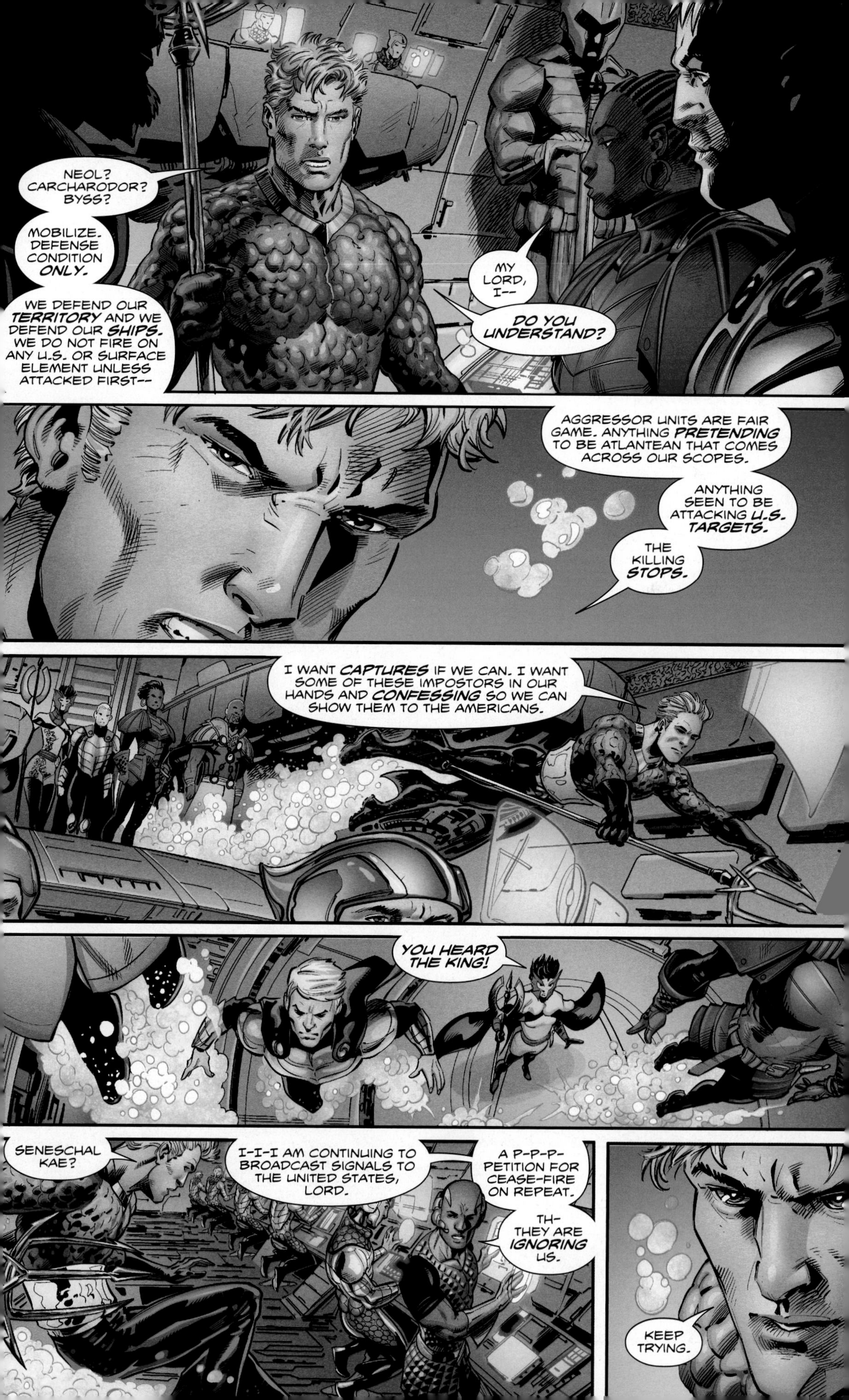
NEOL? CARCHARODOR? BYSS?
MOBILIZE. DEFENSE CONDITION ONLY.
WE DEFEND OUR TERRITORY AND WE DEFEND OUR SHIPS. WE DO NOT FIRE ON ANY U.S. OR SURFACE ELEMENT UNLESS ATTACKED FIRST--
MY LORD, I--
DO YOU UNDERSTAND?
AGGRESSOR UNITS ARE FAIR GAME. ANYTHING PRETENDING TO BE ATLANTEAN THAT COMES ACROSS OUR SCOPES.
ANYTHING SEEN TO BE ATTACKING U.S. TARGETS.
THE KILLING STOPS.
I WANT CAPTURES IF WE CAN. I WANT SOME OF THESE IMPOSTORS IN OUR HANDS AND CONFESSING SO WE CAN SHOW THEM TO THE AMERICANS.
YOU HEARD THE KING!
SENESCHAL KAE?
I-I-I AM CONTINUING TO BROADCAST SIGNALS TO THE UNITED STATES, LORD.
A P-P-P-PETITION FOR CEASE-FIRE ON REPEAT.
TH-THEY ARE IGNORING US.
KEEP TRYING.

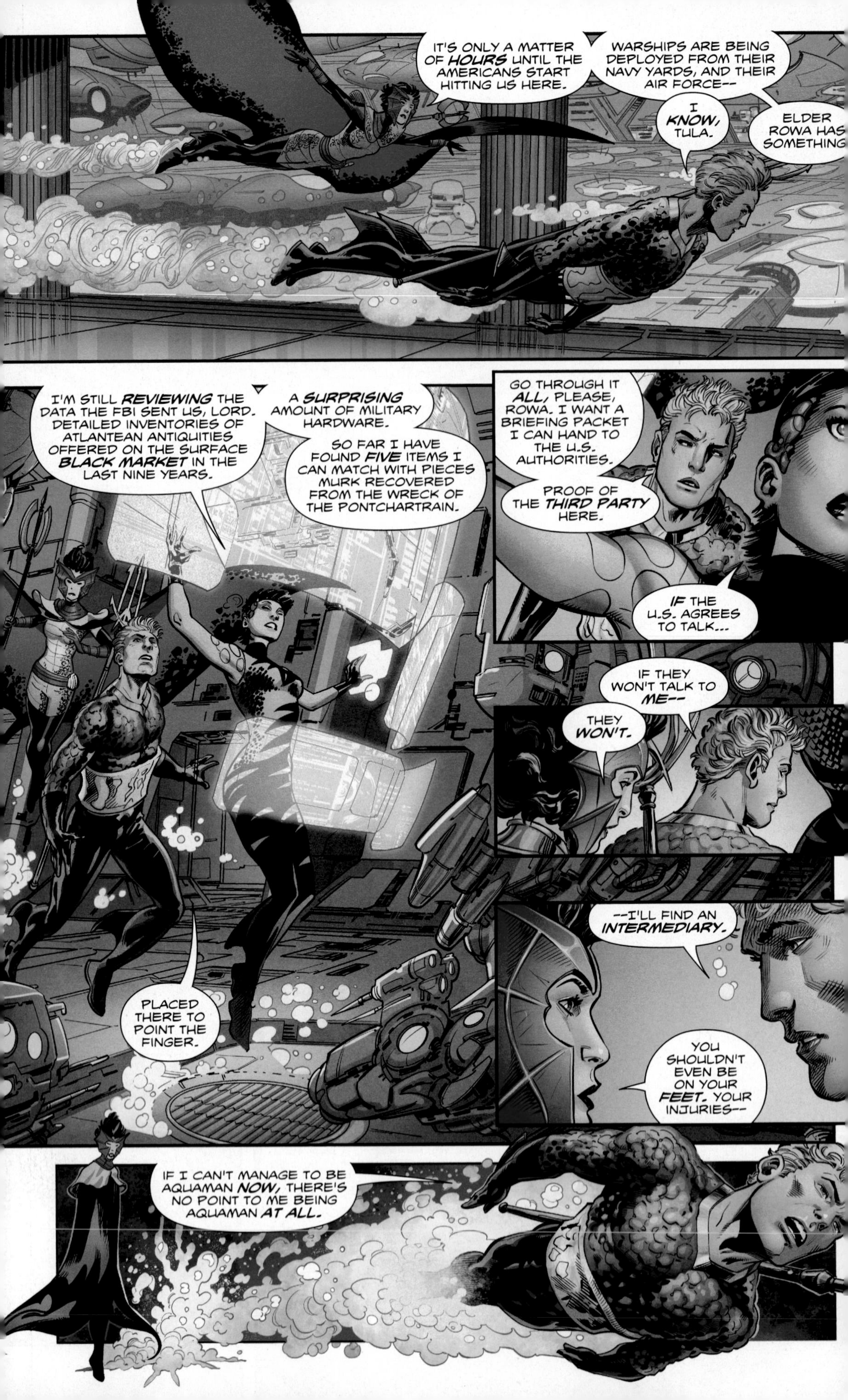
IT'S ONLY A MATTER OF HOURS UNTIL THE AMERICANS START HITTING US HERE.
WARSHIPS ARE BEING DEPLOYED FROM THEIR NAVY YARDS, AND THEIR AIR FORCE--
I KNOW, TULA.
ELDER ROWA HAS SOMETHING
I'M STILL REVIEWING THE DATA THE FBI SENT US, LORD. DETAILED INVENTORIES OF ATLANTEAN ANTIQUITIES OFFERED ON THE SURFACE BLACK MARKET IN THE LAST NINE YEARS.
A SURPRISING AMOUNT OF MILITARY HARDWARE.
SO FAR I HAVE FOUND FIVE ITEMS I CAN MATCH WITH PIECES MURK RECOVERED FROM THE WRECK OF THE PONTCHARTRAIN.
PLACED THERE TO POINT THE FINGER.
GO THROUGH IT ALL, PLEASE, ROWA. I WANT A BRIEFING PACKET I CAN HAND TO THE U.S. AUTHORITIES.
PROOF OF THE THIRD PARTY HERE.
IF THE U.S. AGREES TO TALK...
IF THEY WON'T TALK TO ME--
THEY WON'T.
--I'LL FIND AN INTERMEDIARY.
YOU SHOULDN'T EVEN BE ON YOUR FEET. YOUR INJURIES--
IF I CAN'T MANAGE TO BE AQUAMAN NOW, THERE'S NO POINT TO ME BEING AQUAMAN AT ALL.

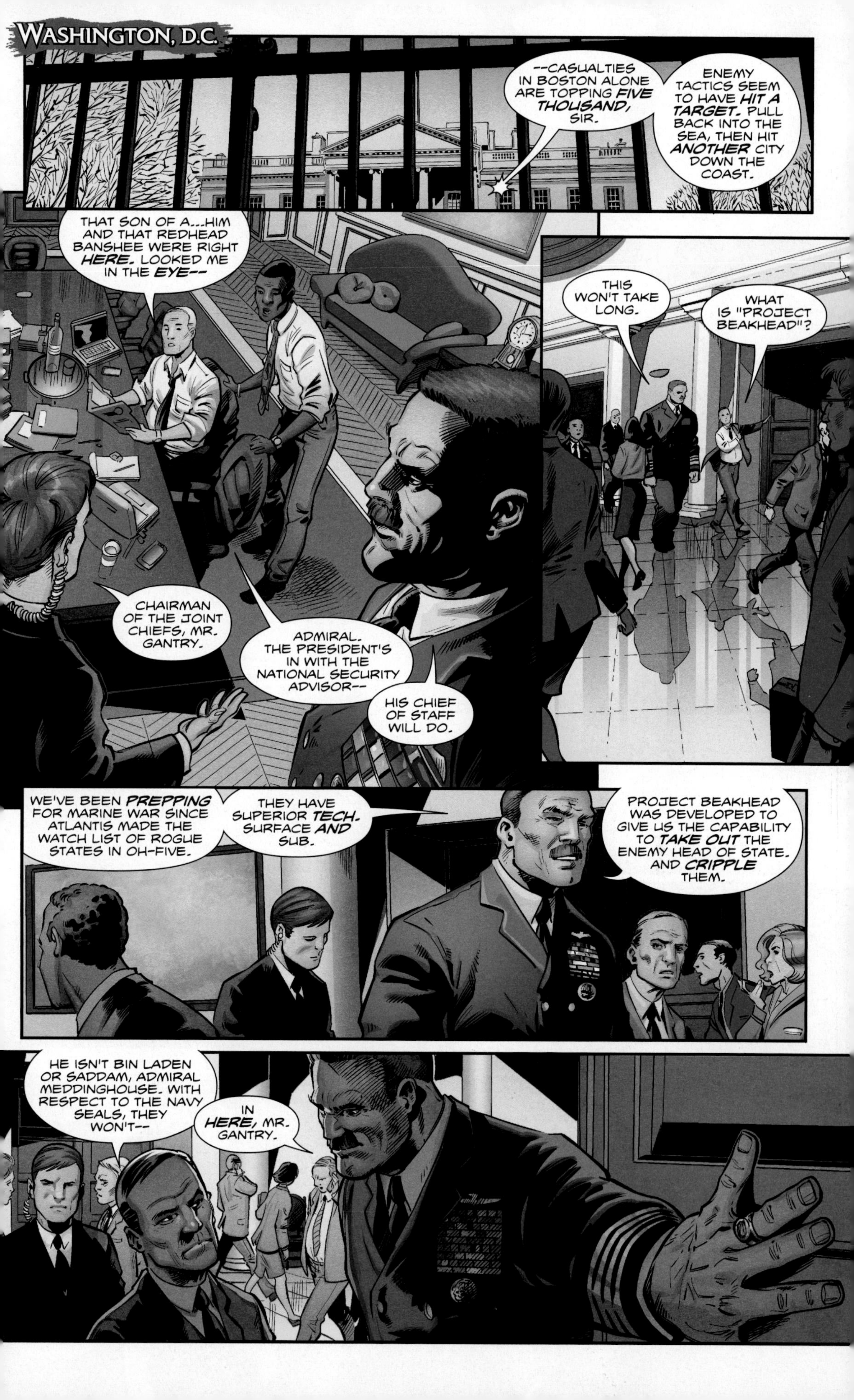
WASHINGTON, D.C.
--CASUALTIES IN BOSTON ALONE ARE TOPPING FIVE THOUSAND, SIR.
ENEMY TACTICS SEEM TO HAVE HIT A TARGET. PULL BACK INTO THE SEA, THEN HIT ANOTHER CITY DOWN THE COAST.
THAT SON OF A...HIM AND THAT REDHEAD BANSHEE WERE RIGHT HERE. LOOKED ME IN THE EYE--
CHAIRMAN OF THE JOINT CHIEFS, MR. GANTRY.
ADMIRAL. THE PRESIDENT'S IN WITH THE NATIONAL SECURITY ADVISOR--
HIS CHIEF OF STAFF WILL DO.
THIS WON'T TAKE LONG.
WHAT IS "PROJECT BEAKHEAD"?
WE'VE BEEN PREPPING FOR MARINE WAR SINCE ATLANTIS MADE THE WATCH LIST OF ROGUE STATES IN OH-FIVE.
THEY HAVE SUPERIOR TECH. SURFACE AND SUB.
PROJECT BEAKHEAD WAS DEVELOPED TO GIVE US THE CAPABILITY TO TAKE OUT THE ENEMY HEAD OF STATE. AND CRIPPLE THEM.
HE ISN'T BIN LADEN OR SADDAM, ADMIRAL MEDDINGHOUSE. WITH RESPECT TO THE NAVY SEALS, THEY WON'T--
IN HERE, MR. GANTRY.

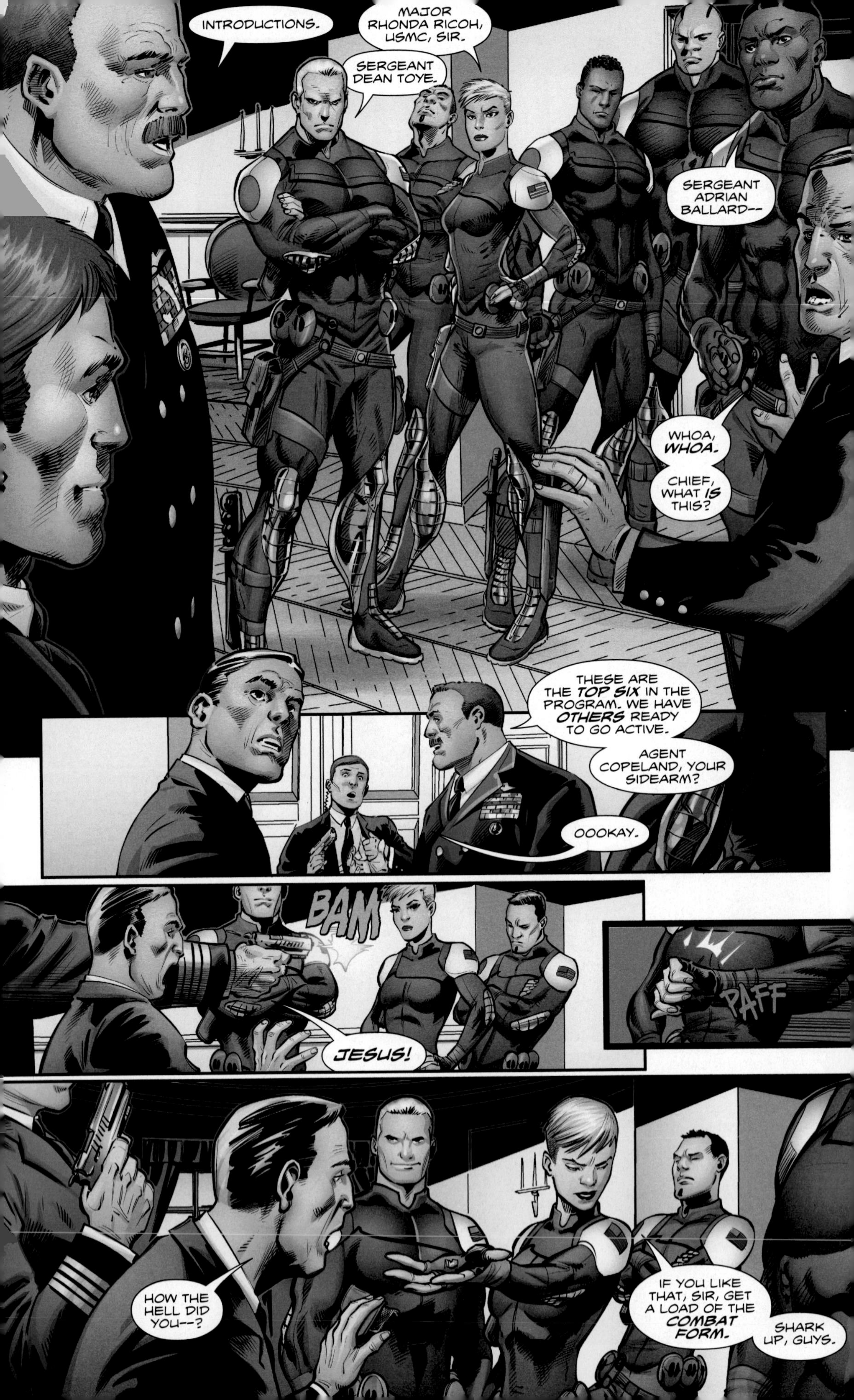
INTRODUCTIONS.
MAJOR RHONDA RICOH, USMC, SIR.
SERGEANT DEAN TOYE.
SERGEANT ADRIAN BALLARD--
WHOA, WHOA.
CHIEF, WHAT IS THIS?
THESE ARE THE TOP SIX IN THE PROGRAM. WE HAVE OTHERS READY TO GO ACTIVE.
AGENT COPELAND, YOUR SIDEARM?
OOOKAY.
BAM
JESUS!
PAFF
HOW THE HELL DID YOU--?
IF YOU LIKE THAT, SIR, GET A LOAD OF THE COMBAT FORM.
SHARK UP, GUYS.

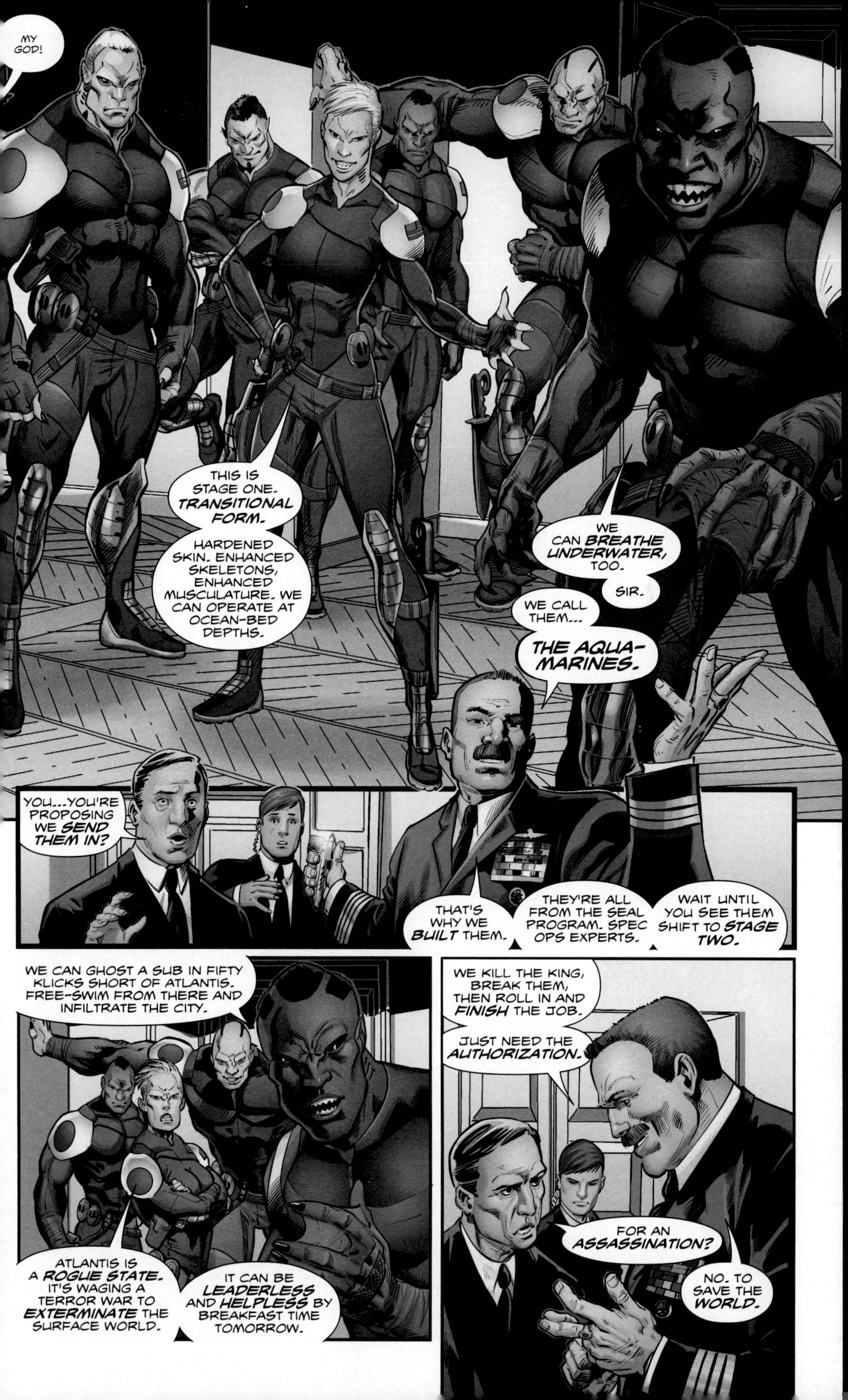

MY GOD!
THIS IS STAGE ONE. TRANSITIONAL FORM.
HARDENED SKIN. ENHANCED SKELETONS, ENHANCED MUSCULATURE. WE CAN OPERATE AT OCEAN-BED DEPTHS.
WE CAN BREATHE UNDERWATER, TOO.
SIR.
WE CALL THEM...
THE AQUA-MARINES.
YOU...YOU'RE PROPOSING WE SEND THEM IN?
THAT'S WHY WE BUILT THEM.
THEY'RE ALL FROM THE SEAL PROGRAM. SPEC OPS EXPERTS.
WAIT UNTIL YOU SEE THEM SHIFT TO STAGE TWO.
WE CAN GHOST A SUB IN FIFTY KLICKS SHORT OF ATLANTIS. FREE-SWIM FROM THERE AND INFILTRATE THE CITY.
ATLANTIS IS A ROGUE STATE. IT'S WAGING A TERROR WAR TO EXTERMINATE THE SURFACE WORLD.
IT CAN BE LEADERLESS AND HELPLESS BY BREAKFAST TIME TOMORROW.
WE KILL THE KING, BREAK THEM, THEN ROLL IN AND FINISH THE JOB.
JUST NEED THE AUTHORIZATION.
FOR AN ASSASSINATION?
NO. TO SAVE THE WORLD.

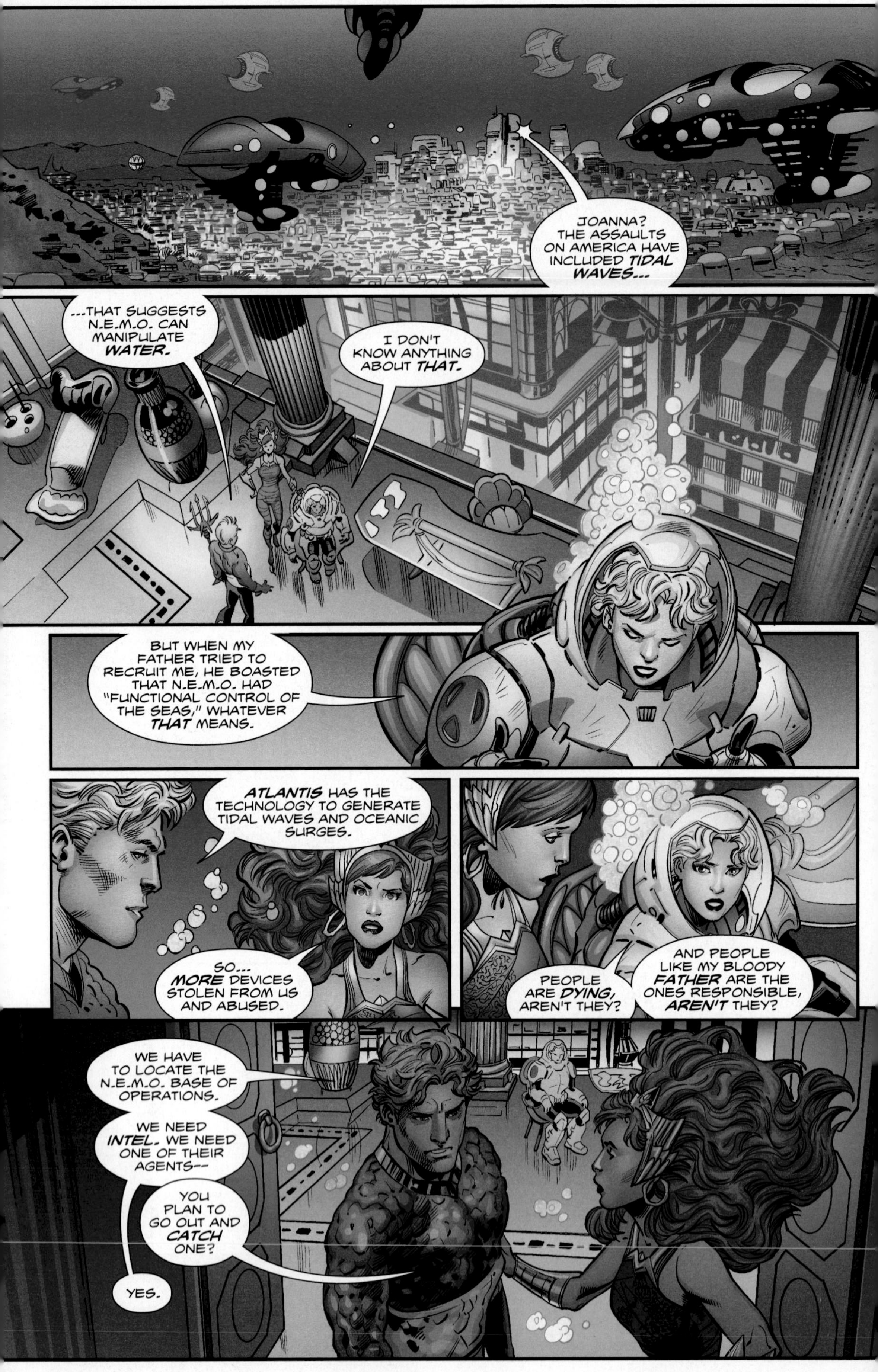
JOANNA? THE ASSAULTS ON AMERICA HAVE INCLUDED TIDAL WAVES...
...THAT SUGGESTS N.E.M.O. CAN MANIPULATE WATER.
I DON'T KNOW ANYTHING ABOUT THAT.
BUT WHEN MY FATHER TRIED TO RECRUIT ME, HE BOASTED THAT N.E.M.O. HAD "FUNCTIONAL CONTROL OF THE SEAS," WHATEVER THAT MEANS.
ATLANTIS HAS THE TECHNOLOGY TO GENERATE TIDAL WAVES AND OCEANIC SURGES.
SO... MORE DEVICES STOLEN FROM US AND ABUSED.
PEOPLE ARE DYING, AREN'T THEY?
AND PEOPLE LIKE MY BLOODY FATHER ARE THE ONES RESPONSIBLE, AREN'T THEY?
WE HAVE TO LOCATE THE N.E.M.O. BASE OF OPERATIONS.
WE NEED INTEL. WE NEED ONE OF THEIR AGENTS--
YOU PLAN TO GO OUT AND CATCH ONE?
YES.

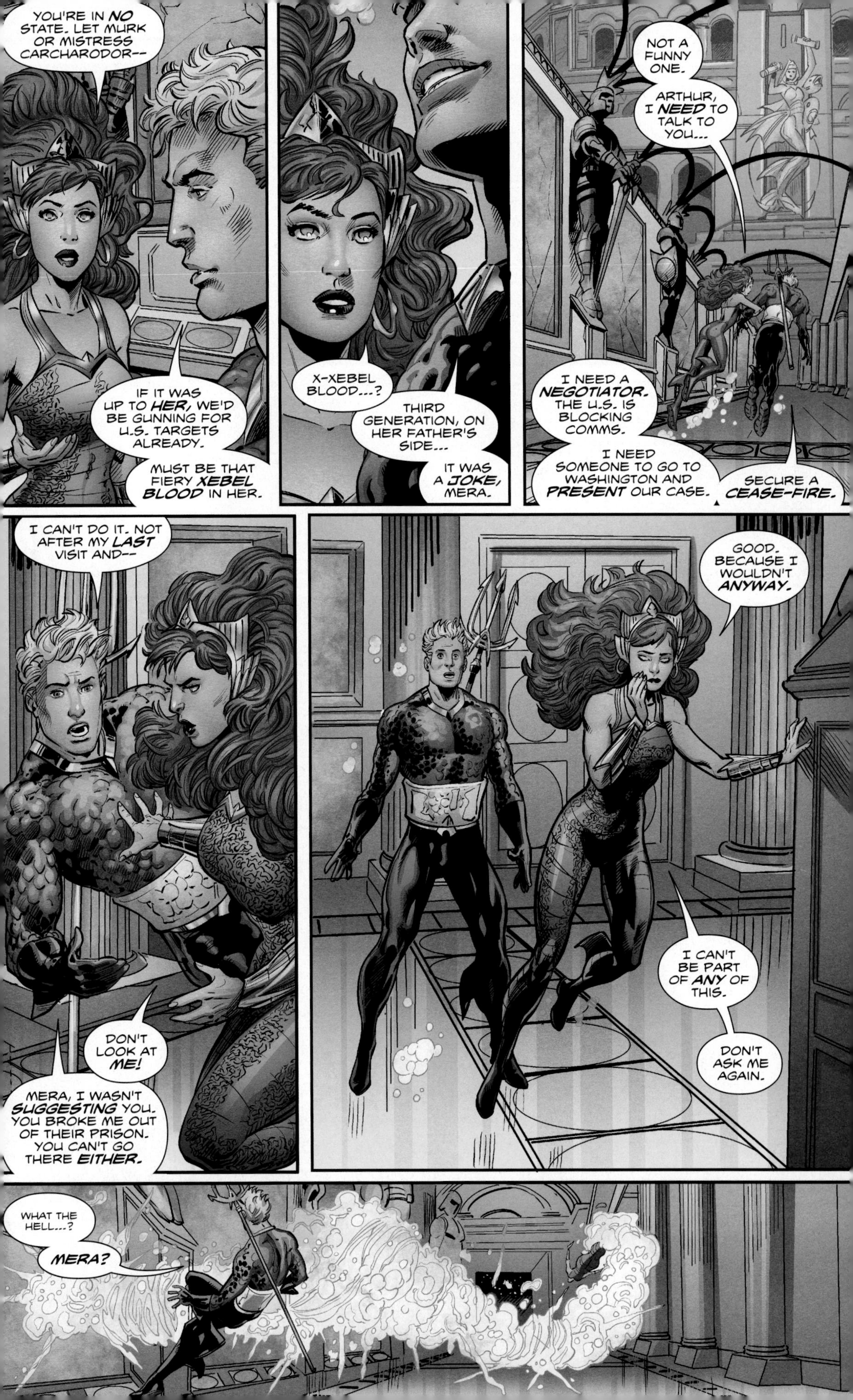

YOU'RE IN NO STATE. LET MURK OR MISTRESS CARCHARODOR--
IF IT WAS UP TO HER, WE'D BE GUNNING FOR U.S. TARGETS ALREADY.
MUST BE THAT FIERY XEBEL BLOOD IN HER.
X-XEBEL BLOOD...?
THIRD GENERATION, ON HER FATHER'S SIDE...
IT WAS A JOKE, MERA.
NOT A FUNNY ONE.
ARTHUR, I NEED TO TALK TO YOU...
I NEED A NEGOTIATOR. THE U.S. IS BLOCKING COMMS.
I NEED SOMEONE TO GO TO WASHINGTON AND PRESENT OUR CASE.
SECURE A CEASE-FIRE.
I CAN'T DO IT. NOT AFTER MY LAST VISIT AND--
DON'T LOOK AT ME!
MERA, I WASN'T SUGGESTING YOU. YOU BROKE ME OUT OF THEIR PRISON. YOU CAN'T GO THERE EITHER.
GOOD. BECAUSE I WOULDN'T ANYWAY.
I CAN'T BE PART OF ANY OF THIS.
DON'T ASK ME AGAIN.
WHAT THE HELL...?
MERA?

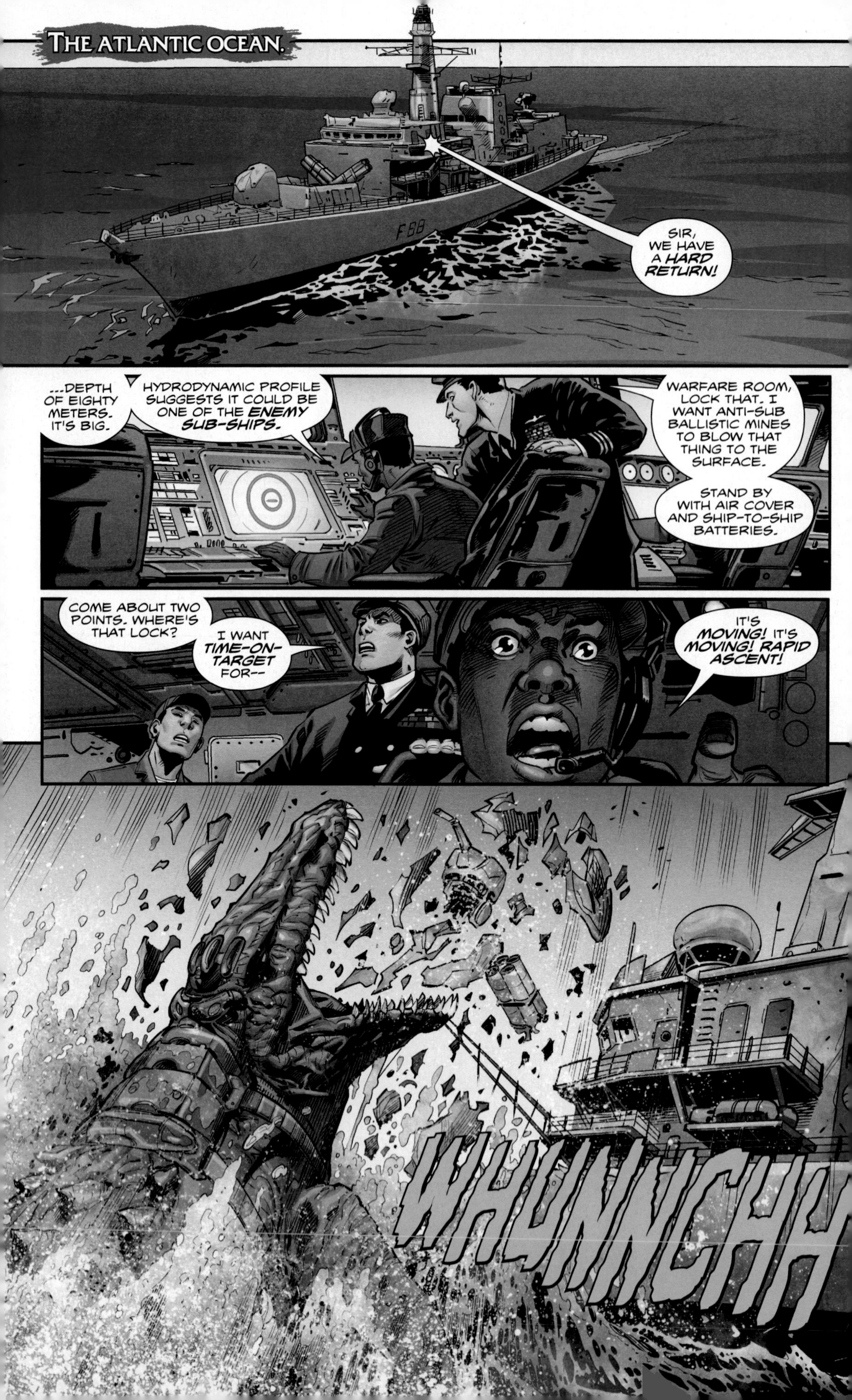

THE ATLANTIC OCEAN.
F88
SIR, WE HAVE A HARD RETURN!
...DEPTH OF EIGHTY METERS. IT'S BIG.
HYDRODYNAMIC PROFILE SUGGESTS IT COULD BE ONE OF THE ENEMY SUB-SHIPS.
WARFARE ROOM, LOCK THAT. I WANT ANTI-SUB BALLISTIC MINES TO BLOW THAT THING TO THE SURFACE.
STAND BY WITH AIR COVER AND SHIP-TO-SHIP BATTERIES.
COME ABOUT TWO POINTS. WHERE'S THAT LOCK?
I WANT TIME-ON-TARGET FOR--
IT'S MOVING! IT'S MOVING! RAPID ASCENT!
WHUNNCHH

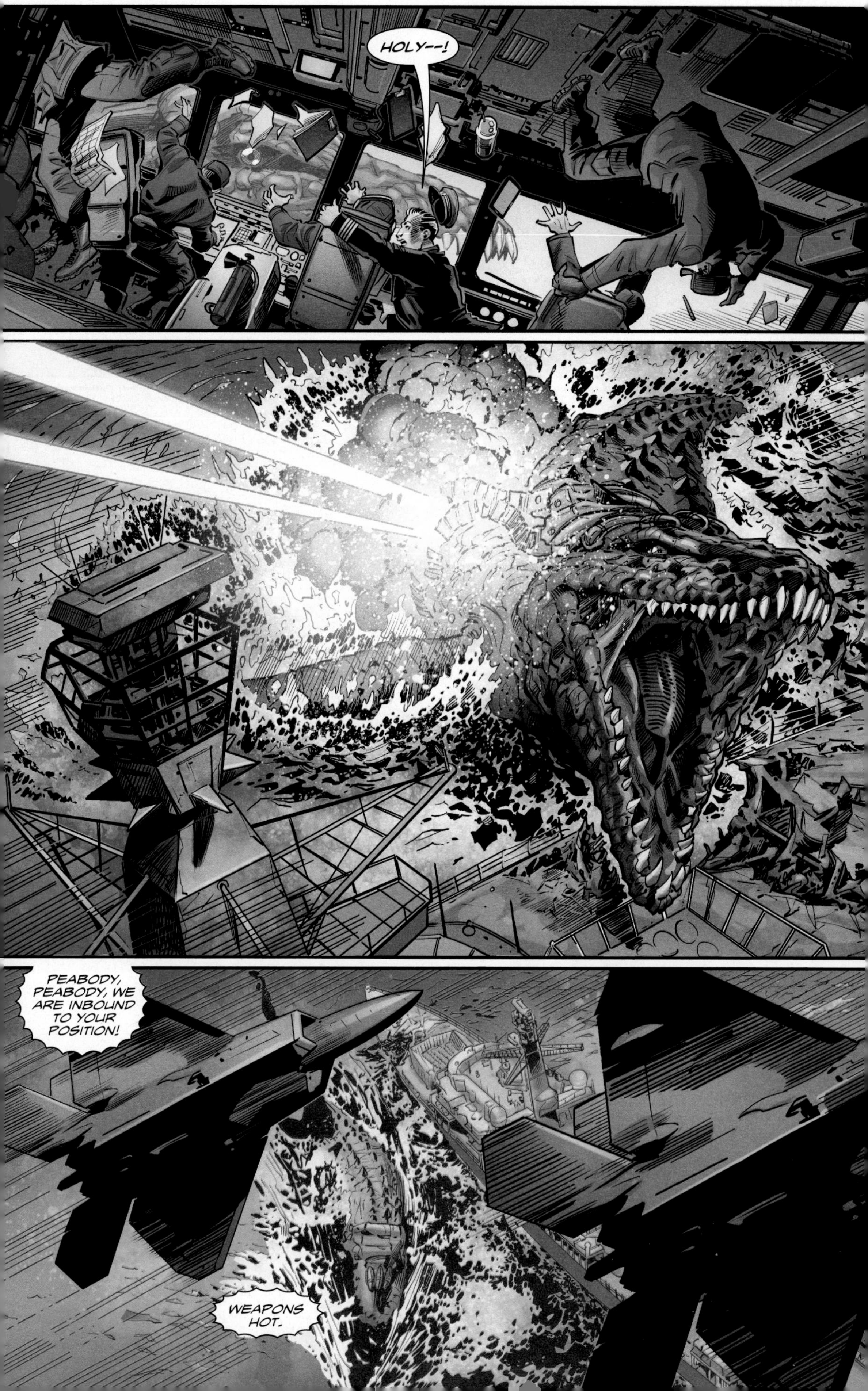
HOLY--!
PEABODY, PEABODY, WE ARE INBOUND TO YOUR POSITION!
WEAPONS HOT.

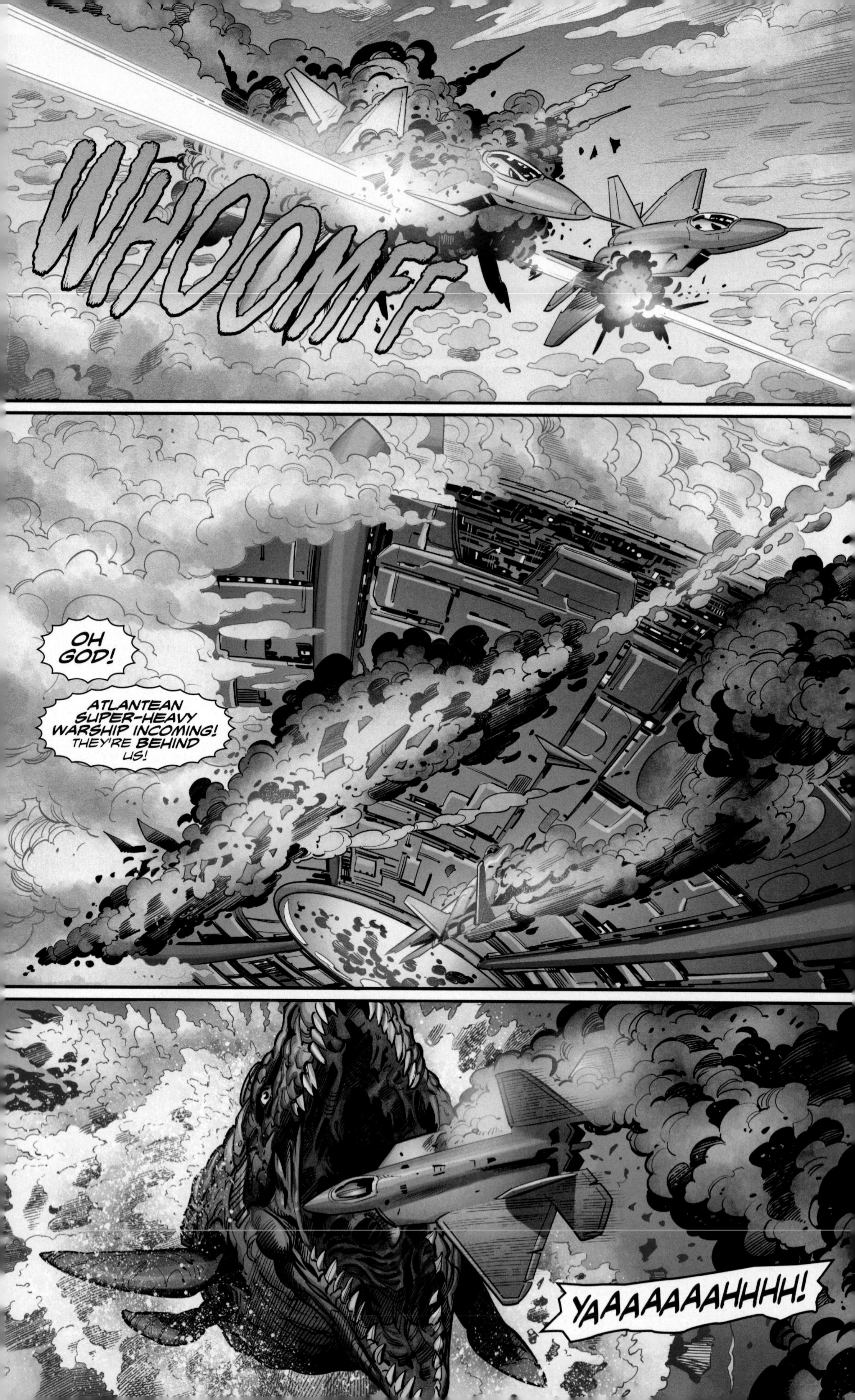
WHOOOMFF
OH GOD!
ATLANTEAN SUPER-HEAVY WARSHIP INCOMING! THEY'RE BEHIND US!
YAAAAAAAHHHH!

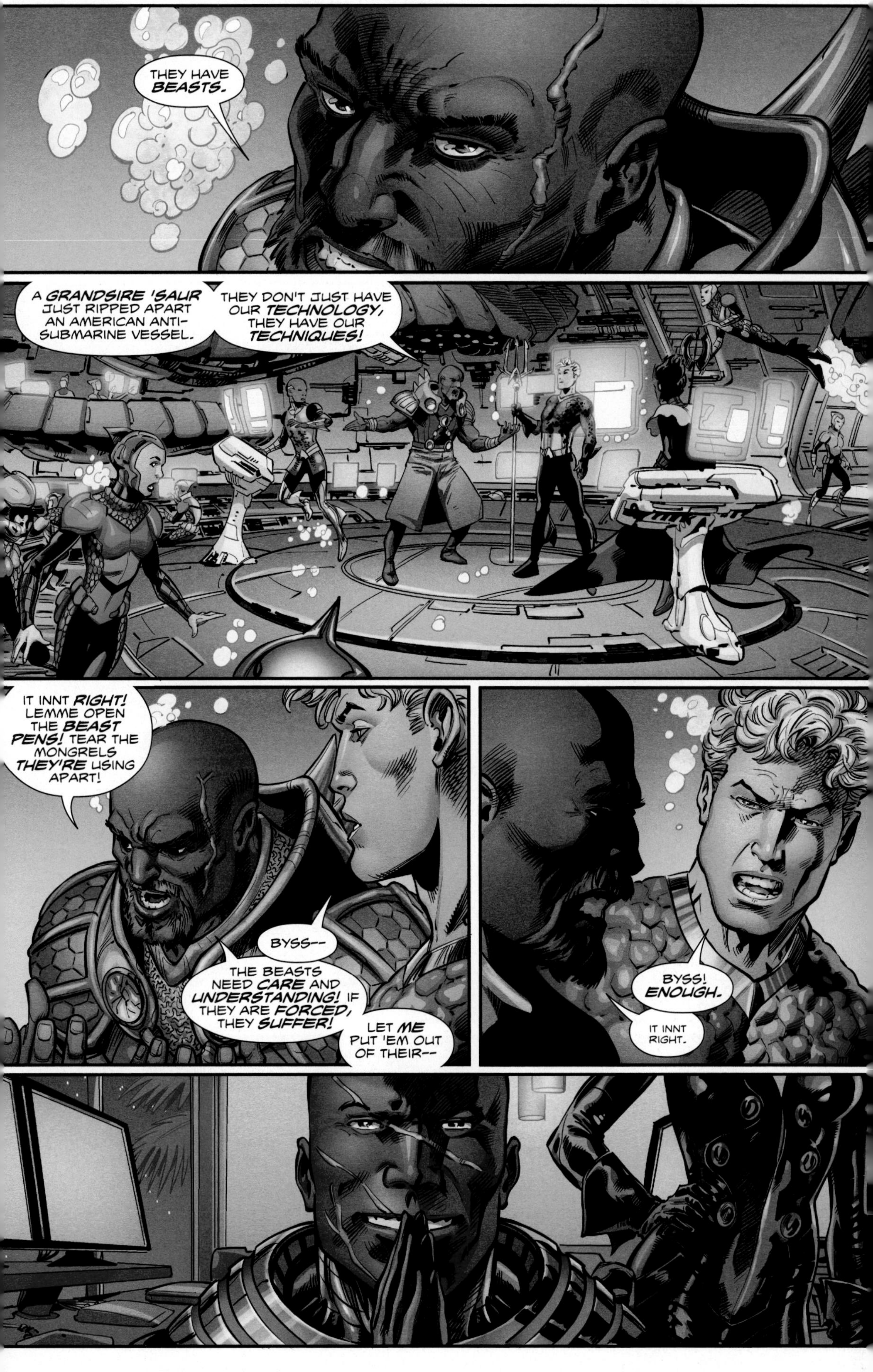
THEY HAVE BEASTS.
A GRANDSIRE 'SAUR JUST RIPPED APART AN AMERICAN ANTI-SUBMARINE VESSEL.
THEY DON'T JUST HAVE OUR TECHNOLOGY, THEY HAVE OUR TECHNIQUES!
IT INNT RIGHT! LEMME OPEN THE BEAST PENS! TEAR THE MONGRELS THEY'RE USING APART!
BYSS--
THE BEASTS NEED CARE AND UNDERSTANDING! IF THEY ARE FORCED, THEY SUFFER!
LET ME PUT 'EM OUT OF THEIR--
BYSS! ENOUGH.
IT INNT RIGHT.

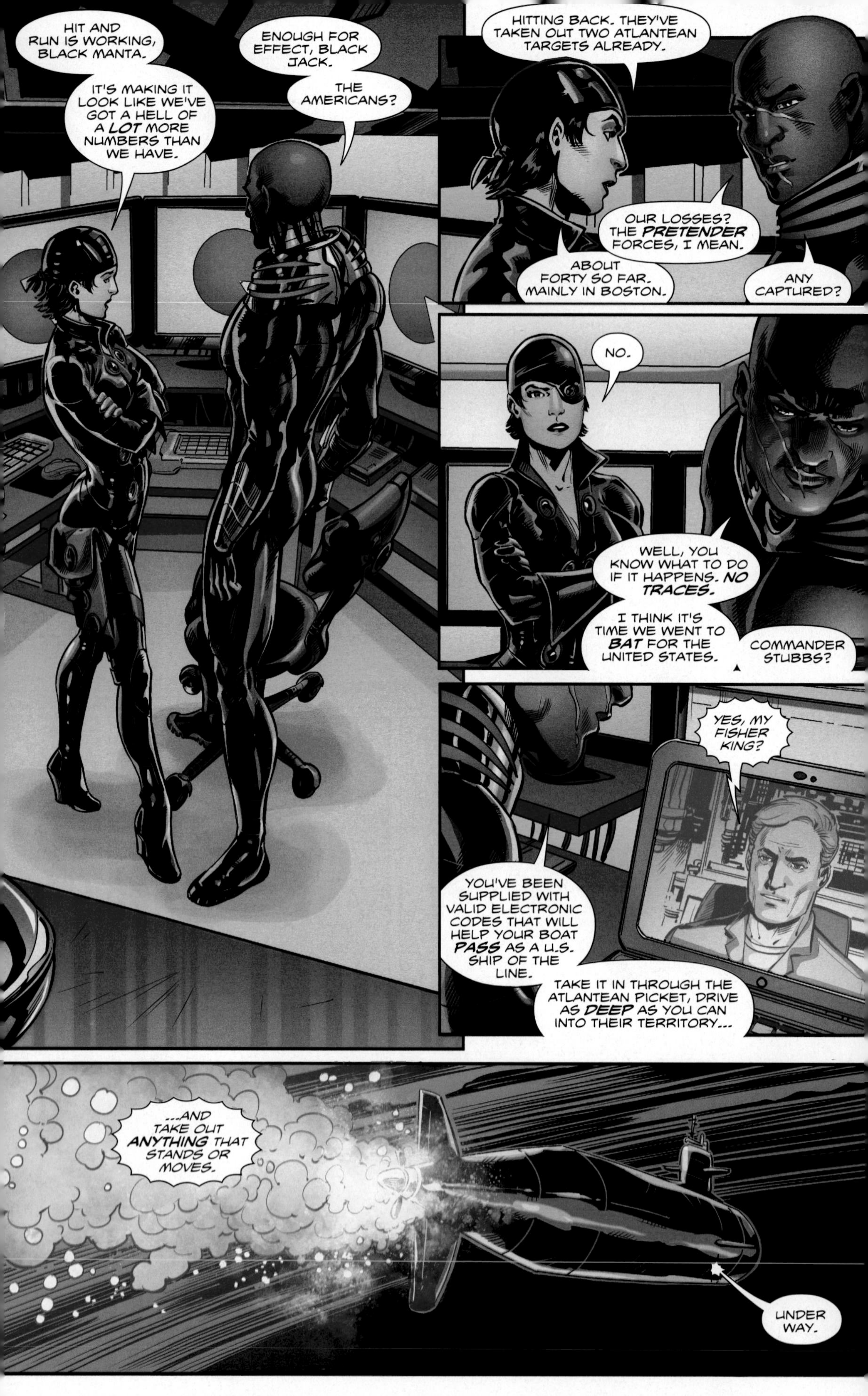
HIT AND RUN IS WORKING, BLACK MANTA.
IT'S MAKING IT LOOK LIKE WE'VE GOT A HELL OF A LOT MORE NUMBERS THAN WE HAVE.
ENOUGH FOR EFFECT, BLACK JACK.
THE AMERICANS?
HITTING BACK. THEY'VE TAKEN OUT TWO ATLANTEAN TARGETS ALREADY.
OUR LOSSES? THE PRETENDER FORCES, I MEAN.
ABOUT FORTY SO FAR. MAINLY IN BOSTON.
ANY CAPTURED?
NO.
WELL, YOU KNOW WHAT TO DO IF IT HAPPENS. NO TRACES.
I THINK IT'S TIME WE WENT TO BAT FOR THE UNITED STATES.
COMMANDER STUBBS?
YES, MY FISHER KING?
YOU'VE BEEN SUPPLIED WITH VALID ELECTRONIC CODES THAT WILL HELP YOUR BOAT PASS AS A U.S. SHIP OF THE LINE.
TAKE IT IN THROUGH THE ATLANTEAN PICKET, DRIVE AS DEEP AS YOU CAN INTO THEIR TERRITORY...
...AND TAKE OUT ANYTHING THAT STANDS OR MOVES.
UNDER WAY.

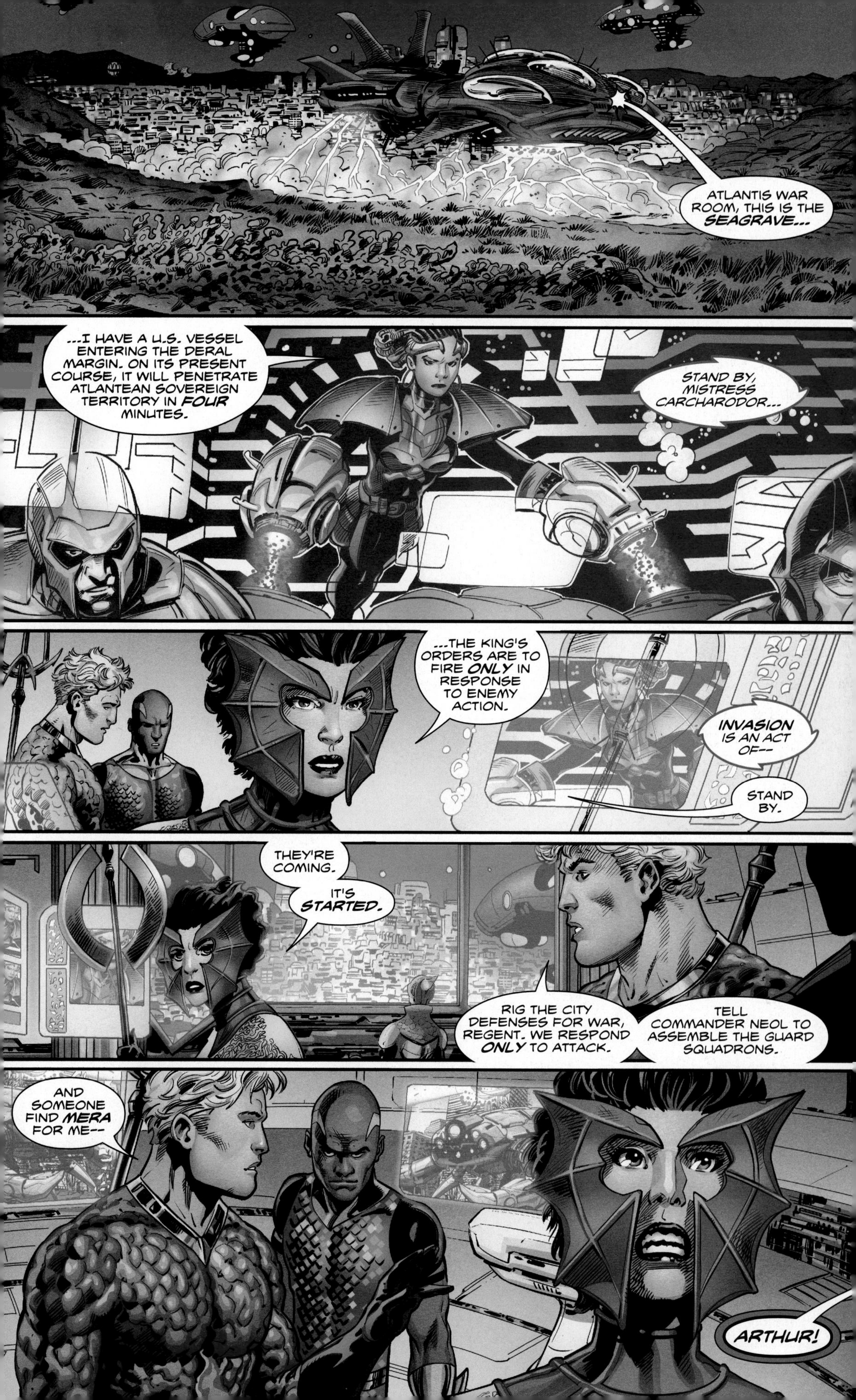
ATLANTIS WAR ROOM, THIS IS THE SEAGRAVE...
...I HAVE A U.S. VESSEL ENTERING THE DERAL MARGIN. ON ITS PRESENT COURSE, IT WILL PENETRATE ATLANTEAN SOVEREIGN TERRITORY IN FOUR MINUTES.
STAND BY, MISTRESS CARCHARODOR...
...THE KING'S ORDERS ARE TO FIRE ONLY IN RESPONSE TO ENEMY ACTION.
INVASION IS AN ACT OF--
STAND BY.
THEY'RE COMING.
IT'S STARTED.
RIG THE CITY DEFENSES FOR WAR, REGENT. WE RESPOND ONLY TO ATTACK.
TELL COMMANDER NEOL TO ASSEMBLE THE GUARD SQUADRONS.
AND SOMEONE FIND MERA FOR ME--
ARTHUR!

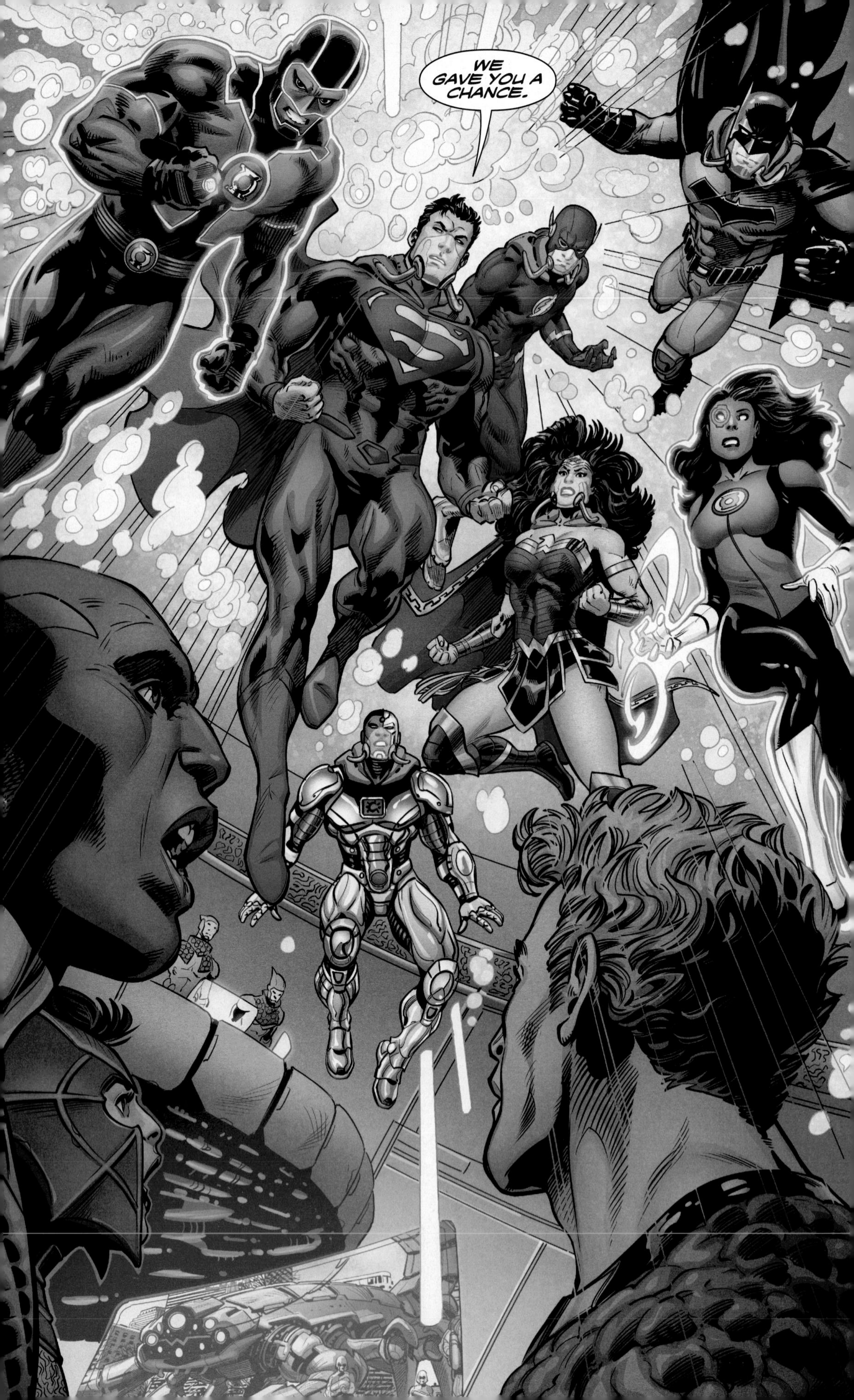
WE GAVE YOU A CHANCE.

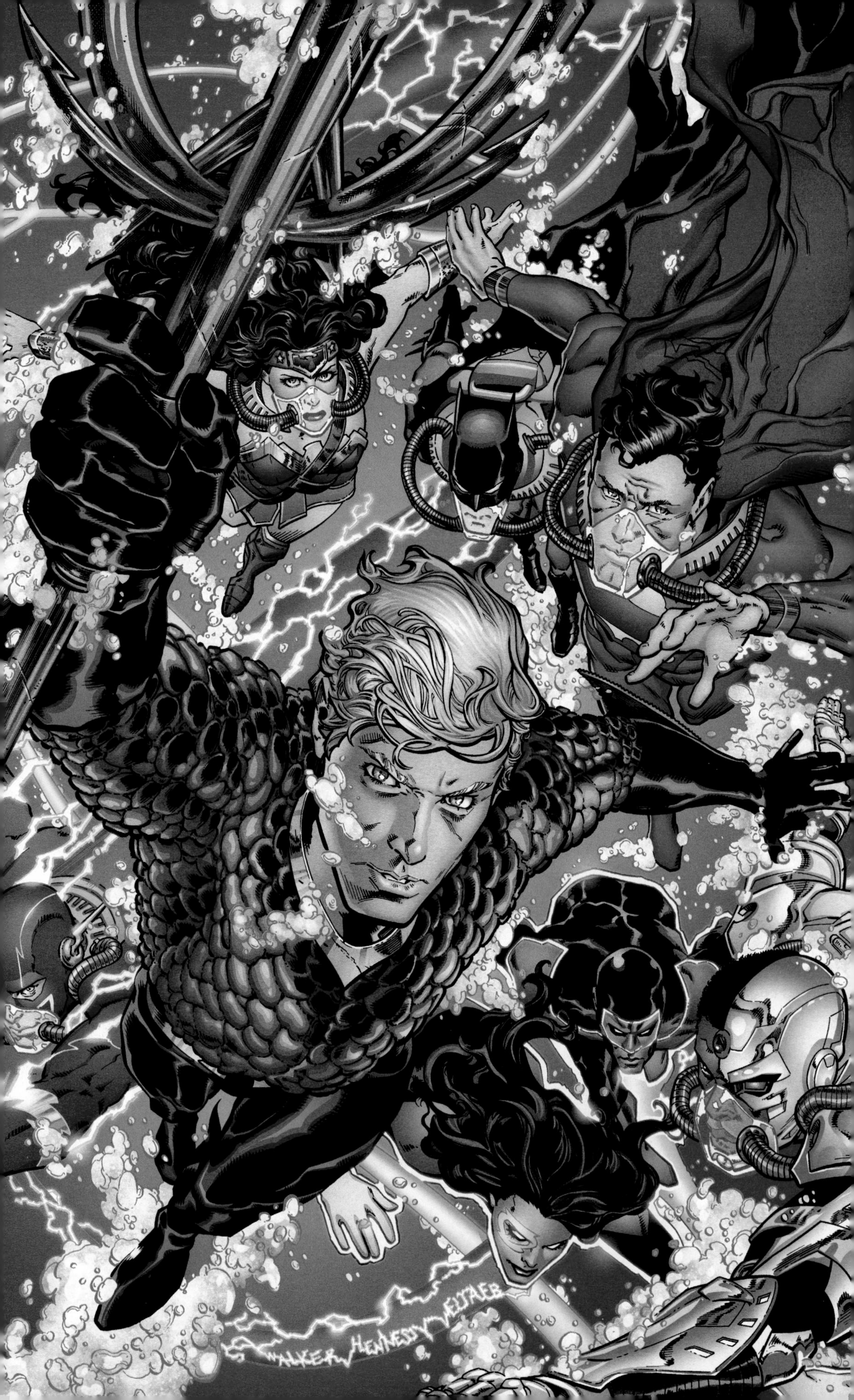
WALKER HENNESSY ELTAEB

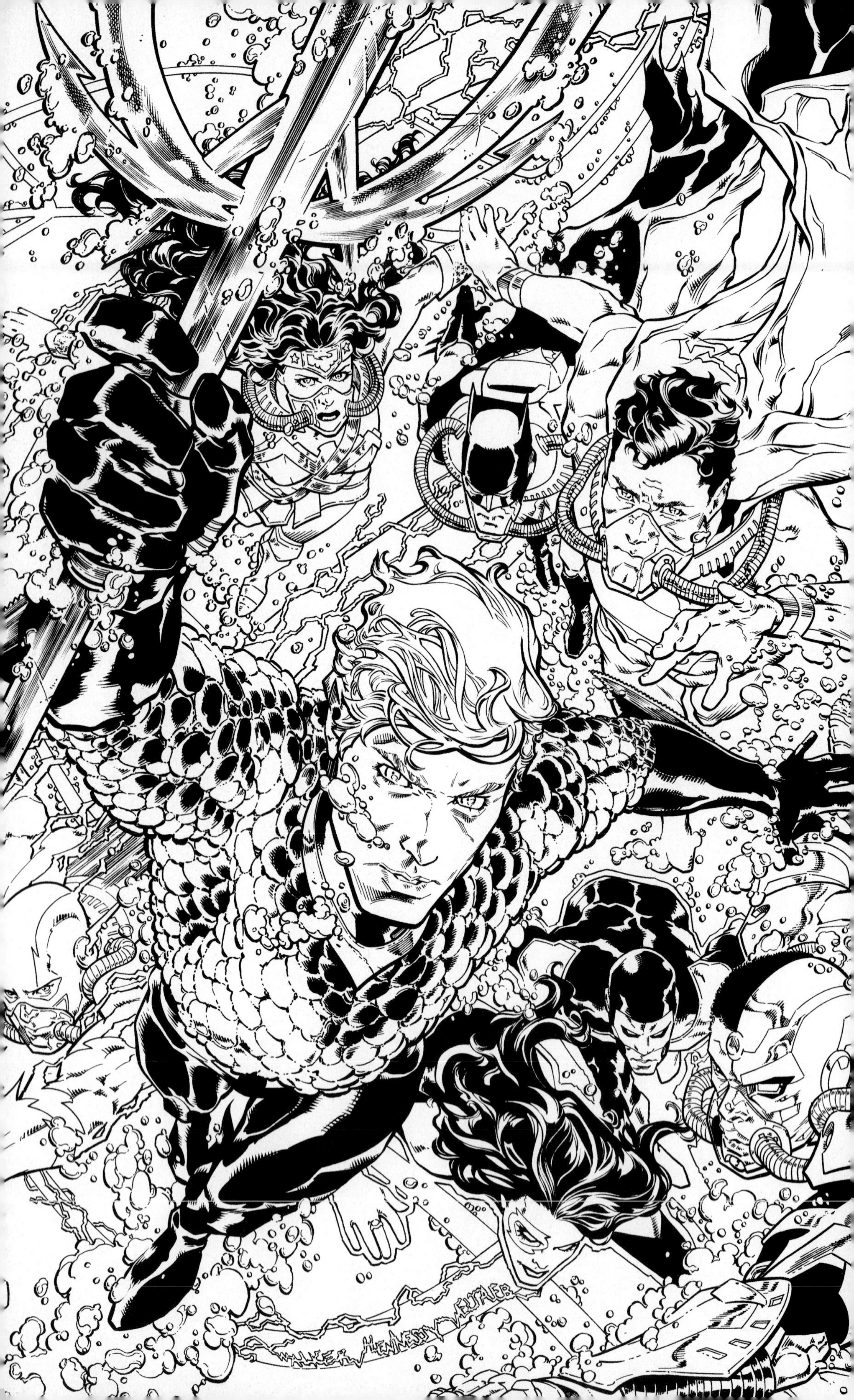

WALKER
HENNESSY

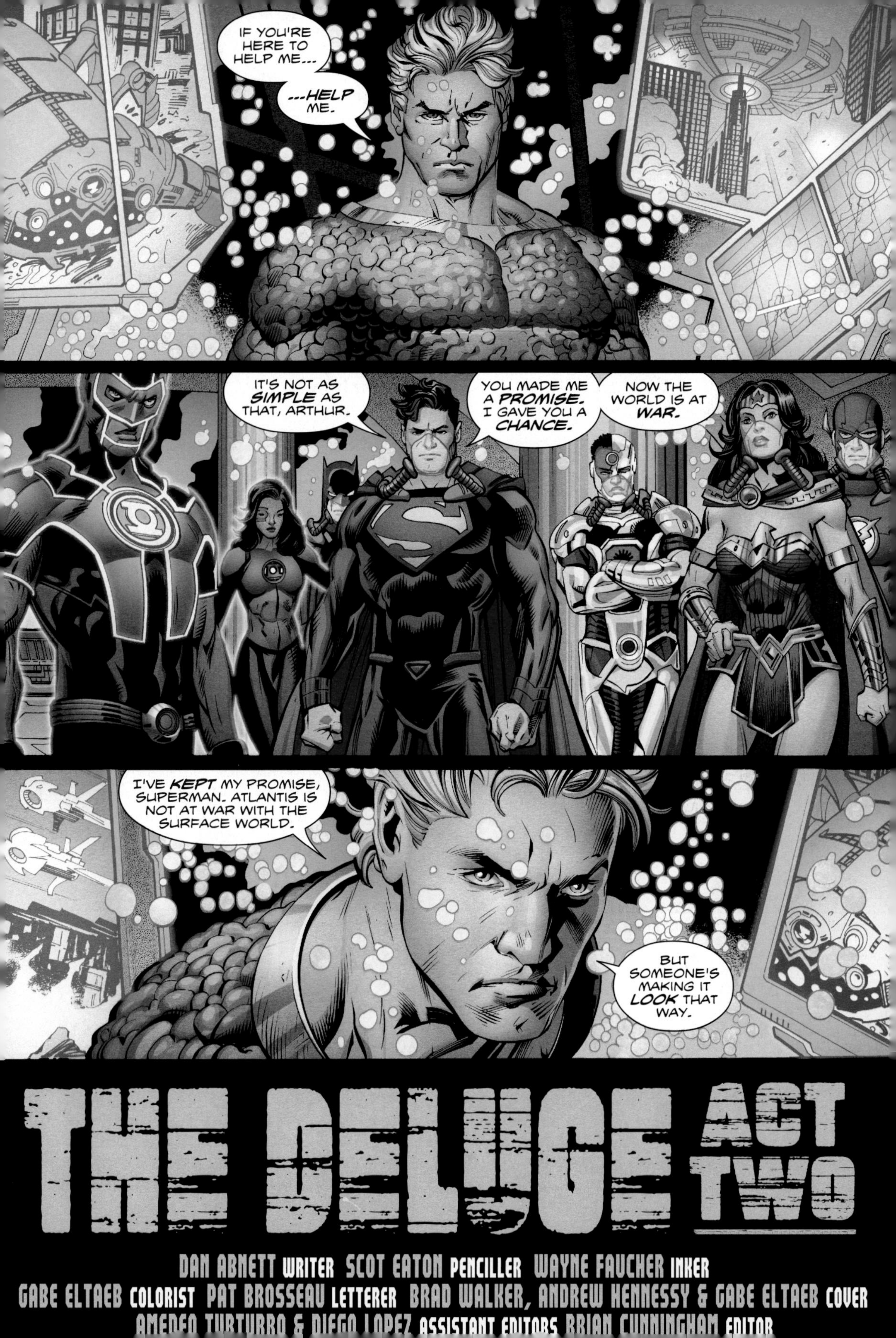
IF YOU'RE HERE TO HELP ME...
...HELP ME.
IT'S NOT AS SIMPLE AS THAT, ARTHUR.
YOU MADE ME A PROMISE. I GAVE YOU A CHANCE.
NOW THE WORLD IS AT WAR.
I'VE KEPT MY PROMISE, SUPERMAN. ATLANTIS IS NOT AT WAR WITH THE SURFACE WORLD.
BUT SOMEONE'S MAKING IT LOOK THAT WAY.

THE DELUGE ACT TWO

DAN ABNETT WRITER SCOT EATON PENCILLER WAYNE FAUCHER INKER
GABE ELTAEB COLORIST PAT BROSSEAU LETTERER BRAD WALKER, ANDREW HENNESSY & GABE ELTAEB COVER
AMEDEO TURTURRO & DIEGO LOPEZ ASSISTANT EDITORS BRIAN CUNNINGHAM EDITOR

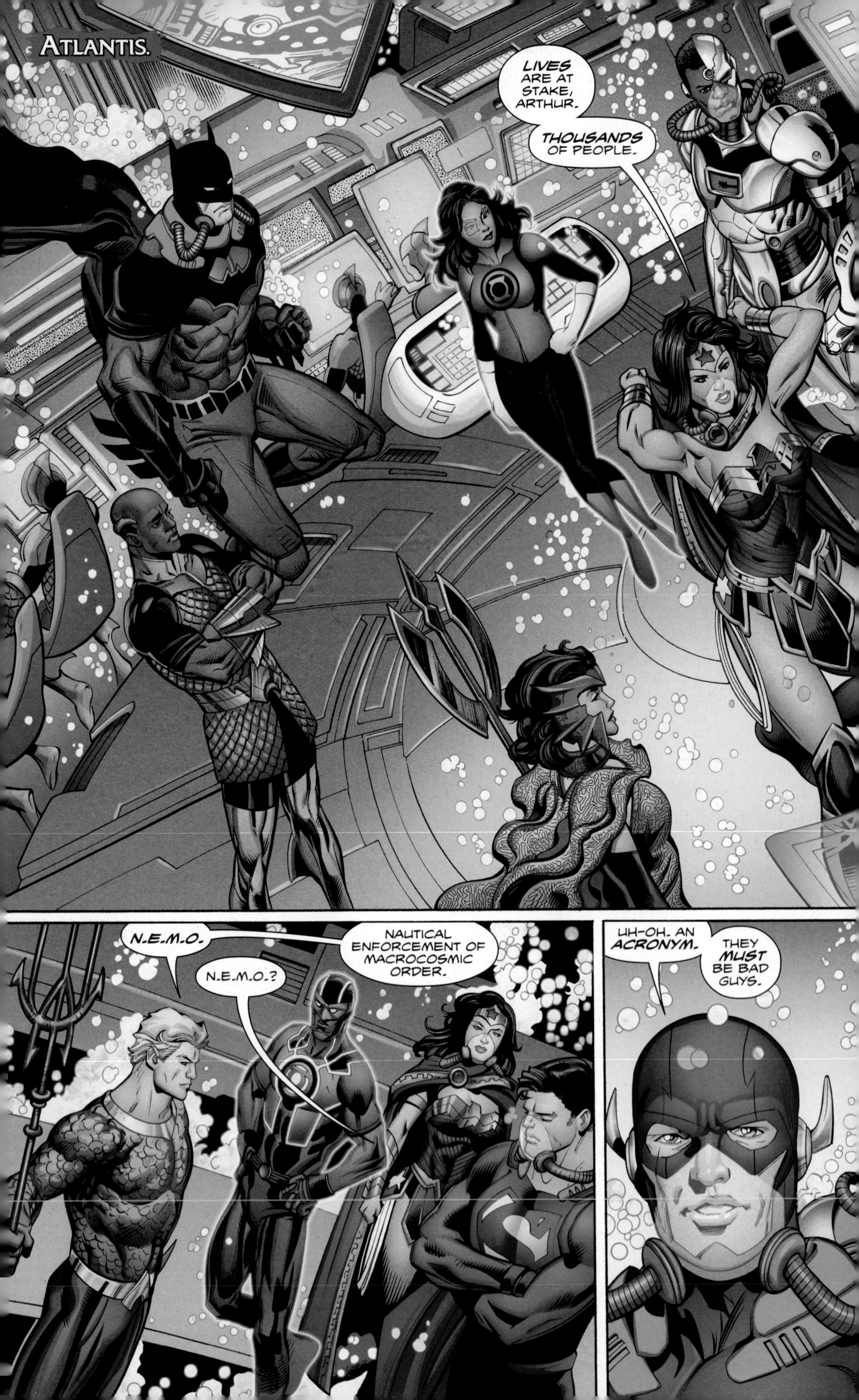
ATLANTIS.
LIVES ARE AT STAKE, ARTHUR.
THOUSANDS OF PEOPLE.
N.E.M.O.
N.E.M.O.?
NAUTICAL ENFORCEMENT OF MACROCOSMIC ORDER.
UH-OH. AN ACRONYM.
THEY MUST BE BAD GUYS.

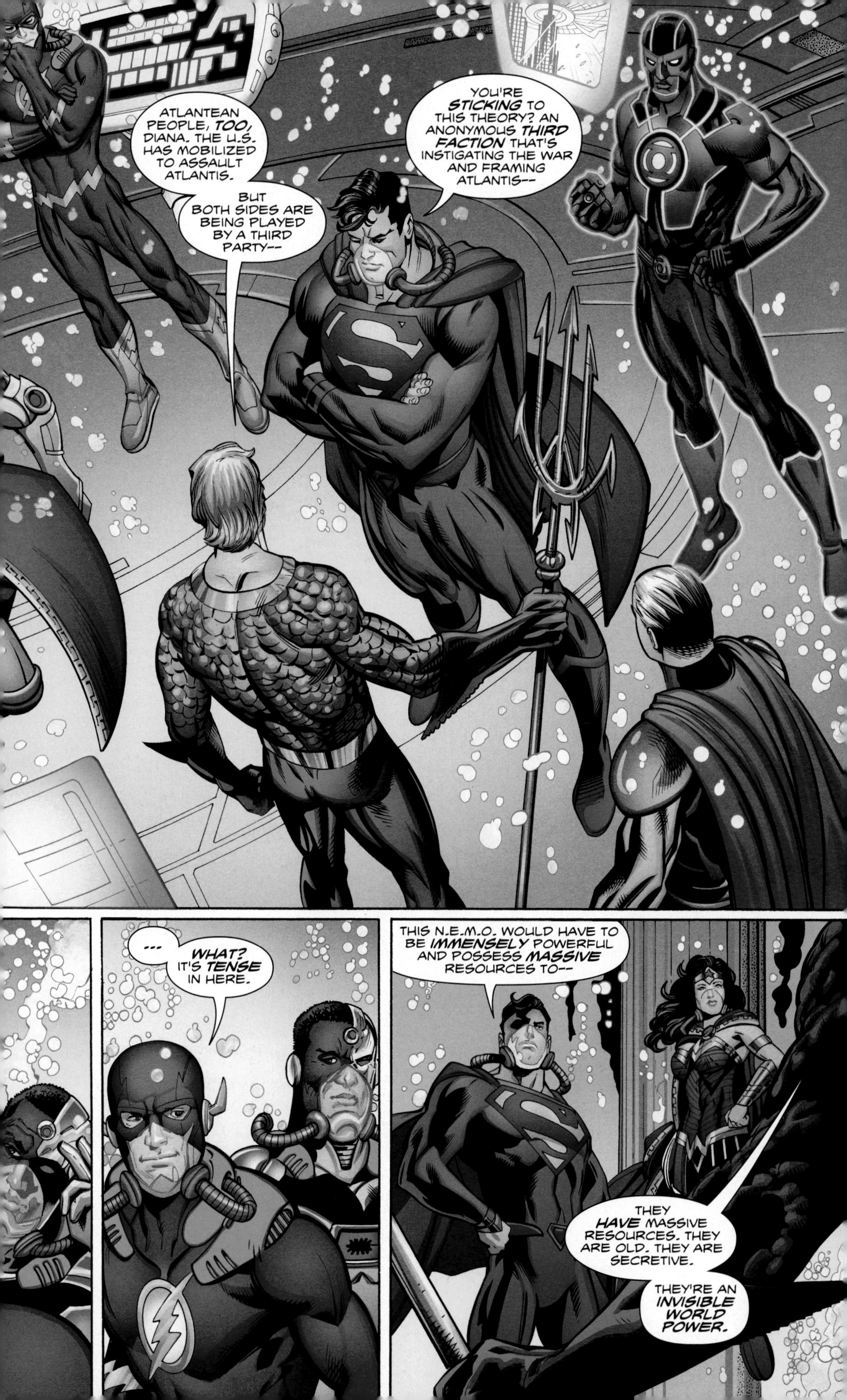
ATLANTEAN PEOPLE, TOO, DIANA. THE U.S. HAS MOBILIZED TO ASSAULT ATLANTIS.
BUT BOTH SIDES ARE BEING PLAYED BY A THIRD PARTY--
YOU'RE STICKING TO THIS THEORY? AN ANONYMOUS THIRD FACTION THAT'S INSTIGATING THE WAR AND FRAMING ATLANTIS--
...WHAT? IT'S TENSE IN HERE.
THIS N.E.M.O. WOULD HAVE TO BE IMMENSELY POWERFUL AND POSSESS MASSIVE RESOURCES TO--
THEY HAVE MASSIVE RESOURCES. THEY ARE OLD. THEY ARE SECRETIVE.
THEY'RE AN INVISIBLE WORLD POWER.

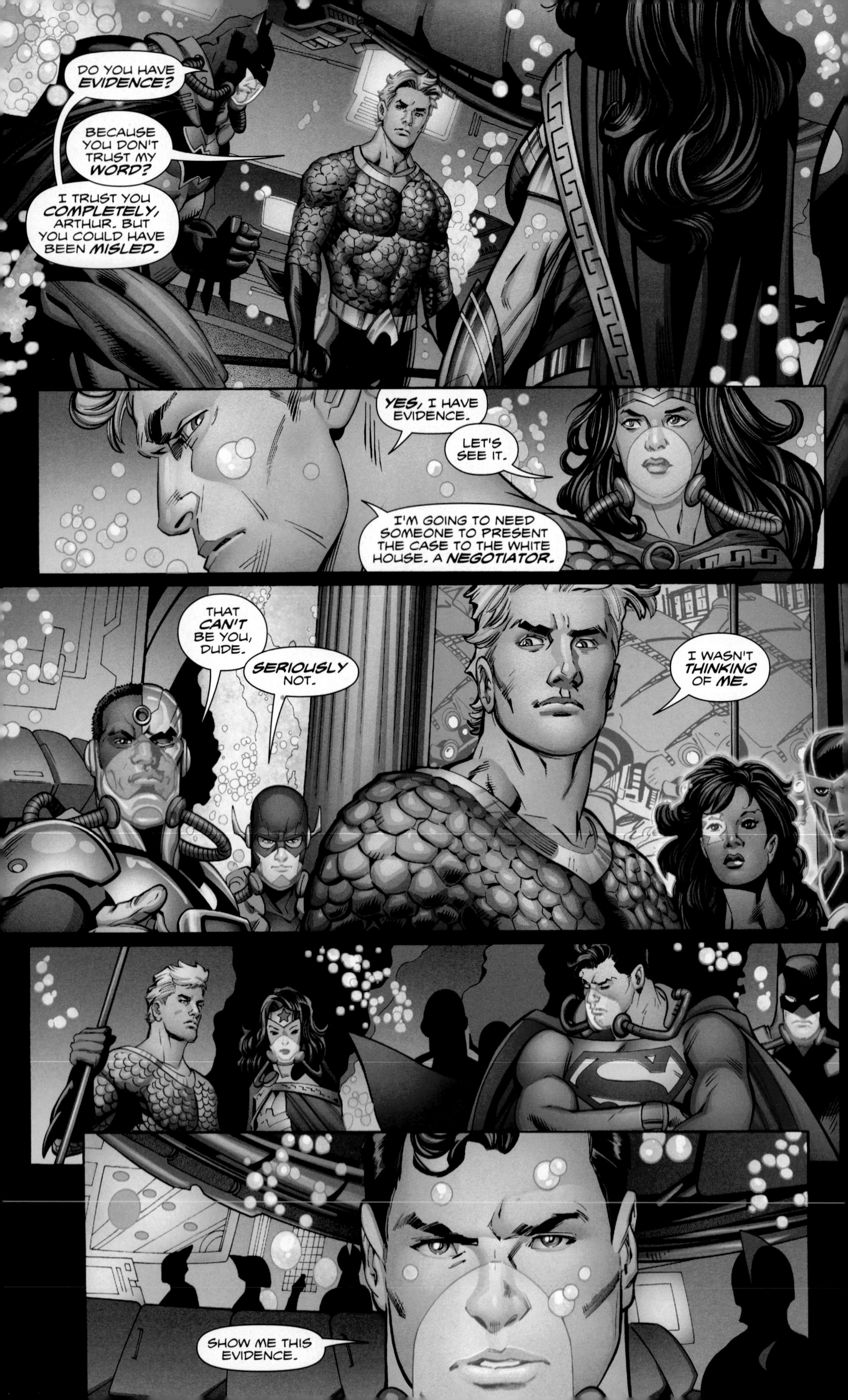
DO YOU HAVE EVIDENCE?
BECAUSE YOU DON'T TRUST MY WORD?
I TRUST YOU COMPLETELY, ARTHUR. BUT YOU COULD HAVE BEEN MISLED.
YES, I HAVE EVIDENCE.
LET'S SEE IT.
I'M GOING TO NEED SOMEONE TO PRESENT THE CASE TO THE WHITE HOUSE. A NEGOTIATOR.
THAT CAN'T BE YOU, DUDE.
SERIOUSLY NOT.
I WASN'T THINKING OF ME.
SHOW ME THIS EVIDENCE.

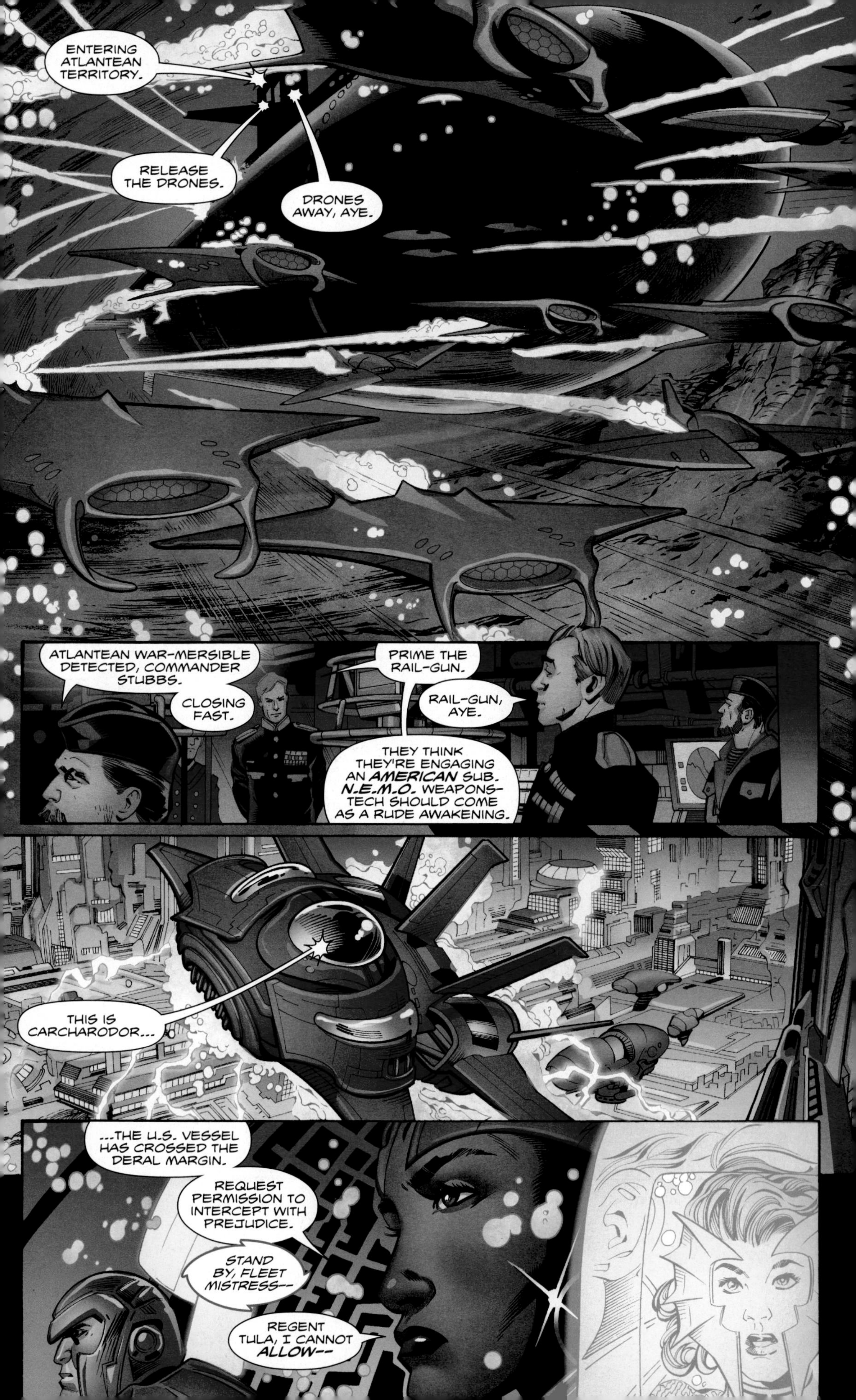
ENTERING ATLANTEAN TERRITORY.
RELEASE THE DRONES.
DRONES AWAY, AYE.
ATLANTEAN WAR-MERSIBLE DETECTED, COMMANDER STUBBS.
CLOSING FAST.
PRIME THE RAIL-GUN.
RAIL-GUN, AYE.
THEY THINK THEY'RE ENGAGING AN AMERICAN SUB. N.E.M.O. WEAPONS-TECH SHOULD COME AS A RUDE AWAKENING.
THIS IS CARCHARODOR...
...THE U.S. VESSEL HAS CROSSED THE DERAL MARGIN.
REQUEST PERMISSION TO INTERCEPT WITH PREJUDICE.
STAND BY, FLEET MISTRESS--
REGENT TULA, I CANNOT ALLOW--

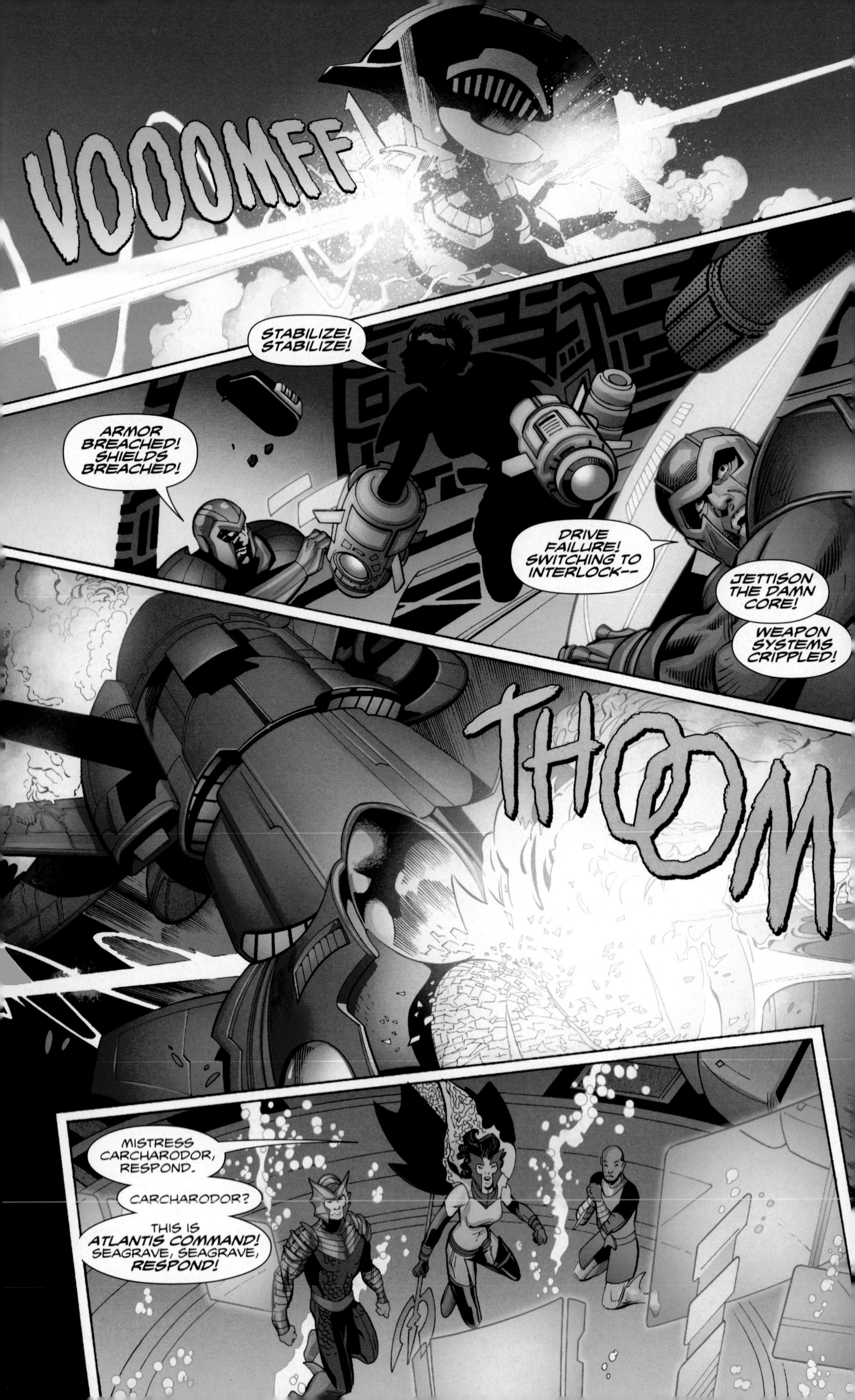
VOOOMFF
STABILIZE! STABILIZE!
ARMOR BREACHED! SHIELDS BREACHED!
DRIVE FAILURE! SWITCHING TO INTERLOCK--
JETTISON THE DAMN CORE!
WEAPON SYSTEMS CRIPPLED!
THOOM
MISTRESS CARCHARODOR, RESPOND.
CARCHARODOR?
THIS IS ATLANTIS COMMAND! SEAGRAVE, SEAGRAVE, RESPOND!

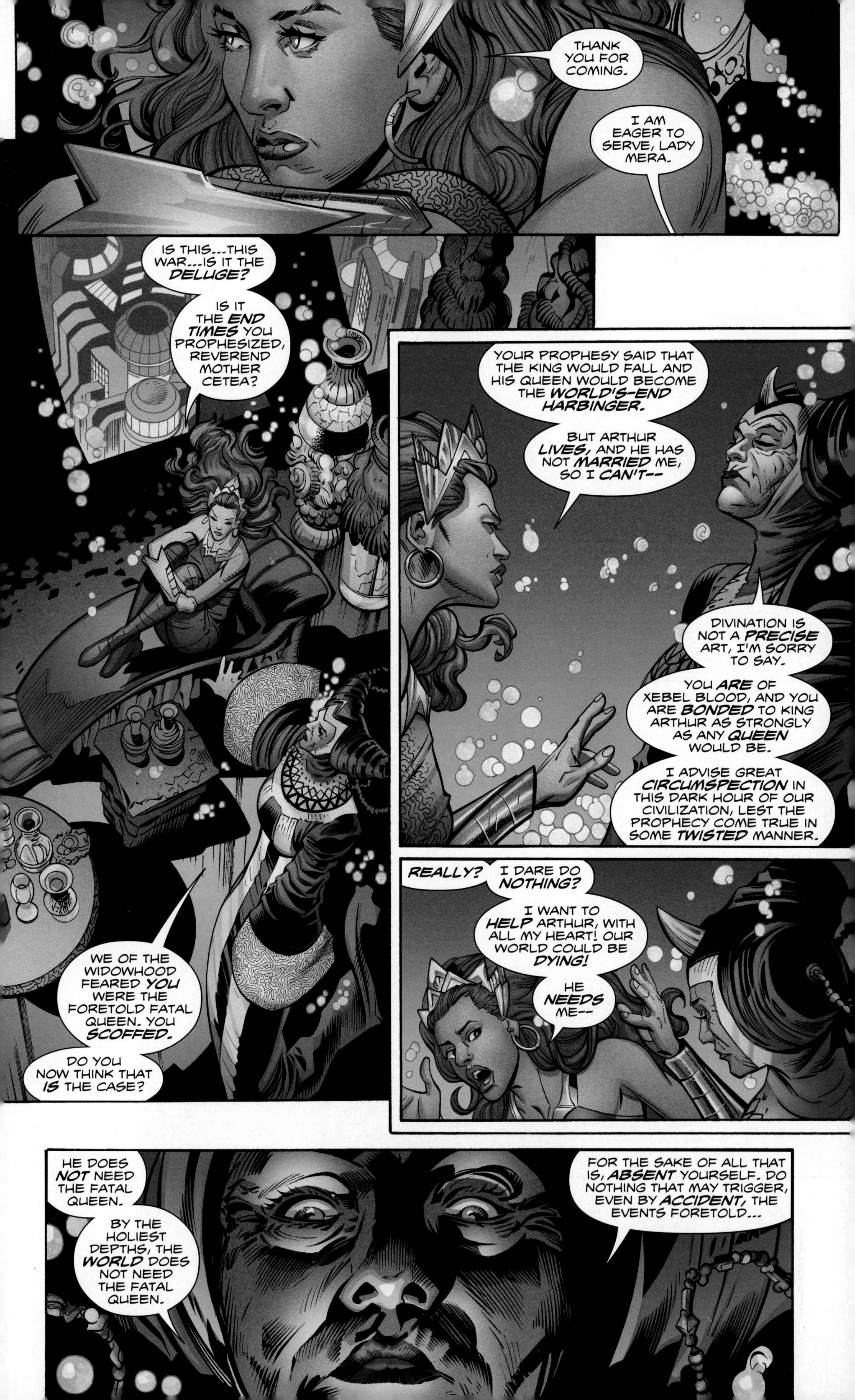
THANK YOU FOR COMING.
I AM EAGER TO SERVE, LADY MERA.
IS THIS...THIS WAR...IS IT THE DELUGE?
IS IT THE END TIMES YOU PROPHESIZED, REVEREND MOTHER CETEA?
WE OF THE WIDOWHOOD FEARED YOU WERE THE FORETOLD FATAL QUEEN. YOU SCOFFED.
DO YOU NOW THINK THAT IS THE CASE?
YOUR PROPHESY SAID THAT THE KING WOULD FALL AND HIS QUEEN WOULD BECOME THE WORLD'S-END HARBINGER.
BUT ARTHUR LIVES, AND HE HAS NOT MARRIED ME, SO I CAN'T--
DIVINATION IS NOT A PRECISE ART, I'M SORRY TO SAY.
YOU ARE OF XEBEL BLOOD, AND YOU ARE BONDED TO KING ARTHUR AS STRONGLY AS ANY QUEEN WOULD BE.
I ADVISE GREAT CIRCUMSPECTION IN THIS DARK HOUR OF OUR CIVILIZATION, LEST THE PROPHECY COME TRUE IN SOME TWISTED MANNER.
REALLY?
I DARE DO NOTHING?
I WANT TO HELP ARTHUR, WITH ALL MY HEART! OUR WORLD COULD BE DYING!
HE NEEDS ME--
HE DOES NOT NEED THE FATAL QUEEN.
BY THE HOLIEST DEPTHS, THE WORLD DOES NOT NEED THE FATAL QUEEN.
FOR THE SAKE OF ALL THAT IS, ABSENT YOURSELF. DO NOTHING THAT MAY TRIGGER, EVEN BY ACCIDENT, THE EVENTS FORETOLD...

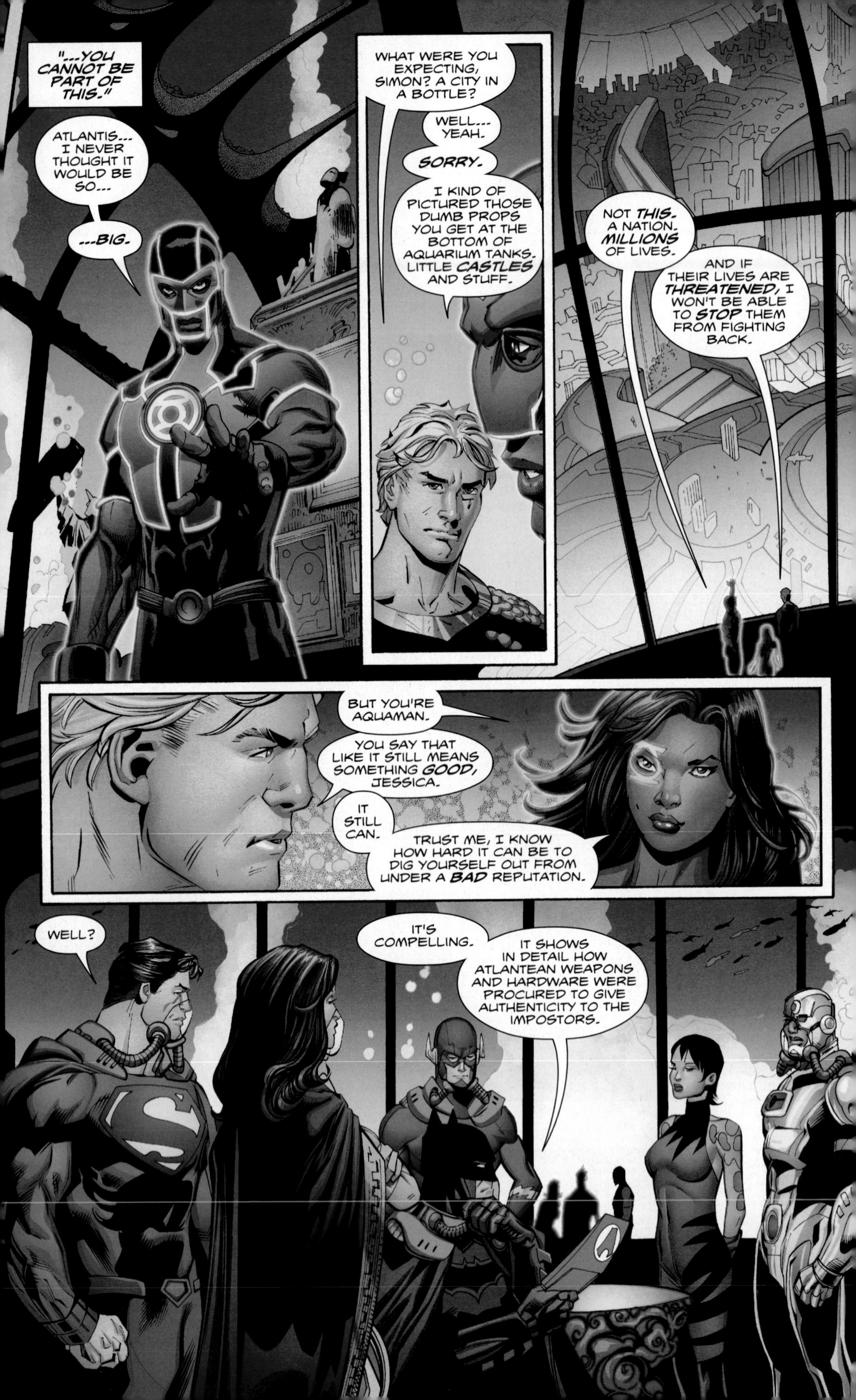
"...YOU CANNOT BE PART OF THIS."
ATLANTIS... I NEVER THOUGHT IT WOULD BE SO...
...BIG.
WHAT WERE YOU EXPECTING, SIMON? A CITY IN A BOTTLE?
WELL... YEAH.
SORRY.
I KIND OF PICTURED THOSE DUMB PROPS YOU GET AT THE BOTTOM OF AQUARIUM TANKS. LITTLE CASTLES AND STUFF.
NOT THIS. A NATION. MILLIONS OF LIVES.
AND IF THEIR LIVES ARE THREATENED, I WON'T BE ABLE TO STOP THEM FROM FIGHTING BACK.
BUT YOU'RE AQUAMAN.
YOU SAY THAT LIKE IT STILL MEANS SOMETHING GOOD, JESSICA.
IT STILL CAN.
TRUST ME, I KNOW HOW HARD IT CAN BE TO DIG YOURSELF OUT FROM UNDER A BAD REPUTATION.
WELL?
IT'S COMPELLING.
IT SHOWS IN DETAIL HOW ATLANTEAN WEAPONS AND HARDWARE WERE PROCURED TO GIVE AUTHENTICITY TO THE IMPOSTORS.

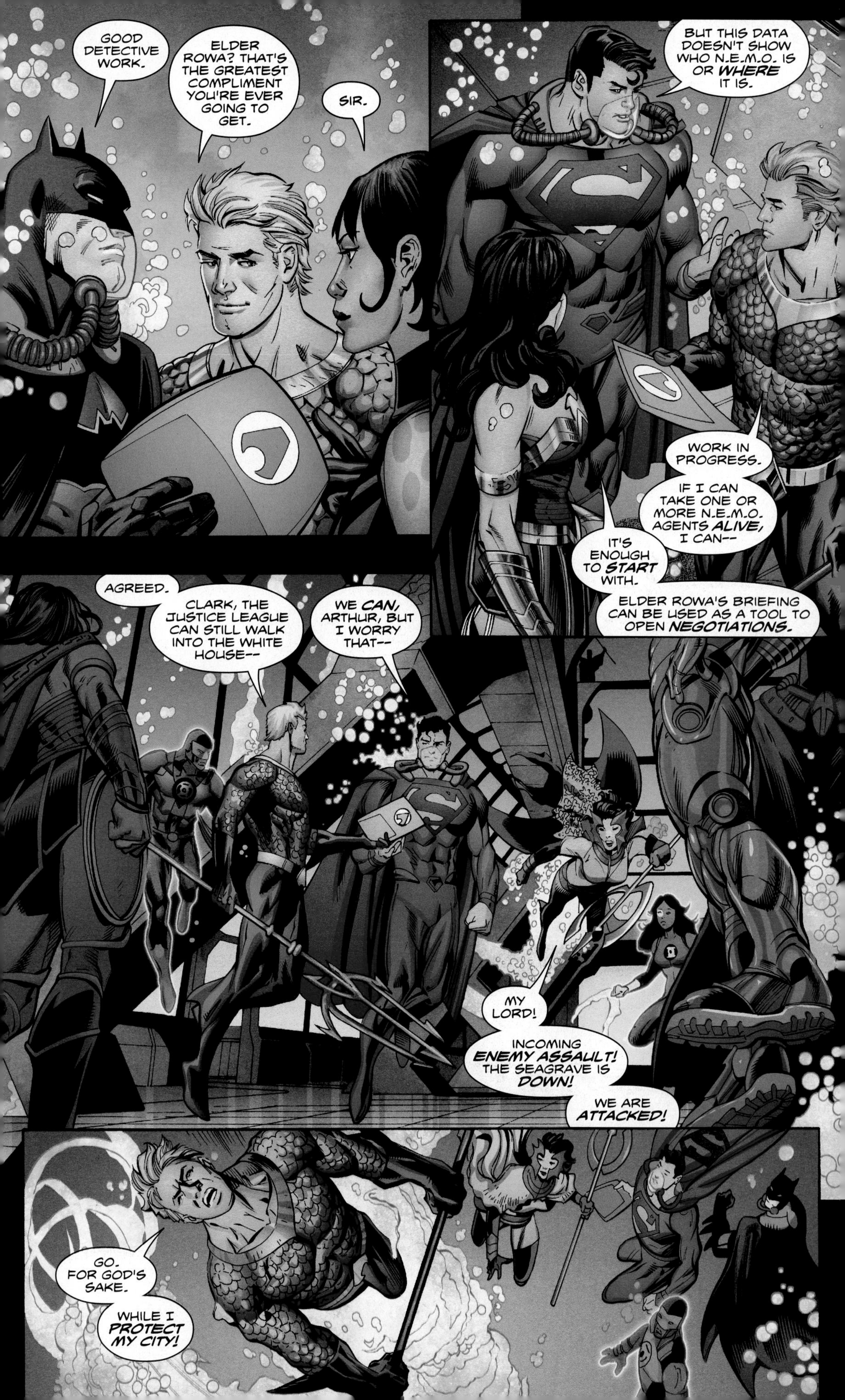
GOOD DETECTIVE WORK.
ELDER ROWA? THAT'S THE GREATEST COMPLIMENT YOU'RE EVER GOING TO GET.
SIR.
BUT THIS DATA DOESN'T SHOW WHO N.E.M.O. IS OR WHERE IT IS.
WORK IN PROGRESS.
IF I CAN TAKE ONE OR MORE N.E.M.O. AGENTS ALIVE, I CAN--
IT'S ENOUGH TO START WITH.
ELDER ROWA'S BRIEFING CAN BE USED AS A TOOL TO OPEN NEGOTIATIONS.
AGREED.
CLARK, THE JUSTICE LEAGUE CAN STILL WALK INTO THE WHITE HOUSE--
WE CAN, ARTHUR, BUT I WORRY THAT--
MY LORD!
INCOMING ENEMY ASSAULT! THE SEAGRAVE IS DOWN!
WE ARE ATTACKED!
GO. FOR GOD'S SAKE.
WHILE I PROTECT MY CITY!

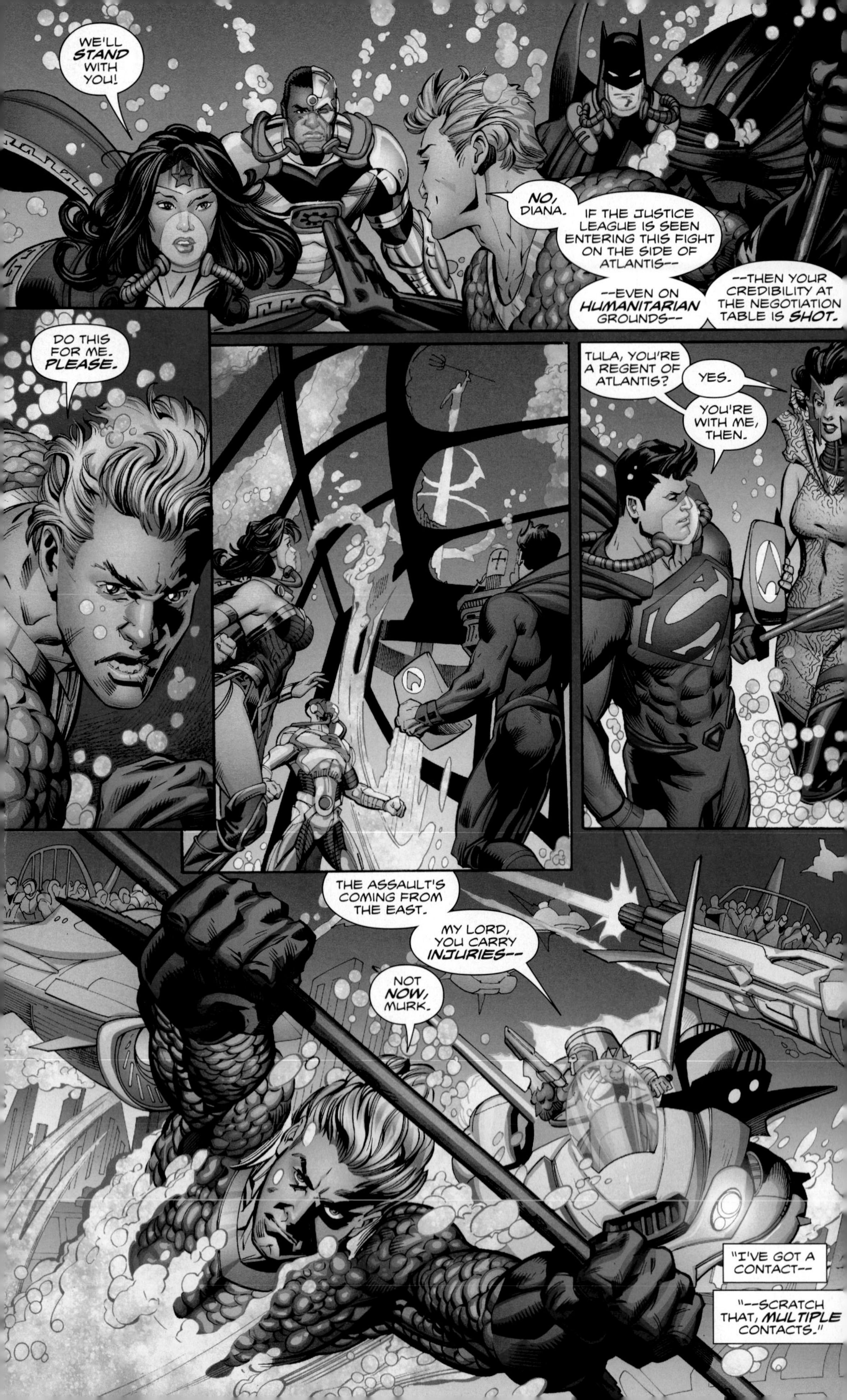
WE'LL STAND WITH YOU!
NO, DIANA.
IF THE JUSTICE LEAGUE IS SEEN ENTERING THIS FIGHT ON THE SIDE OF ATLANTIS--
--EVEN ON HUMANITARIAN GROUNDS--
--THEN YOUR CREDIBILITY AT THE NEGOTIATION TABLE IS SHOT.
DO THIS FOR ME. PLEASE.
TULA, YOU'RE A REGENT OF ATLANTIS?
YES.
YOU'RE WITH ME, THEN.
THE ASSAULT'S COMING FROM THE EAST.
MY LORD, YOU CARRY INJURIES--
NOT NOW, MURK.
"I'VE GOT A CONTACT--
"--SCRATCH THAT, MULTIPLE CONTACTS."

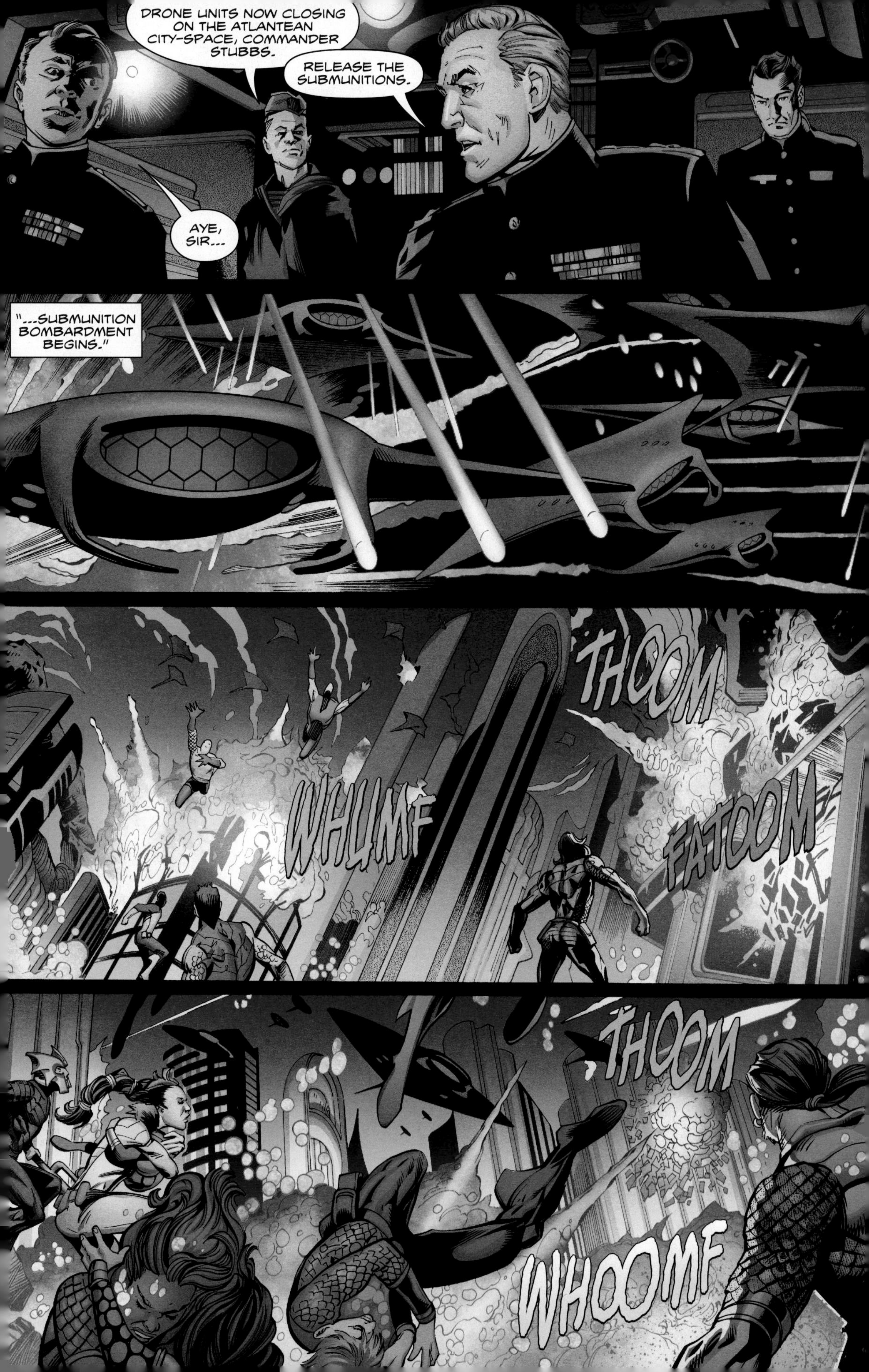
DRONE UNITS NOW CLOSING ON THE ATLANTEAN CITY-SPACE, COMMANDER STUBBS.
RELEASE THE SUBMUNITIONS.
AYE, SIR...
"...SUBMUNITION BOMBARDMENT BEGINS."
THOOM
WHUMF
FATOOM
THOOM
WHOOMF

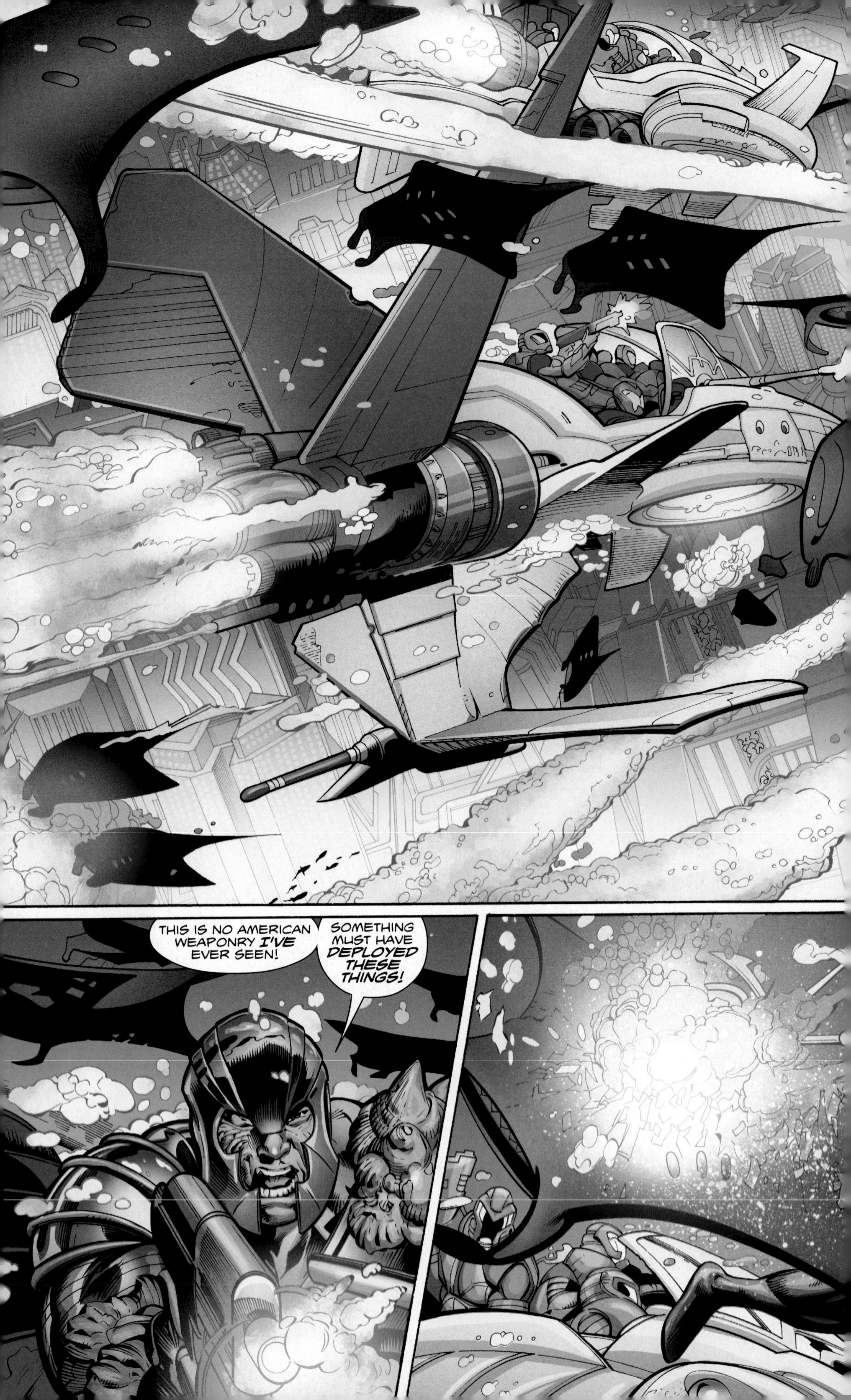

THIS IS NO AMERICAN WEAPONRY I'VE EVER SEEN!
SOMETHING MUST HAVE DEPLOYED THESE THINGS!

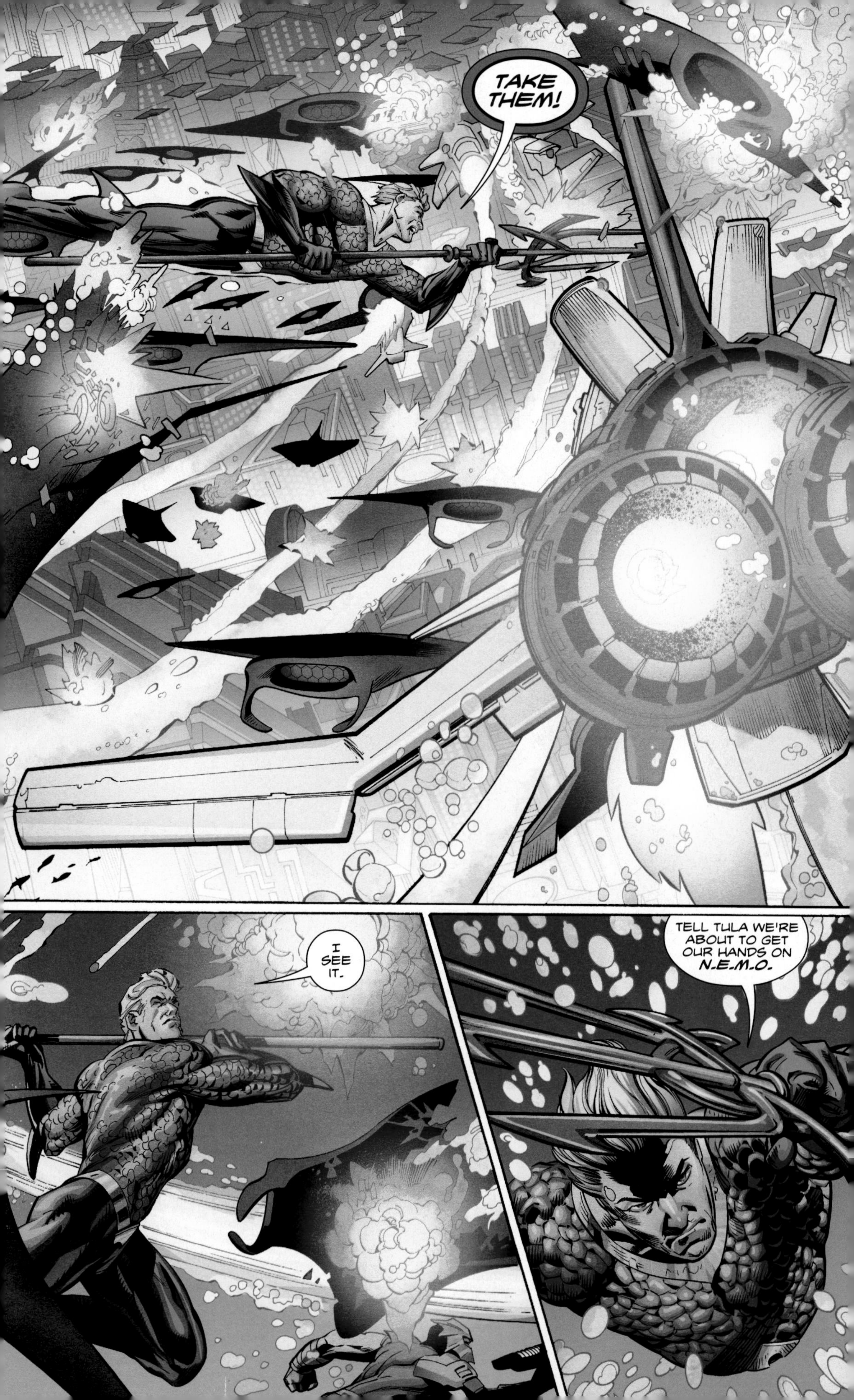
TAKE THEM!
I SEE IT.
TELL TULA WE'RE ABOUT TO GET OUR HANDS ON N.E.M.O.

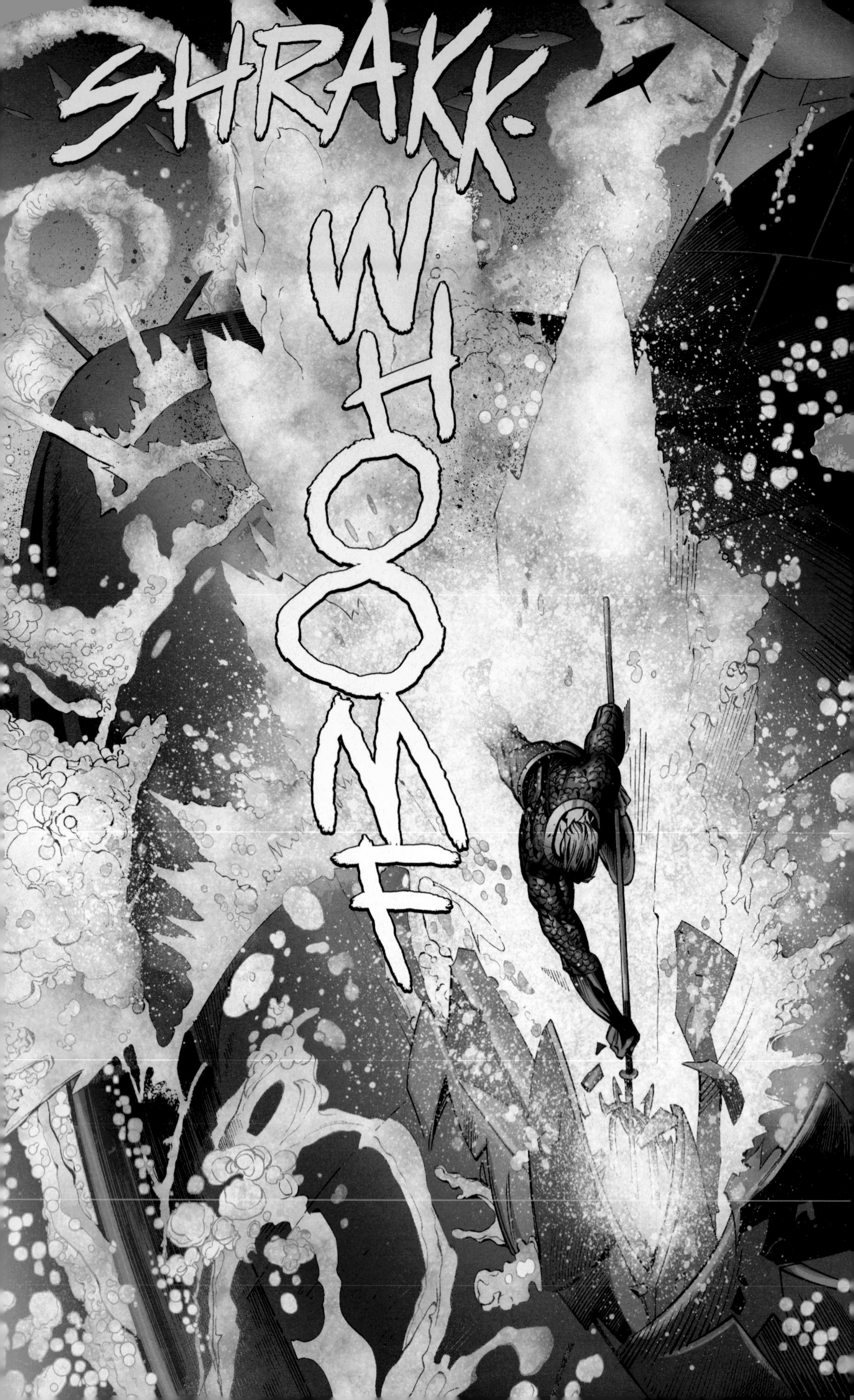
SHRAKK-

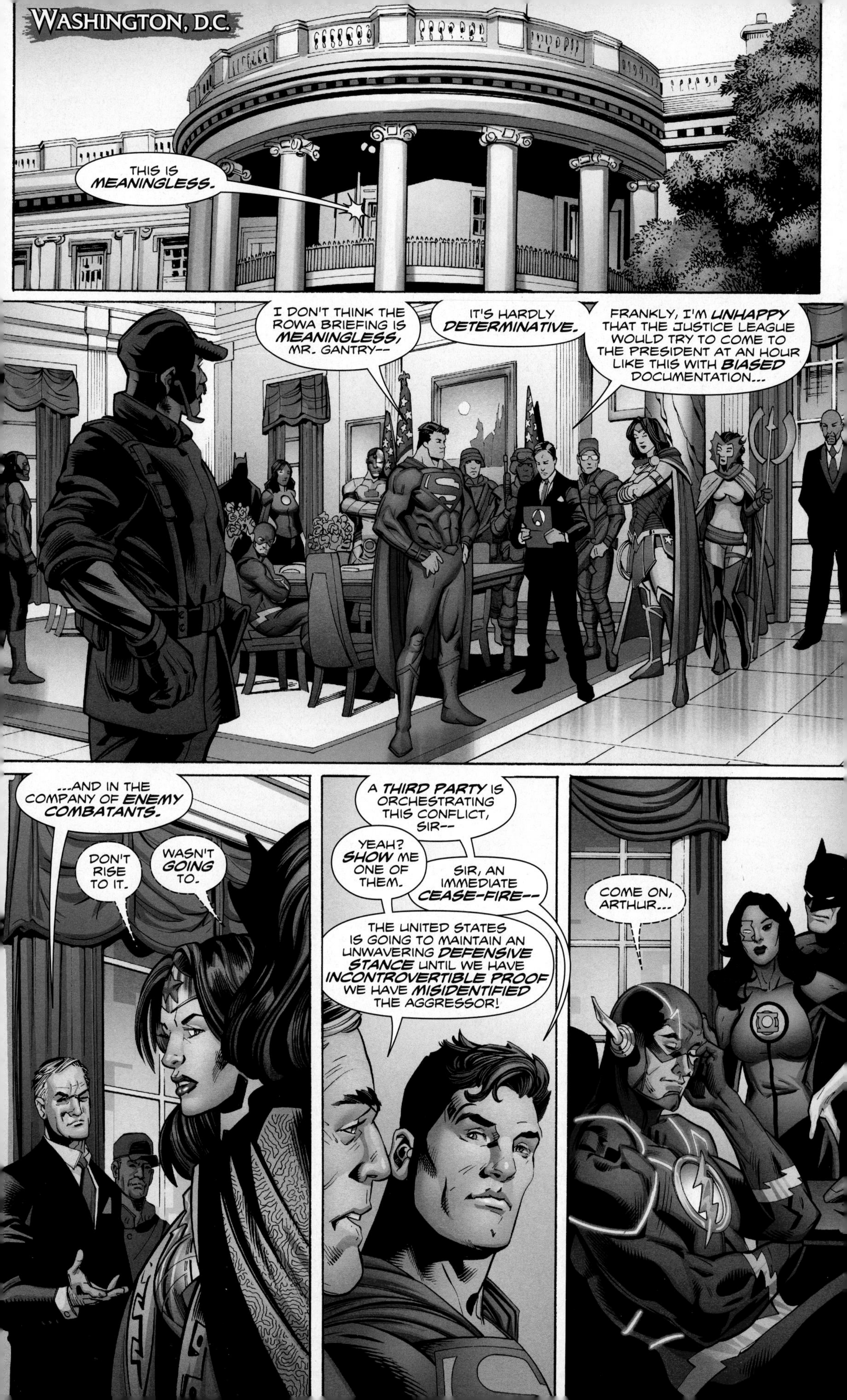
WASHINGTON, D.C.
THIS IS MEANINGLESS.
I DON'T THINK THE ROWA BRIEFING IS MEANINGLESS, MR. GANTRY--
IT'S HARDLY DETERMINATIVE.
FRANKLY, I'M UNHAPPY THAT THE JUSTICE LEAGUE WOULD TRY TO COME TO THE PRESIDENT AT AN HOUR LIKE THIS WITH BIASED DOCUMENTATION...
...AND IN THE COMPANY OF ENEMY COMBATANTS.
DON'T RISE TO IT.
WASN'T GOING TO.
A THIRD PARTY IS ORCHESTRATING THIS CONFLICT, SIR--
YEAH? SHOW ME ONE OF THEM.
SIR, AN IMMEDIATE CEASE-FIRE--
THE UNITED STATES IS GOING TO MAINTAIN AN UNWAVERING DEFENSIVE STANCE UNTIL WE HAVE INCONTROVERTIBLE PROOF WE HAVE MISIDENTIFIED THE AGGRESSOR!
COME ON, ARTHUR...

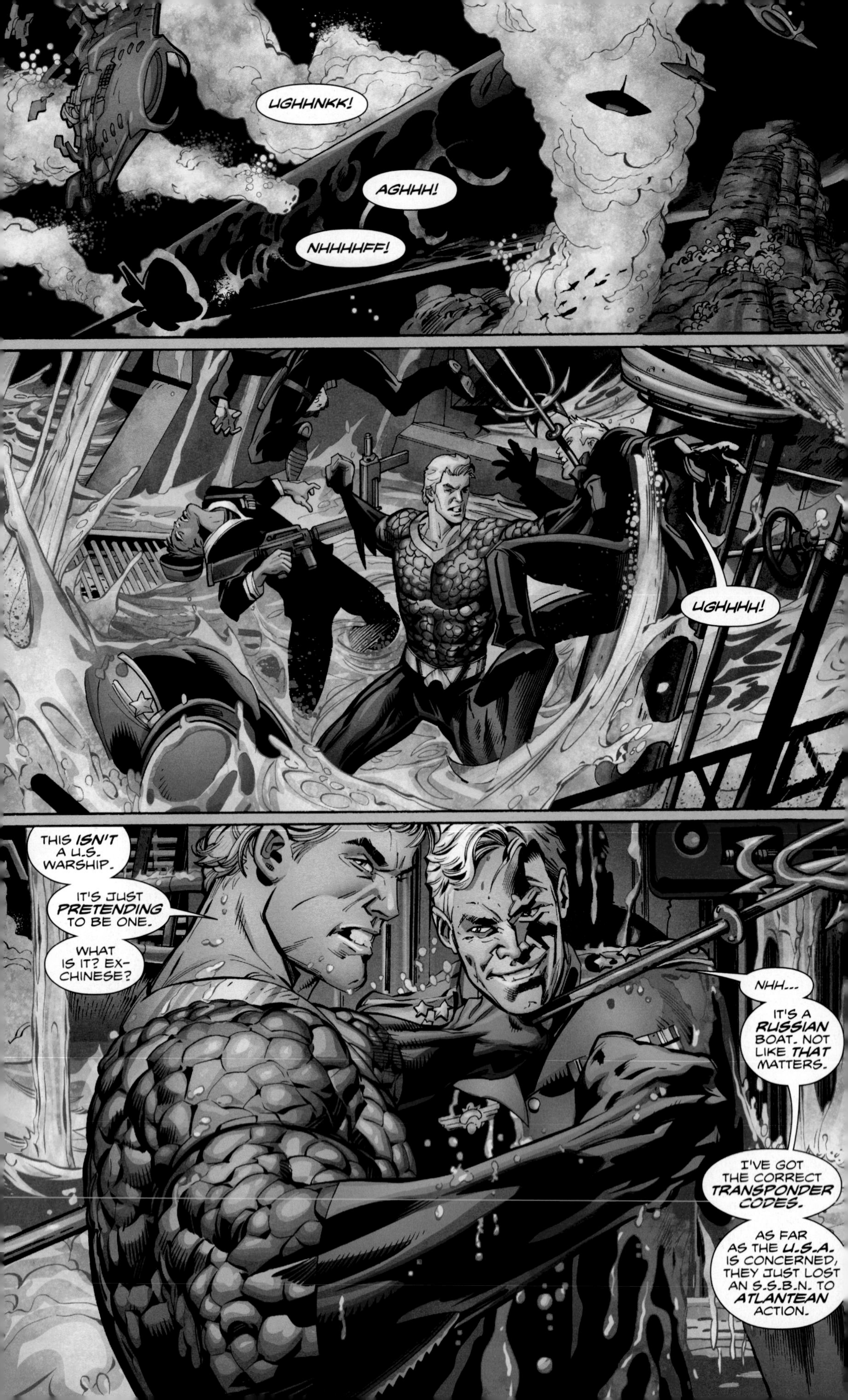
UGHHNKK!
AGHHH!
NHHHHFF!
UGHHHH!
THIS ISN'T A U.S. WARSHIP.
IT'S JUST PRETENDING TO BE ONE.
WHAT IS IT? EX-CHINESE?
NHH...
IT'S A RUSSIAN BOAT. NOT LIKE THAT MATTERS.
I'VE GOT THE CORRECT TRANSPONDER CODES.
AS FAR AS THE U.S.A. IS CONCERNED, THEY JUST LOST AN S.S.B.N. TO ATLANTEAN ACTION.

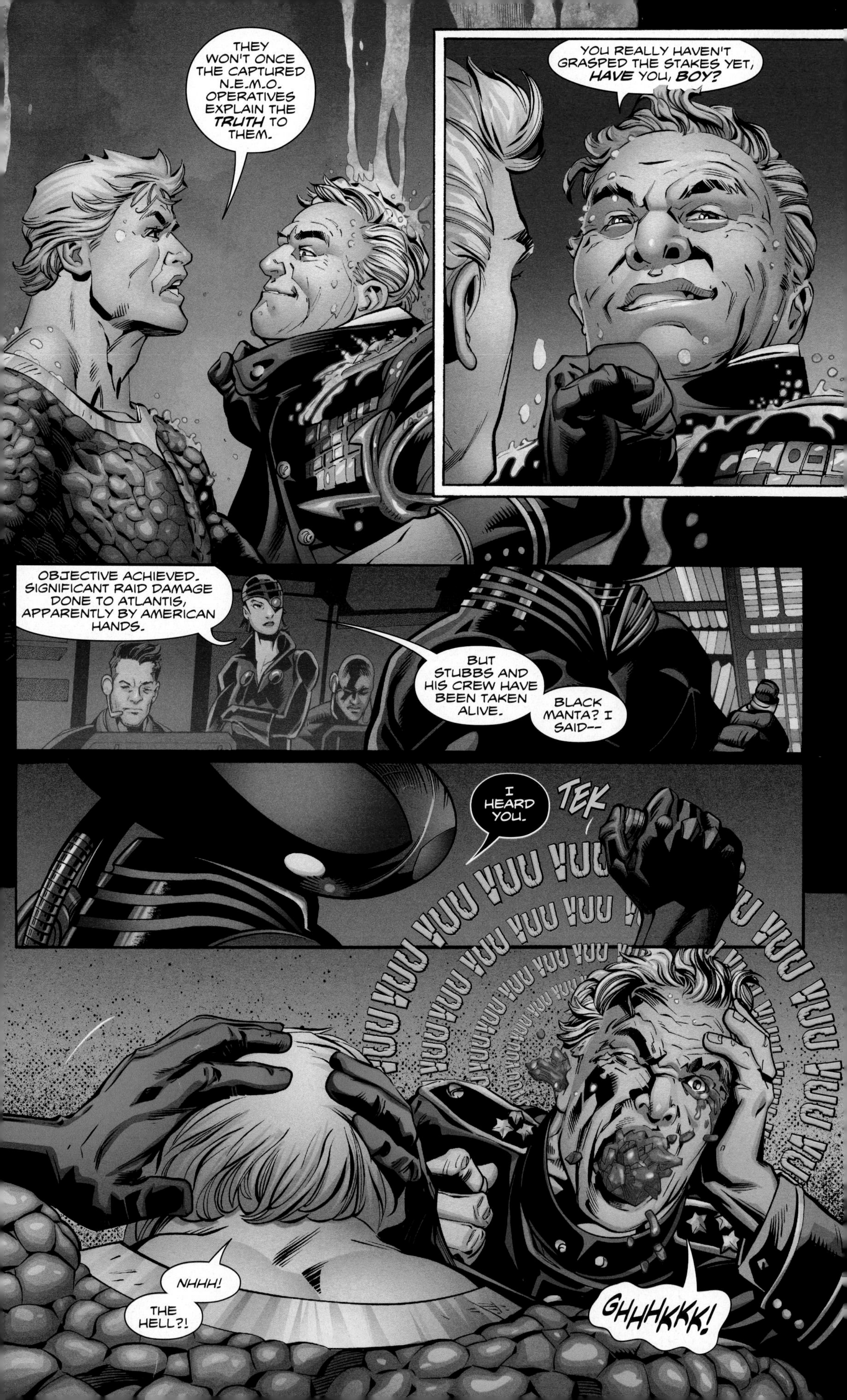
THEY WON'T ONCE THE CAPTURED N.E.M.O. OPERATIVES EXPLAIN THE TRUTH TO THEM.
YOU REALLY HAVEN'T GRASPED THE STAKES YET, HAVE YOU, BOY?
OBJECTIVE ACHIEVED. SIGNIFICANT RAID DAMAGE DONE TO ATLANTIS, APPARENTLY BY AMERICAN HANDS.
BUT STUBBS AND HIS CREW HAVE BEEN TAKEN ALIVE.
BLACK MANTA? I SAID--
I HEARD YOU.
TEK
NHHH!
THE HELL?!
GHHHKKK!

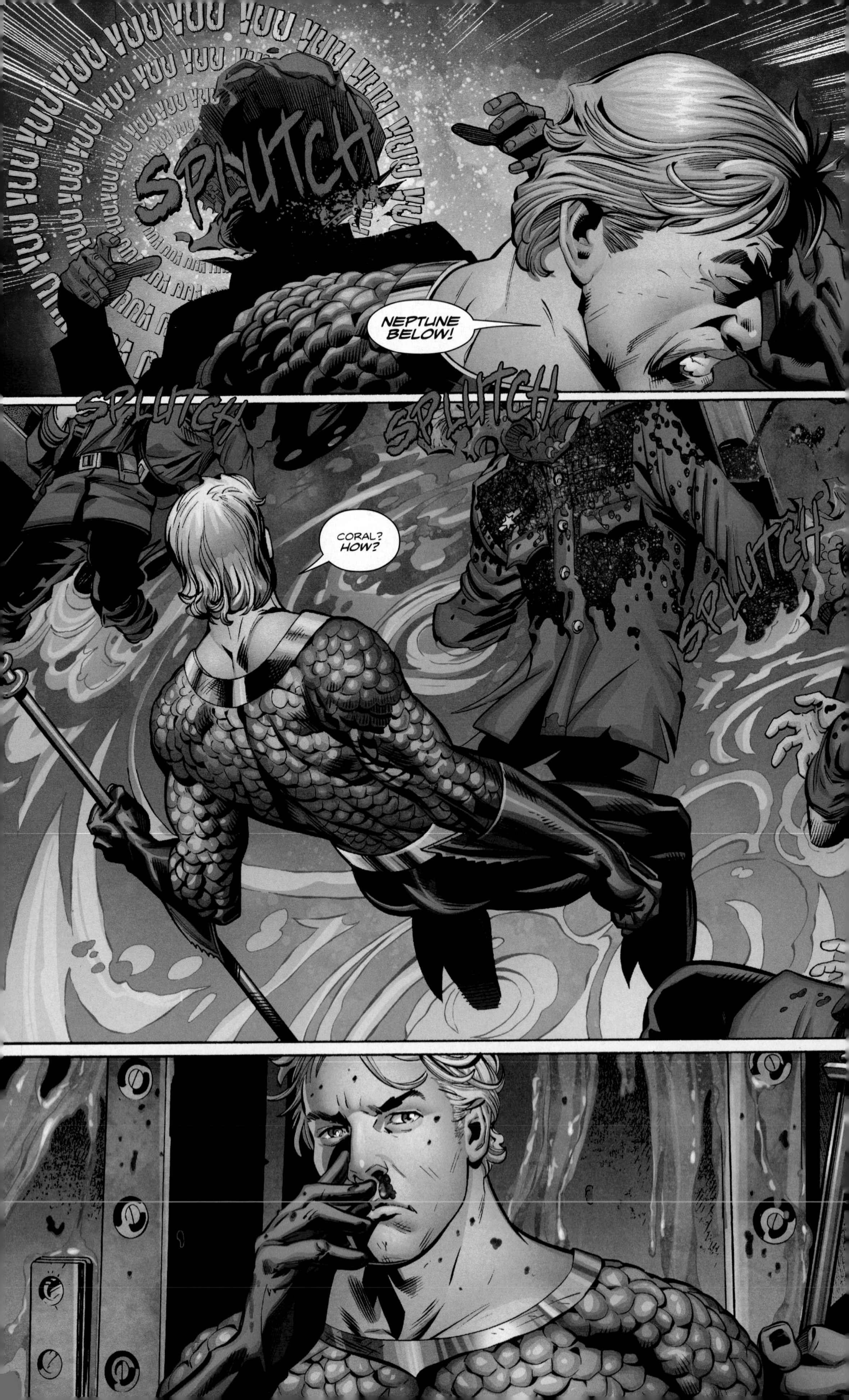
SPLUTCH
NEPTUNE BELOW!
SPLUTCH
SPLUTCH
CORAL? HOW?
SPLUTCH

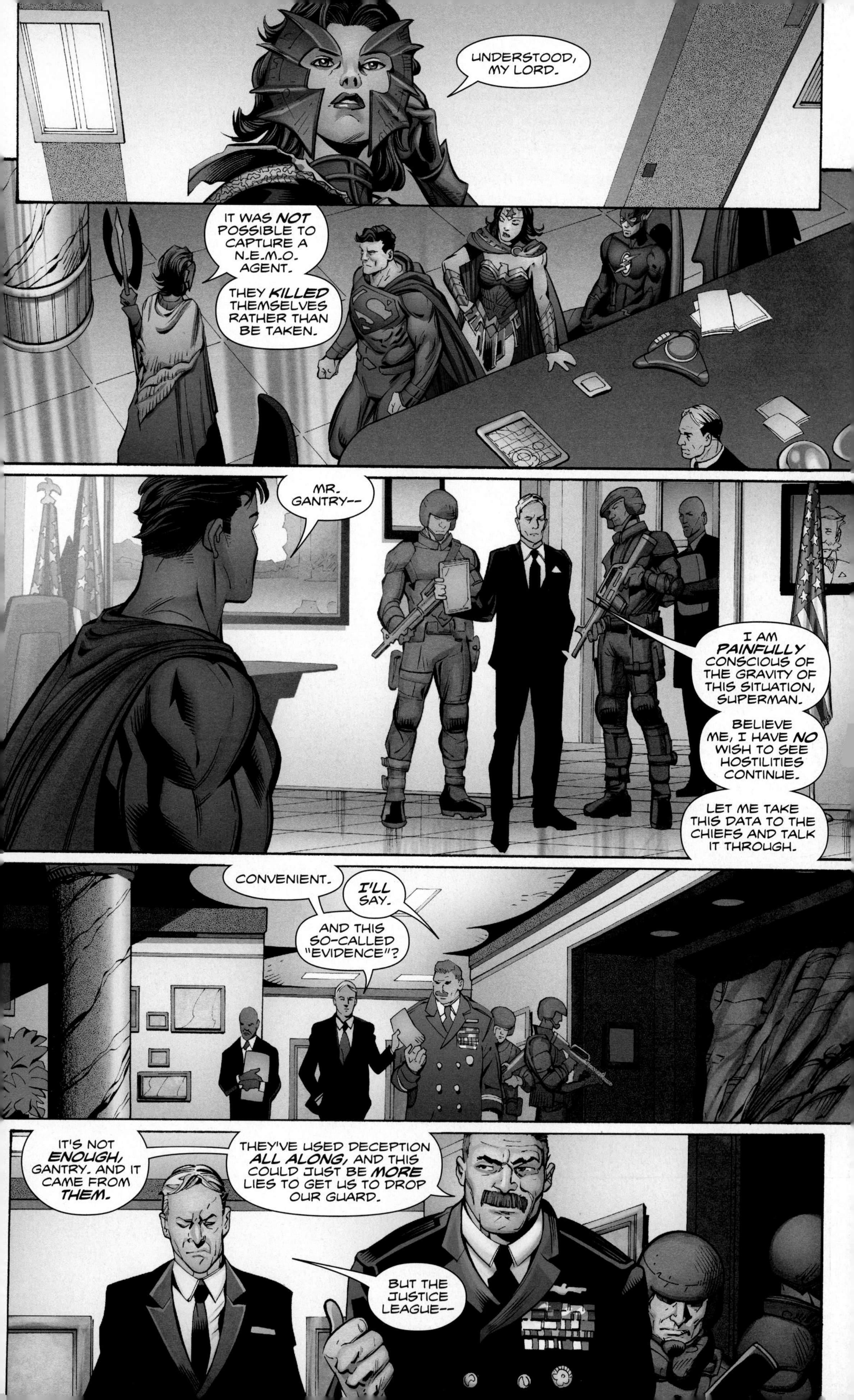
UNDERSTOOD, MY LORD.
IT WAS NOT POSSIBLE TO CAPTURE A N.E.M.O. AGENT.
THEY KILLED THEMSELVES RATHER THAN BE TAKEN.
MR. GANTRY--
I AM PAINFULLY CONSCIOUS OF THE GRAVITY OF THIS SITUATION, SUPERMAN.
BELIEVE ME, I HAVE NO WISH TO SEE HOSTILITIES CONTINUE.
LET ME TAKE THIS DATA TO THE CHIEFS AND TALK IT THROUGH.
CONVENIENT.
I'LL SAY.
AND THIS SO-CALLED "EVIDENCE"?
IT'S NOT ENOUGH, GANTRY. AND IT CAME FROM THEM.
THEY'VE USED DECEPTION ALL ALONG, AND THIS COULD JUST BE MORE LIES TO GET US TO DROP OUR GUARD.
BUT THE JUSTICE LEAGUE--

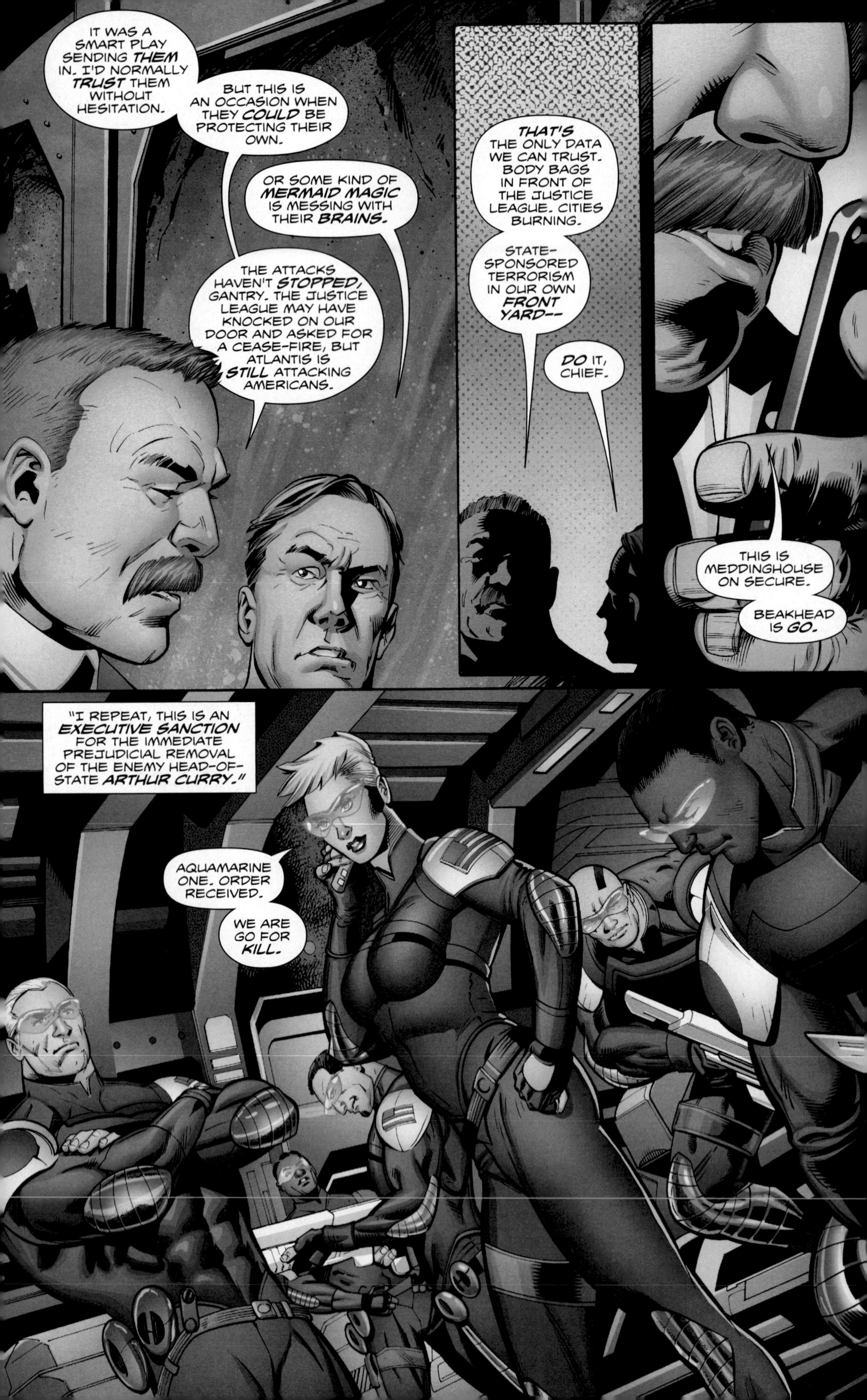
IT WAS A SMART PLAY SENDING THEM IN. I'D NORMALLY TRUST THEM WITHOUT HESITATION.
BUT THIS IS AN OCCASION WHEN THEY COULD BE PROTECTING THEIR OWN.
OR SOME KIND OF MERMAID MAGIC IS MESSING WITH THEIR BRAINS.
THE ATTACKS HAVEN'T STOPPED, GANTRY. THE JUSTICE LEAGUE MAY HAVE KNOCKED ON OUR DOOR AND ASKED FOR A CEASE-FIRE, BUT ATLANTIS IS STILL ATTACKING AMERICANS.
THAT'S THE ONLY DATA WE CAN TRUST. BODY BAGS IN FRONT OF THE JUSTICE LEAGUE. CITIES BURNING.
STATE-SPONSORED TERRORISM IN OUR OWN FRONT YARD--
DO IT, CHIEF.
THIS IS MEDDINGHOUSE ON SECURE.
BEAKHEAD IS GO.
"I REPEAT, THIS IS AN EXECUTIVE SANCTION FOR THE IMMEDIATE PREJUDICIAL REMOVAL OF THE ENEMY HEAD-OF-STATE ARTHUR CURRY."
AQUAMARINE ONE. ORDER RECEIVED.
WE ARE GO FOR KILL.

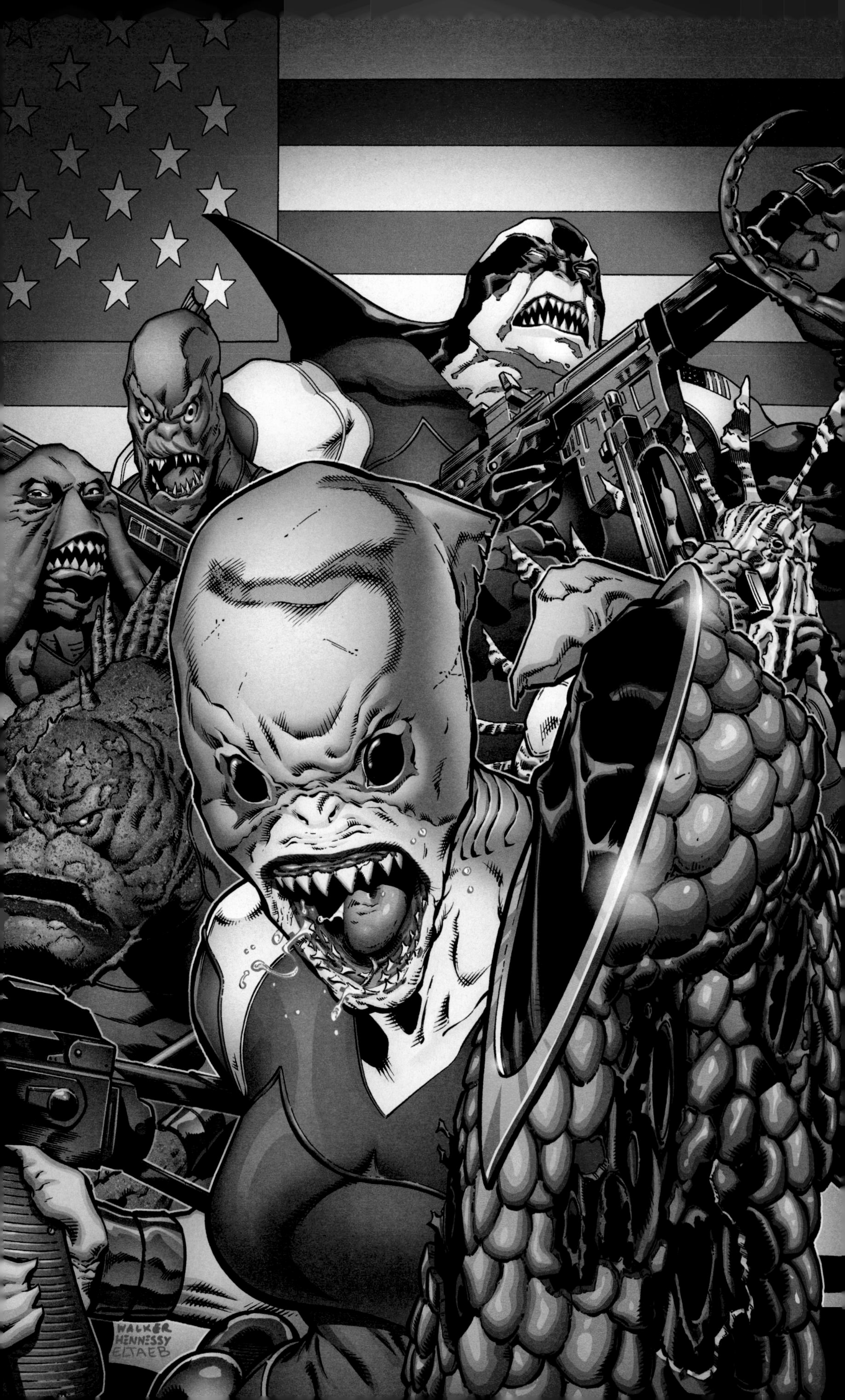
WALKER
HENNESSY
ELTAEB

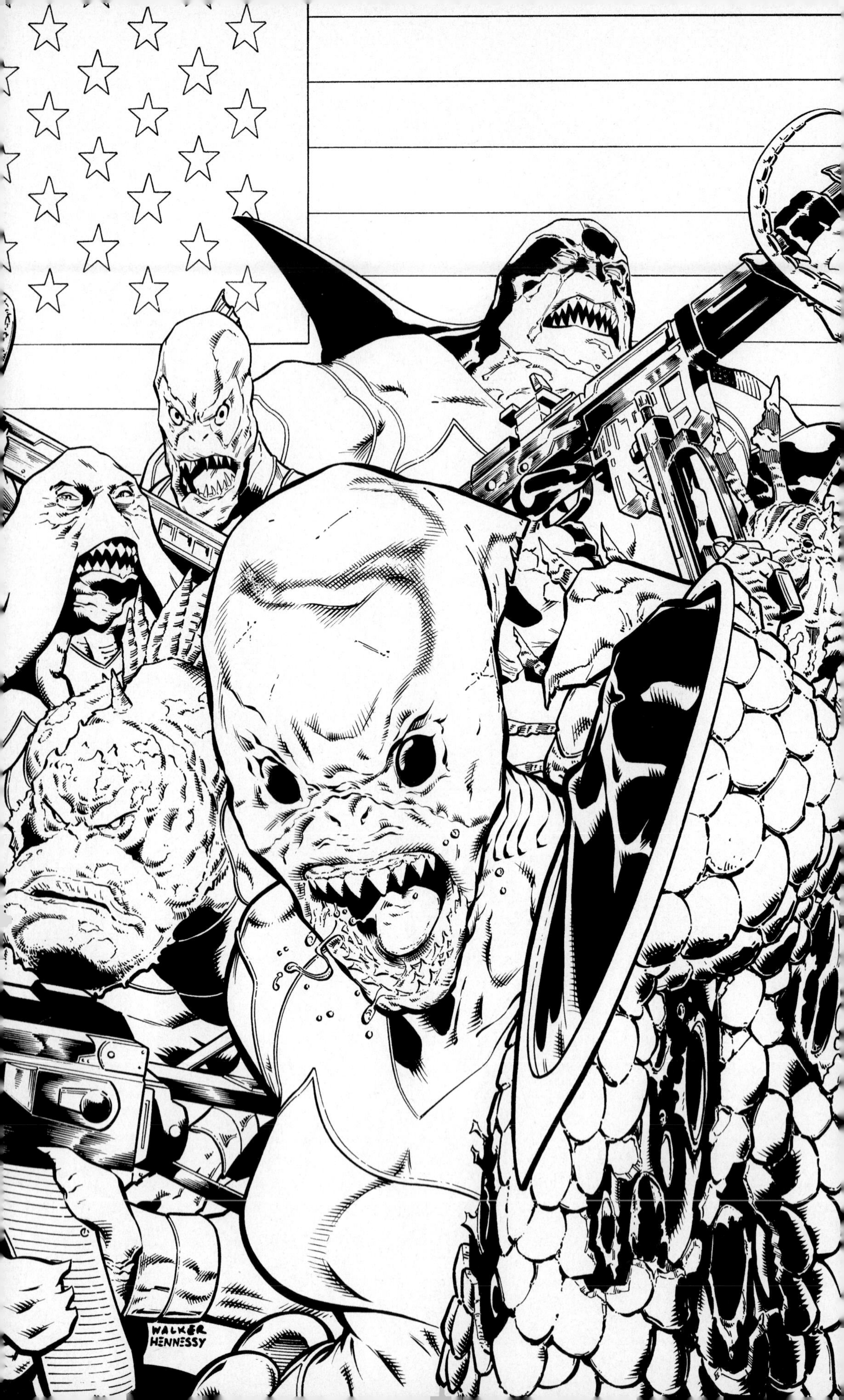
WALKER
HENNESSY

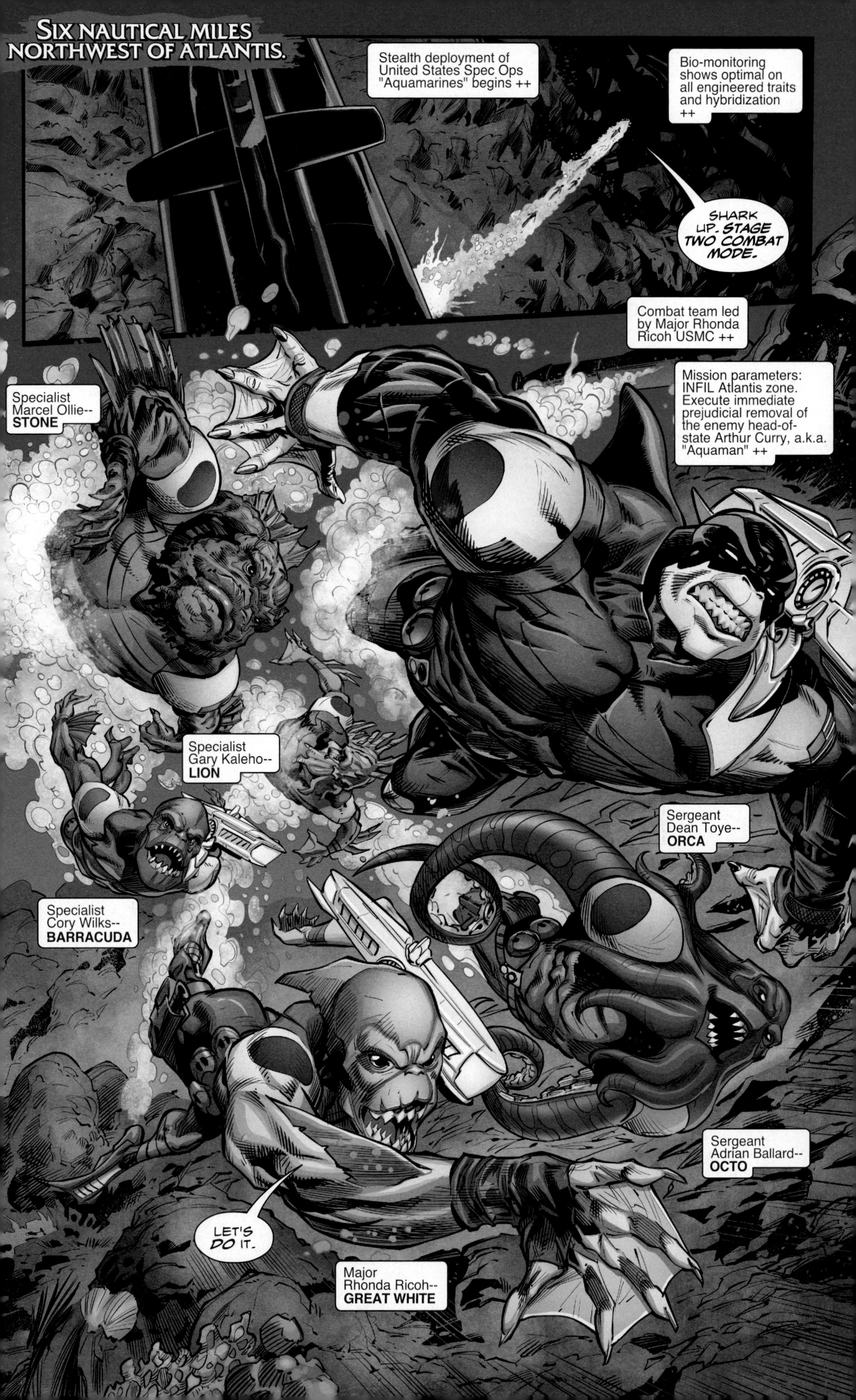
SIX NAUTICAL MILES NORTHWEST OF ATLANTIS.
Stealth deployment of United States Spec Ops "Aquamarines" begins ++
Bio-monitoring shows optimal on all engineered traits and hybridization ++
SHARK UP. STAGE TWO COMBAT MODE.
Combat team led by Major Rhonda Ricoh USMC ++
Mission parameters: INFIL Atlantis zone. Execute immediate prejudicial removal of the enemy head-of-state Arthur Curry, a.k.a. "Aquaman" ++
Specialist Marcel Ollie-- STONE
Specialist Gary Kaleho-- LION
Sergeant Dean Toye-- ORCA
Specialist Cory Wilks-- BARRACUDA
Sergeant Adrian Ballard-- OCTO
LET'S DO IT.
Major Rhonda Ricoh-- GREAT WHITE

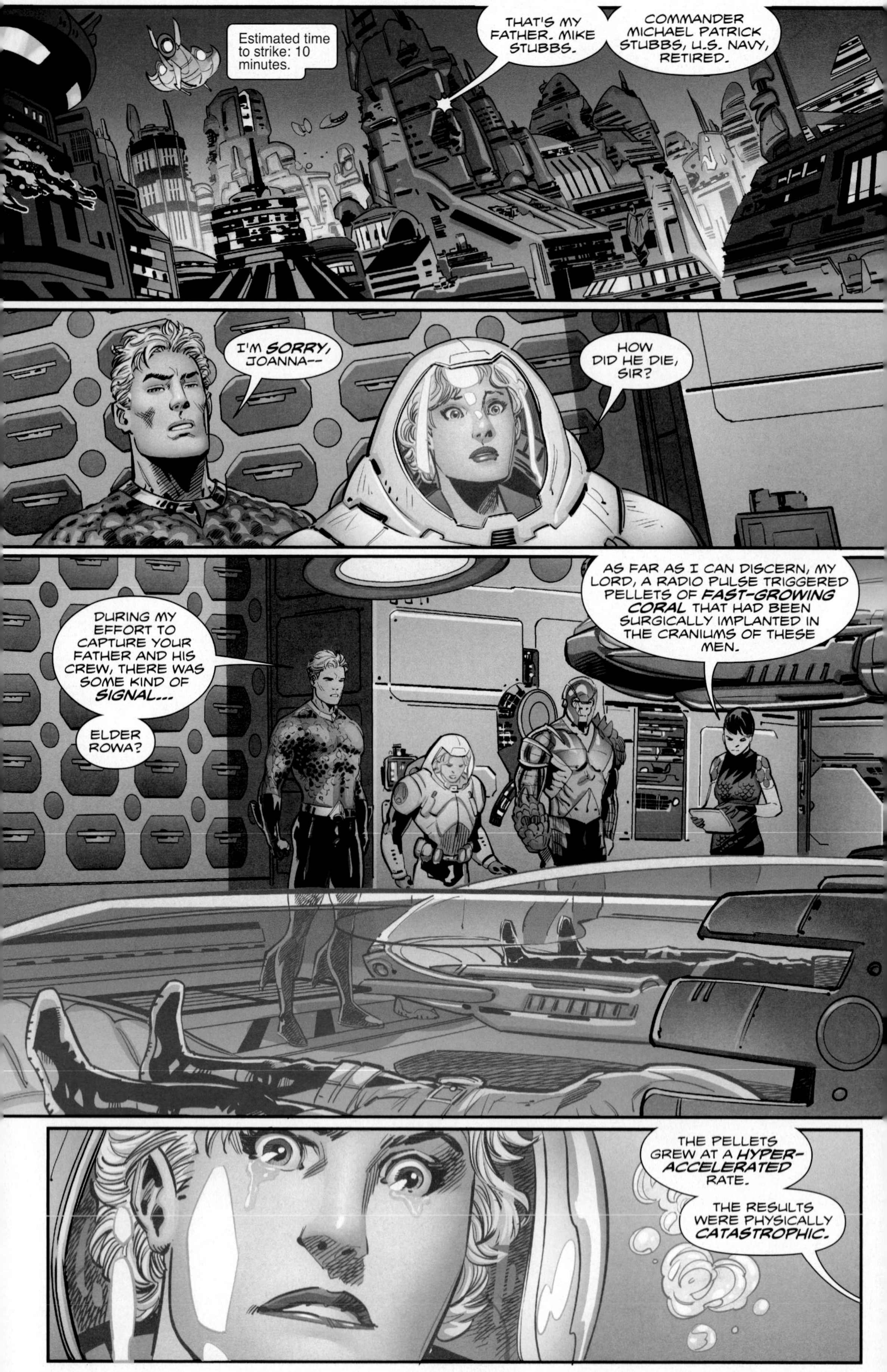

Estimated time to strike: 10 minutes.
THAT'S MY FATHER. MIKE STUBBS.
COMMANDER MICHAEL PATRICK STUBBS, U.S. NAVY, RETIRED.
I'M SORRY, JOANNA--
HOW DID HE DIE, SIR?
DURING MY EFFORT TO CAPTURE YOUR FATHER AND HIS CREW, THERE WAS SOME KIND OF SIGNAL...
ELDER ROWA?
AS FAR AS I CAN DISCERN, MY LORD, A RADIO PULSE TRIGGERED PELLETS OF FAST-GROWING CORAL THAT HAD BEEN SURGICALLY IMPLANTED IN THE CRANIUMS OF THESE MEN.
THE PELLETS GREW AT A HYPER-ACCELERATED RATE.
THE RESULTS WERE PHYSICALLY CATASTROPHIC.

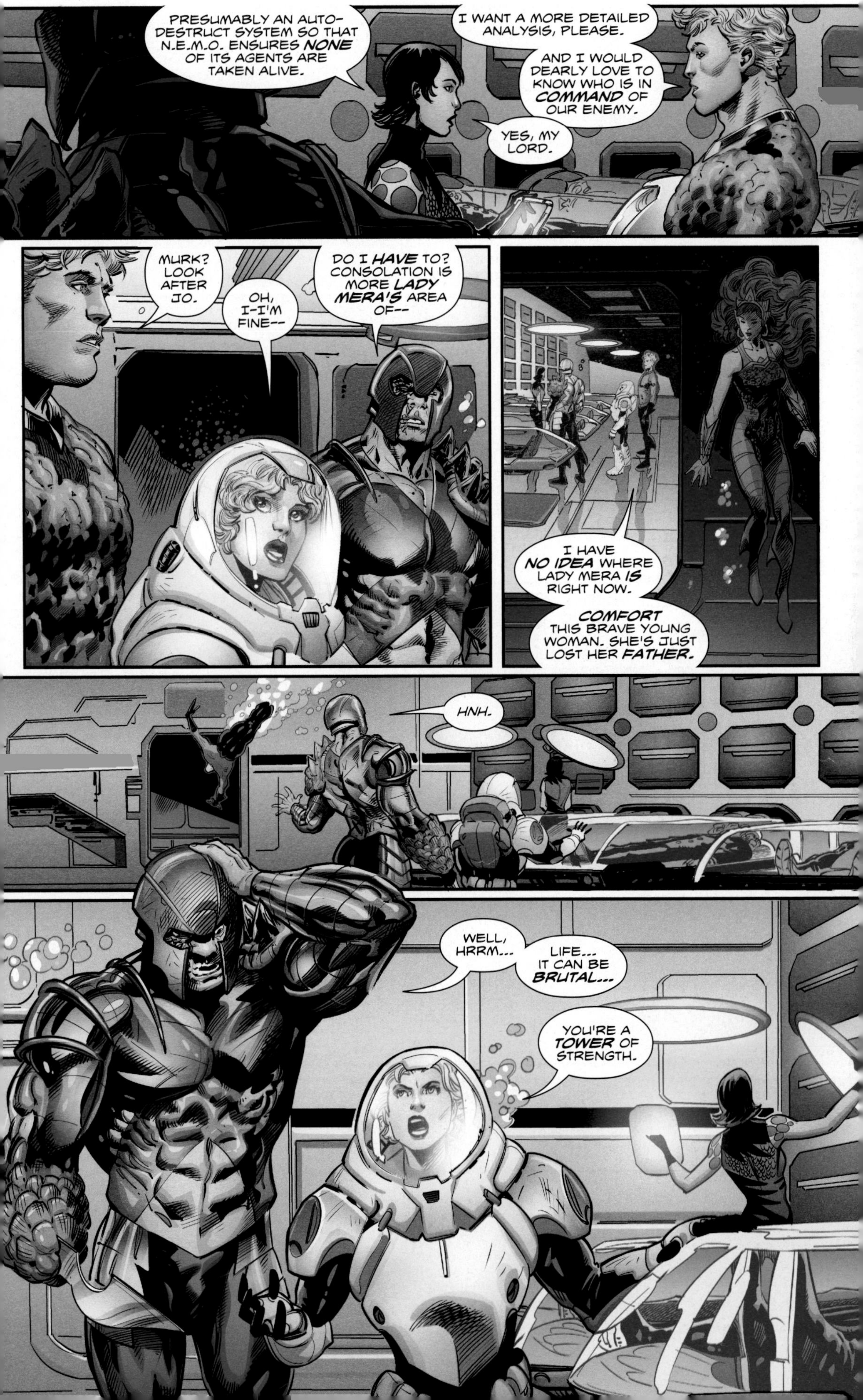
PRESUMABLY AN AUTO-DESTRUCT SYSTEM SO THAT N.E.M.O. ENSURES NONE OF ITS AGENTS ARE TAKEN ALIVE.
I WANT A MORE DETAILED ANALYSIS, PLEASE.
AND I WOULD DEARLY LOVE TO KNOW WHO IS IN COMMAND OF OUR ENEMY.
YES, MY LORD.
MURK? LOOK AFTER JO.
OH, I-I'M FINE--
DO I HAVE TO? CONSOLATION IS MORE LADY MERA'S AREA OF--
I HAVE NO IDEA WHERE LADY MERA IS RIGHT NOW.
COMFORT THIS BRAVE YOUNG WOMAN. SHE'S JUST LOST HER FATHER.
HNH.
WELL, HRRM...
LIFE... IT CAN BE BRUTAL...
YOU'RE A TOWER OF STRENGTH.

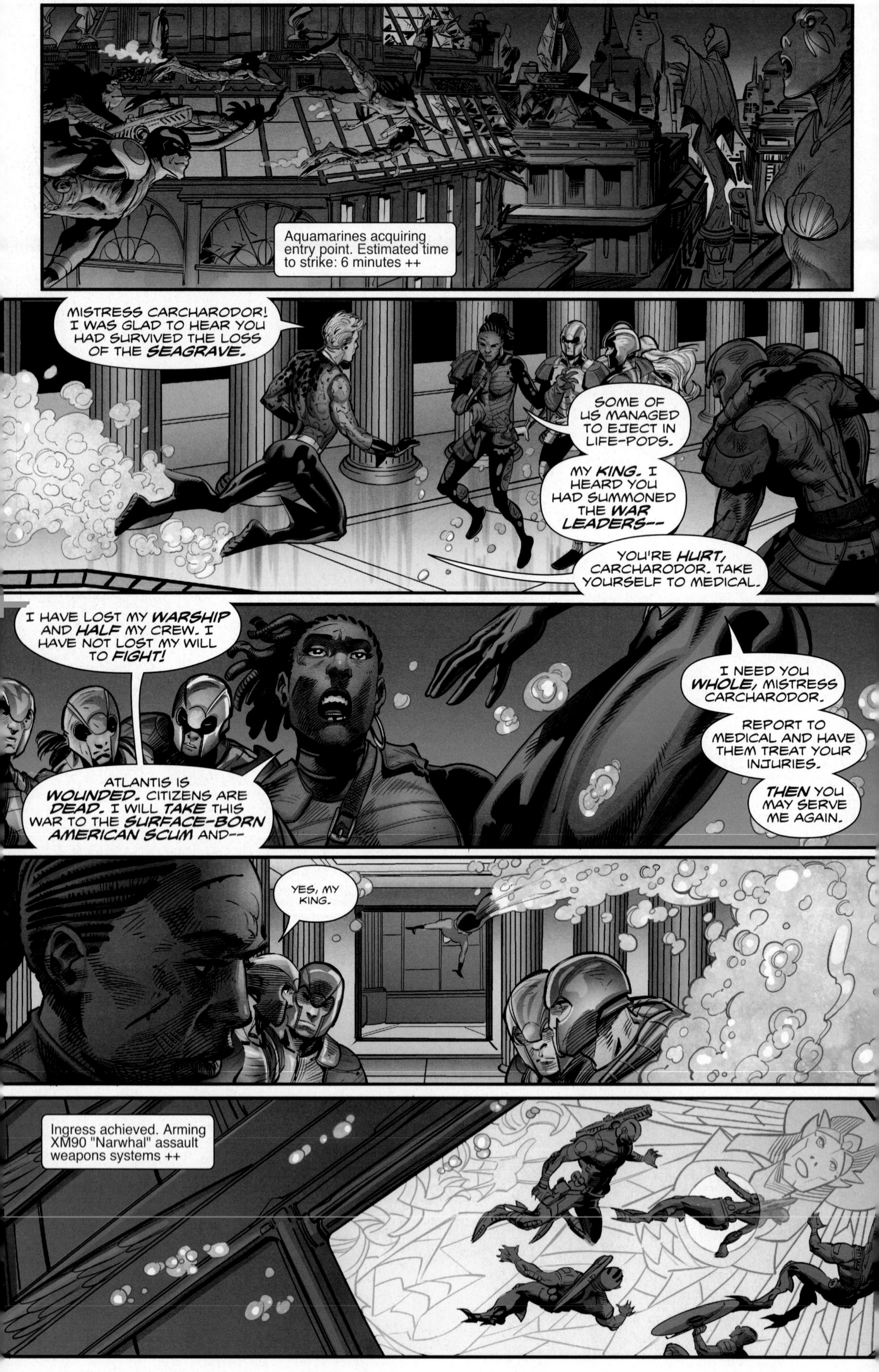
Aquamarines acquiring entry point. Estimated time to strike: 6 minutes ++
MISTRESS CARCHARODOR! I WAS GLAD TO HEAR YOU HAD SURVIVED THE LOSS OF THE SEAGRAVE.
SOME OF US MANAGED TO EJECT IN LIFE-PODS.
MY KING. I HEARD YOU HAD SUMMONED THE WAR LEADERS--
YOU'RE HURT, CARCHARODOR. TAKE YOURSELF TO MEDICAL.
I HAVE LOST MY WARSHIP AND HALF MY CREW. I HAVE NOT LOST MY WILL TO FIGHT!
ATLANTIS IS WOUNDED. CITIZENS ARE DEAD. I WILL TAKE THIS WAR TO THE SURFACE-BORN AMERICAN SCUM AND--
I NEED YOU WHOLE, MISTRESS CARCHARODOR.
REPORT TO MEDICAL AND HAVE THEM TREAT YOUR INJURIES.
THEN YOU MAY SERVE ME AGAIN.
YES, MY KING.
Ingress achieved. Arming XM90 "Narwhal" assault weapons systems ++

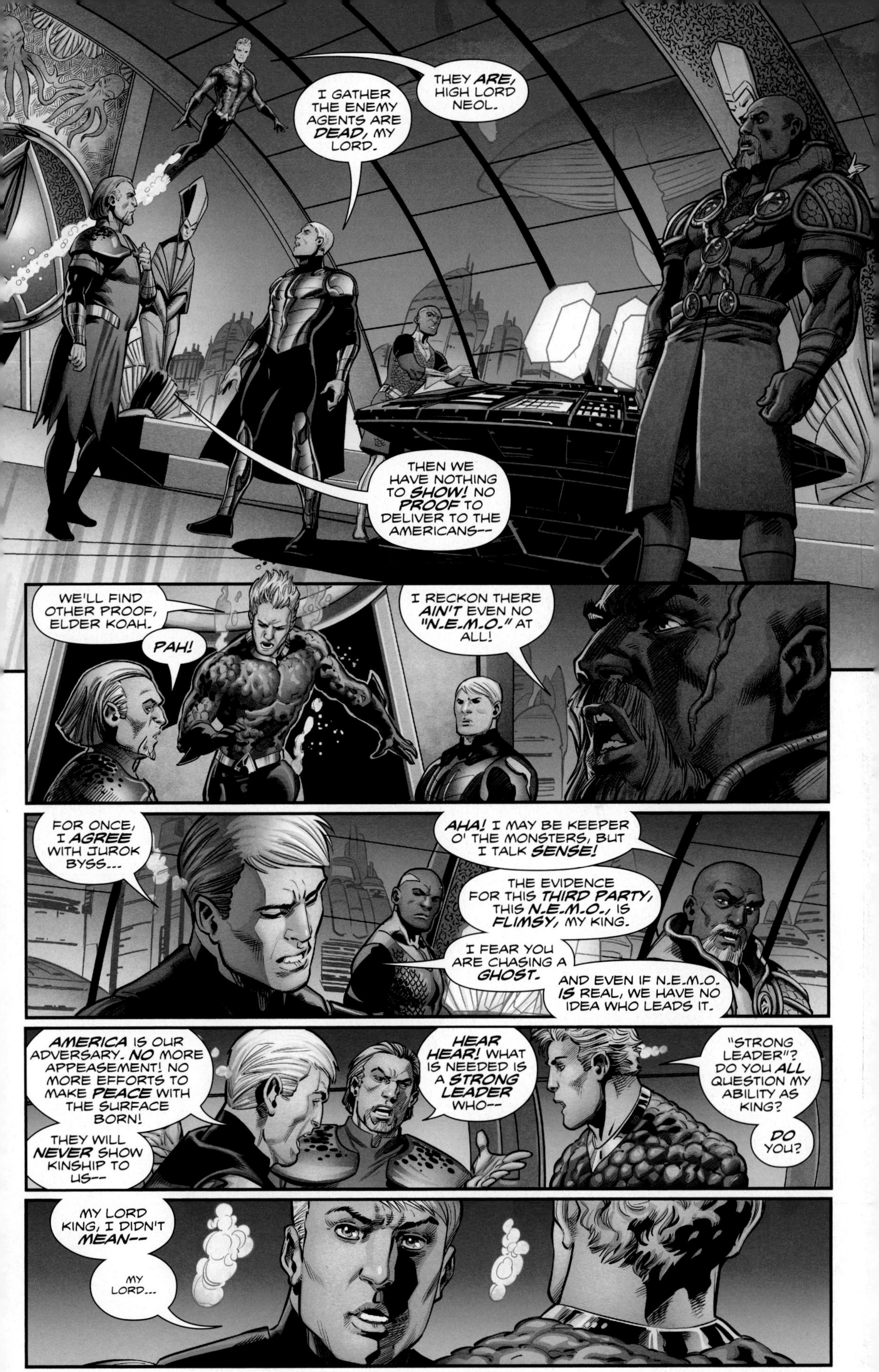

I GATHER THE ENEMY AGENTS ARE DEAD, MY LORD.
THEY ARE, HIGH LORD NEOL.
THEN WE HAVE NOTHING TO SHOW! NO PROOF TO DELIVER TO THE AMERICANS--
WE'LL FIND OTHER PROOF, ELDER KOAH.
PAH!
I RECKON THERE AIN'T EVEN NO "N.E.M.O." AT ALL!
FOR ONCE, I AGREE WITH JUROK BYSS...
AHA! I MAY BE KEEPER O' THE MONSTERS, BUT I TALK SENSE!
THE EVIDENCE FOR THIS THIRD PARTY, THIS N.E.M.O., IS FLIMSY, MY KING.
I FEAR YOU ARE CHASING A GHOST.
AND EVEN IF N.E.M.O. IS REAL, WE HAVE NO IDEA WHO LEADS IT.
AMERICA IS OUR ADVERSARY. NO MORE APPEASEMENT! NO MORE EFFORTS TO MAKE PEACE WITH THE SURFACE BORN!
THEY WILL NEVER SHOW KINSHIP TO US--
HEAR HEAR! WHAT IS NEEDED IS A STRONG LEADER WHO--
"STRONG LEADER"? DO YOU ALL QUESTION MY ABILITY AS KING?
DO YOU?
MY LORD KING, I DIDN'T MEAN--
MY LORD...

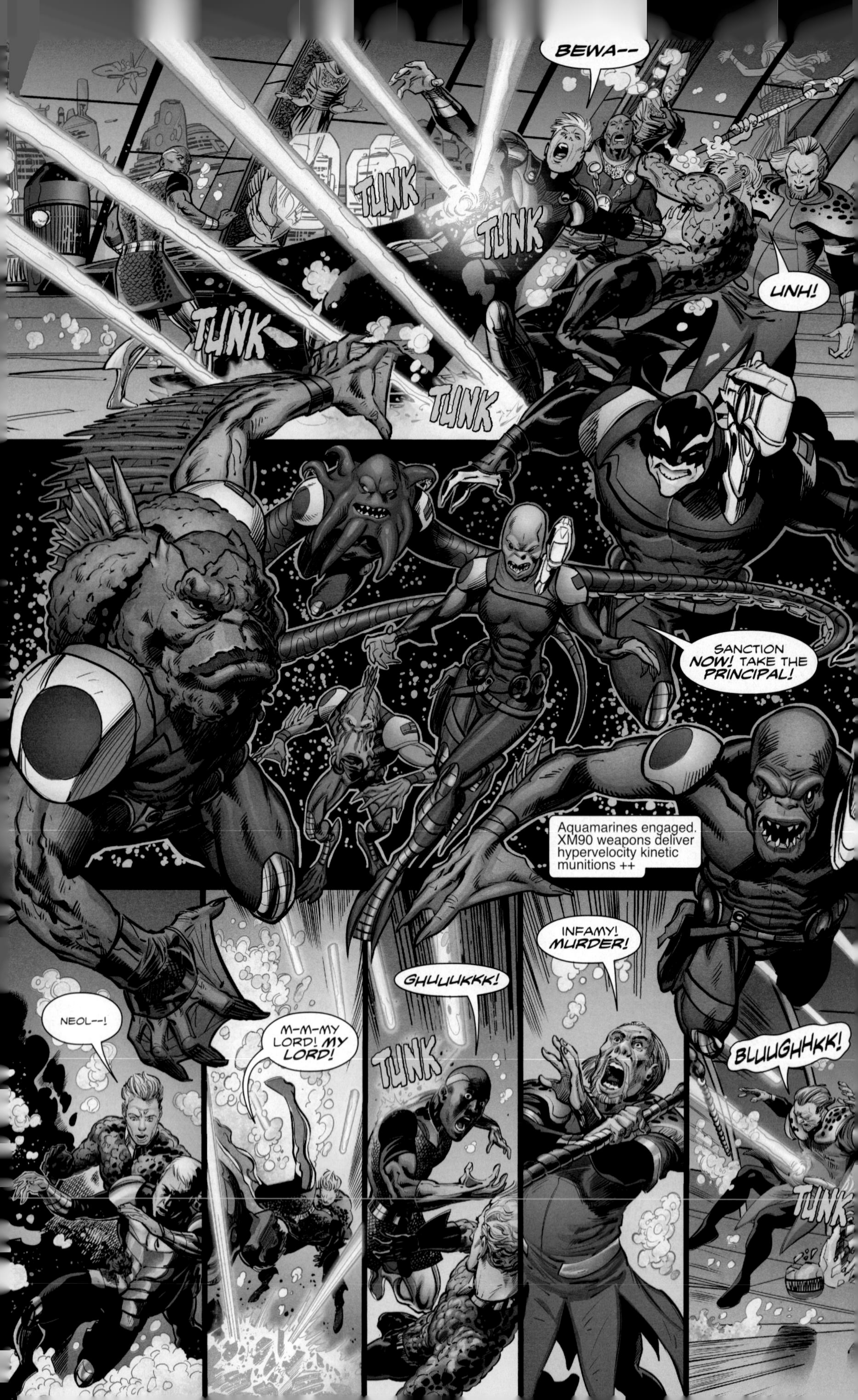
BEWA--
TUNK
TUNK
TUNK
TUNK
UNH!
SANCTION NOW! TAKE THE PRINCIPAL!
Aquamarines engaged. XM90 weapons deliver hypervelocity kinetic munitions ++
NEOL--!
M-M-MY LORD! MY LORD!
GHUUUKKK!
TUNK
INFAMY! MURDER!
BLUUGHHKK!
TUNK

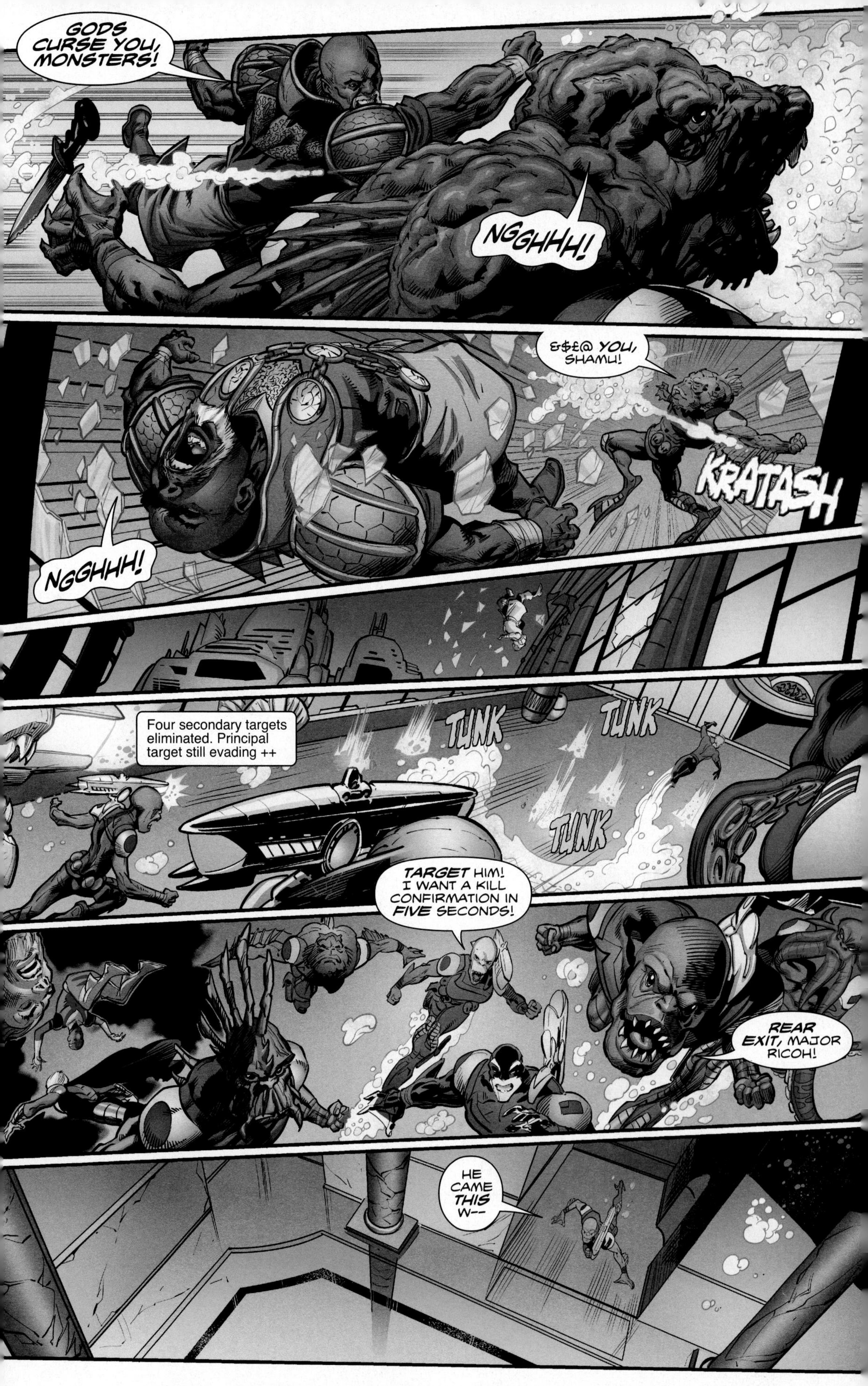
GODS CURSE YOU, MONSTERS!
NGGHHH!
&$£@ YOU, SHAMU!
KRATASH
NGGHHH!
Four secondary targets eliminated. Principal target still evading ++
TUNK
TUNK
TUNK
TARGET HIM! I WANT A KILL CONFIRMATION IN FIVE SECONDS!
REAR EXIT, MAJOR RICOH!
HE CAME THIS W--

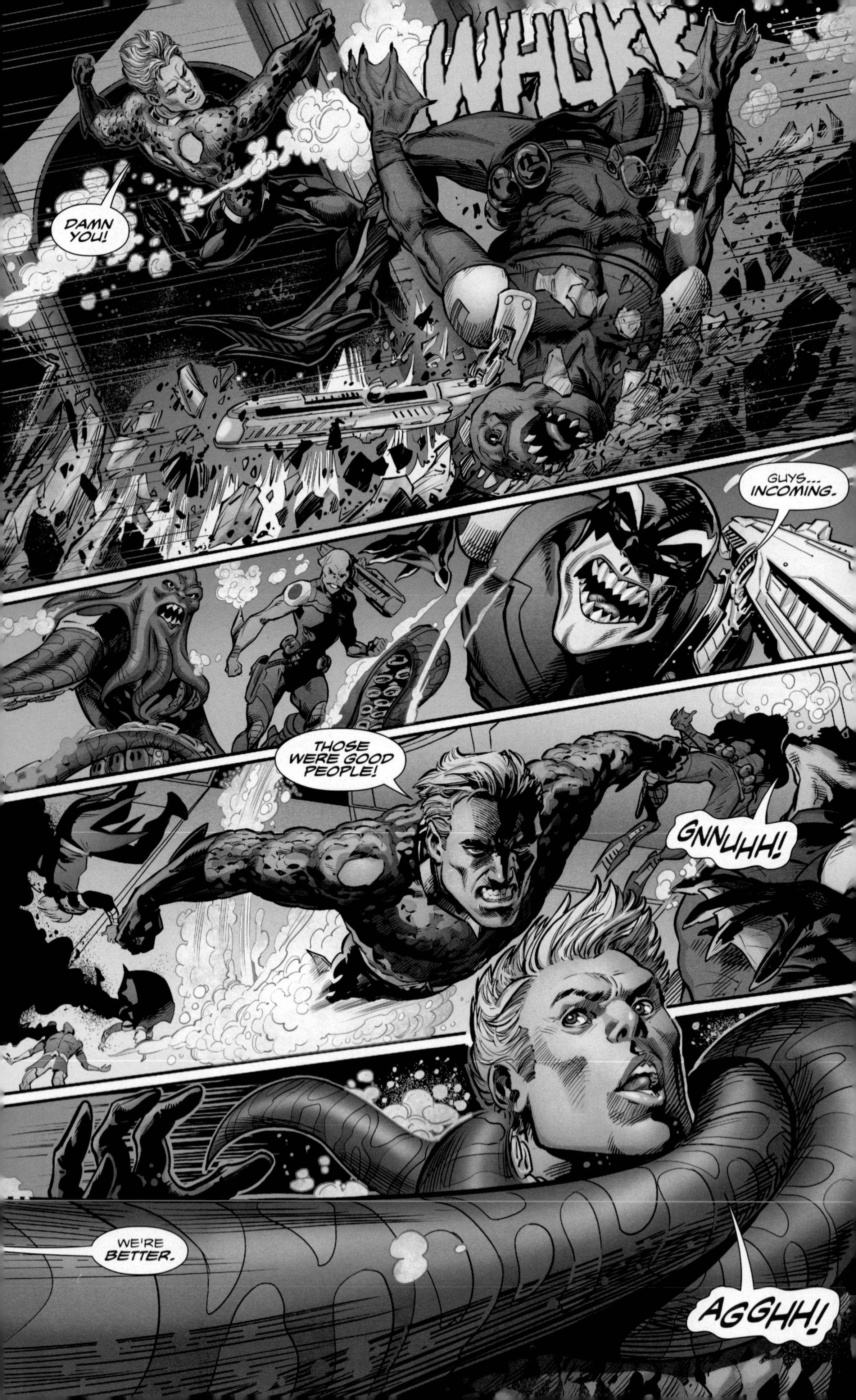
WHUK!
DAMN YOU!
GUYS... INCOMING.
THOSE WERE GOOD PEOPLE!
GNNUHH!
WE'RE BETTER.
AGGHH!

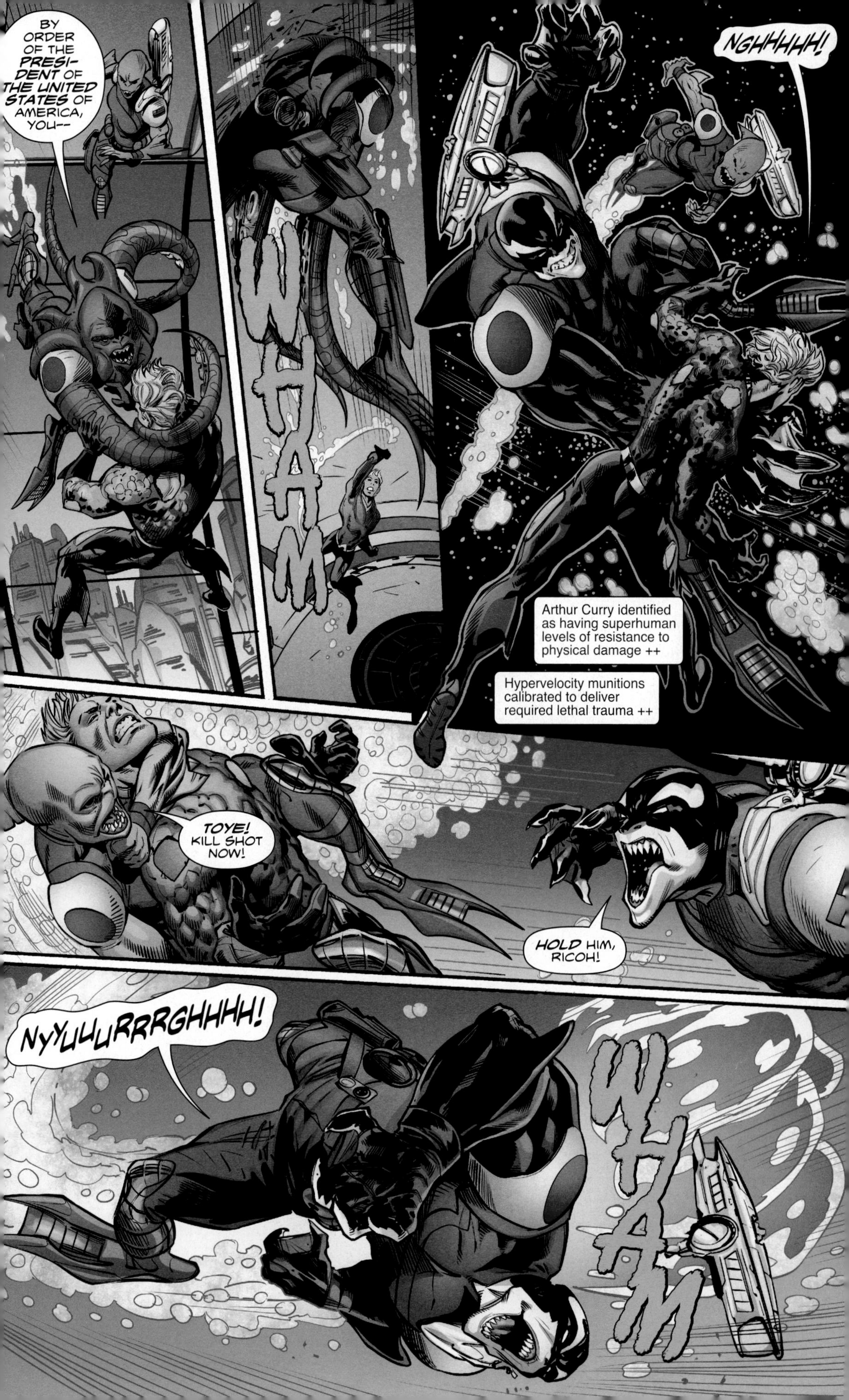
BY ORDER OF THE PRESIDENT OF THE UNITED STATES OF AMERICA, YOU--
WHAM
NGHHHHH!
Arthur Curry identified as having superhuman levels of resistance to physical damage ++
Hypervelocity munitions calibrated to deliver required lethal trauma ++
TOYE! KILL SHOT NOW!
HOLD HIM, RICOH!
NYYUURRRGHHHH!
WHAM

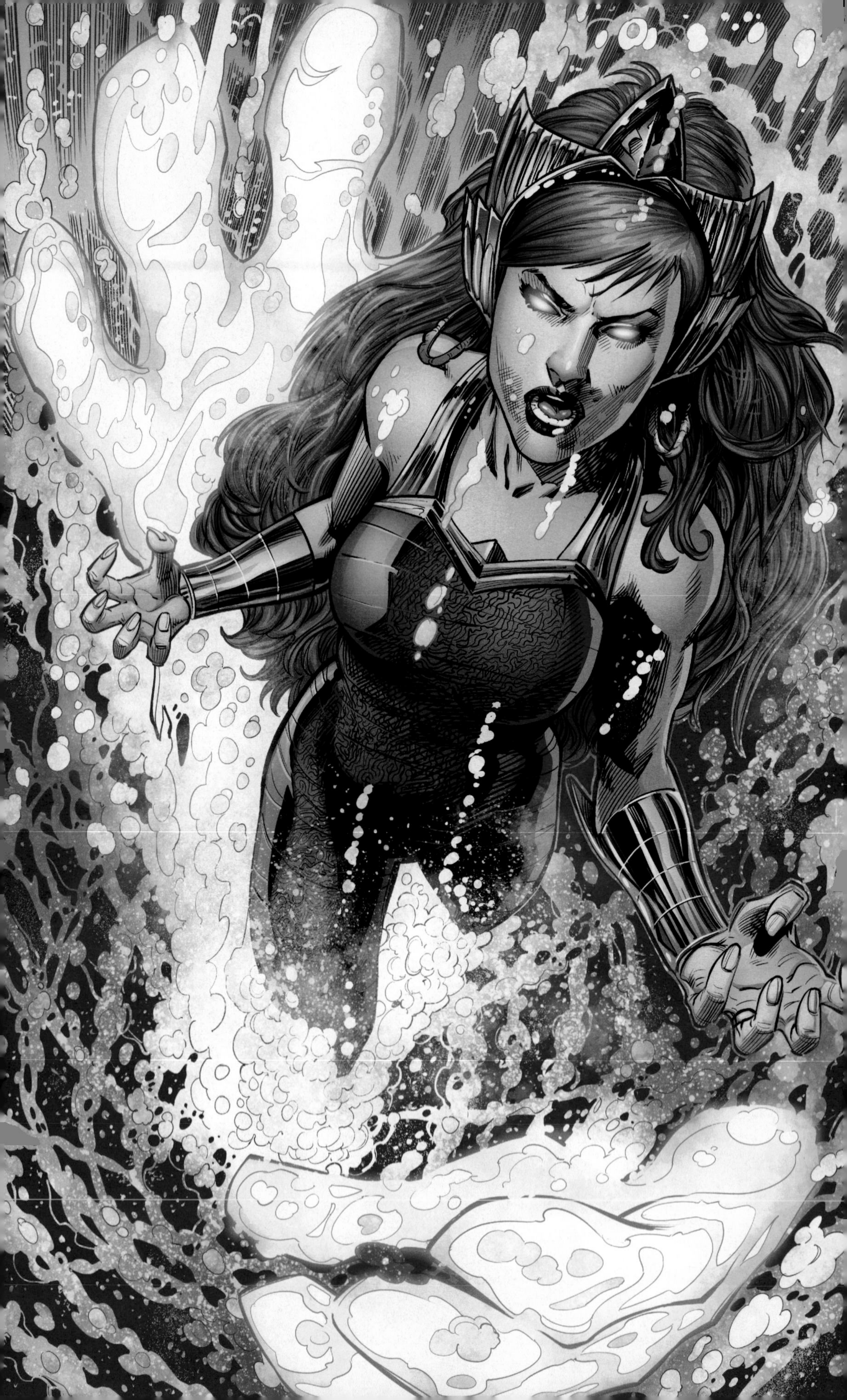

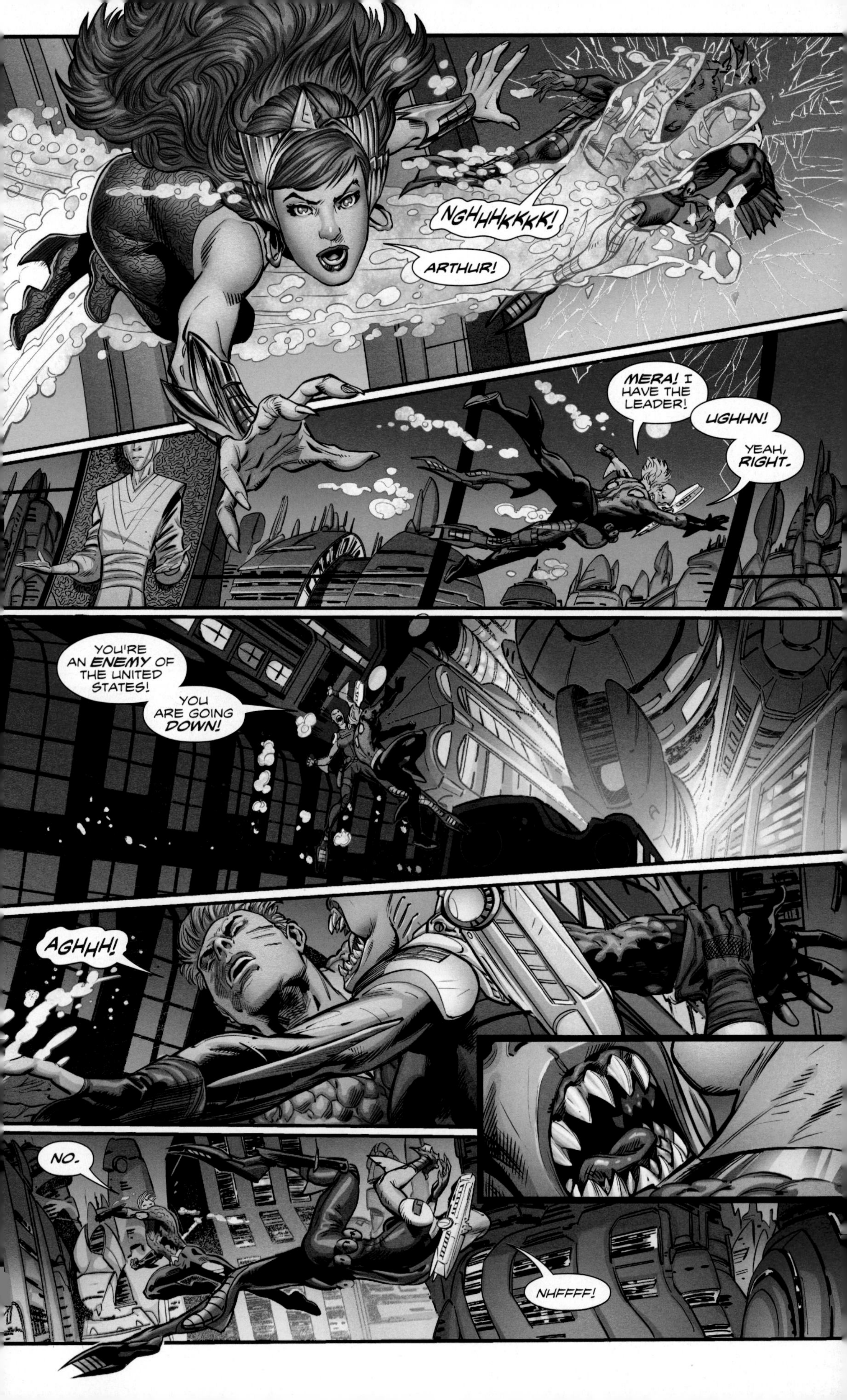
NGHHHKKKK!
ARTHUR!
MERA! I HAVE THE LEADER!
UGHHN!
YEAH, RIGHT.
YOU'RE AN ENEMY OF THE UNITED STATES!
YOU ARE GOING DOWN!
AGHHH!
NO.
NHFFFF!

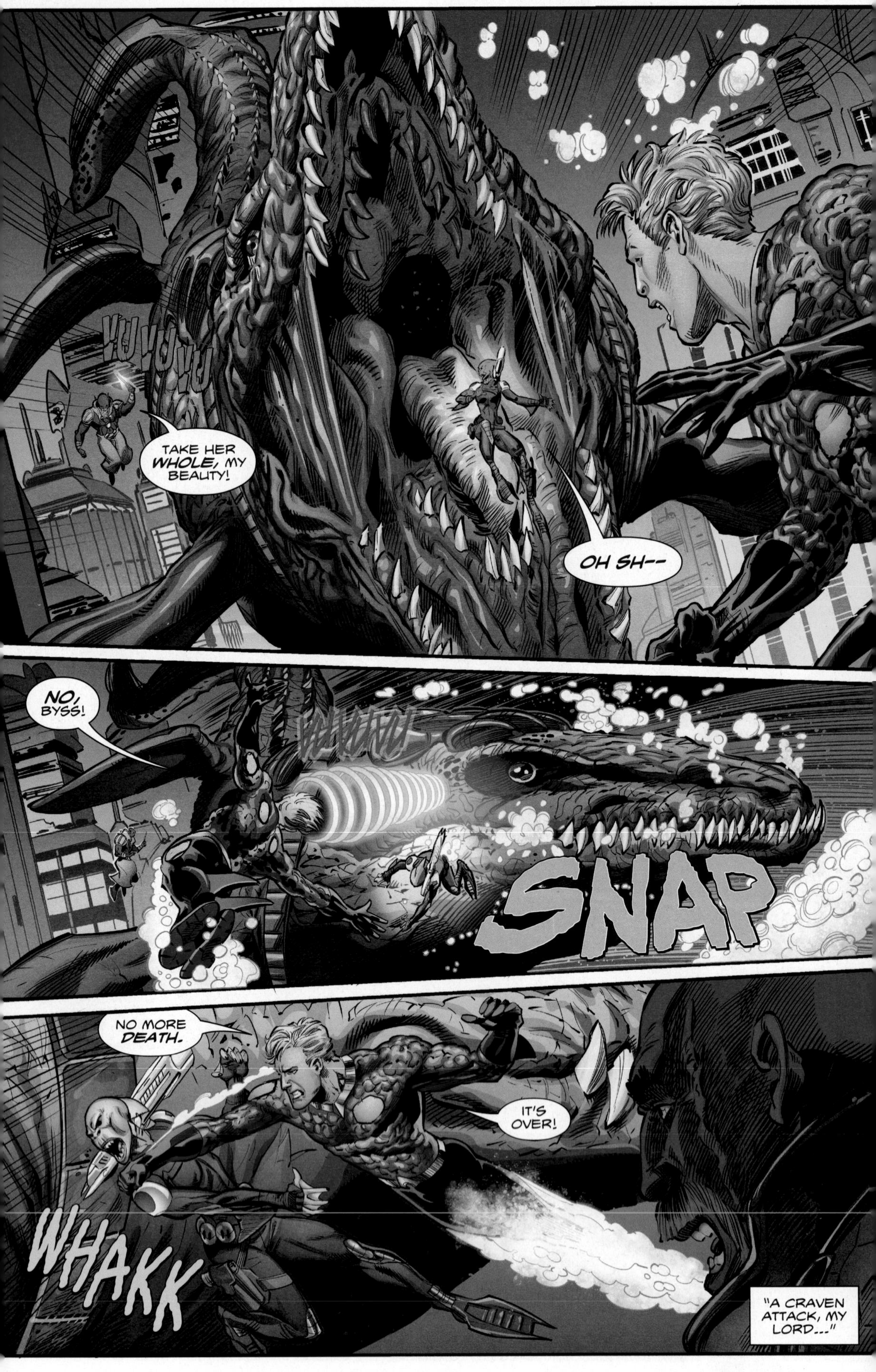
TAKE HER WHOLE, MY BEAUTY!
OH SH--
NO, BYSS!
SNAP
NO MORE DEATH.
IT'S OVER!
WHAKK
"A CRAVEN ATTACK, MY LORD..."

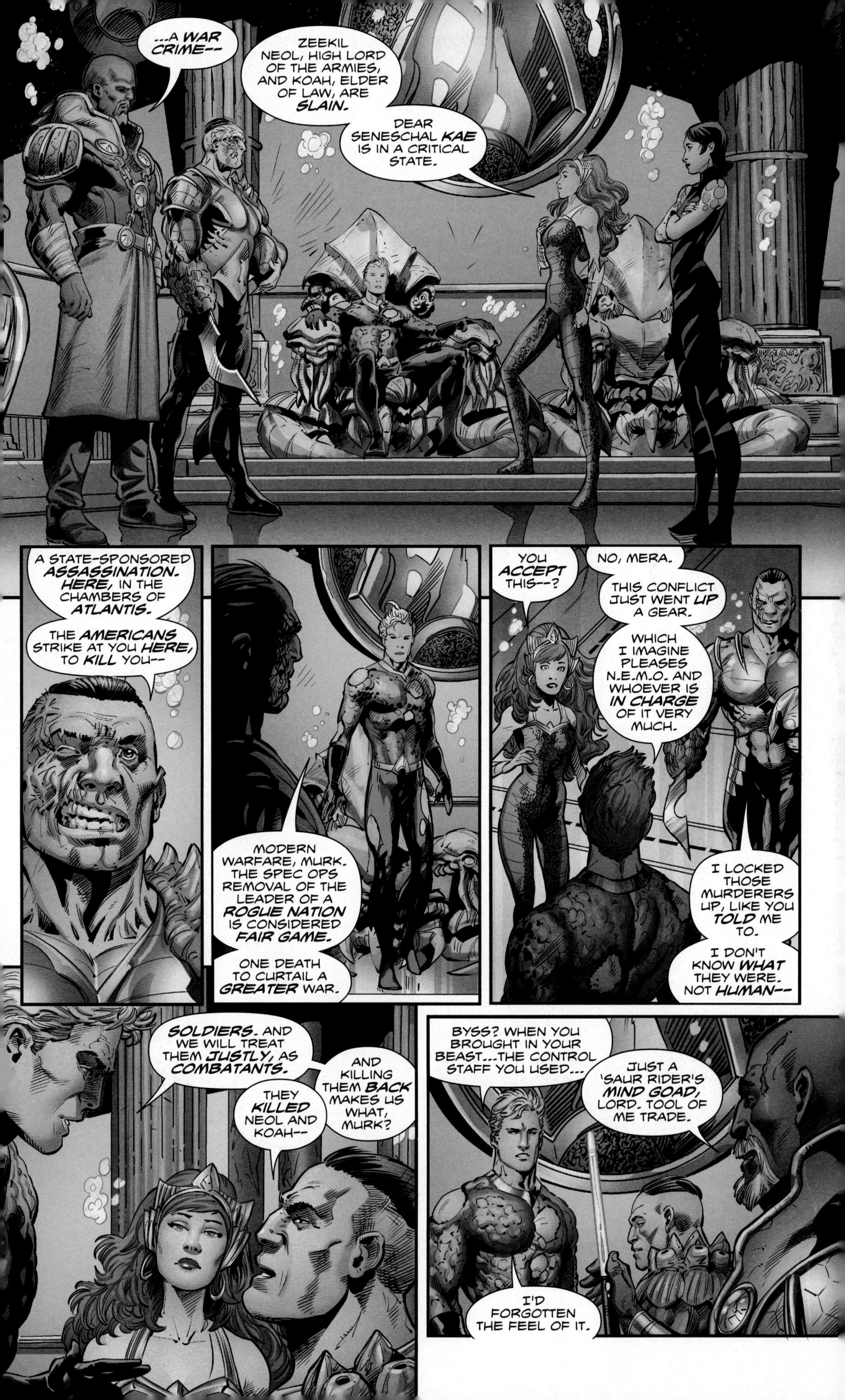
...A WAR CRIME--
ZEEKIL NEOL, HIGH LORD OF THE ARMIES, AND KOAH, ELDER OF LAW, ARE SLAIN.
DEAR SENESCHAL KAE IS IN A CRITICAL STATE.
A STATE-SPONSORED ASSASSINATION. HERE, IN THE CHAMBERS OF ATLANTIS.
THE AMERICANS STRIKE AT YOU HERE, TO KILL YOU--
MODERN WARFARE, MURK. THE SPEC OPS REMOVAL OF THE LEADER OF A ROGUE NATION IS CONSIDERED FAIR GAME.
ONE DEATH TO CURTAIL A GREATER WAR.
YOU ACCEPT THIS--?
NO, MERA.
THIS CONFLICT JUST WENT UP A GEAR.
WHICH I IMAGINE PLEASES N.E.M.O. AND WHOEVER IS IN CHARGE OF IT VERY MUCH.
I LOCKED THOSE MURDERERS UP, LIKE YOU TOLD ME TO.
I DON'T KNOW WHAT THEY WERE. NOT HUMAN--
SOLDIERS. AND WE WILL TREAT THEM JUSTLY, AS COMBATANTS.
THEY KILLED NEOL AND KOAH--
AND KILLING THEM BACK MAKES US WHAT, MURK?
BYSS? WHEN YOU BROUGHT IN YOUR BEAST...THE CONTROL STAFF YOU USED...
JUST A 'SAUR RIDER'S MIND GOAD, LORD. TOOL OF ME TRADE.
I'D FORGOTTEN THE FEEL OF IT.

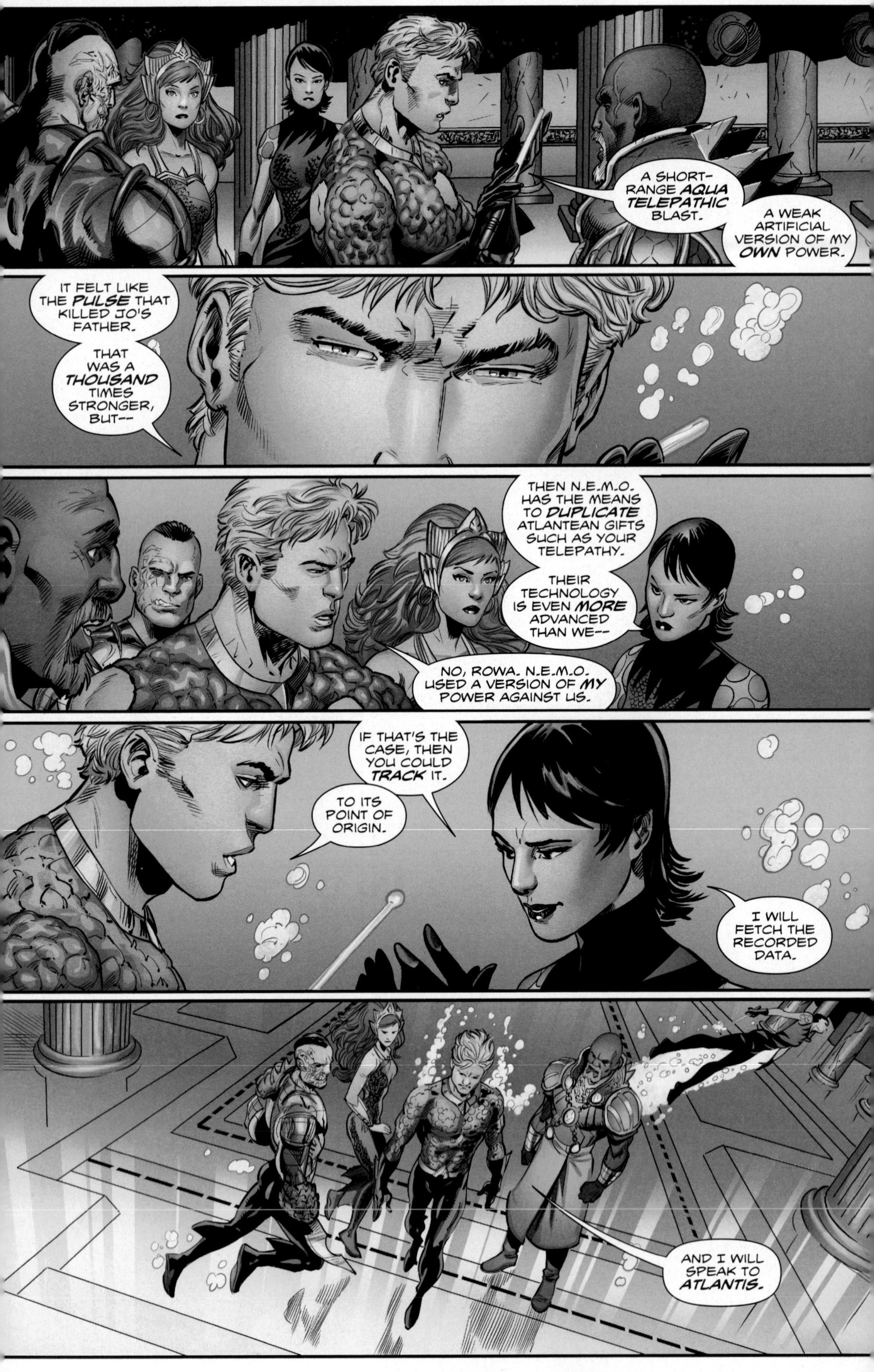
A SHORT-RANGE AQUA TELEPATHIC BLAST.
A WEAK ARTIFICIAL VERSION OF MY OWN POWER.
IT FELT LIKE THE PULSE THAT KILLED JO'S FATHER.
THAT WAS A THOUSAND TIMES STRONGER, BUT--
THEN N.E.M.O. HAS THE MEANS TO DUPLICATE ATLANTEAN GIFTS SUCH AS YOUR TELEPATHY.
THEIR TECHNOLOGY IS EVEN MORE ADVANCED THAN WE--
NO, ROWA. N.E.M.O. USED A VERSION OF MY POWER AGAINST US.
IF THAT'S THE CASE, THEN YOU COULD TRACK IT.
TO ITS POINT OF ORIGIN.
I WILL FETCH THE RECORDED DATA.
AND I WILL SPEAK TO ATLANTIS.

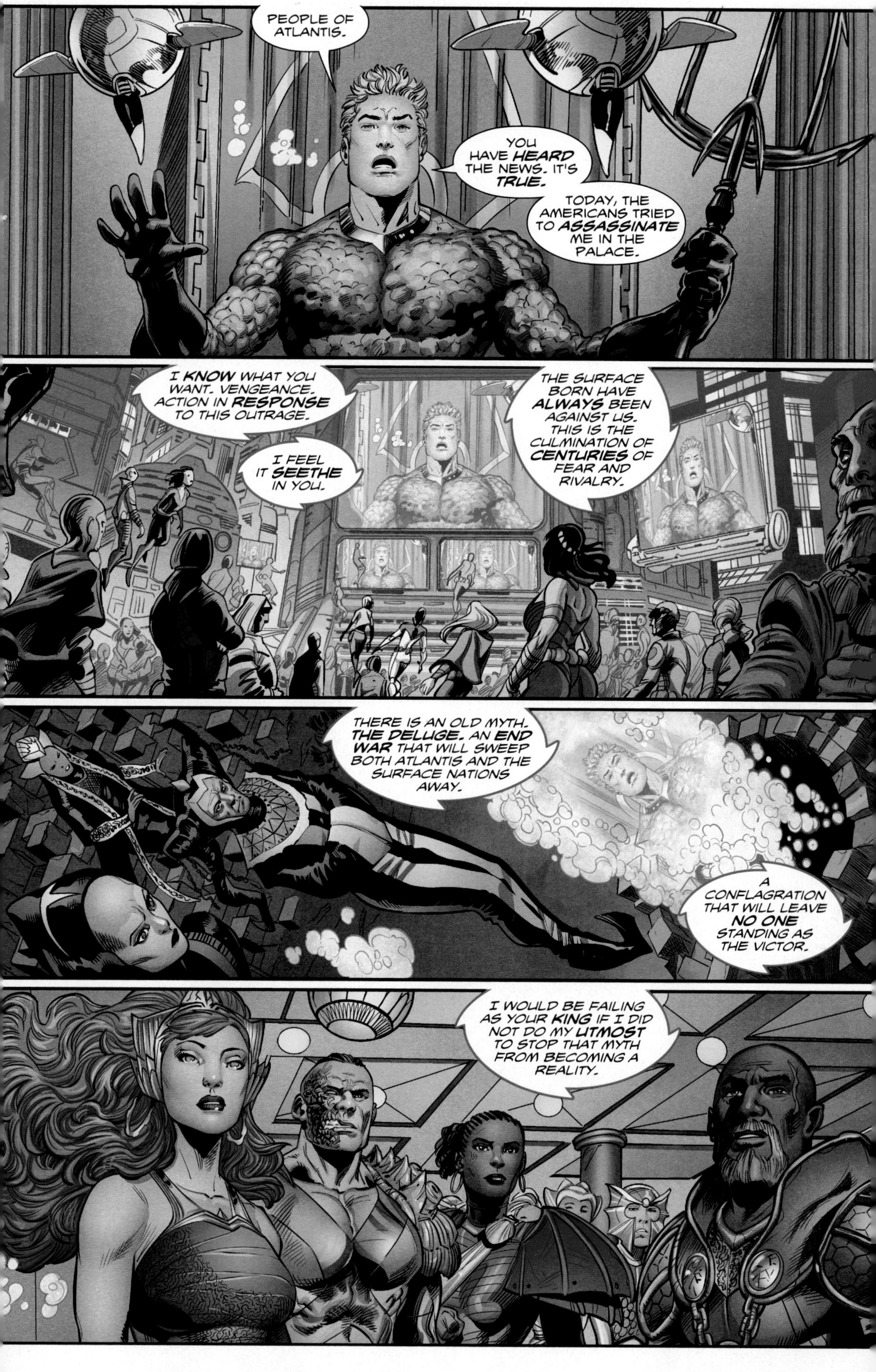
PEOPLE OF ATLANTIS.
YOU HAVE HEARD THE NEWS. IT'S TRUE.
TODAY, THE AMERICANS TRIED TO ASSASSINATE ME IN THE PALACE.
I KNOW WHAT YOU WANT. VENGEANCE. ACTION IN RESPONSE TO THIS OUTRAGE.
I FEEL IT SEETHE IN YOU.
THE SURFACE BORN HAVE ALWAYS BEEN AGAINST US. THIS IS THE CULMINATION OF CENTURIES OF FEAR AND RIVALRY.
THERE IS AN OLD MYTH. THE DELUGE. AN END WAR THAT WILL SWEEP BOTH ATLANTIS AND THE SURFACE NATIONS AWAY.
A CONFLAGRATION THAT WILL LEAVE NO ONE STANDING AS THE VICTOR.
I WOULD BE FAILING AS YOUR KING IF I DID NOT DO MY UTMOST TO STOP THAT MYTH FROM BECOMING A REALITY.

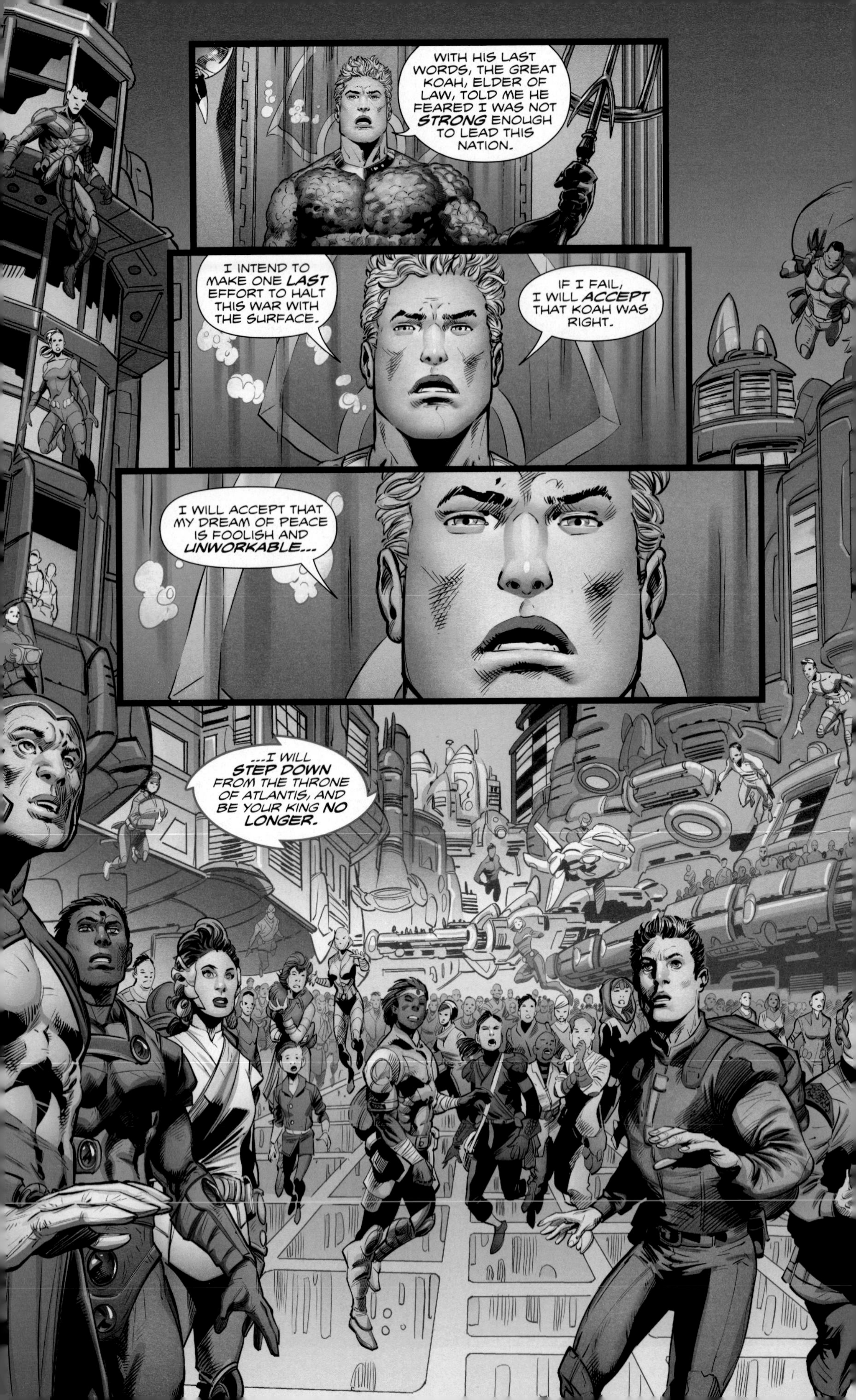
WITH HIS LAST WORDS, THE GREAT KOAH, ELDER OF LAW, TOLD ME HE FEARED I WAS NOT STRONG ENOUGH TO LEAD THIS NATION.
I INTEND TO MAKE ONE LAST EFFORT TO HALT THIS WAR WITH THE SURFACE.
IF I FAIL, I WILL ACCEPT THAT KOAH WAS RIGHT.
I WILL ACCEPT THAT MY DREAM OF PEACE IS FOOLISH AND UNWORKABLE...
...I WILL STEP DOWN FROM THE THRONE OF ATLANTIS, AND BE YOUR KING NO LONGER.

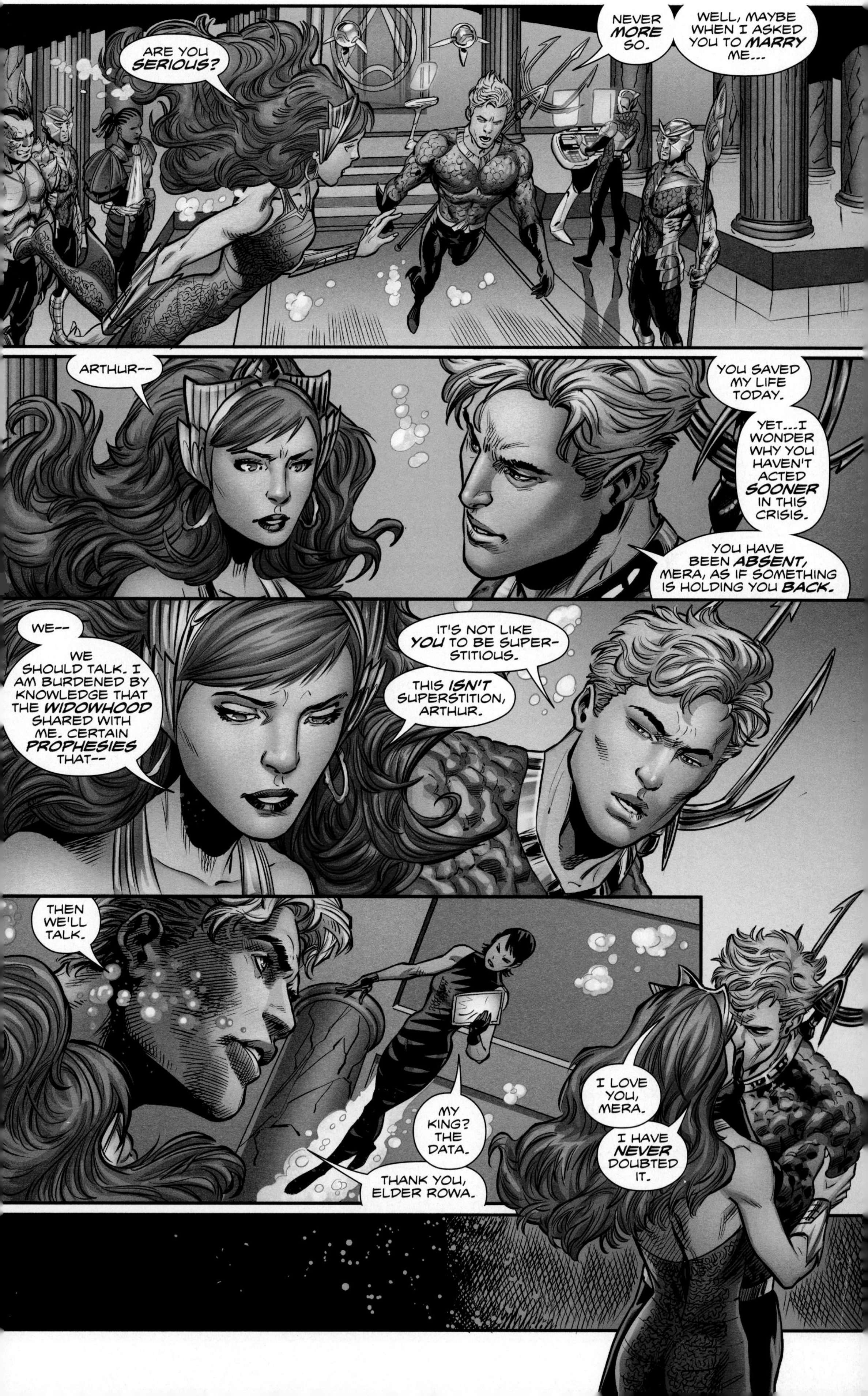
ARE YOU SERIOUS?
NEVER MORE SO.
WELL, MAYBE WHEN I ASKED YOU TO MARRY ME...
ARTHUR--
YOU SAVED MY LIFE TODAY.
YET...I WONDER WHY YOU HAVEN'T ACTED SOONER IN THIS CRISIS.
YOU HAVE BEEN ABSENT, MERA, AS IF SOMETHING IS HOLDING YOU BACK.
WE--
WE SHOULD TALK. I AM BURDENED BY KNOWLEDGE THAT THE WIDOWHOOD SHARED WITH ME. CERTAIN PROPHESIES THAT--
IT'S NOT LIKE YOU TO BE SUPER-STITIOUS.
THIS ISN'T SUPERSTITION, ARTHUR.
THEN WE'LL TALK.
MY KING? THE DATA.
THANK YOU, ELDER ROWA.
I LOVE YOU, MERA.
I HAVE NEVER DOUBTED IT.

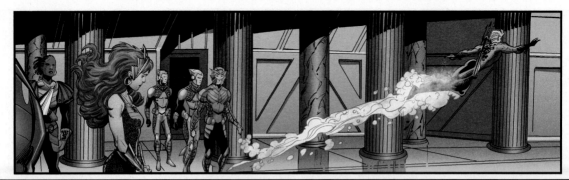

PONTA DA ALTA, THE AZORES.

TEMPORARY N.E.M.O. BASE OF OPERATIONS.

AMPLIFIED TIDAL SURGE JUST *SWAMPED* GALVESTON.

PRETENDER UNITS ARE *CONTINUING* THE HIT-AND- RUN ALONG THE EAST COAST...

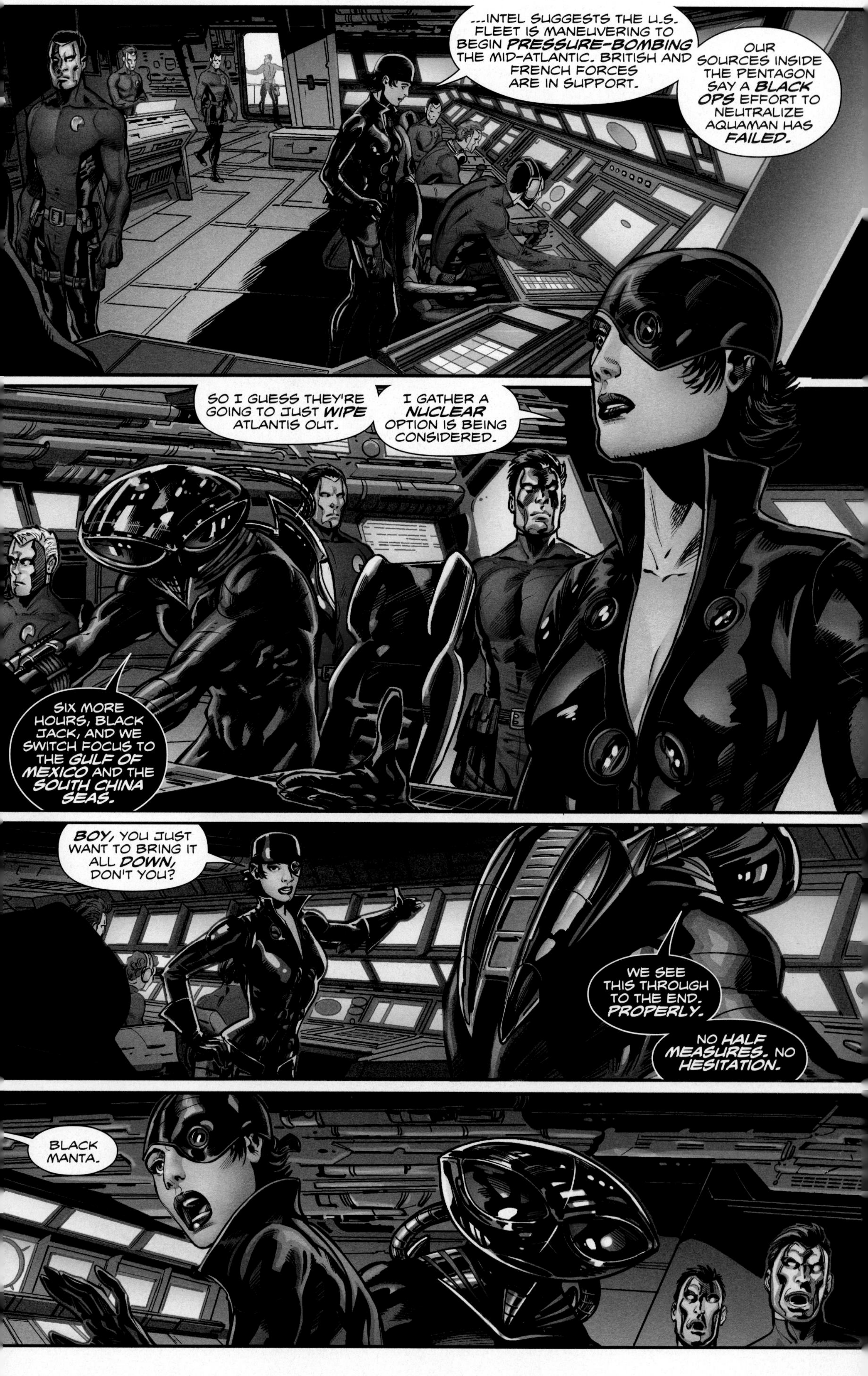
...INTEL SUGGESTS THE U.S. FLEET IS MANEUVERING TO BEGIN PRESSURE-BOMBING THE MID-ATLANTIC. BRITISH AND FRENCH FORCES ARE IN SUPPORT.
OUR SOURCES INSIDE THE PENTAGON SAY A BLACK OPS EFFORT TO NEUTRALIZE AQUAMAN HAS FAILED.
SO I GUESS THEY'RE GOING TO JUST WIPE ATLANTIS OUT.
I GATHER A NUCLEAR OPTION IS BEING CONSIDERED.
SIX MORE HOURS, BLACK JACK, AND WE SWITCH FOCUS TO THE GULF OF MEXICO AND THE SOUTH CHINA SEAS.
BOY, YOU JUST WANT TO BRING IT ALL DOWN, DON'T YOU?
WE SEE THIS THROUGH TO THE END. PROPERLY.
NO HALF MEASURES. NO HESITATION.
BLACK MANTA.

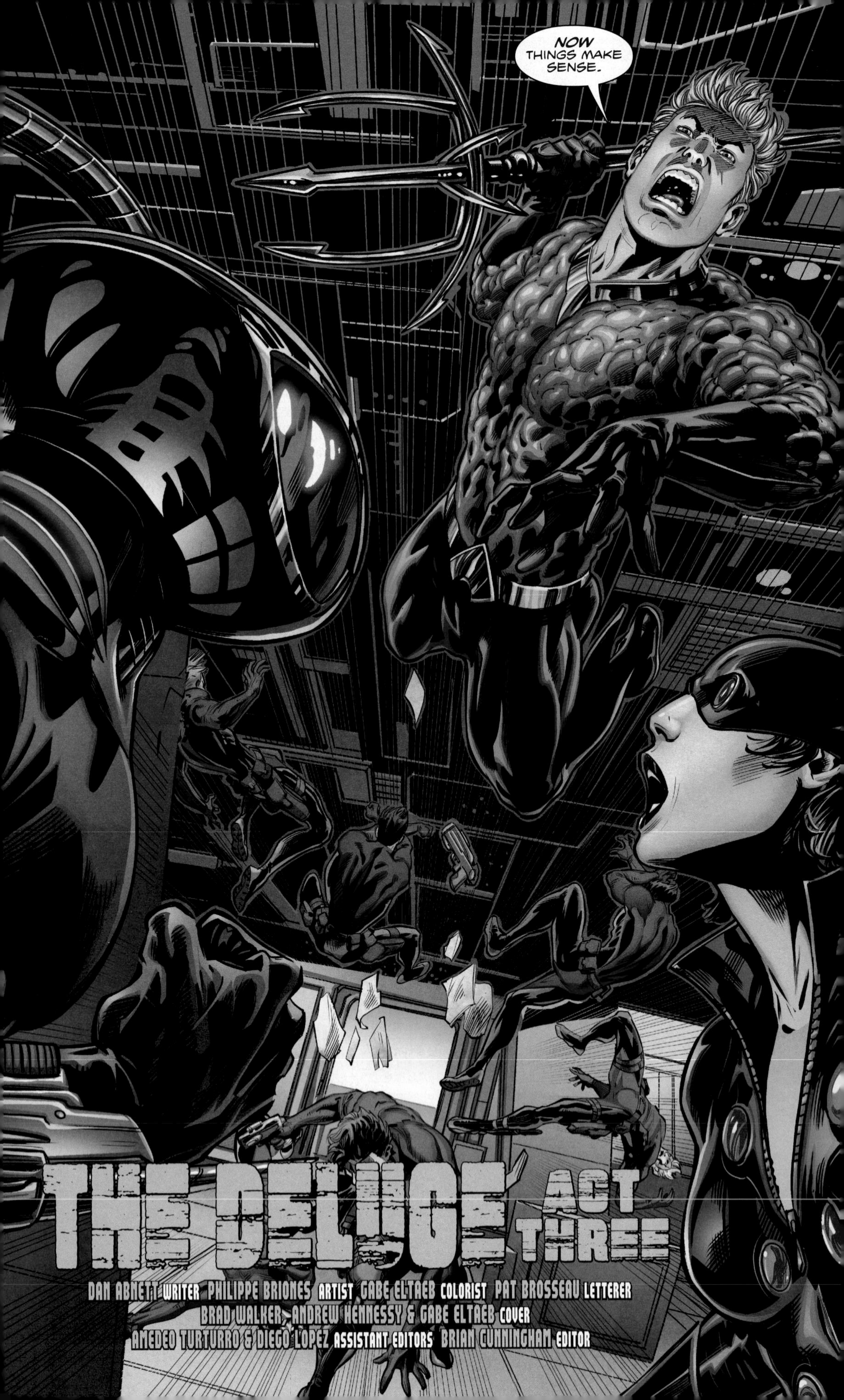
NOW THINGS MAKE SENSE.
THE DELUGE ACT THREE
DAN ABNETT WRITER PHILIPPE BRIONES ARTIST GABE ELTAEB COLORIST PAT BROSSEAU LETTERER
BRAD WALKER, ANDREW HENNESSY & GABE ELTAEB COVER
AMEDEO TURTURRO & DIEGO LOPEZ ASSISTANT EDITORS BRIAN CUNNINGHAM EDITOR

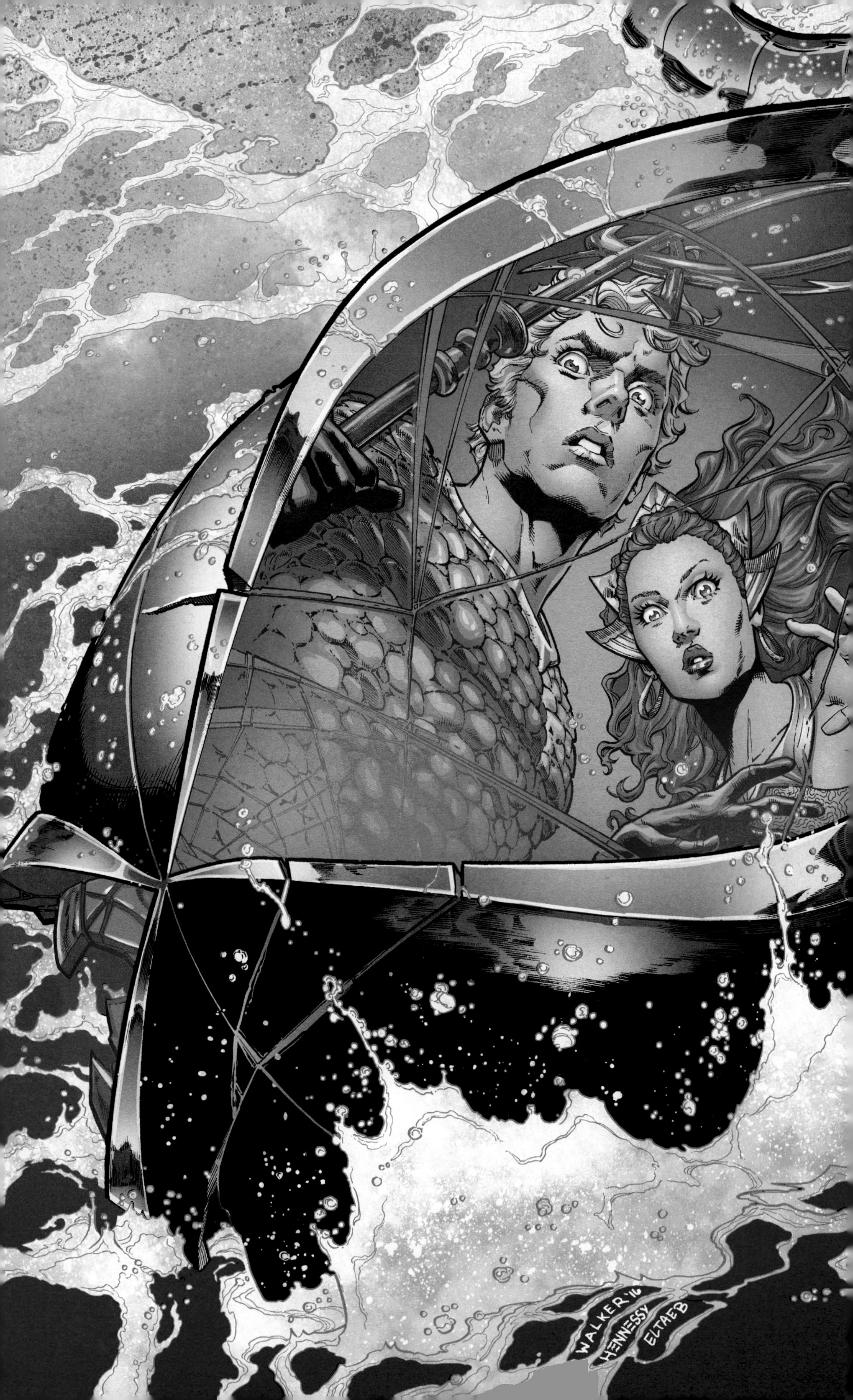
WALKER '16
HENNESSY
ELTAEB

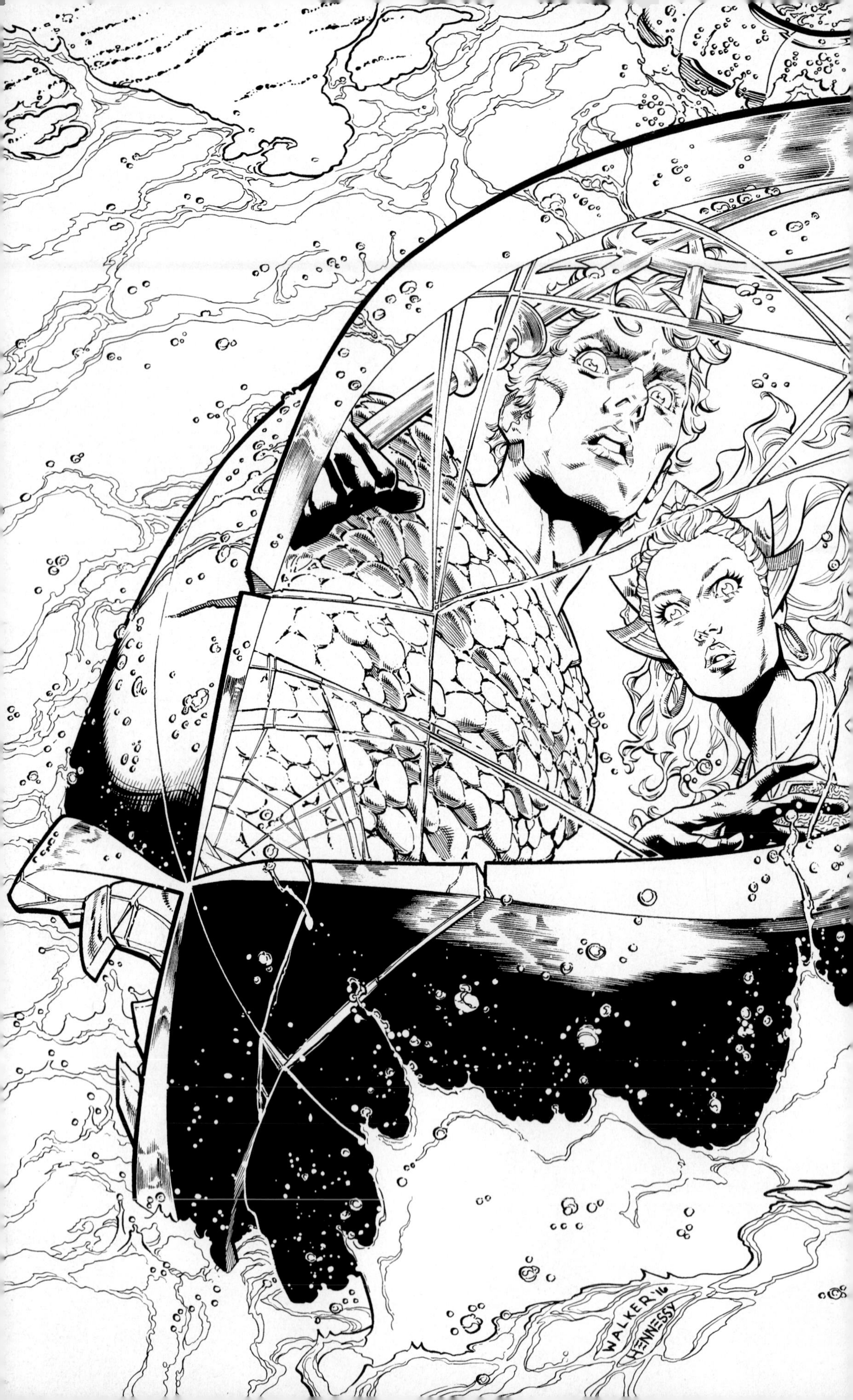
WALKER '16
HENNESSY

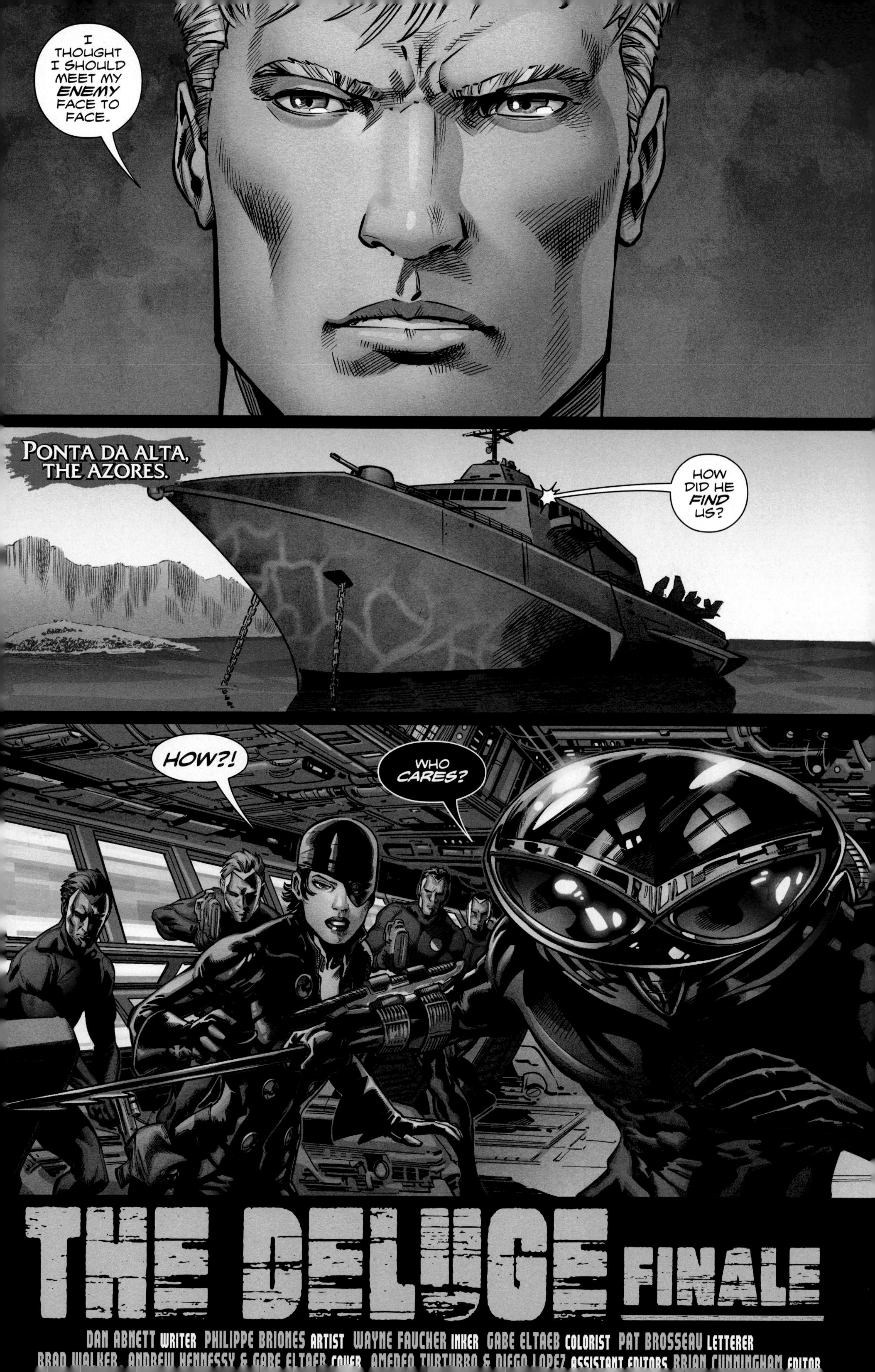

I THOUGHT I SHOULD MEET MY ENEMY FACE TO FACE.
PONTA DA ALTA, THE AZORES.
HOW DID HE FIND US?
HOW?!
WHO CARES?
THE DELUGE FINALE
DAN ABNETT WRITER PHILIPPE BRIONES ARTIST WAYNE FAUCHER INKER GABE ELTAEB COLORIST PAT BROSSEAU LETTERER
BRAD WALKER, ANDREW HENNESSY & GABE ELTAEB COVER AMEDEO TURTURRO & DIEGO LOPEZ ASSISTANT EDITORS BRIAN CUNNINGHAM EDITOR

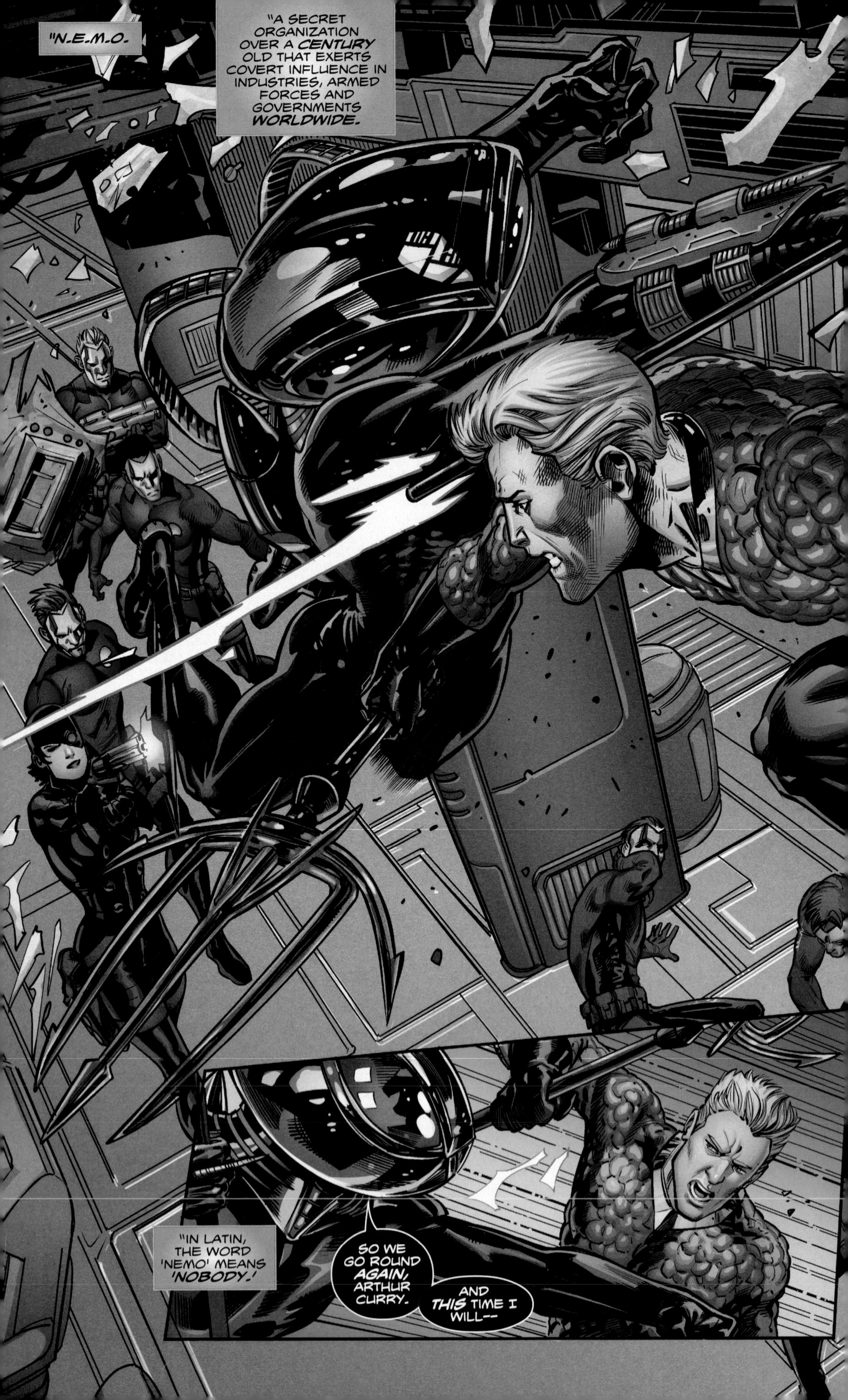
"N.E.M.O.
"A SECRET ORGANIZATION OVER A CENTURY OLD THAT EXERTS COVERT INFLUENCE IN INDUSTRIES, ARMED FORCES AND GOVERNMENTS WORLDWIDE.
"IN LATIN, THE WORD 'NEMO' MEANS 'NOBODY.'
SO WE GO ROUND AGAIN, ARTHUR CURRY.
AND THIS TIME I WILL--

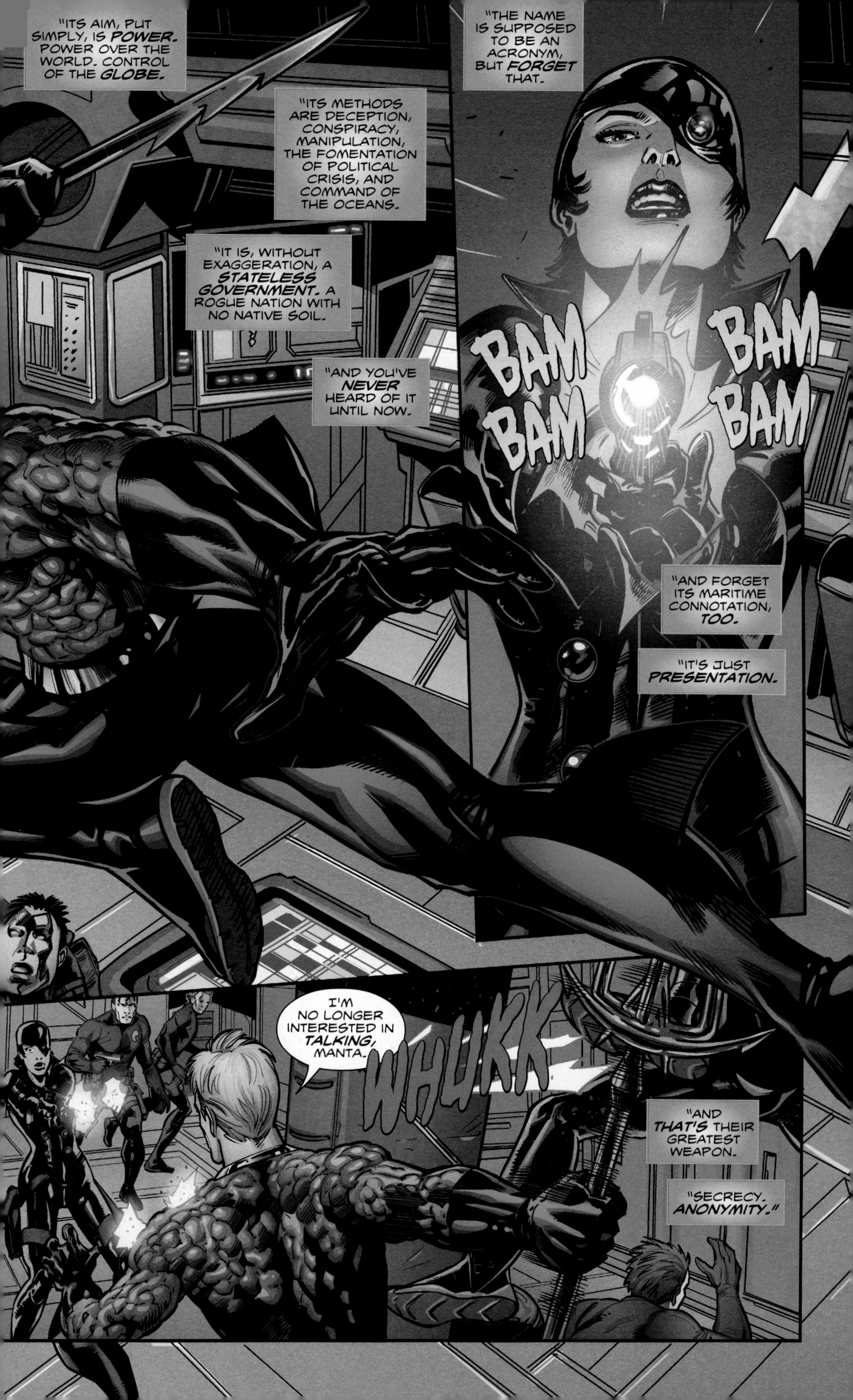
"ITS AIM, PUT SIMPLY, IS POWER. POWER OVER THE WORLD. CONTROL OF THE GLOBE.
"ITS METHODS ARE DECEPTION, CONSPIRACY, MANIPULATION, THE FOMENTATION OF POLITICAL CRISIS, AND COMMAND OF THE OCEANS.
"IT IS, WITHOUT EXAGGERATION, A STATELESS GOVERNMENT. A ROGUE NATION WITH NO NATIVE SOIL.
"AND YOU'VE NEVER HEARD OF IT UNTIL NOW.
"THE NAME IS SUPPOSED TO BE AN ACRONYM, BUT FORGET THAT.
BAM BAM
BAM BAM
"AND FORGET ITS MARITIME CONNOTATION, TOO.
"IT'S JUST PRESENTATION.
I'M NO LONGER INTERESTED IN TALKING, MANTA.
WHUKK
"AND THAT'S THEIR GREATEST WEAPON.
"SECRECY. ANONYMITY."

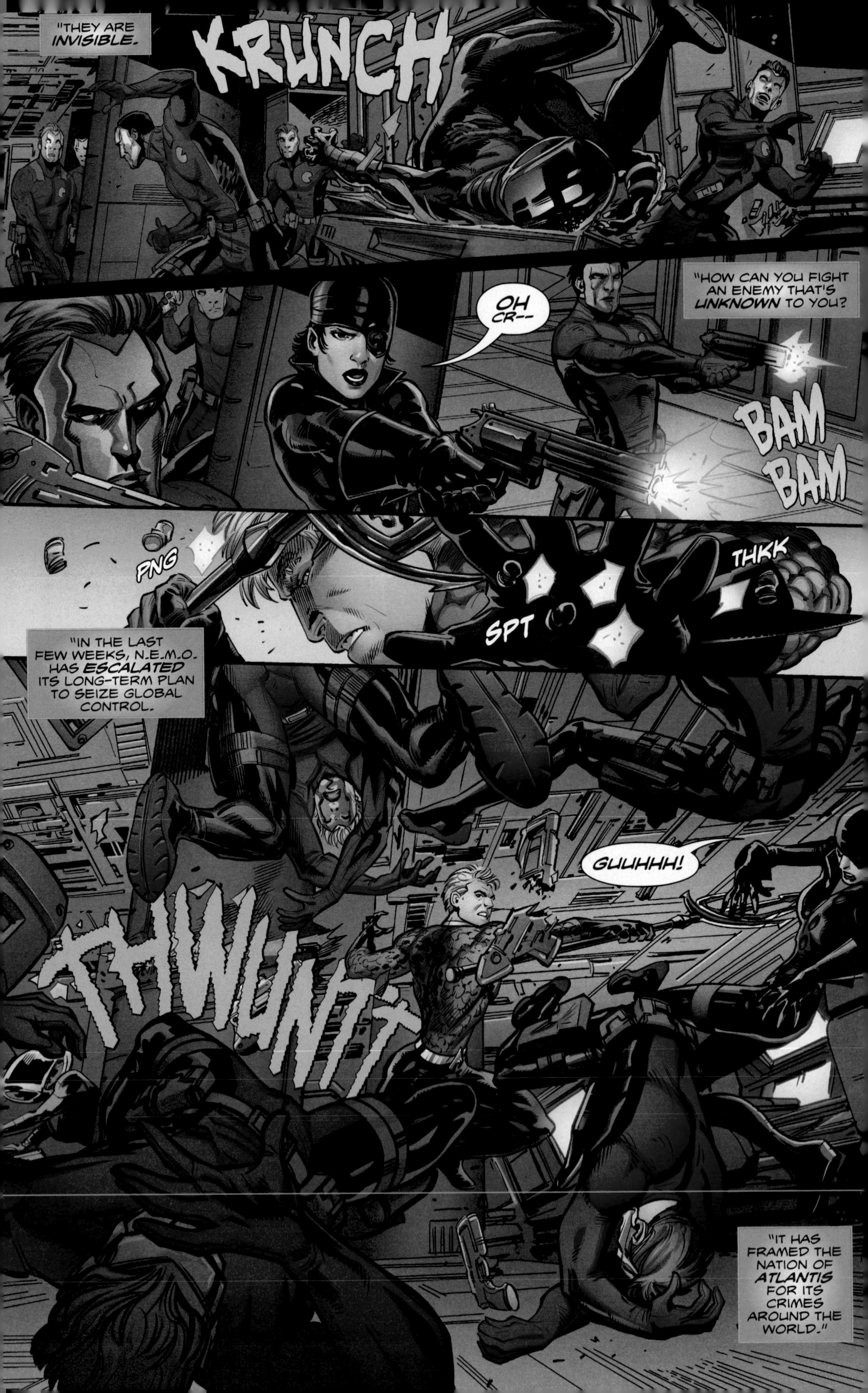
"THEY ARE INVISIBLE.
KRUNCH
OH CR--
"HOW CAN YOU FIGHT AN ENEMY THAT'S UNKNOWN TO YOU?
BAM BAM
PNG
THKK
SPT
"IN THE LAST FEW WEEKS, N.E.M.O. HAS ESCALATED ITS LONG-TERM PLAN TO SEIZE GLOBAL CONTROL.
GUUHHH!
THWUNT
"IT HAS FRAMED THE NATION OF ATLANTIS FOR ITS CRIMES AROUND THE WORLD."

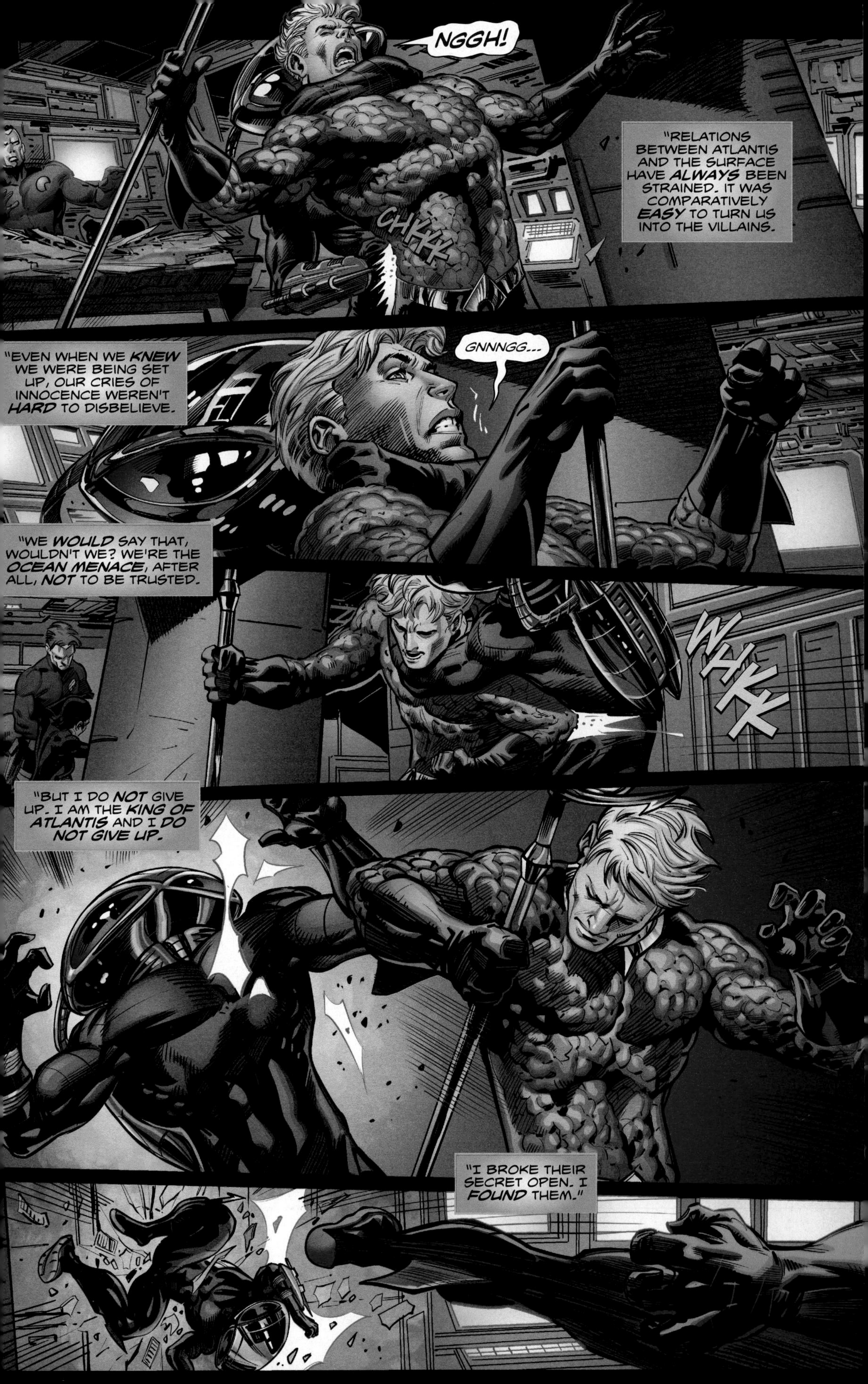
NGGH!
CHKKK
"RELATIONS BETWEEN ATLANTIS AND THE SURFACE HAVE ALWAYS BEEN STRAINED. IT WAS COMPARATIVELY EASY TO TURN US INTO THE VILLAINS.
"EVEN WHEN WE KNEW WE WERE BEING SET UP, OUR CRIES OF INNOCENCE WEREN'T HARD TO DISBELIEVE.
GNNNGG...
"WE WOULD SAY THAT, WOULDN'T WE? WE'RE THE OCEAN MENACE, AFTER ALL, NOT TO BE TRUSTED.
WHKK
"BUT I DO NOT GIVE UP. I AM THE KING OF ATLANTIS AND I DO NOT GIVE UP.
"I BROKE THEIR SECRET OPEN. I FOUND THEM."

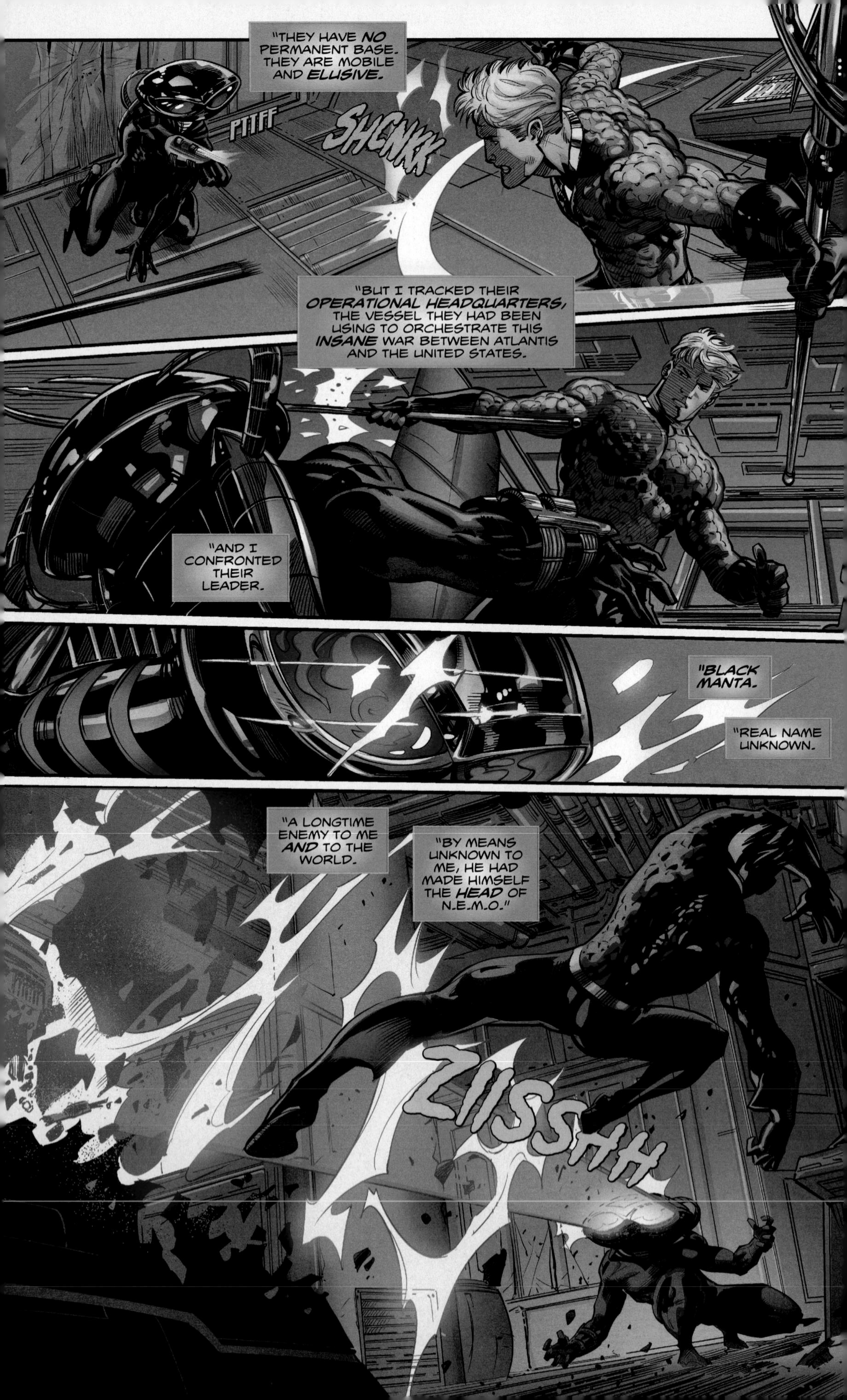
"THEY HAVE NO PERMANENT BASE. THEY ARE MOBILE AND ELUSIVE.
PTTFF
SHCNKK
"BUT I TRACKED THEIR OPERATIONAL HEADQUARTERS, THE VESSEL THEY HAD BEEN USING TO ORCHESTRATE THIS INSANE WAR BETWEEN ATLANTIS AND THE UNITED STATES.
"AND I CONFRONTED THEIR LEADER.
"BLACK MANTA.
"REAL NAME UNKNOWN.
"A LONGTIME ENEMY TO ME AND TO THE WORLD.
"BY MEANS UNKNOWN TO ME, HE HAD MADE HIMSELF THE HEAD OF N.E.M.O."
ZIISSHH

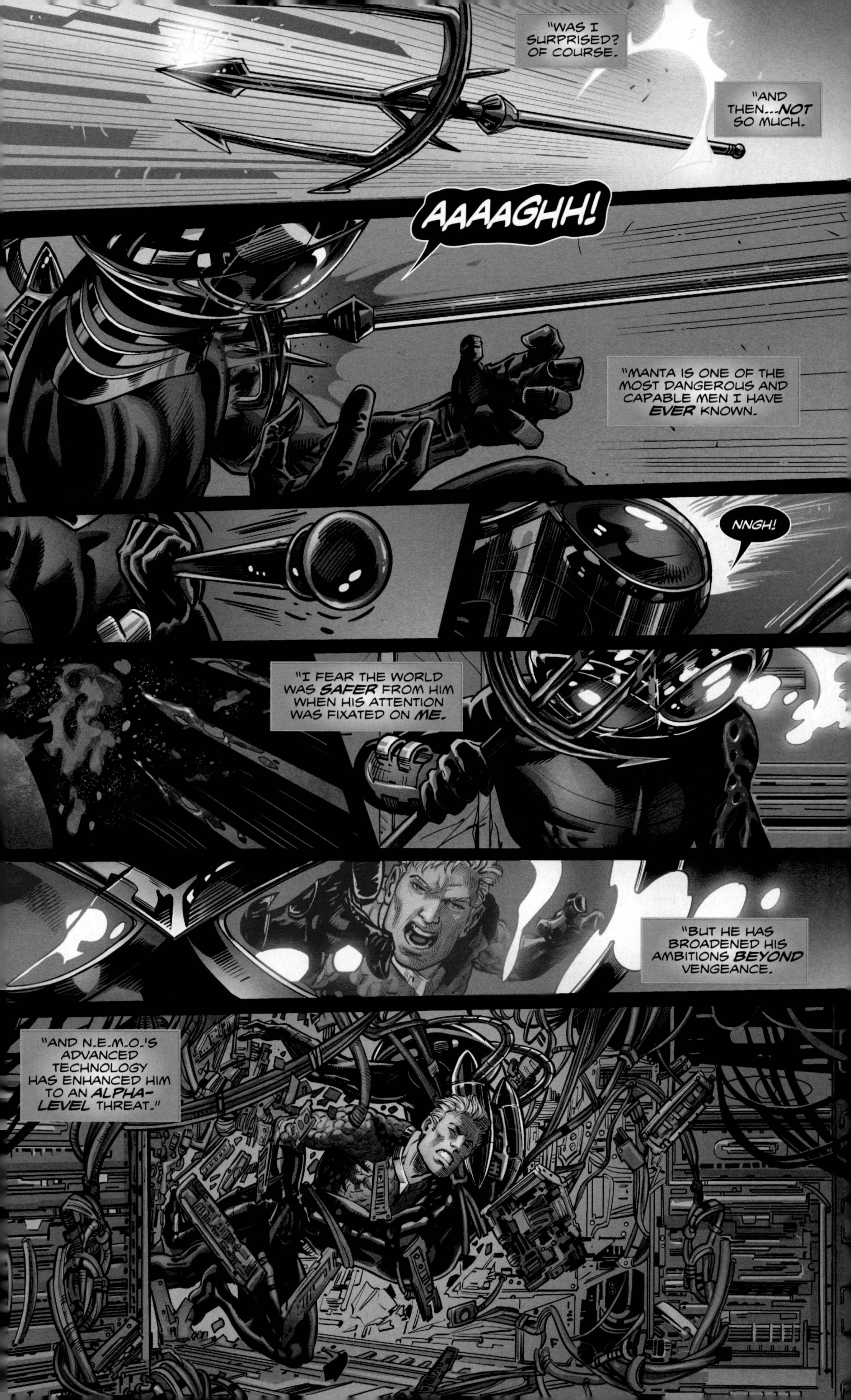
"WAS I SURPRISED? OF COURSE.
"AND THEN...NOT SO MUCH.
AAAAGHH!
"MANTA IS ONE OF THE MOST DANGEROUS AND CAPABLE MEN I HAVE EVER KNOWN.
NNGH!
"I FEAR THE WORLD WAS SAFER FROM HIM WHEN HIS ATTENTION WAS FIXATED ON ME.
"BUT HE HAS BROADENED HIS AMBITIONS BEYOND VENGEANCE.
"AND N.E.M.O.'S ADVANCED TECHNOLOGY HAS ENHANCED HIM TO AN ALPHA-LEVEL THREAT."

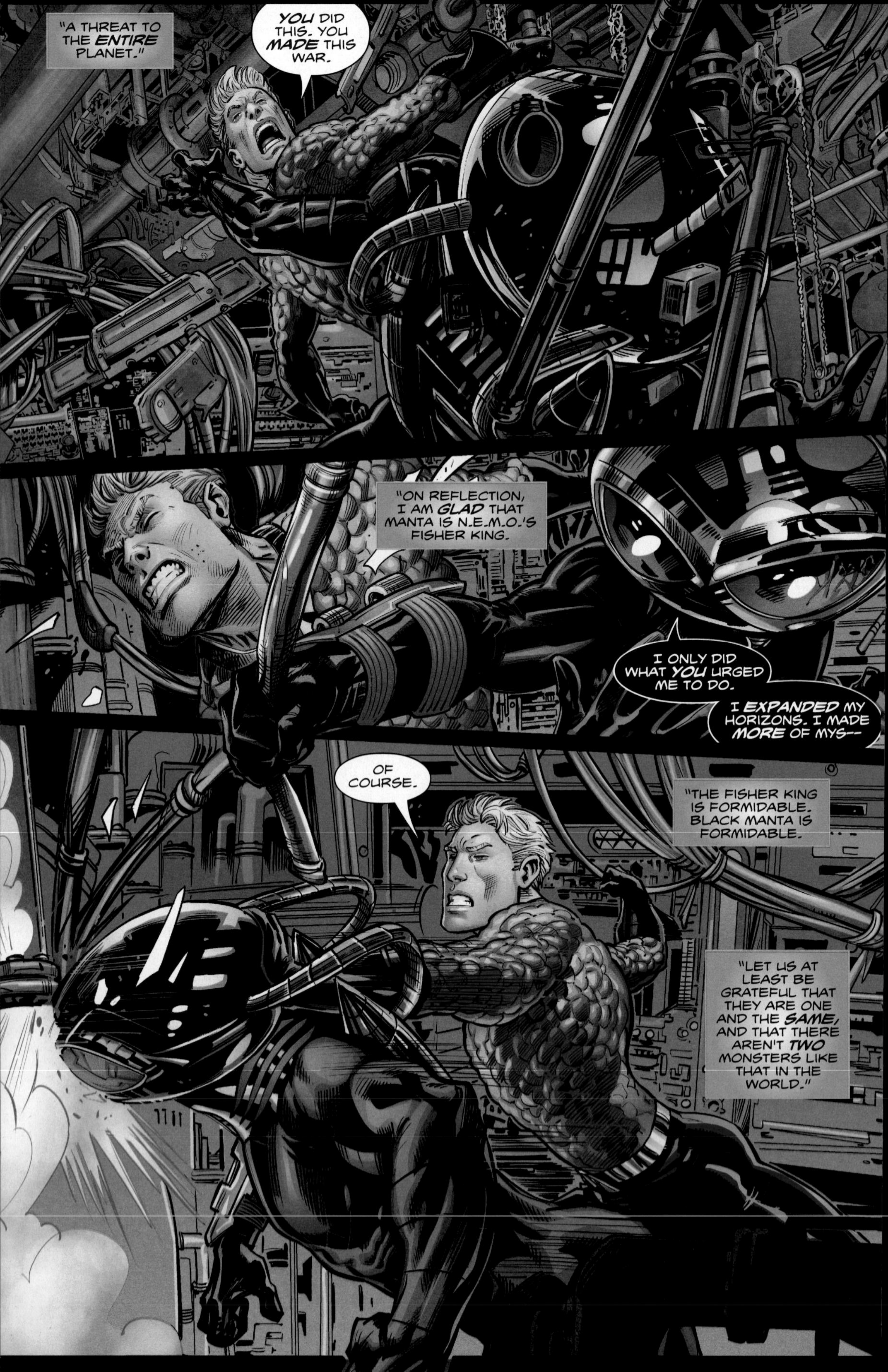
"A THREAT TO THE ENTIRE PLANET."
YOU DID THIS. YOU MADE THIS WAR.
"ON REFLECTION, I AM GLAD THAT MANTA IS N.E.M.O.'S FISHER KING.
I ONLY DID WHAT YOU URGED ME TO DO.
I EXPANDED MY HORIZONS. I MADE MORE OF MYS--
OF COURSE.
"THE FISHER KING IS FORMIDABLE. BLACK MANTA IS FORMIDABLE.
"LET US AT LEAST BE GRATEFUL THAT THEY ARE ONE AND THE SAME, AND THAT THERE AREN'T TWO MONSTERS LIKE THAT IN THE WORLD."

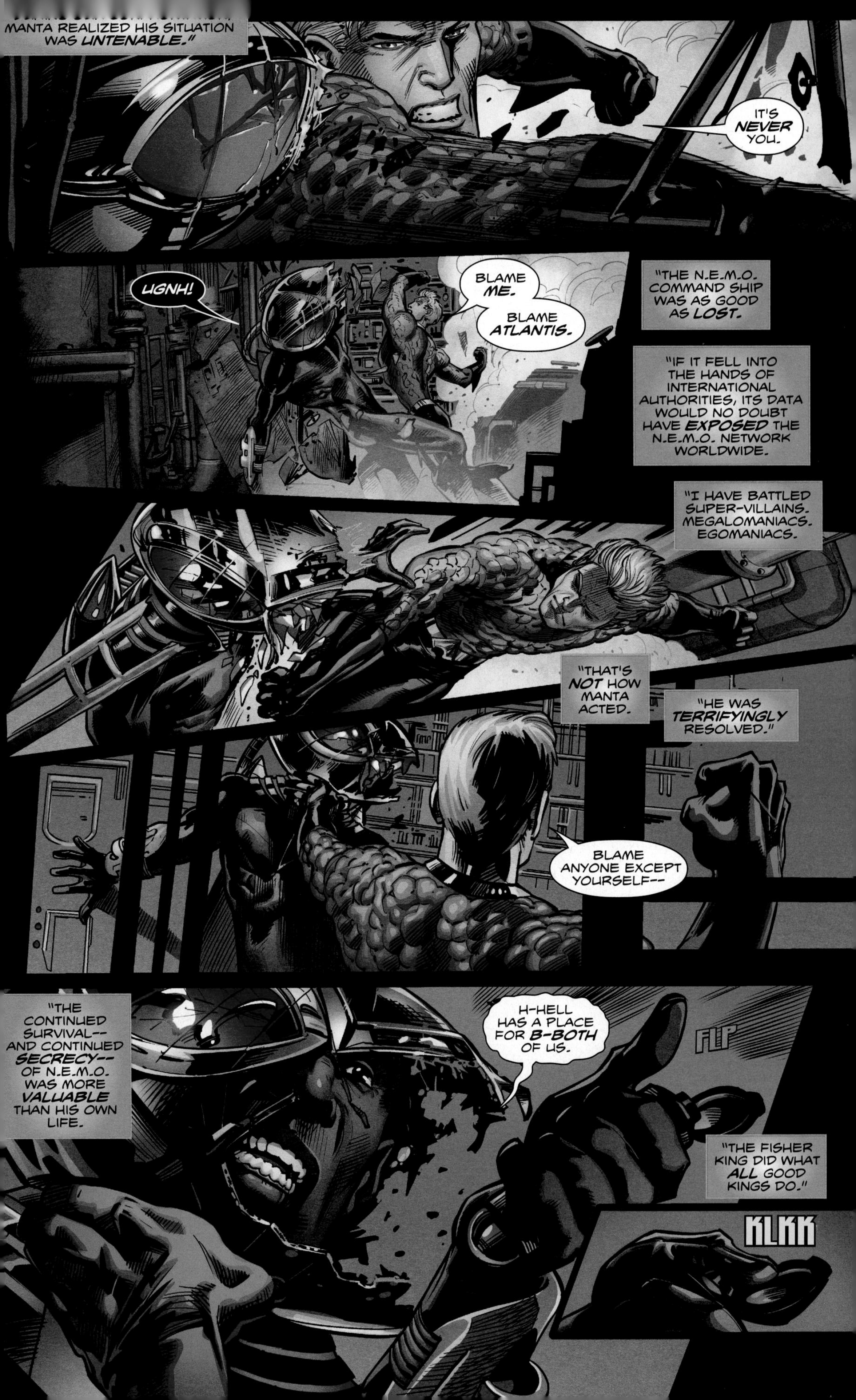

MANTA REALIZED HIS SITUATION WAS UNTENABLE."
IT'S NEVER YOU.
UGNH!
BLAME ME.
BLAME ATLANTIS.
"THE N.E.M.O. COMMAND SHIP WAS AS GOOD AS LOST.
"IF IT FELL INTO THE HANDS OF INTERNATIONAL AUTHORITIES, ITS DATA WOULD NO DOUBT HAVE EXPOSED THE N.E.M.O. NETWORK WORLDWIDE.
"I HAVE BATTLED SUPER-VILLAINS. MEGALOMANIACS. EGOMANIACS.
"THAT'S NOT HOW MANTA ACTED.
"HE WAS TERRIFYINGLY RESOLVED."
BLAME ANYONE EXCEPT YOURSELF--
"THE CONTINUED SURVIVAL-- AND CONTINUED SECRECY-- OF N.E.M.O. WAS MORE VALUABLE THAN HIS OWN LIFE.
H-HELL HAS A PLACE FOR B-BOTH OF US.
FLP
"THE FISHER KING DID WHAT ALL GOOD KINGS DO."
KLKK

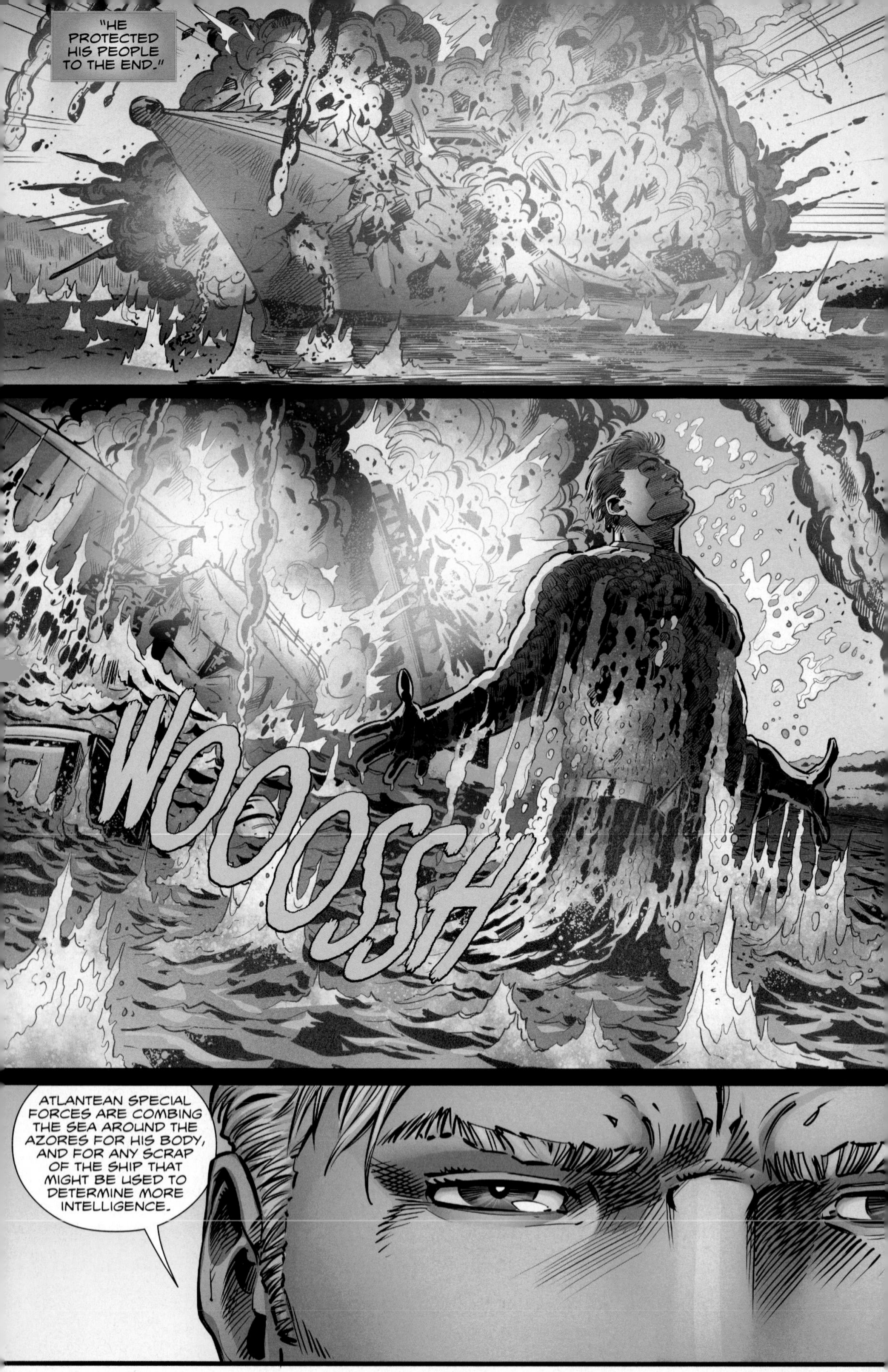
"HE PROTECTED HIS PEOPLE TO THE END."
WOOOSSH
ATLANTEAN SPECIAL FORCES ARE COMBING THE SEA AROUND THE AZORES FOR HIS BODY, AND FOR ANY SCRAP OF THE SHIP THAT MIGHT BE USED TO DETERMINE MORE INTELLIGENCE.

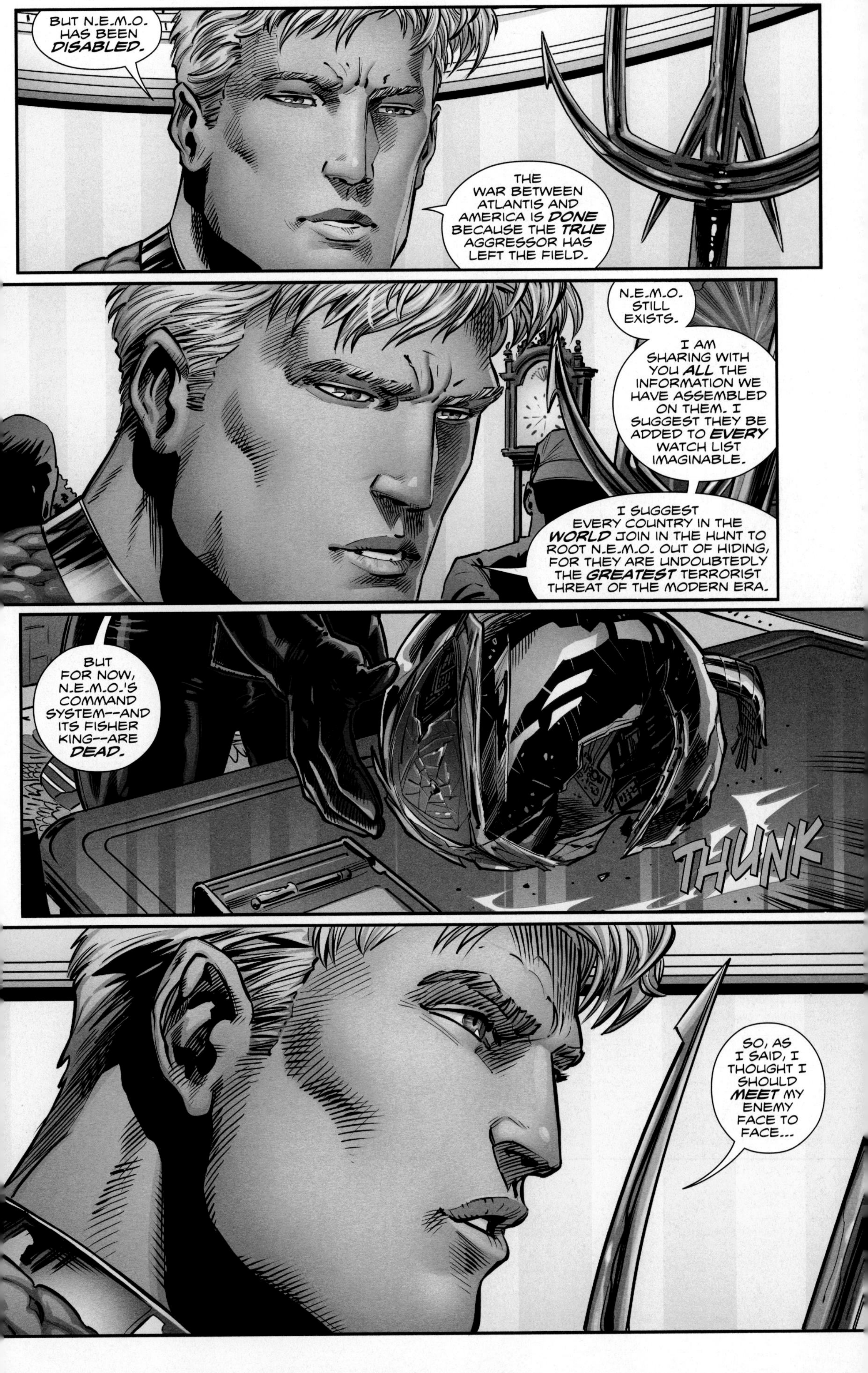
BUT N.E.M.O. HAS BEEN DISABLED.
THE WAR BETWEEN ATLANTIS AND AMERICA IS DONE BECAUSE THE TRUE AGGRESSOR HAS LEFT THE FIELD.
N.E.M.O. STILL EXISTS.
I AM SHARING WITH YOU ALL THE INFORMATION WE HAVE ASSEMBLED ON THEM. I SUGGEST THEY BE ADDED TO EVERY WATCH LIST IMAGINABLE.
I SUGGEST EVERY COUNTRY IN THE WORLD JOIN IN THE HUNT TO ROOT N.E.M.O. OUT OF HIDING, FOR THEY ARE UNDOUBTEDLY THE GREATEST TERRORIST THREAT OF THE MODERN ERA.
BUT FOR NOW, N.E.M.O.'S COMMAND SYSTEM--AND ITS FISHER KING--ARE DEAD.
THUNK
SO, AS I SAID, I THOUGHT I SHOULD MEET MY ENEMY FACE TO FACE...

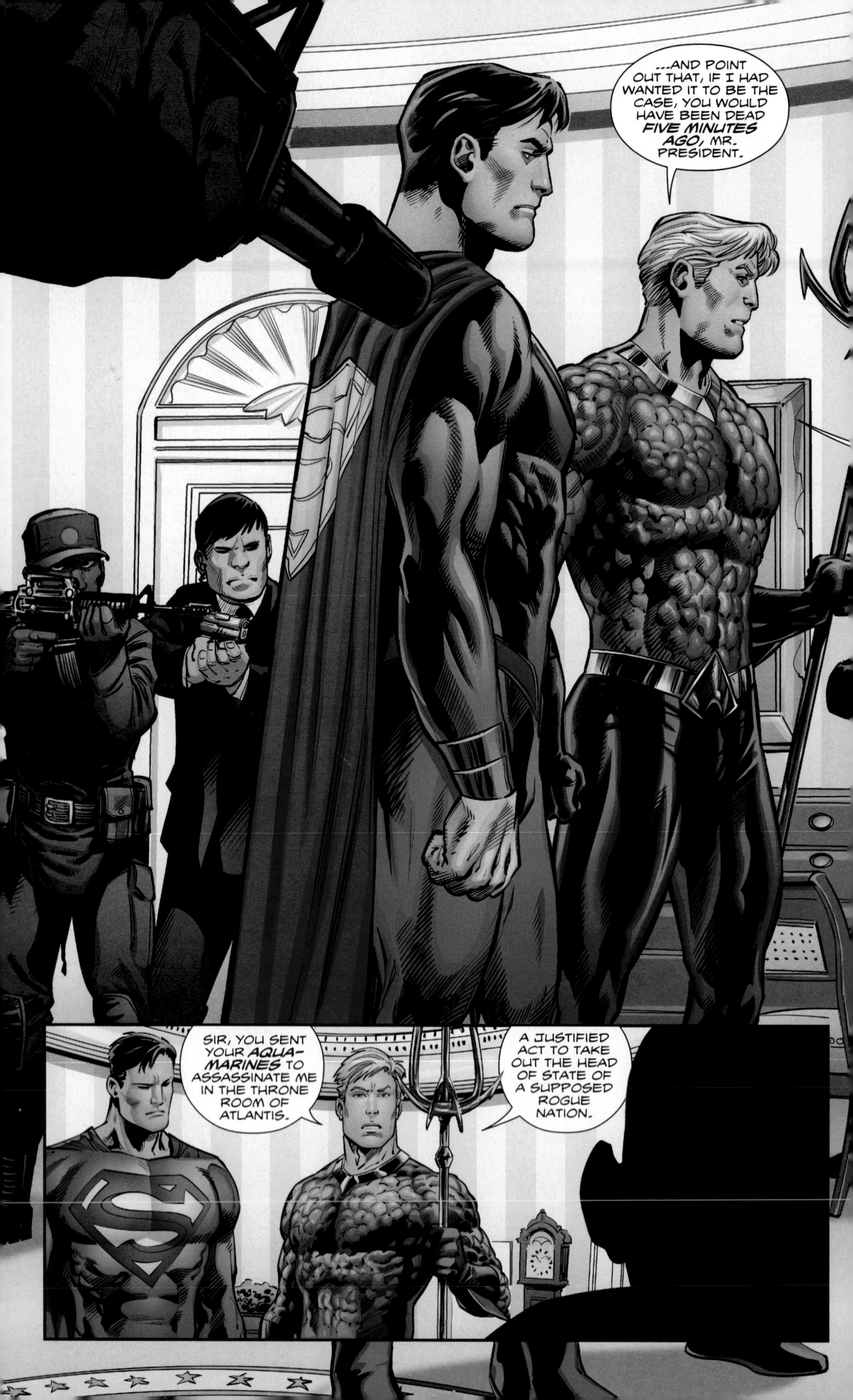

...AND POINT OUT THAT, IF I HAD WANTED IT TO BE THE CASE, YOU WOULD HAVE BEEN DEAD FIVE MINUTES AGO, MR. PRESIDENT.
SIR, YOU SENT YOUR AQUA-MARINES TO ASSASSINATE ME IN THE THRONE ROOM OF ATLANTIS.
A JUSTIFIED ACT TO TAKE OUT THE HEAD OF STATE OF A SUPPOSED ROGUE NATION.

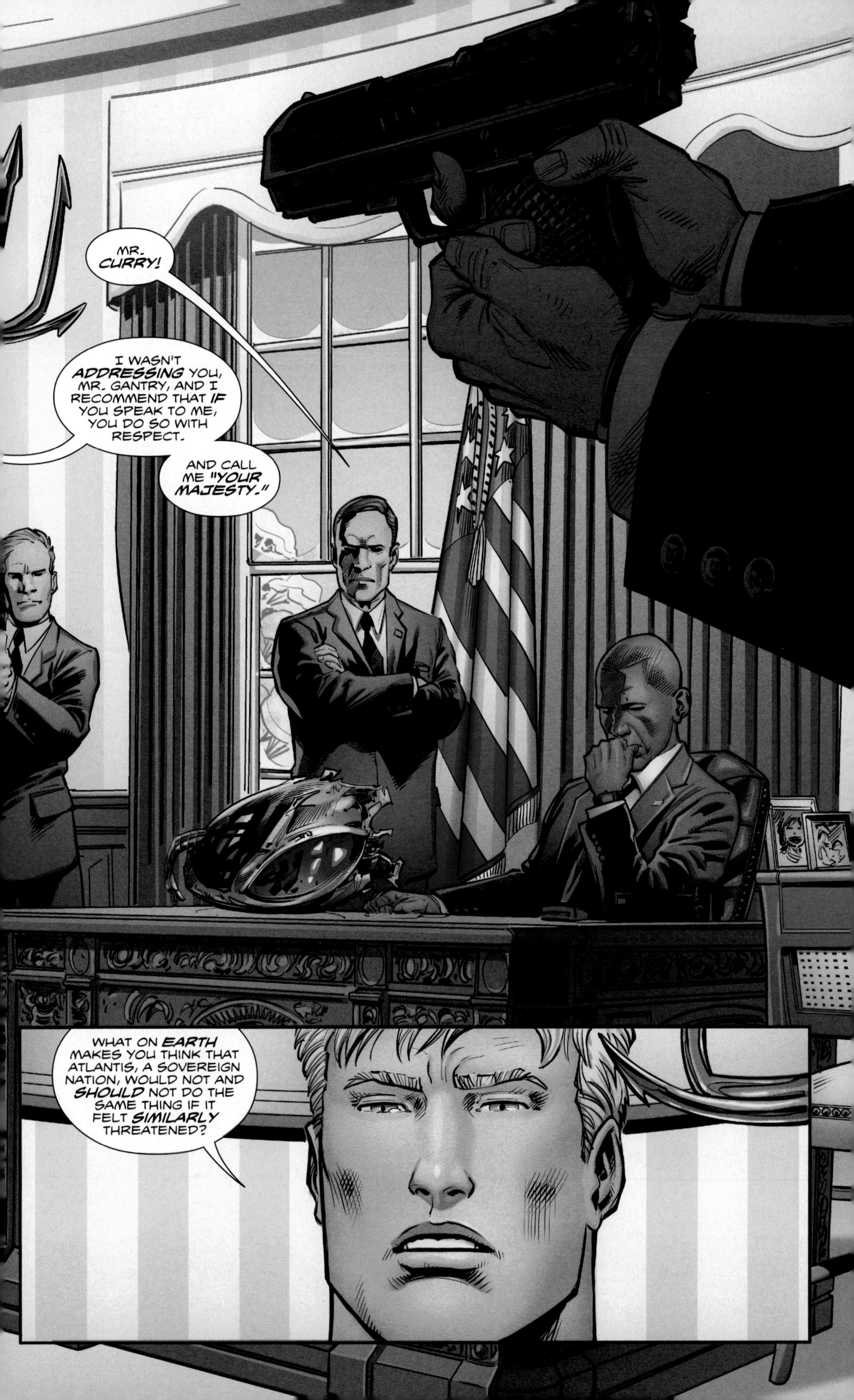
MR. CURRY!
I WASN'T ADDRESSING YOU, MR. GANTRY, AND I RECOMMEND THAT IF YOU SPEAK TO ME, YOU DO SO WITH RESPECT.
AND CALL ME "YOUR MAJESTY."
WHAT ON EARTH MAKES YOU THINK THAT ATLANTIS, A SOVEREIGN NATION, WOULD NOT AND SHOULD NOT DO THE SAME THING IF IT FELT SIMILARLY THREATENED?

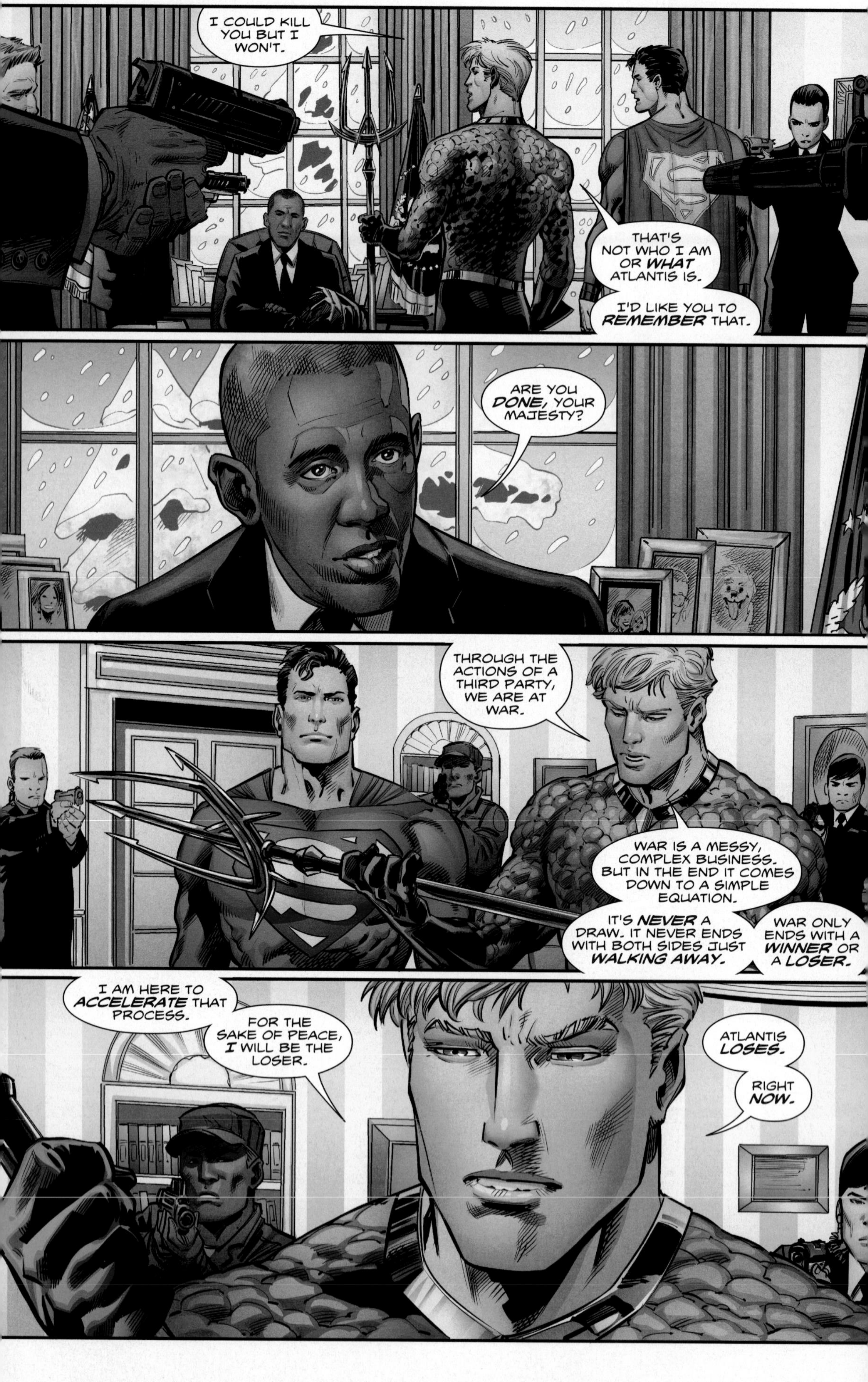
I COULD KILL YOU BUT I WON'T.
THAT'S NOT WHO I AM OR WHAT ATLANTIS IS.
I'D LIKE YOU TO REMEMBER THAT.
ARE YOU DONE, YOUR MAJESTY?
THROUGH THE ACTIONS OF A THIRD PARTY, WE ARE AT WAR.
WAR IS A MESSY, COMPLEX BUSINESS. BUT IN THE END IT COMES DOWN TO A SIMPLE EQUATION.
IT'S NEVER A DRAW. IT NEVER ENDS WITH BOTH SIDES JUST WALKING AWAY.
WAR ONLY ENDS WITH A WINNER OR A LOSER.
I AM HERE TO ACCELERATE THAT PROCESS.
FOR THE SAKE OF PEACE, I WILL BE THE LOSER.
ATLANTIS LOSES.
RIGHT NOW.

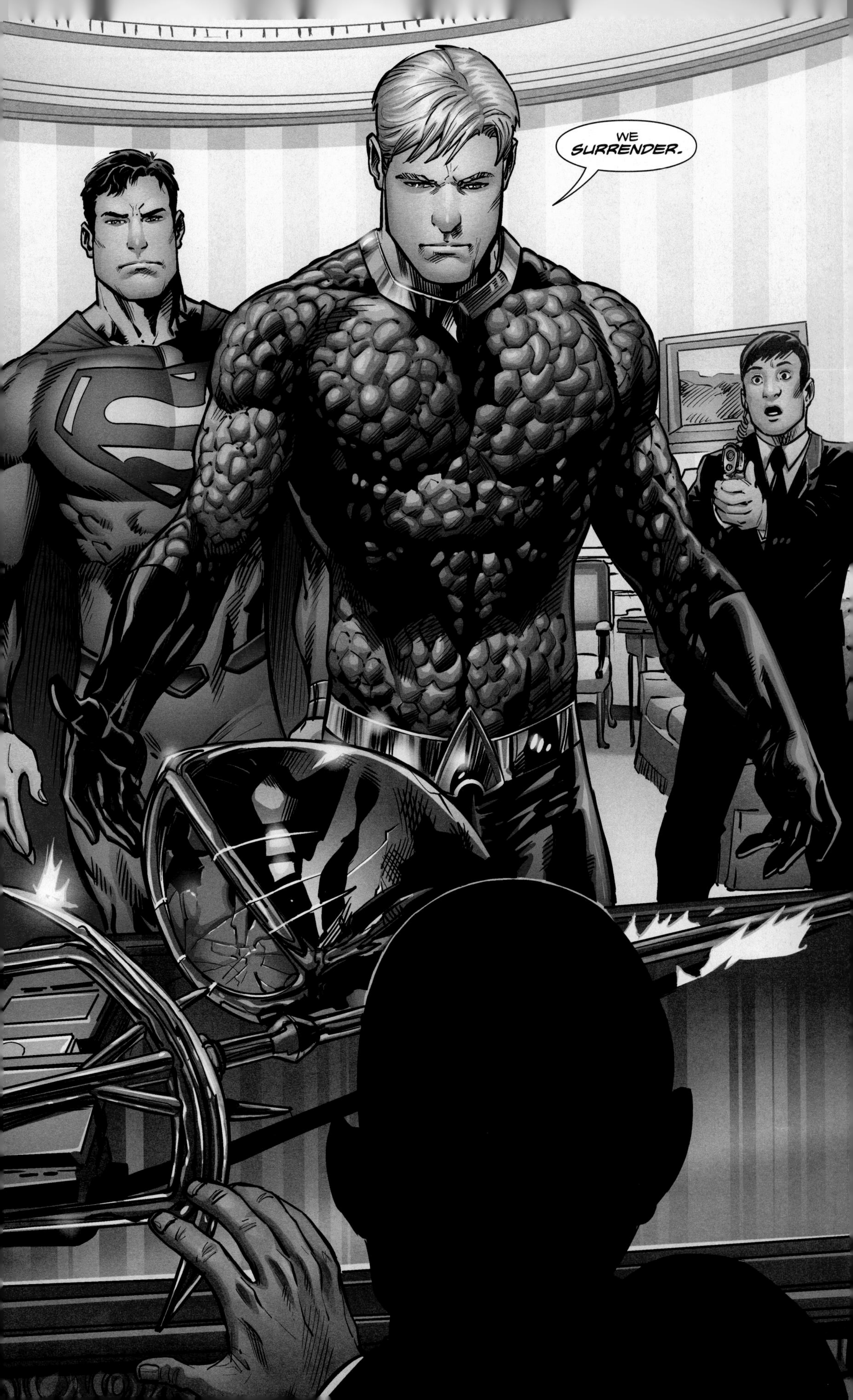
WE SURRENDER.

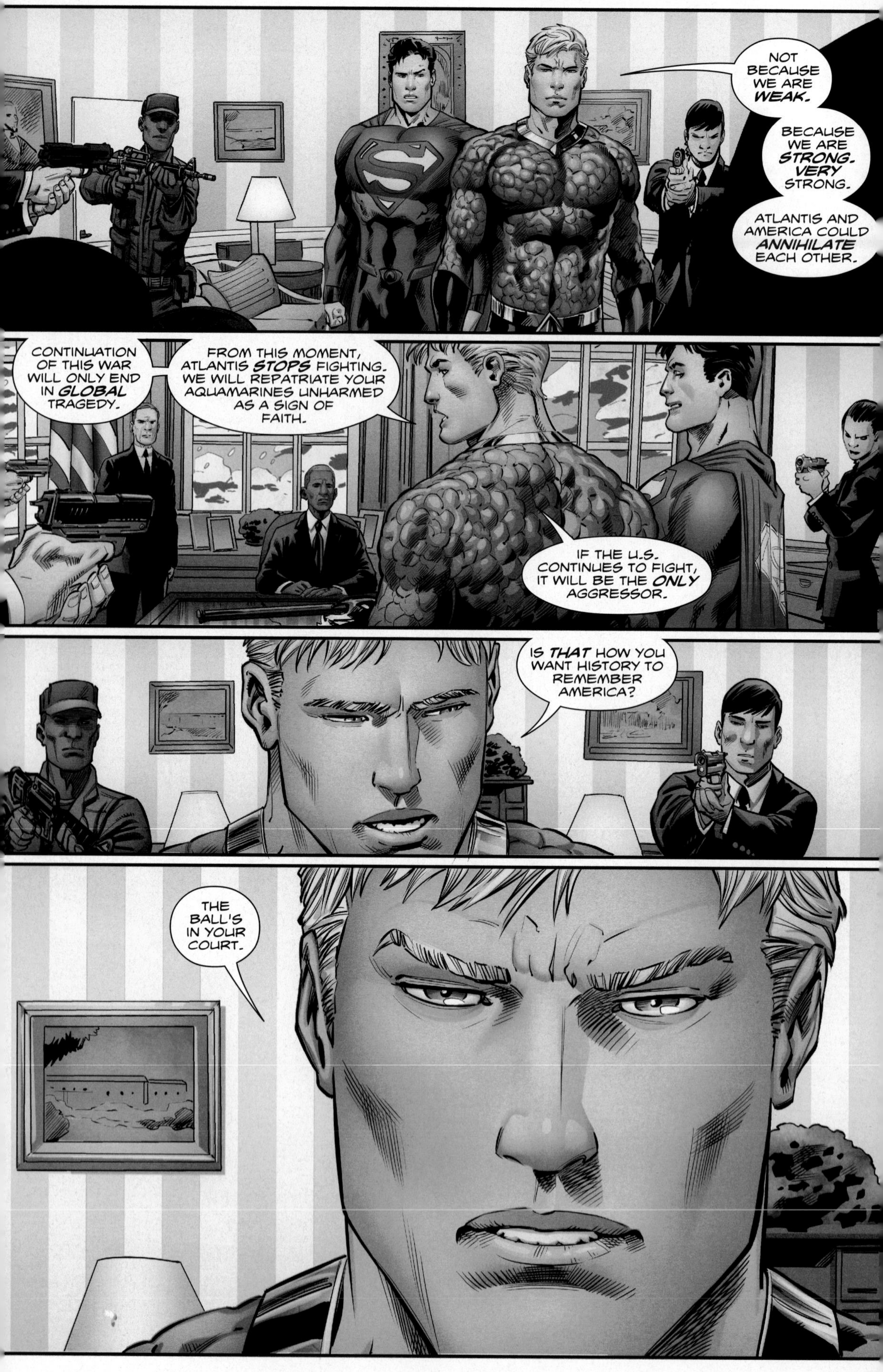
NOT BECAUSE WE ARE WEAK.
BECAUSE WE ARE STRONG. VERY STRONG.
ATLANTIS AND AMERICA COULD ANNIHILATE EACH OTHER.
CONTINUATION OF THIS WAR WILL ONLY END IN GLOBAL TRAGEDY.
FROM THIS MOMENT, ATLANTIS STOPS FIGHTING. WE WILL REPATRIATE YOUR AQUAMARINES UNHARMED AS A SIGN OF FAITH.
IF THE U.S. CONTINUES TO FIGHT, IT WILL BE THE ONLY AGGRESSOR.
IS THAT HOW YOU WANT HISTORY TO REMEMBER AMERICA?
THE BALL'S IN YOUR COURT.

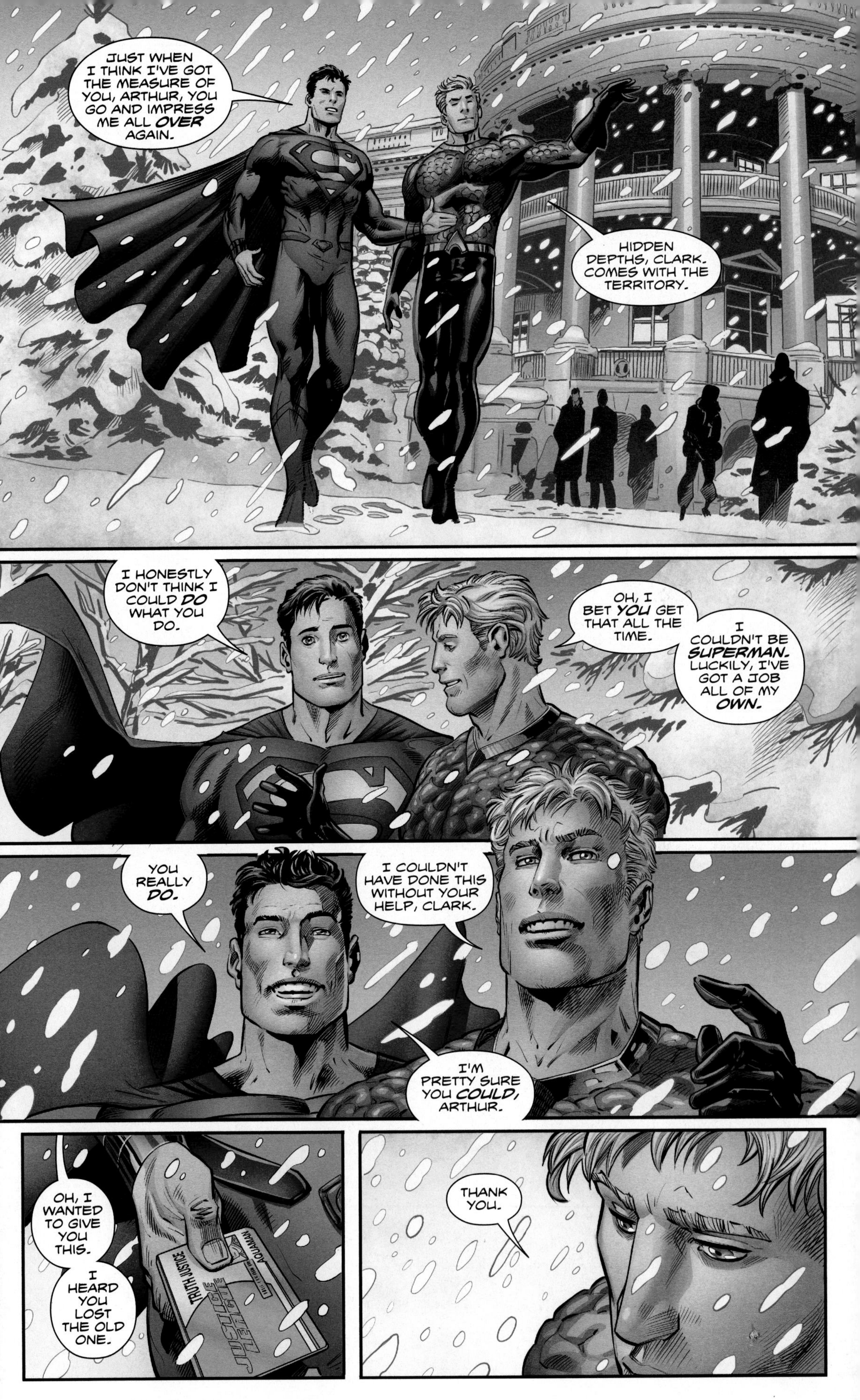
JUST WHEN I THINK I'VE GOT THE MEASURE OF YOU, ARTHUR, YOU GO AND IMPRESS ME ALL OVER AGAIN.
HIDDEN DEPTHS, CLARK. COMES WITH THE TERRITORY.
I HONESTLY DON'T THINK I COULD DO WHAT YOU DO.
OH, I BET YOU GET THAT ALL THE TIME.
I COULDN'T BE SUPERMAN. LUCKILY, I'VE GOT A JOB ALL OF MY OWN.
YOU REALLY DO.
I COULDN'T HAVE DONE THIS WITHOUT YOUR HELP, CLARK.
I'M PRETTY SURE YOU COULD, ARTHUR.
OH, I WANTED TO GIVE YOU THIS.
I HEARD YOU LOST THE OLD ONE.
TRUTH JUSTICE
AQUAMAN
THANK YOU.

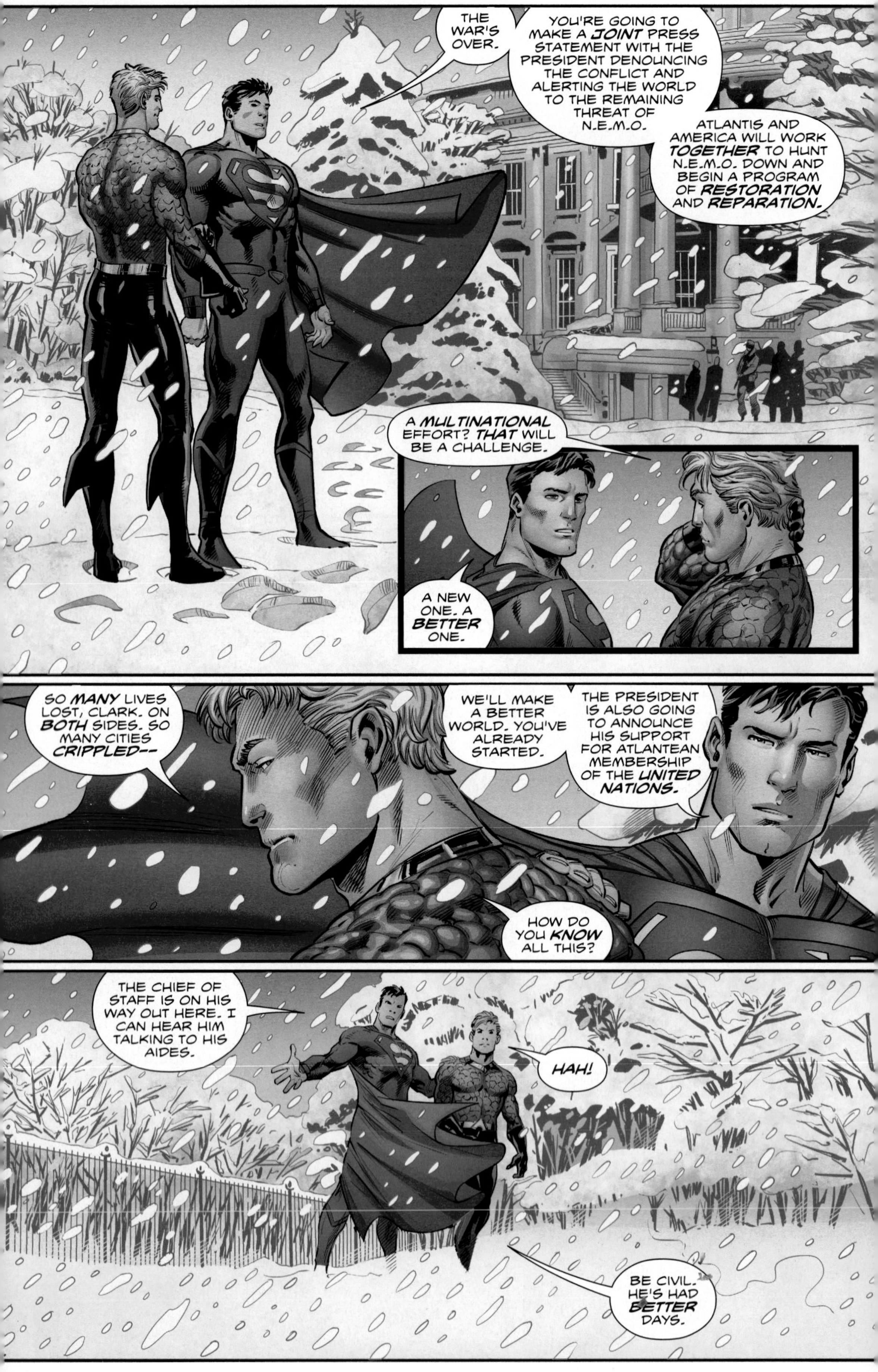
THE WAR'S OVER.
YOU'RE GOING TO MAKE A JOINT PRESS STATEMENT WITH THE PRESIDENT DENOUNCING THE CONFLICT AND ALERTING THE WORLD TO THE REMAINING THREAT OF N.E.M.O.
ATLANTIS AND AMERICA WILL WORK TOGETHER TO HUNT N.E.M.O. DOWN AND BEGIN A PROGRAM OF RESTORATION AND REPARATION.
A MULTINATIONAL EFFORT? THAT WILL BE A CHALLENGE.
A NEW ONE. A BETTER ONE.
SO MANY LIVES LOST, CLARK. ON BOTH SIDES. SO MANY CITIES CRIPPLED--
WE'LL MAKE A BETTER WORLD. YOU'VE ALREADY STARTED.
THE PRESIDENT IS ALSO GOING TO ANNOUNCE HIS SUPPORT FOR ATLANTEAN MEMBERSHIP OF THE UNITED NATIONS.
HOW DO YOU KNOW ALL THIS?
THE CHIEF OF STAFF IS ON HIS WAY OUT HERE. I CAN HEAR HIM TALKING TO HIS AIDES.
HAH!
BE CIVIL. HE'S HAD BETTER DAYS.

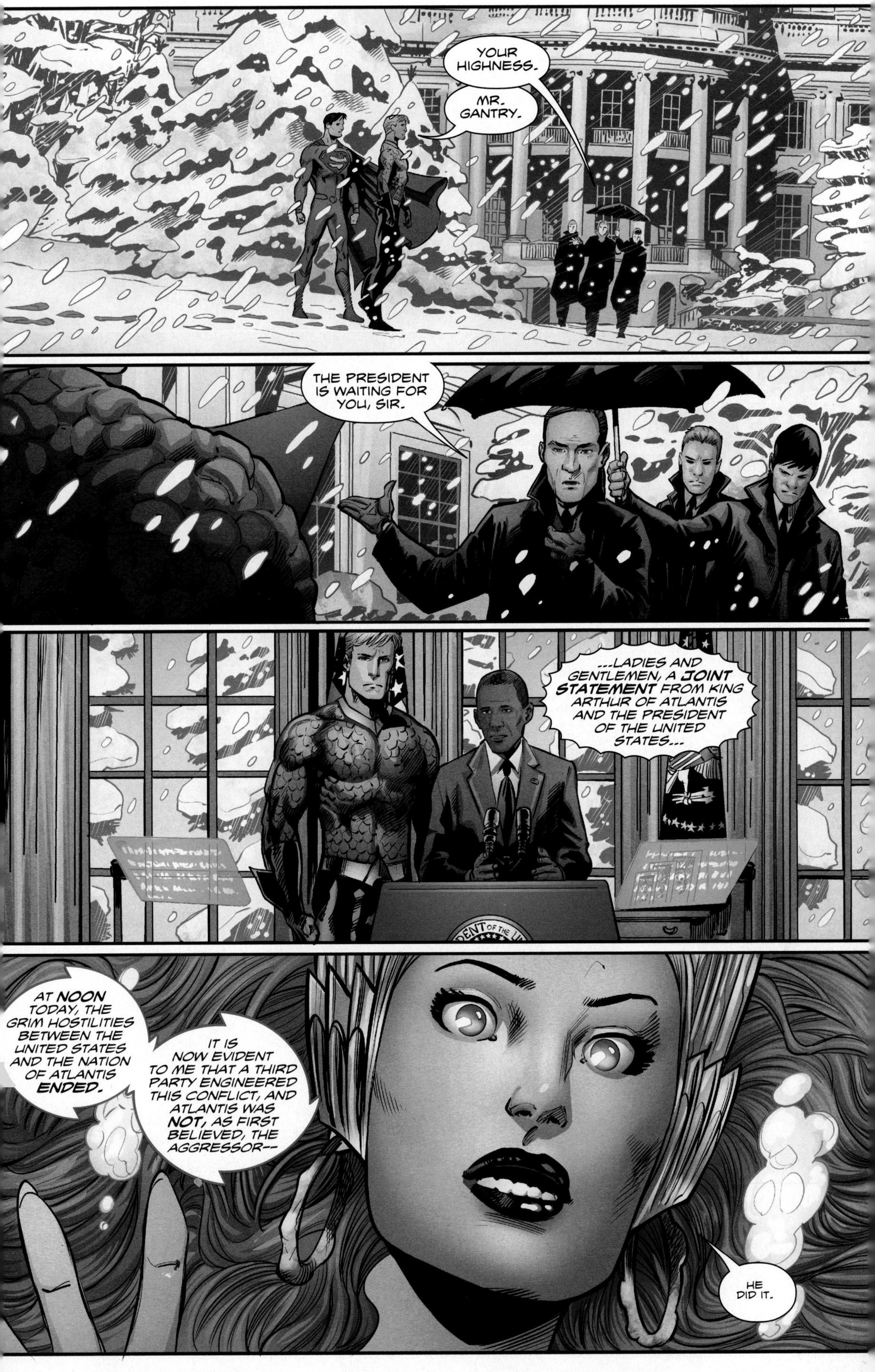
YOUR HIGHNESS.
MR. GANTRY.
THE PRESIDENT IS WAITING FOR YOU, SIR.
...LADIES AND GENTLEMEN, A **JOINT STATEMENT** FROM KING ARTHUR OF ATLANTIS AND THE PRESIDENT OF THE UNITED STATES...
AT **NOON** TODAY, THE GRIM HOSTILITIES BETWEEN THE UNITED STATES AND THE NATION OF ATLANTIS **ENDED.**
IT IS NOW EVIDENT TO ME THAT A THIRD PARTY ENGINEERED THIS CONFLICT, AND ATLANTIS WAS **NOT,** AS FIRST BELIEVED, THE AGGRESSOR--
HE DID IT.

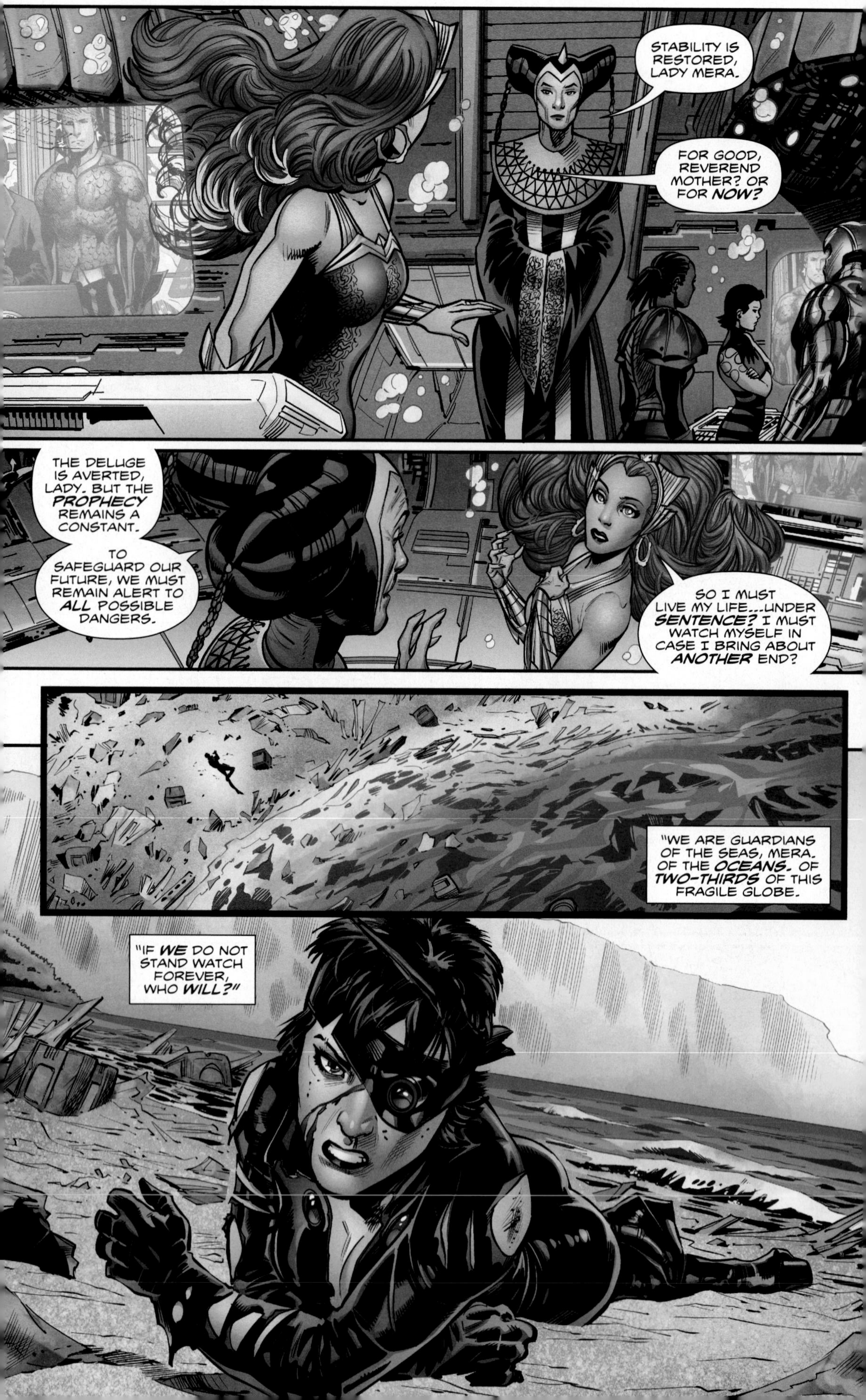
STABILITY IS RESTORED, LADY MERA.
FOR GOOD, REVEREND MOTHER? OR FOR NOW?
THE DELUGE IS AVERTED, LADY. BUT THE PROPHECY REMAINS A CONSTANT.
TO SAFEGUARD OUR FUTURE, WE MUST REMAIN ALERT TO ALL POSSIBLE DANGERS.
SO I MUST LIVE MY LIFE...UNDER SENTENCE? I MUST WATCH MYSELF IN CASE I BRING ABOUT ANOTHER END?
"WE ARE GUARDIANS OF THE SEAS, MERA. OF THE OCEANS. OF TWO-THIRDS OF THIS FRAGILE GLOBE.
"IF WE DO NOT STAND WATCH FOREVER, WHO WILL?"

AQUAMAN #7 variant cover by JOSHUA MIDDLETON

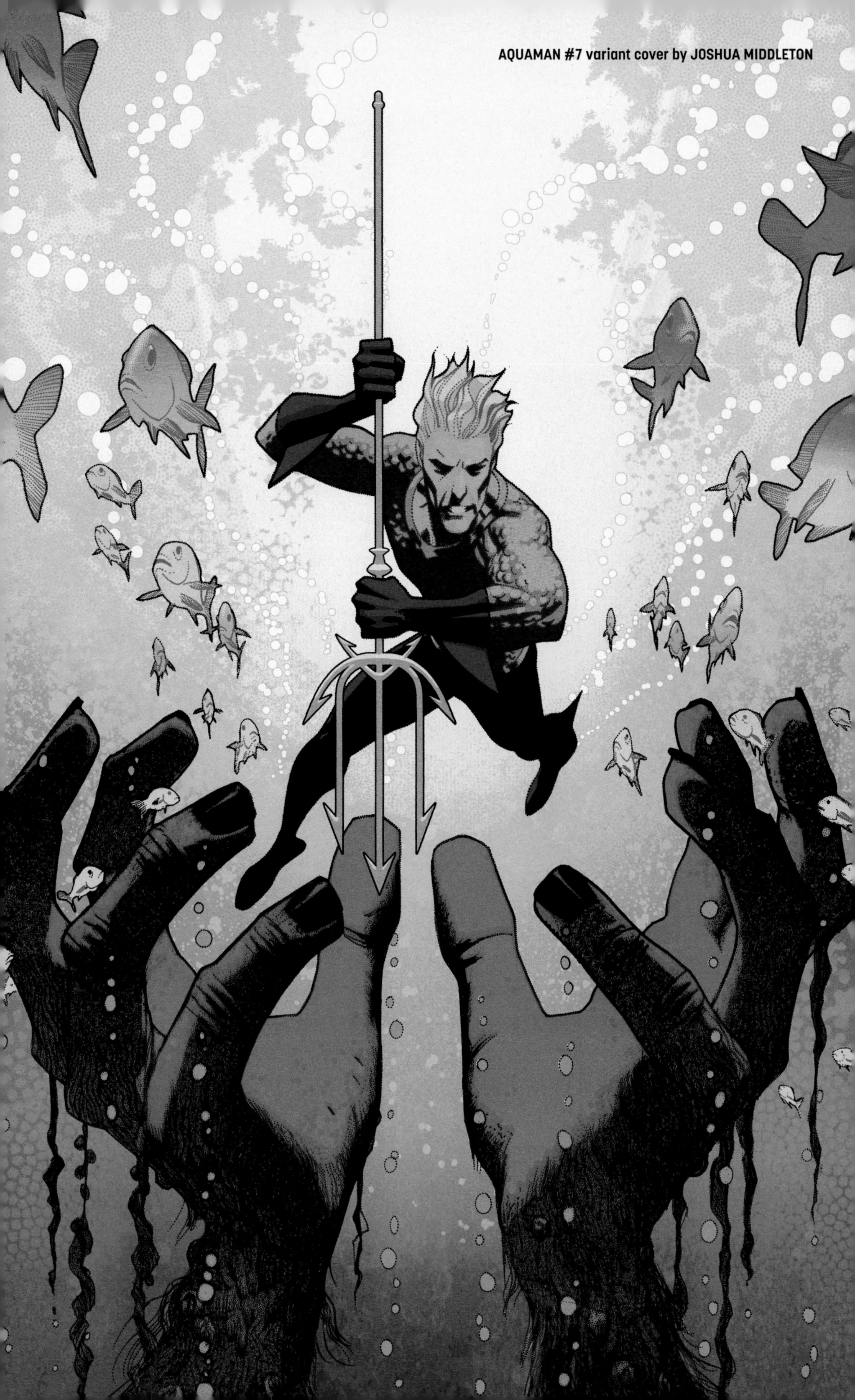

AQUAMAN #8 variant cover by JOSHUA MIDDLETON

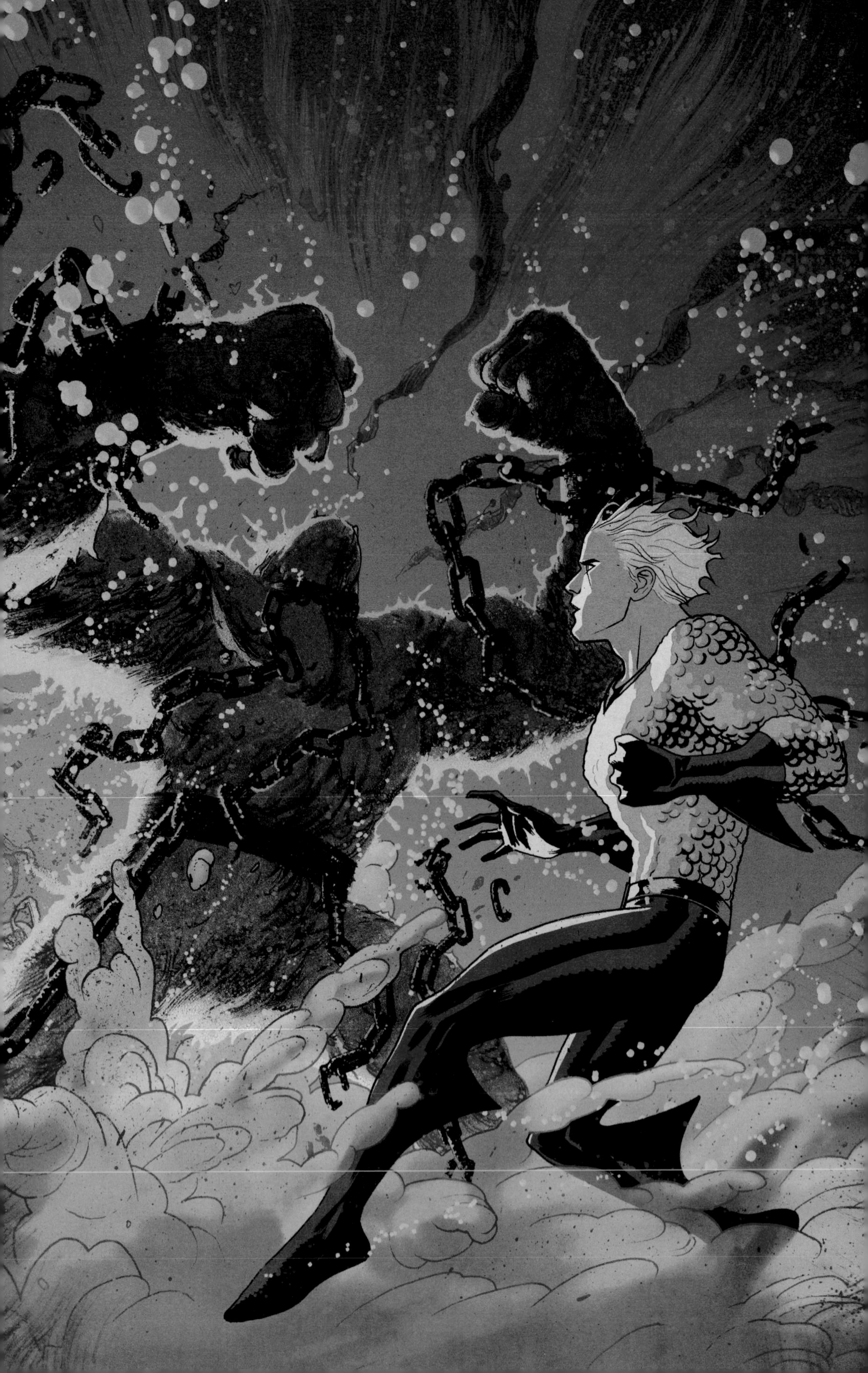

AQUAMAN #9 variant cover by JOSHUA MIDDLETON

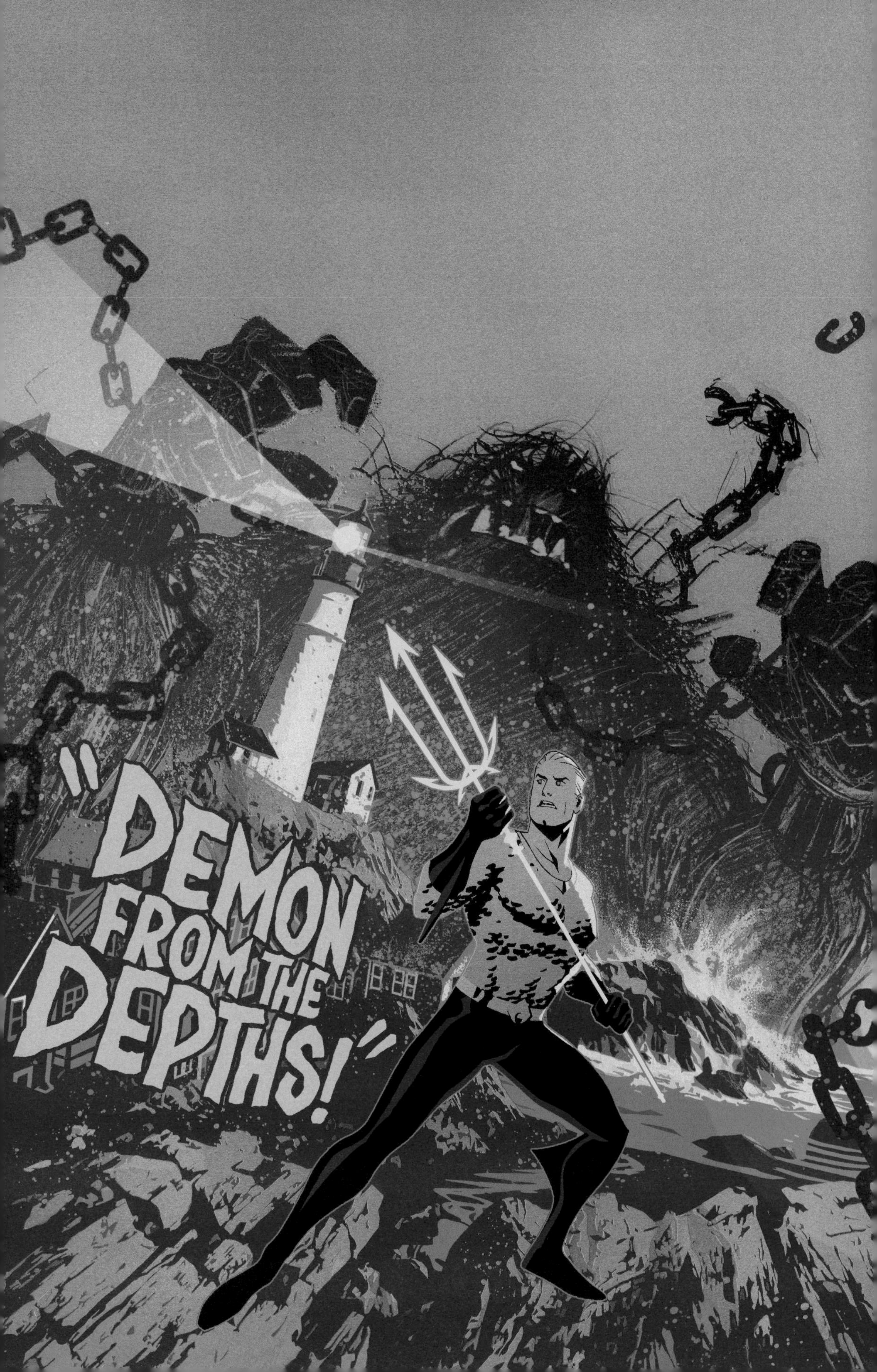
"DEMON FROM THE DEPTHS!"

AQUAMAN #10 variant cover by JOSHUA MIDDLETON

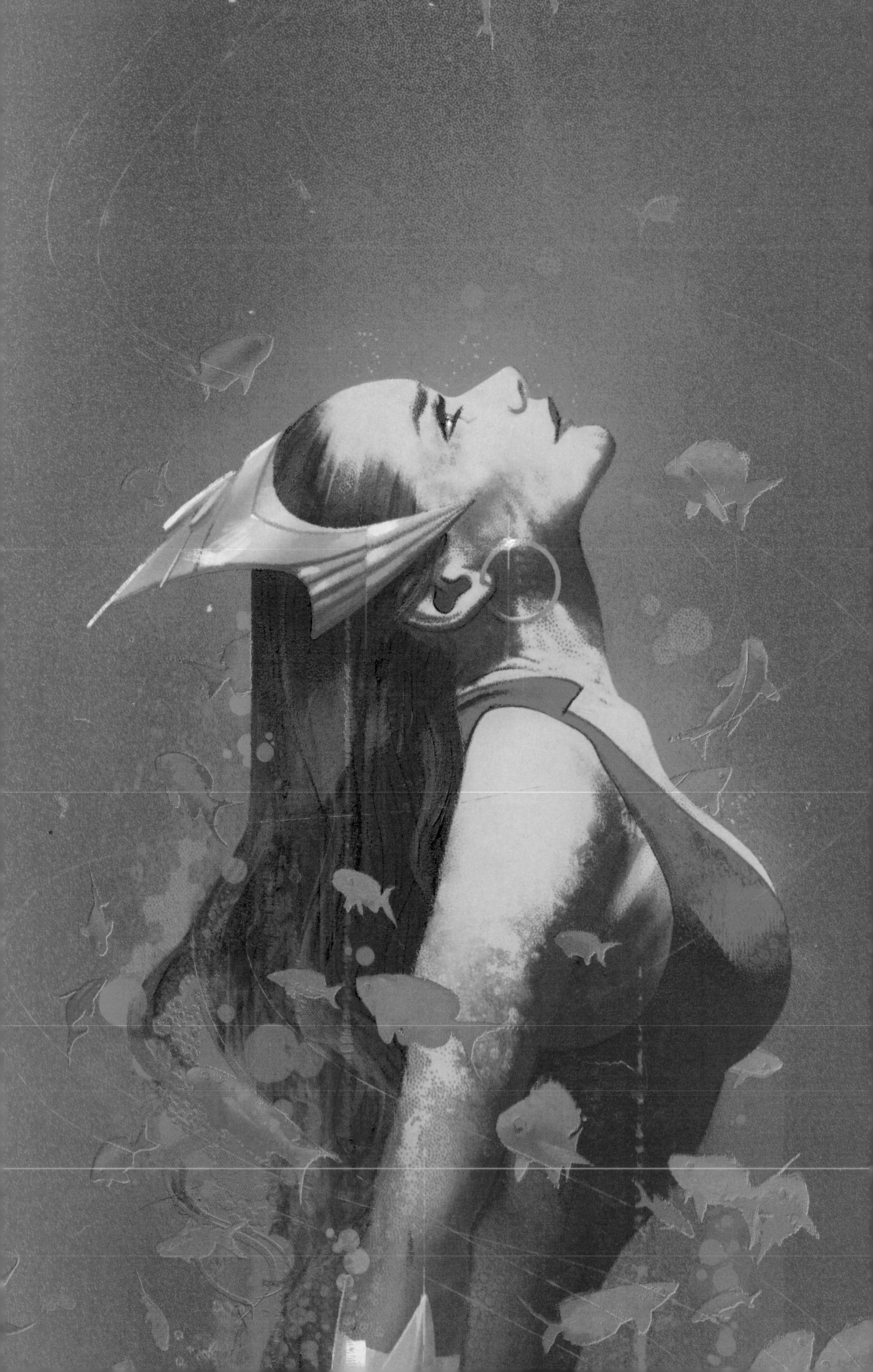

AQUAMAN #11 variant cover by JOSHUA MIDDLETON

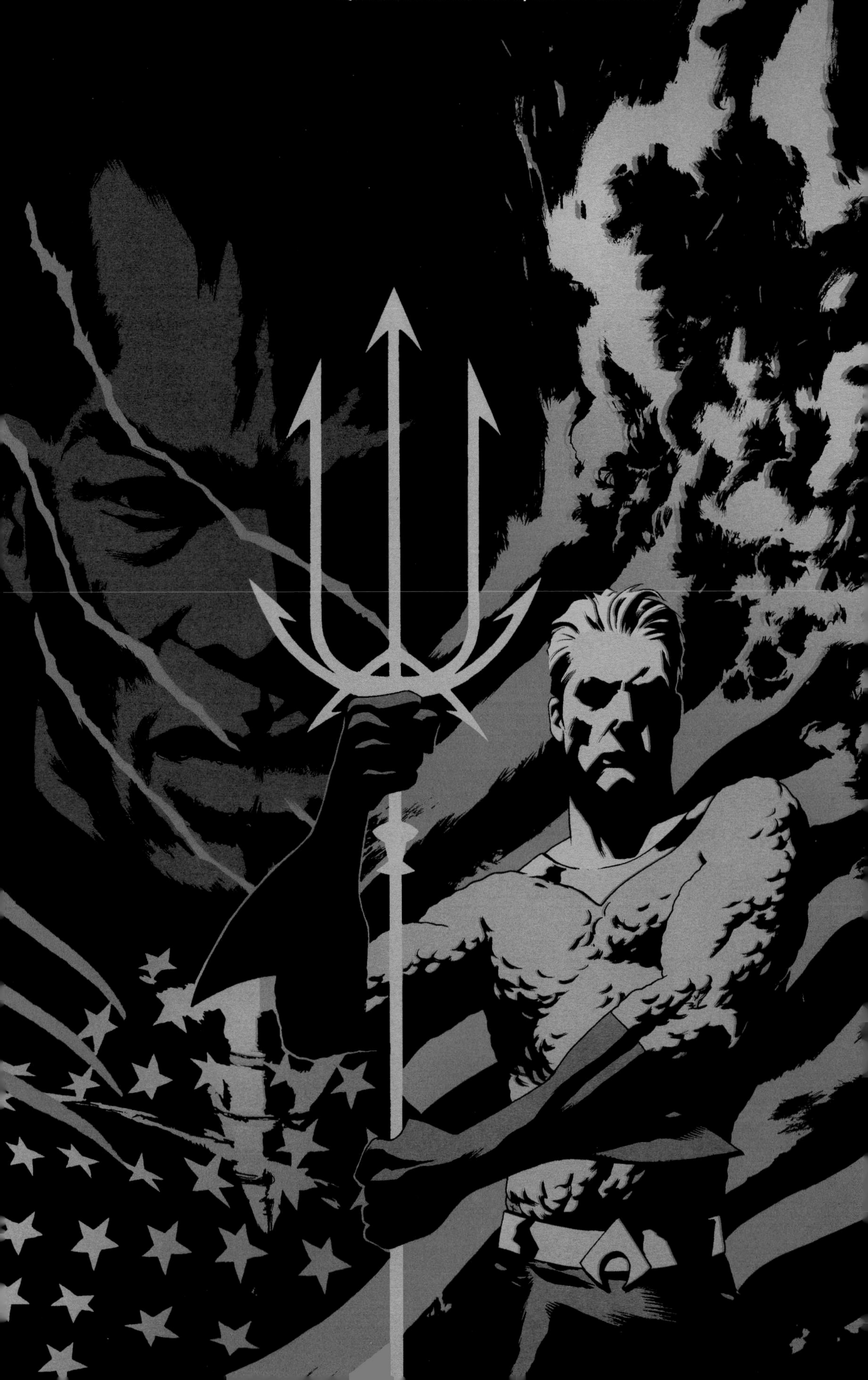

AQUAMAN #12 variant cover by JOSHUA MIDDLETON

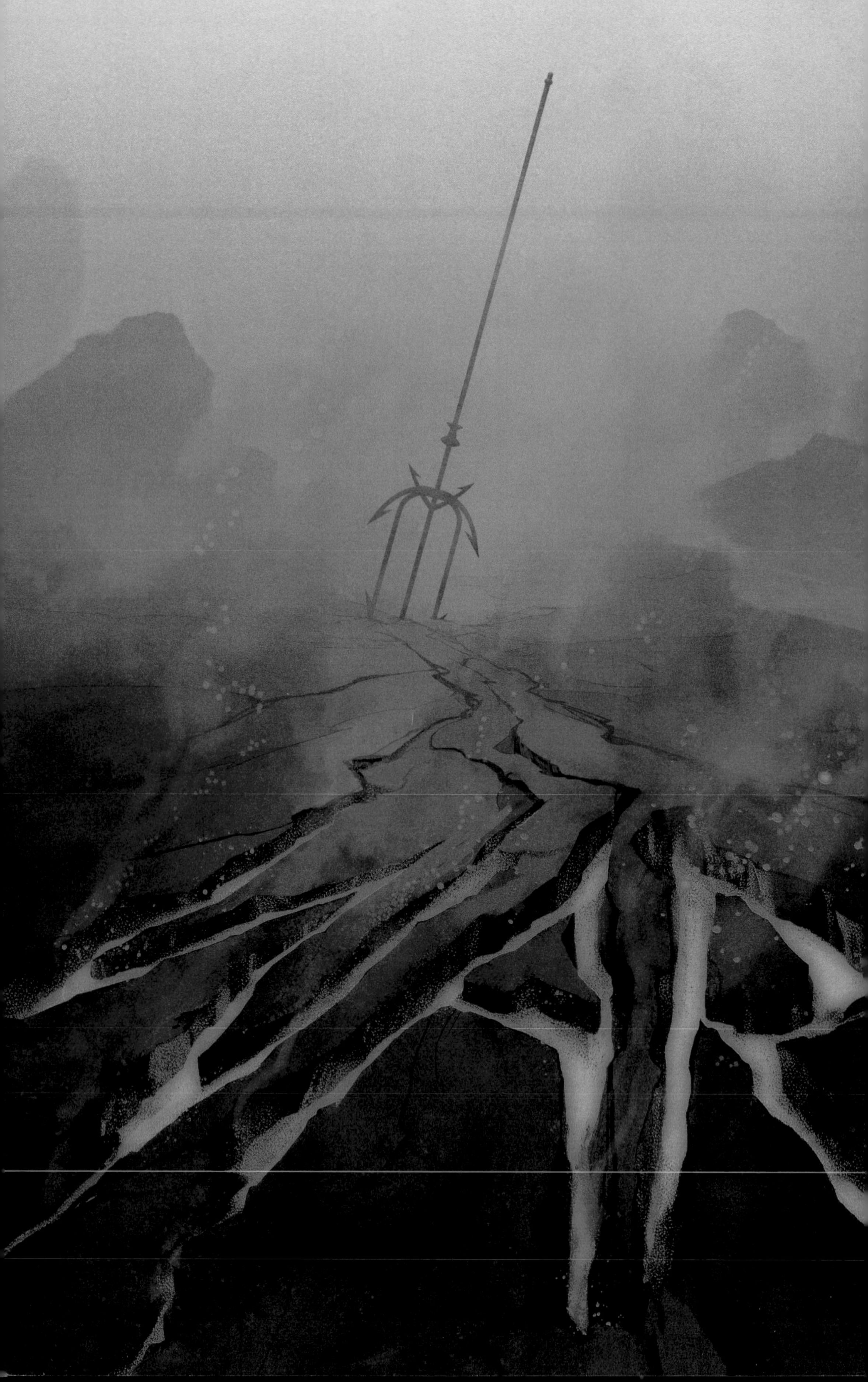

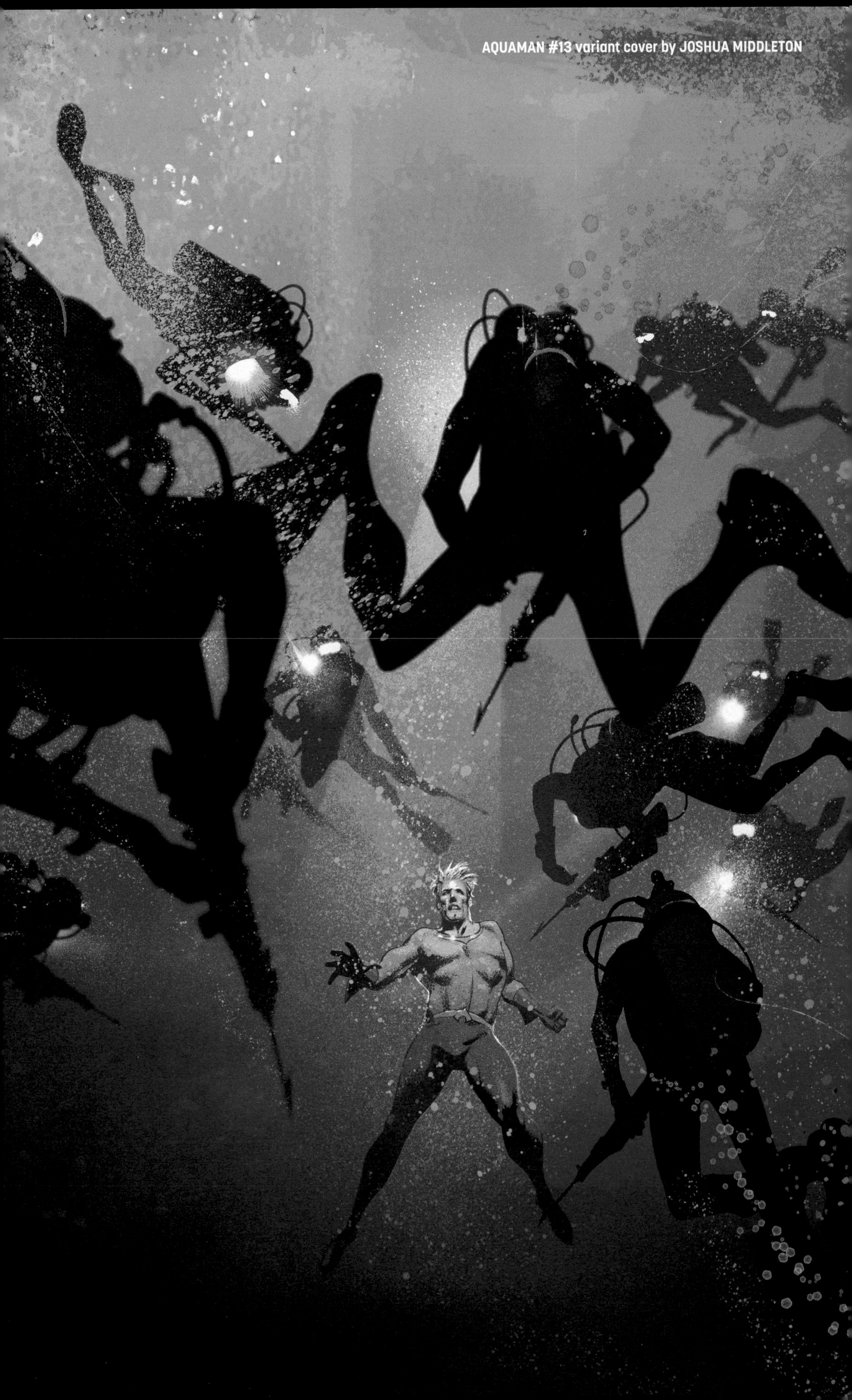
AQUAMAN #13 variant cover by JOSHUA MIDDLETON

AQUAMAN #14 variant cover by JOSHUA MIDDLETON

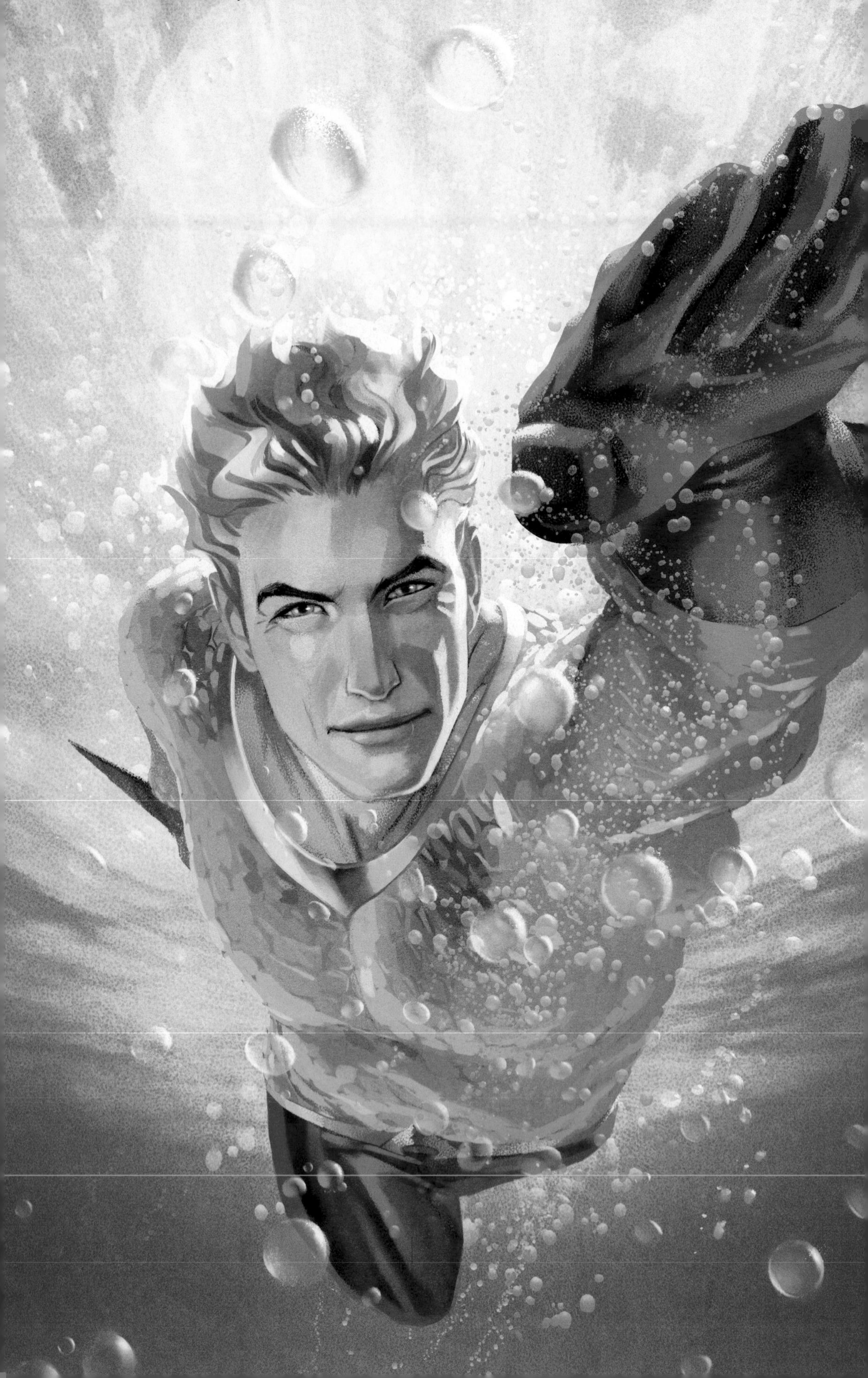

AQUAMAN #15 variant cover by JOSHUA MIDDLETON

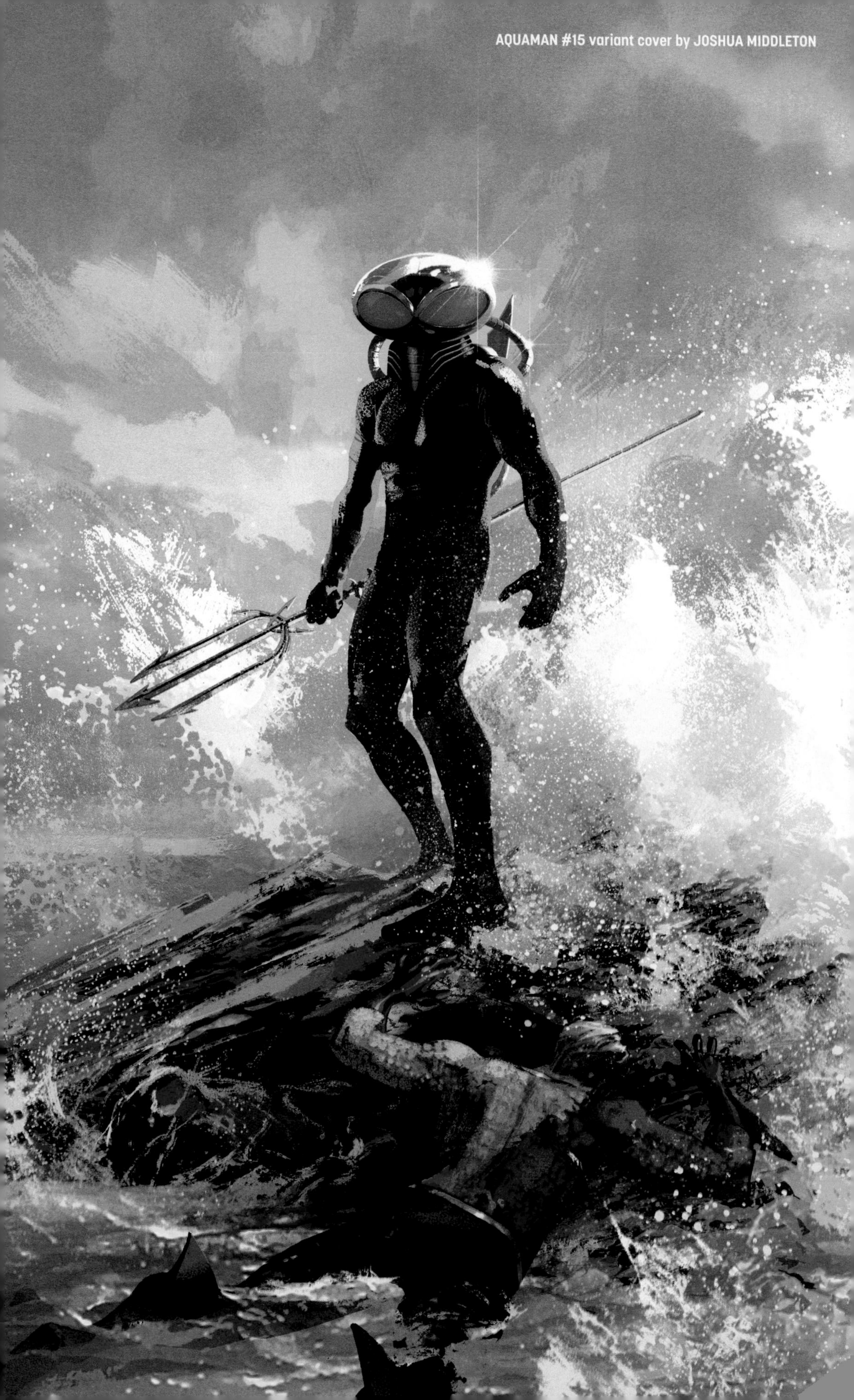

Designs by Brad Walker

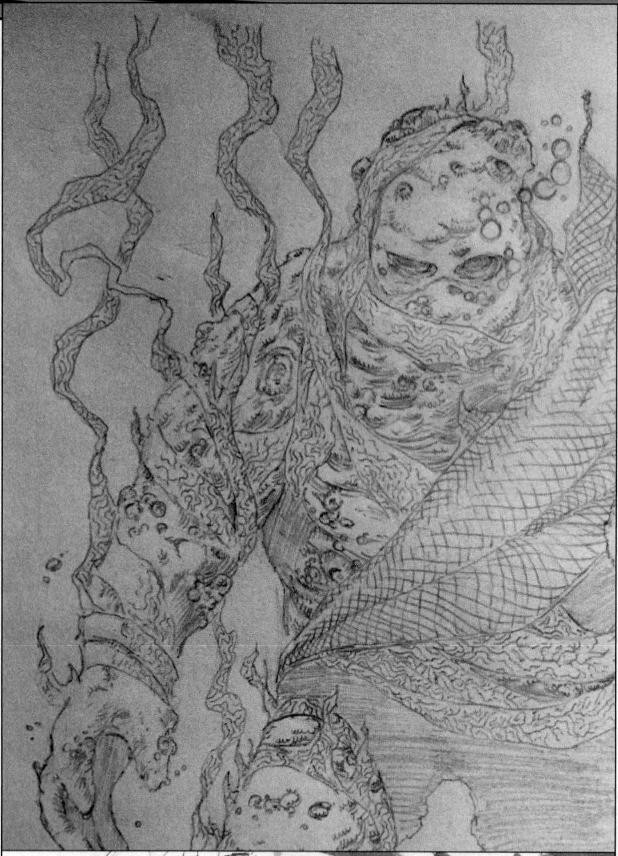

Shaggy Man

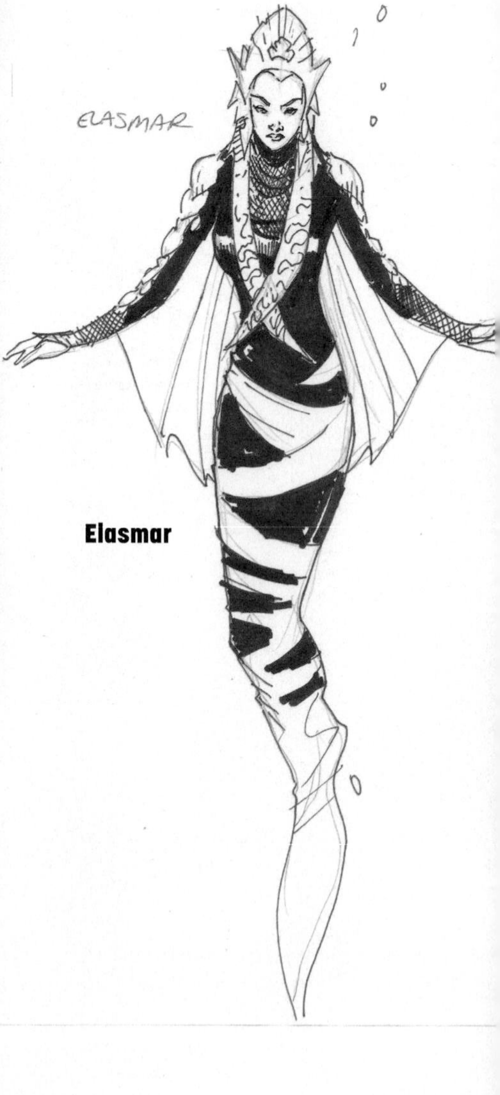
ELASMAR

Elasmar

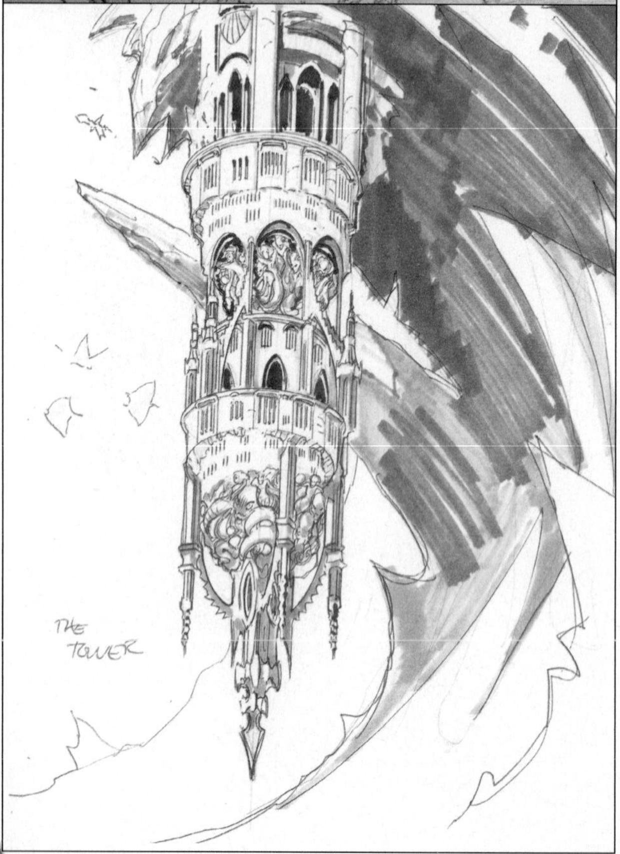
THE
TOWER

The Tower of the Widowhood

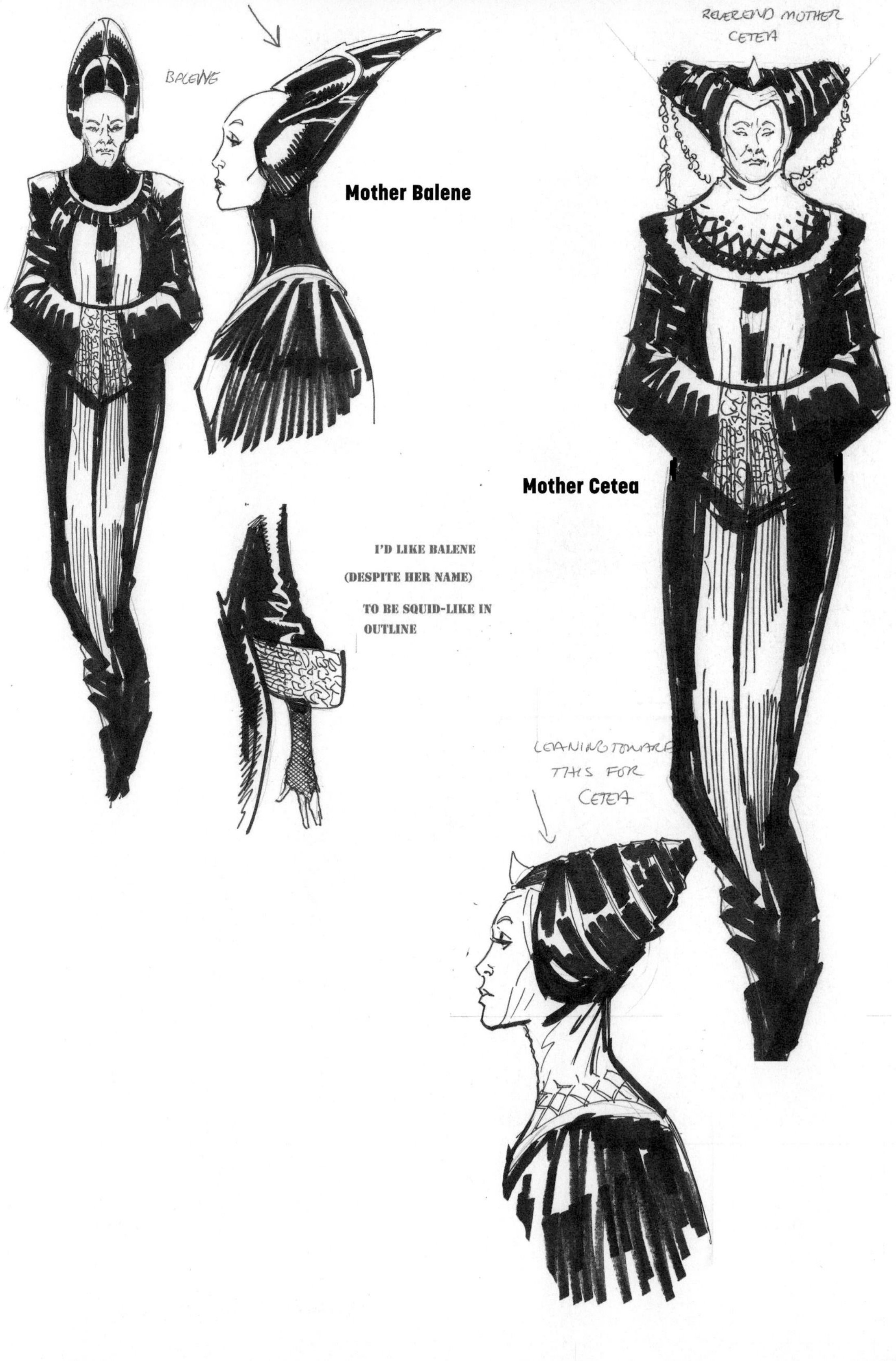
BALENE
Mother Balene
REVEREND MOTHER CETEA
Mother Cetea
I'D LIKE BALENE
(DESPITE HER NAME)
TO BE SQUID-LIKE IN
OUTLINE
LEANING TOWARD
THIS FOR
CETEA

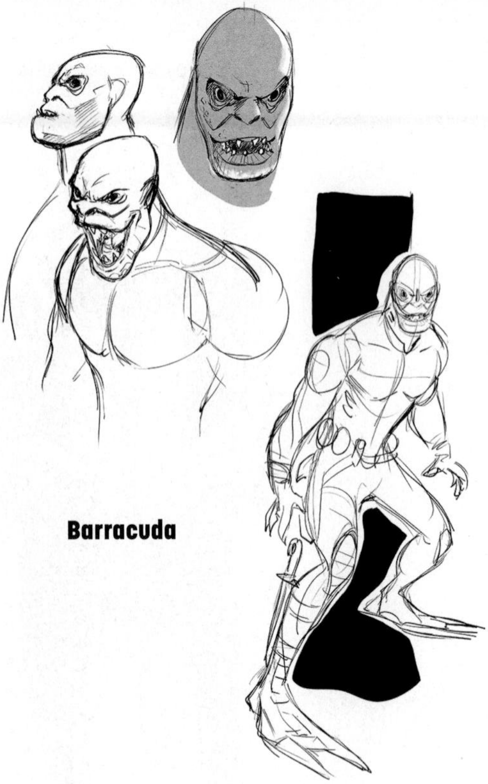

Barracuda

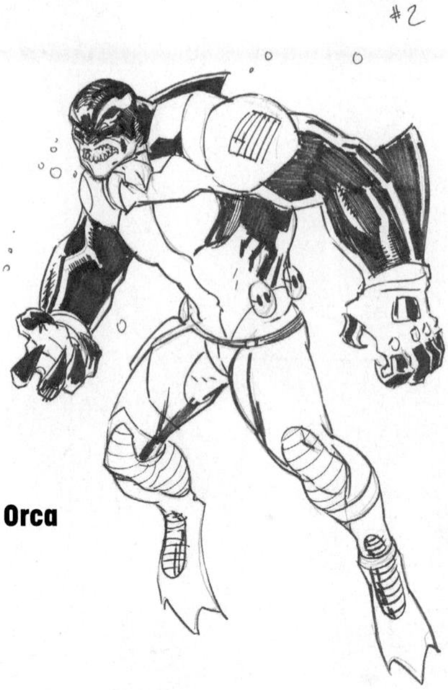
#2

Orca

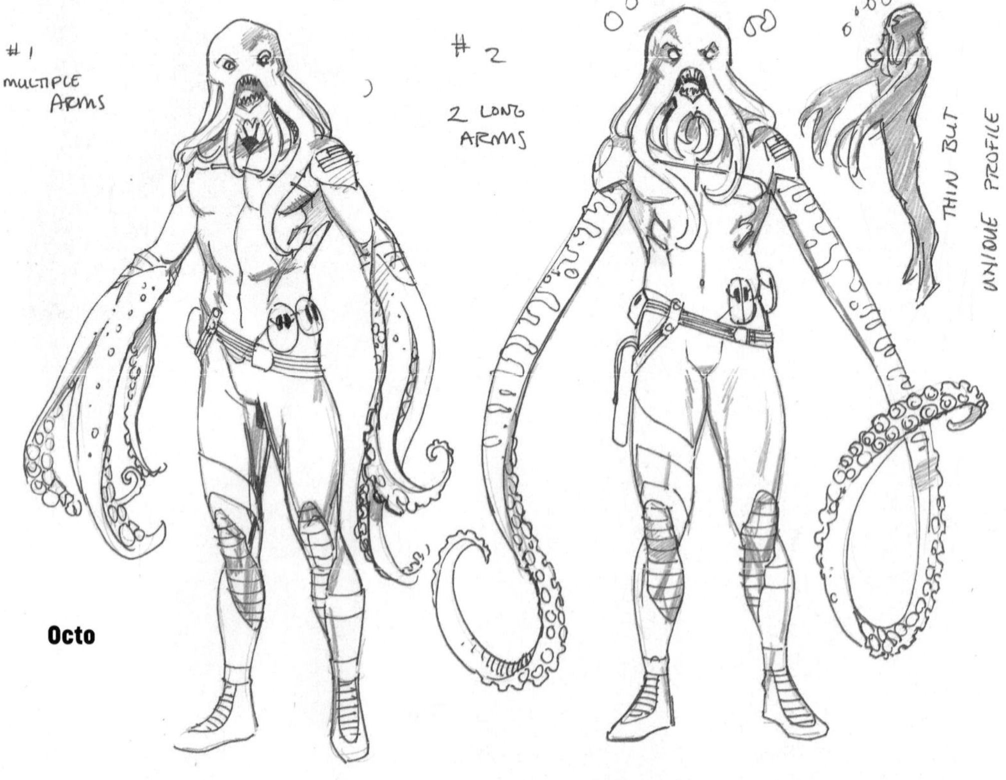
OCTO-MAN
#1
MULTIPLE ARMS
#2
2 LONG ARMS
THIN BUT UNIQUE PROFILE

Octo

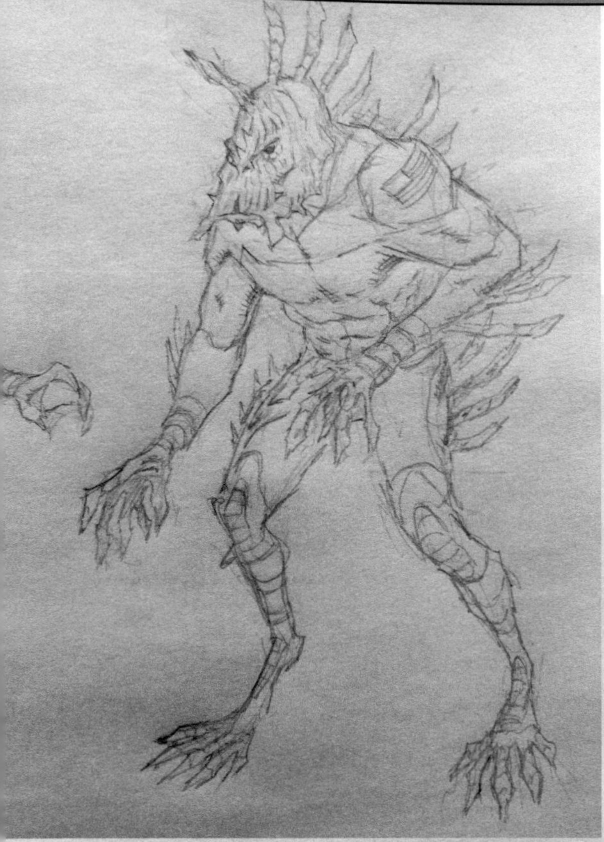

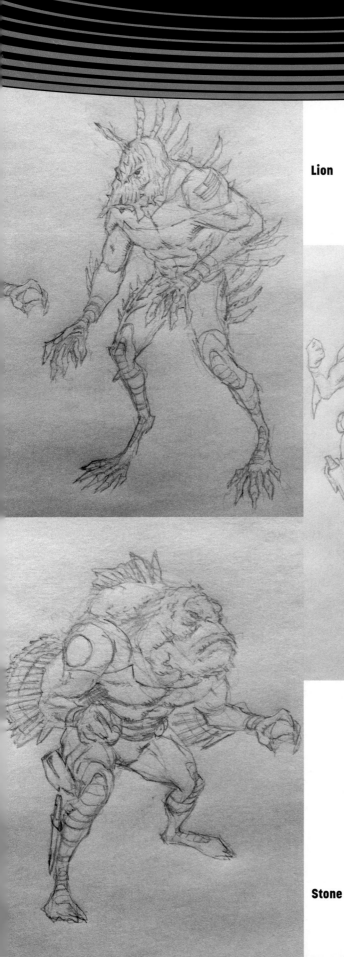

Lion

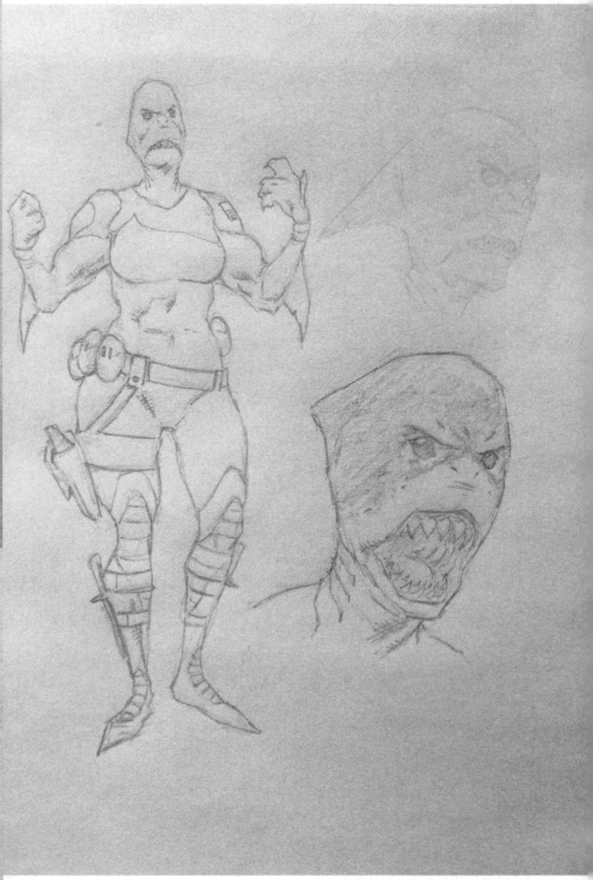

Great White

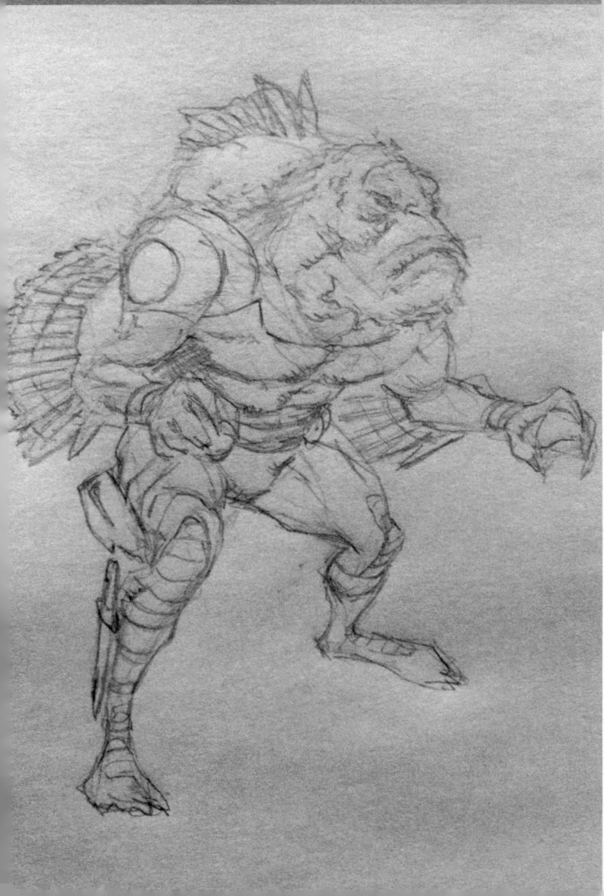

Stone

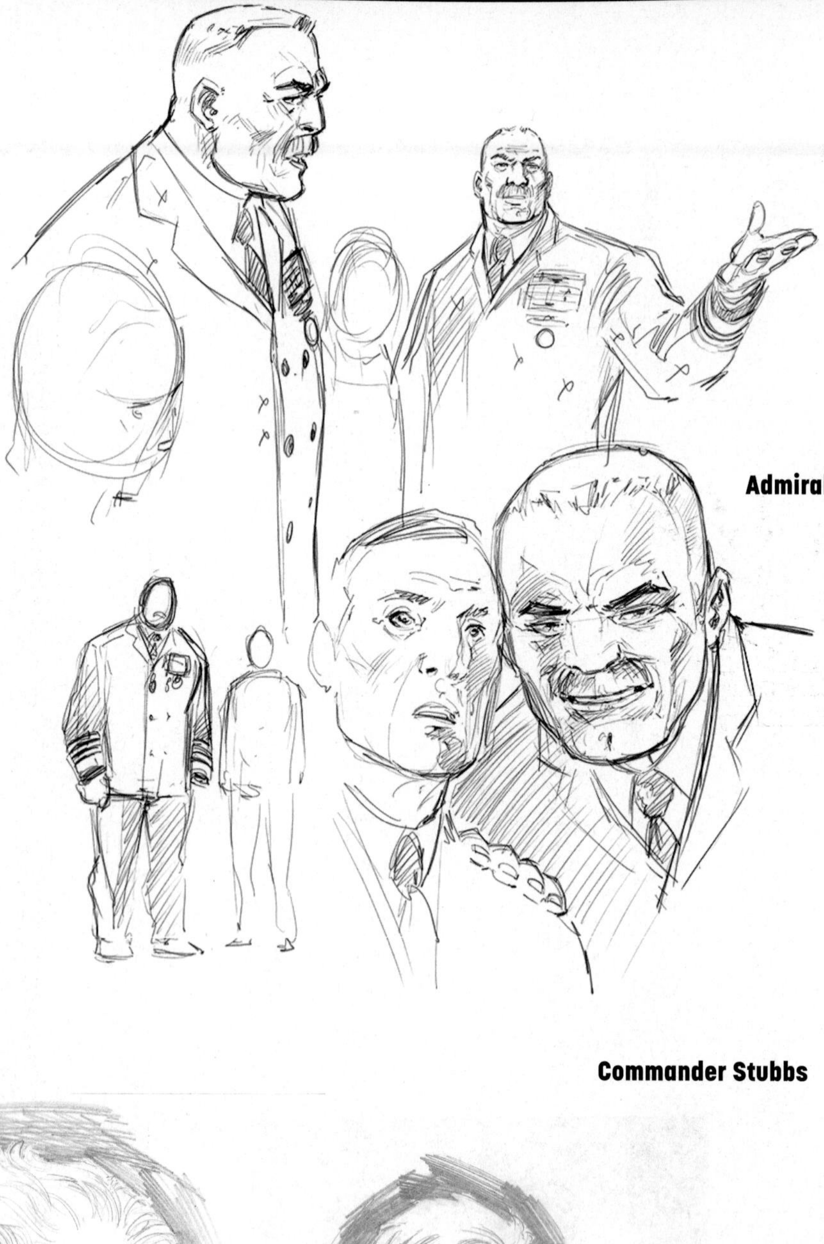

Admiral Meddinghouse

Commander Stubbs

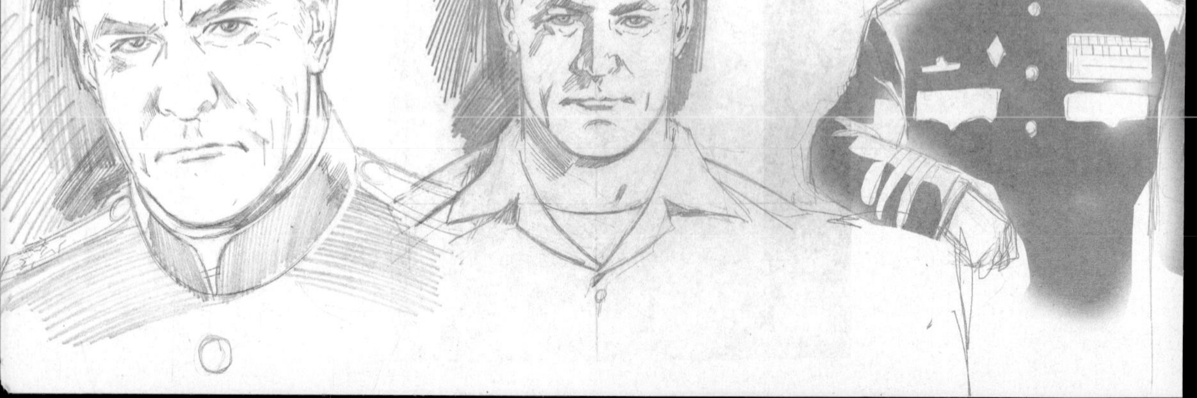

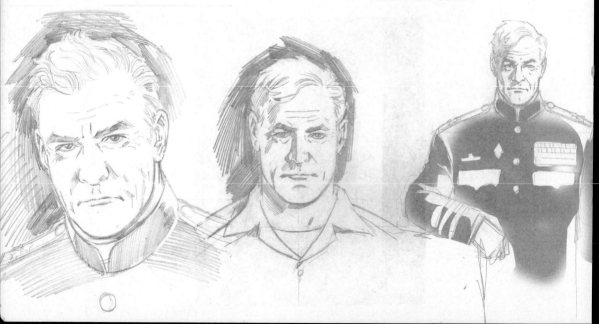